Structural Unemployment in Western Europe:
Reasons and Remedies

Structural Unemployment in Western Europe

Reasons and Remedies

Martin Werding, editor

CESifo Seminar Series

The MIT Press
Cambridge, Massachusetts
London, England

MIT Press books may be purchased at special quantity discounts for business or sales promotional use. For information, please email special_sales@mitpress.mit.edu or write to Special Sales Department, The MIT Press, 55 Hayward Street, Cambridge, MA 02142.

This book was set in Palatino on 3B2 by Asco Typesetters, Hong Kong. Printed and bound in the United States of America.

Library of Congress Cataloging-in-Publication Data

Structural unemployment in Western Europe : reasons and remedies / Martin Werding, editor.
  p.   cm. — (CESifo seminar series)
Includes bibliographical references and index.
ISBN 0-262-23246-4 (alk. paper)
1. Structural unemployment—Europe, Western. I. Werding, Martin. II. Series.
HD5708.47.E5S77   2006
331.13′7041094—dc22   2005054483

10 9 8 7 6 5 4 3 2 1

Contents

Contributors

Torben M. Andersen
Department of Economics
University of Aarhus

Samuel Bentolila
Centro de Estudios Monetarios y
Financieros (CEMFI), Madrid

Norbert Berthold
Department of Economics and
Business Administration
University of Würzburg

Giuseppe Bertola
Department of Economics and
Public Finance
University of Torino

Rainer Fehn†
Ifo Institute for Economic
Research and Department of
Economics
University of Munich

Pietro Garibaldi
Department of Economics and
Public Finance
University of Torino

Bertil Holmlund
Department of Economics
Uppsala University

Juan F. Jimeno
Directorate General Economics,
Statistics and Research
Bank of Spain, Madrid

Erkki Koskela
Department of Economics
University of Helsinki

Stephen Nickell
Department of Economics
London School of Economics

Jan C. van Ours
Center for Economic Research
(CentER)
Tilburg University

Edmund S. Phelps
Department of Economics
Columbia University, New York

Jean Pisani-Ferry
Brussels European and Global
Economic Laboratory (Bruegel),
Brussels

Christopher A. Pissarides
Department of Economics
London School of Economics

Roope Uusitalo
Labour Institute for Economic
Research, Helsinki

Brendan Walsh
Department of Economics
University College, Dublin

Martin Werding
Ifo Institute for Economic
Research, Munich

Main Book Title:

CESifo Seminar Series
Foreword

Y 20

This book is part of the CESifo Seminar Series in Economic Policy, which aims to cover topical policy issues in economics from a largely European perspective. The books in this series are the products of the papers presented and discussed at seminars hosted by CESifo, an international research network of renowned economists supported jointly by the Center for Economic Studies at Ludwig-Maximilians University, Munich, and the Ifo Institute for Economic Research. All publications in this series have been carefully selected and refereed by members of the CESifo research network.

Hans-Werner Sinn

1   Introduction: Still More Questions Than Answers

Martin Werding

It is a common experience across industrialized countries that unemployment is not just a cyclical phenomenon. Underlying all fluctuations of unemployment that follow the ups and downs of economic activity during a typical business cycle, countercyclically and often with some time lag, there is a trend component of unemployment that can go up and sometimes down over much longer periods of time.

The precise pattern of these movements differs a lot across countries, and the experience diverges at national levels. During the 1980s the United States, for instance, now often considered a model for other countries, was faced with much higher levels of unemployment, exceeding 10 percent of the labor force, than most of continental Europe. In the late 1990s, however, US unemployment went down to around 4 percent, and over this decade employment grew remarkably fast as conditions for job creation and matches between labor supply and labor demand substantially changed. Quite a number of other OECD countries underwent similar long-term shifts over time. Indeed, the only industrialized country with a consistent labor market performance for the last three decades is Germany. Unfortunately, in the German case performance has been consistently poor, and since the late 1960s trend unemployment has been continuously rising from virtually zero to about 10 percent of the labor force at the present time.[1]

Autoregressive time-series models can be used to identify long-term trends in unemployment among its other components—those related to the business cycle, seasonal movements, and the like. These models are helpful in that they may tell us something about the relative strengths of these different components. Accordingly, trend unemployment often accounts for 75 percent or more of total unemployment when, during a period of recession, the latter reaches its cyclical peak.[2] If aggregate unemployment is then 10 percent of the labor force or higher, any hope that a short-term economic recovery will bring the labor market back into balance is wholly misguided. At the same time decompositions and estimates of this kind do not tell us a lot about the determinants of, and the mechanisms behind, the different patterns and long-term trends in unemployment observed at an international level. To continue in this direction, we first need to develop material explanations for unemployment to arise and to persist, and then to exploit the richness of experience gathered in different countries.

In early contributions Friedman (1968) and Phelps (1968) coined the term "natural rate" of unemployment, suggesting that there might be an exceptionally high level of search unemployment, or frictional unemployment, associated with "actual structural characteristics of the labor and commodity markets" that deviate from those implied in the notion of perfect markets. Building on Tobin (1972), numerous other authors (e.g., see Modigliani and Papademos 1975 who might be the earliest reference, or the influential book by Layard, Nickell, and Jackman 1991) stressed that for a given economy and a given period of time, there is a certain rate of unemployment that is "non-accelerating inflation" or, as the OECD prefers to put it (see Elmeskov and Mac-Farland 1993), "non-accelerating wages."[3]

Today the term that is most commonly used to label the trend component of unemployment, at least when economists attempt to communicate their ideas to a greater public, is "structural unemployment." In the research literature there is no single author to whom this notion can be traced and certainly no single definition of "structural unemployment."[4] Often, and this is the practice I am going to adopt here, the term is used in a less technical sense, largely substituting, or embedding, the other notions I introduced above. I will argue in what follows that the imprecise, but allusive, nature of this term may have important merits of its own.

In discussing the types of market imperfections that may matter for "natural" unemployment to be high, or the economic and institutional determinants of measures of the NAIRU/NAWRU, all the contributions mentioned before and a host of follow-ups and applications have gone quite some way toward explaining the nature of long-term trends in unemployment. Theorists have worked themselves through a list of potential explanations: the usual being procedures of wage determination and the role of social partners, public intervention in search and matching processes in labor markets, and virtually all fiscal activities of the state, including the introduction and specific design of unemployment benefits. What is less well understood, however, is the empirical side of these explanations. Up until today there appears to be no single model, nor even a distinct family of models, that fits the data equally well both over time and across countries. As a consequence there is still considerable uncertainty about how to reduce persistent high-level unemployment wherever this constitutes a pressing problem.

Even though the political questions related to high levels of unemployment can be really urgent, a lot more research, comparative work in particular, is called for. For this purpose it is precisely the ambiguity—or, rather, multiplicity—of both the empirical evidence and the policy implications behind it that render the notion of structural unemployment so useful. What is seen as a weakness may also be a strength: *structural* unemployment has meant different things in different places and at different points in time.

In economic theory structural unemployment should always be understood as an *equilibrium* phenomenon arising *endogenously*— meaning from within a given economy and its institutional framework. These are two characteristics that clearly dissociate structural unemployment from temporary disequilibria associated with cyclical swings in both external and domestic demand that, with similar regularity, also affect the labor market. Structural unemployment is stable as long as the determinants are unchanged. These determinants must further be structural features of an economy that can influence the economy's capability to adjust to all kinds of endogenous and exogenous shocks, including business-cycle fluctuations, but that, by definition, do not change over short-term periods such as a few months or even a few years. Beyond this merely formal, and almost tautological, description, the concept lacks the specific content by which structural unemployment can be defined and, eventually, defeated.

Yet this is not nearly all one can say about why the notion of structural unemployment is so useful. The many implications of the term "structural" make it a powerful heuristic device. In applied work, and even in theory-building, researchers can make use of the relevant subissues, in attending to the questions that lead to at least preliminarily valid answers. Whether the conclusions hold more generally for earlier periods of time and for other places is then a matter that can be clarified in separate steps.

Over time as well as across countries, unemployment has had many faces, and there is no one way to analysing the causes and the best means for combating the unemployment. The contributions in this volume are restricted to Western Europe with the case of the United States used for comparison. In general, the structural features and structural determinants of unemployment are treated as a common point of departure for labor market research. In the first stage, both the causes and the solutions are necessarily limited to a specific locality. At a second stage, researchers who have considered just a single country can then broaden their analysis to account for trends observed elsewhere.

There are many structural dimensions to observed unemployment. All are potentially of interest when investigating the determinants of high-level trend unemployment. Unemployment can be broken down by fields and levels of professional training, by education and general skill levels, by age groups, gender, ethnic groups, regions, and so on. Whatever shows up in such structural breakdowns as a deviation from economywide or cross-country averages involves questions that probe closer to the true causes of trend unemployment. The immediate answers come from the most visible causes—such as low mobility, occupational or regional, particular patterns of wages and their distribution—and they are then traced back to more fundamental structural developments. Even if visible structures of unemployment differ, the fundamental explanations may overlap.

Structural unemployment has also a subtext. As was mentioned above, there are many ways by which economic life in general and labor market interactions in particular are "structured": by public and social institutions, by a regulatory framework, and by actual use. Mainly structural unemployment is due to failure of labor market institutions—in defining wage bargaining procedures, employment protection, conditions for receiving unemployment benefits, and so forth. However, unemployment can also persist because of social protection and taxation in general, public regulation that primarily addresses markets for goods and services or capital markets, competitiveness in the political sphere, and so forth. Last, and as important, structural unemployment can be due to the way all these structural elements combine. Again, although the single mechanisms generating or perpetuating unemployment in a given country may differ, there may be common patterns of how they work together.

From the taxonomy of types and concepts of unemployment we are right in the middle of the different themes and issues that are addressed in many of the chapters of this volume. The studies collected in this volume originate in a conference on unemployment in Europe held in Munich in December 2002. The conference was jointly organized by the Yrjö Jahnsson Foundation (YJS), Helsinki, and CESifo.[5]

When soliciting contributions to the conference, we were guided by the idea that both labor market research and policy making should try to benefit from the diversity of national experience with unemployment and from how it is being addressed in different countries. In particular, we wanted to benefit from the richness of research conducted at a national level that should be made accessible to an international audience. Outstanding scholars were therefore brought together from a larger number of countries mainly to report on what is going on in their domestic economies. The participants were invited from the United States and ten of the EU-15 countries, in recognition of the fact that unemployment is nowadays a pressing problem in many European countries and that a common, EU-wide stage for policy-oriented research is currently in the making.

For the conference as well as for this volume, two chapters set the stage for the contributions that follow: chapter 2 by Stephen Nickell (London School of Economics and the Bank of England's Monetary Policy Committee), who reviews success and failure in understanding, and combating, European unemployment in its different forms, and chapter 3 by Edmund Phelps (Columbia University), who gives a stylized view on what he thinks are potential explanations of high unemployment prevailing in many parts of Western Europe. Both studies are shaped by many years, if not decades, of research on the wide range of topics covered in other chapters of this book as well. The country studies that follow cover (in an order that is loosely motivated by geographical aspects and also some similarities among the countries grouped together):

- Denmark (chapter 4 by Torben Andersen)
- Sweden (chapter 5 by Bertil Holmlund)
- The Netherlands (chapter 6 by Jan van Ours)
- Finland (chapter 7 by Roope Uusitalo and Erkki Koskela)
- Ireland (chapter 8 by Brendan Walsh)
- United Kingdom (chapter 9 by Christopher Pissarides)
- France (chapter 10 by Jean Pisani-Ferry)
- Germany (chapter 11 by Norbert Berthold and Rainer Fehn)

- Italy (chapter 12 by Giuseppe Bertola and Pietro Garibaldi)
- Spain (chapter 13 by Samuel Bentolila and Juan Jimeno)

At the time of publishing the short-term economic outlook has changed and basically improved. Still in many countries it is not just a matter of time until cyclical movements reach the labor market, thus reducing unemployment and increasing employment by substantial margins. Problems of structural unemployment, where they exist, are not easily solved. Achieving progress in this area can take a long time. This again is an experience common to many countries, despite all the differences that the studies in this book are pointing to.

I thank Erkki Koskela, University of Helsinki, who took the initiative for organizing the conference on Unemployment in Europe: Reasons and Remedies and for collecting the studies presented in this volume. Also I thank all the authors who contributed to this project for the huge amount of expertise and effort that they put into preparing their manuscripts as well as for their patience with the editorial process. Special thanks further go to a number of anonymous referees and to Hannu Vartiainen (YJS) for his valuable help in organizing the conference and in preparing this volume. I am grateful to YJS and CESifo for funding both the conference and this publication. CESifo also hosted the conference, and I wish to thank the CESifo staff, Roisin Hearn in particular, who was extremely attentive to many details of the planning and administrative work and also provided invaluable editorial work.

Martin Werding
Munich, August 2004

Notes

1. For an in-depth analysis of trend unemployment in the United States and Germany, see Flaig (2003).

2. Up to a point, it is a matter of definition whether actual unemployment rates are assumed to *fluctuate around* a measure of trend unemployment or to *fall to* a residual level of unemployment determined by the long-term trend during the peak of a boom period. Here I tend to follow the former way of putting things. In any case, the share of observed unemployment that can be attributed to the trend component will be *smallest* in the situation referred to in the text.

3. One could of course distinguish more carefully between the concepts of a natural rate and a NAI/NAW rate of unemployment (e.g., see Tobin 1998, who points out that the

natural rate is an aspect of a new classical model, while the NAIRU fits into a Keynesian model). Yet the research agendas followed under either label and the issues addressed as potential explanations of trend unemployment widely overlap across the two approaches. (This is perhaps best illustrated by simply comparing the structure of Layard, Nickell and Jackman 1991 with that of Blanchard and Katz 1999.) Here I take them both to be part of a common objective of economists to get to the root of the problem of higher, and more persistent unemployment than experts as well as the greater public would like to accept.

4. Sometimes the understanding is in the narrow sense where "structural unemployment" refers to the mismatch of employment arising during times of structural change. Some professions and skills become obsolete as specific branches of industry decline, or with shifts in economic activity between regions (see Franz 1991).

5. CESifo is a joint initiative of the University of Munich's Center for Economic Studies (CES) and the Ifo Institute for Economic Research, Munich.

References

Blanchard, O., and L. F. Katz. 1997. What we know and do not know about the natural rate of unemployment. *Journal of Economic Perspectives* 11: 51–72.

Elmeskov, J., and M. MacFarland. 1993. Unemployment persistence in OECD countries. *OECD Economic Studies* 21: 59–88.

Flaig, G. 2003. Die Entwicklung der Arbeitslosenquote: Ein langfristiger Vergleich zwischen Deutschland und den USA. *Ifo Schnelldienst* 16/2003: 14–19.

Franz, W. 1991. *Structural Unemployment*. Heidelberg: Physica.

Friedman, M. 1968. The role of monetary policy. *American Economic Review* 58: 1–21.

Layard, R., S. Nickell, and R. Jackman. 1991. *Unemployment: Macroeconomic Perfomance and the Labour Market*. Oxford: Oxford University Press.

Modigliani, F., and L. Papademos. 1975. Targets for monetary policy in the coming year. *Brookings Papers on Economic Activity* 1: 141–65.

Phelps, E. S. 1968. Money-wage dynamics and labor market equilibrium. *Journal of Political Economy* 76: 678–711.

Tobin, J. 1972. Inflation and unemployment. *American Economic Review* 62: 1–18.

Tobin, J. 1998. Supply constraints on employment and output: NAIRU versus natural rate. *Cowles Foundation Discussion Paper* 1150.

2

A Picture of European Unemployment: Success and Failure

Stephen Nickell

E24 H24

J22 J65

2.1 Introduction

The average unemployment rate in Europe in 2002 was 7.6 percent. This is higher than in any developed country of the OECD outside Europe[1] except for Canada. Interestingly the same applies to the average inactivity rate in Europe as well. So, on average, there is a European unemployment problem. But averaging across European countries in this way is silly. Europe, by which we mean the Western half, consists of fifteen countries (we omit Luxembourg) with fifteen more or less independent labor markets. As we will see, it is how these labor markets operate that determines unemployment over the longer term. In 2002 nine of these fifteen labor markets were operating well enough to produce unemployment rates *lower* than in any non-European developed OECD country including the United States. So why is average unemployment in Europe so high? The answer is that unemployment is high in the four largest economies of continental Western Europe, namely France, Germany, Italy, and Spain. Exclude these four countries and the famous European unemployment problem disappears.

The chapter is organized as follows: In the next section, I present an overview of labor supply in the developed OECD countries simply to set the scene for the analysis of unemployment. Then in section 2.3, I discuss the large secular shifts in unemployment and the circumstances where changes in the operation of the labor market can provide an explanation. In section 2.4, I consider the labor market institutions that might be expected to relate to unemployment over the longer term, and in section 2.5, I summarize some of the evidence on this issue. Finally, in section 2.6, I look at what has happened to labor market institutions in a select group of OECD countries over the last four decades. Then I attempt to explain the significant differences in unemployment performance across Europe since the early 1980s.

2.2   An Overall Picture of Labor Supply

Although I will be concentrating on unemployment in what follows, it is helpful to look at some background information on labor supply. Table 2.1 presents the aggregate picture in 2002. From recent unemployment data the first striking point to be noted is that there is no *Eu-*

Table 2.1
Picture of employment and unemployment in the OECD in 2002

	Unemployment (%)	Inactivity rate (%)	Employment rate (%)	Hours per year
Europe				
Austria	4.3	28.3	68.2	—
Belgium	7.3	35.9	59.7	1,559
Denmark	4.5	20.1	76.4	1,499
Finland	9.1	25.5	67.7	1,545
France	8.7	32.0	61.1	1,545
Germany	8.2	28.5	65.3	1,444
Ireland	4.4	32.1	65.0	1,668
Italy	9.0	38.8	55.6	1,619
Netherlands	2.8	24.4	73.2	1,340
Norway	3.9	19.7	77.1	1,342
Portugal	5.1	28.0	68.1	1,719
Spain	11.4	32.9	59.5	1,807
Sweden	4.9	21.0	74.9	1,581
Switzerland	2.5	18.7	78.9	1,541*
United Kingdom	5.1	23.4	72.7	1,707
EU total	7.6	30.2	64.3	—
Non-Europe				
Australia	6.3	26.1	69.4	1,824
Canada	7.7	22.5	71.5	1,778
Japan	5.4	27.7	68.2	1,809*
New Zealand	5.2	23.6	72.4	1,816
United States	5.8	23.6	71.9	1,815

Source: *OECD Employment Outlook 2003*, tables A, B, F.
Note: *refers to 2001. Unemployment is based on OECD standardized rates. These approximate the ILO definition. Hours per year is an average over all workers, part-time and full time.

ropean unemployment problem. Most European economies have lower levels of unemployment than the OECD countries outside Europe, including the United States. The problem lies in the four largest countries: France, Germany, Italy, and Spain, henceforward referred to as the Big Four. Of the eleven other Western European countries in the table, nine currently have relatively low unemployment,[2] the exceptions being Belgium and Finland. By and large, the European countries with high unemployment rates tend to have high inactivity rates and low employment rates as well. The Big Four and Belgium all have employment rates below 66 percent with only Ireland of the rest joining this group. With the exception of Germany, the Big Four and Belgium also have inactivity rates in excess of 30 percent.

Table 2.2
Long-term unemployment in 2001 (over 12 months)

	Long-term unemployment rate	Short-term unemployment rate
Europe		
Austria	0.8	2.8
Belgium	3.4	3.2
Denmark	1.0	3.3
Finland	2.4	6.7
France	3.2	5.4
Germany	4.1	3.8
Ireland	2.1	1.7
Italy	5.7	3.8
Netherlands	0.4	2.0
Norway	0.2	3.4
Portugal	1.6	2.5
Spain	5.7	7.3
Sweden	1.1	4.0
Switzerland	0.8	1.8
United Kingdom	1.4	3.6
EU total	3.3	4.3
Non-Europe		
Australia	1.4	5.3
Canada	0.7	6.5
Japan	1.3	3.7
New Zealand	1.0	4.3
United States	0.3	4.5

Source: *OECD Employment Outlook 2002*, table G.

Table 2.3
Unemployment, inactivity, and employment by age and gender in 2001

	Unemployment (%)				Inactivity rate (%)				Employment rate (%)			
	Men		Women		Men		Women		Men		Women	
	25–54	55–64	25–54	55–64	25–54	55–64	25–54	55–64	25–54	55–64	25–54	55–64
Europe												
Austria	3.4	5.7	3.8	5.2	6.5	59.8	23.1	81.7	90.3	37.9	74.0	17.4
Belgium	4.8	3.9	6.1	0.9	9.1	63.4	29.3	84.2	86.5	35.1	66.4	15.6
Denmark	2.9	4.0	4.1	4.0	8.6	34.3	16.5	48.1	88.7	63.1	80.1	49.8
Finland	6.9	8.9	8.0	8.8	9.0	48.8	15.0	50.5	84.7	46.7	78.2	45.1
France	6.3	5.6	10.1	6.6	5.9	56.2	21.3	65.9	88.1	41.4	70.8	31.8
Germany	7.3	10.3	7.7	12.5	5.7	49.4	21.7	67.6	87.5	45.4	72.2	28.4
Ireland	3.4	2.6	3.0	2.7	8.2	33.6	33.9	70.8	88.7	64.6	64.1	28.4
Italy[a]	6.4	4.6	12.5	4.9	9.6	57.8	42.1	84.1	84.6	40.3	50.7	15.2
Netherlands	1.4	1.7	2.1	1.1	6.0	48.6	25.8	71.7	92.7	50.5	72.6	28.0
Norway	2.7	1.7	2.5	1.4	8.6	26.4	16.7	36.8	88.9	72.3	81.2	62.3
Portugal	2.6	3.2	4.4	3.1	7.2	36.4	21.9	58.1	90.4	61.6	74.7	40.6
Spain	6.3	5.6	13.7	8.0	8.4	38.6	38.8	76.4	85.9	57.9	52.8	21.8
Sweden	4.4	5.3	3.7	4.5	9.4	26.5	14.4	32.7	86.6	69.6	82.5	64.3
Switzerland	1.0	1.8	3.4	1.6	3.7	17.5	20.7	43.8	95.3	81.0	76.6	55.3
United Kingdom	4.1	4.4	3.6	1.8	8.7	35.6	23.6	56.0	87.6	61.6	73.6	43.2
EU total	5.5	6.3	7.9	6.6	8.2	47.8	28.4	68.1	86.8	48.9	66.0	29.8

Non-Europe

Australia	5.5	5.6	5.0	3.3	10.1	40.0	28.6	63.1	85.0	43.3	67.8	35.7
Canada	6.3	6.0	6.0	5.6	8.9	38.8	20.9	58.2	85.4	57.6	74.3	39.4
Japan	4.2	7.0	4.7	3.7	3.1	16.6	32.7	50.8	92.8	77.5	64.1	47.3
New Zealand	4.0	4.0	4.1	2.8	8.7	25.7	25.5	48.2	87.6	71.3	71.5	50.3
United States	3.7	3.4	3.8	2.7	8.7	31.9	23.6	47.0	87.9	65.8	73.5	51.6

Source: *OECD Employment Outlook 2002*, table C.

Note: These data do not include the prison population. This makes little difference except in the United States where counting those in prison would raise the inactivity rate among prime-age men by around 2 percentage points.

a. Data for 2000.

Table 2.4
Youth unemployment rate (%) in 2001, ages 15 to 24

	Total	Men	Women
Europe			
Austria	6.0	6.2	5.8
Belgium	15.3	14.3	16.6
Denmark	8.3	7.3	9.3
Finland	19.9	19.6	20.2
France	18.7	16.2	21.8
Germany	8.4	9.1	7.5
Ireland	6.2	6.4	5.8
Italy	27.0	23.2	32.2
Netherlands	4.4	4.2	4.5
Norway	10.5	10.6	10.3
Portugal	9.2	7.2	11.9
Spain	20.8	16.1	27.0
Sweden	11.8	12.7	10.8
Switzerland	5.6	5.8	5.5
United Kingdom	10.5	12.0	8.7
EU total	13.9	13.1	15.0
Non-Europe			
Australia	12.7	13.3	12.0
Canada	12.8	14.5	11.0
Japan	9.7	10.7	8.7
New Zealand	11.8	12.1	11.5
United States	10.6	11.4	9.7

Source: *OECD Employment Outlook 2002*, table C.

A second point worth noting is the pattern of long-term unemployment rates (over 12 months) set out in table 2.2. Here we see that while the short-term unemployment rate in the European Union is relatively low at 4.3 percent, the long-term rate far exceeds that outside Europe. The Big Four and Belgium have long-term unemployment rates between 3 and 6 percent, many times the equivalent rates of the non-European countries. High long-term rates obviously reflect barriers to re-entry into the job market, once an individual has lost a job.

Tables 2.3 and 2.4 present unemployment, inactivity, and employment rates for a variety of subgroups of the working age population to illustrate the wide variations in the patterns across age and gender groupings. Focusing first on prime working age men (age 25–54), we see that in most countries more of this group are inactive than unemployed. Furthermore the inactivity rate in this group is higher in the United States than in the European Union. Interestingly most inactive men in this age group are classified as sick or disabled, so the majority of these men are claiming some form of state benefits. Note that the size of this disability group has risen substantially since the 1970s in nearly every country, and this increase has typically been driven by changes in the entry rules and the available benefits (see Bound and Burkhauser 1999 for some evidence).

Among older working age men, the unemployment rates are generally much the same as for prime working age men, but inactivity rates are much larger and fluctuate dramatically from country to country. In some European countries, more than half the older men are inactive, whereas in Norway and Sweden, the inactivity rate is closer to one-quarter. As Blondal and Scarpetta (1998) note, these large cross-country variations were not apparent as recently as 1971, when nearly all the countries had inactivity rates for this group below 20 percent, the major exception being Italy with a rate of 41 percent, (see Blondal and Scarpetta 1998, tab. V.1, p. 72). The main explanation for the current variations and the consequent large changes since 1971 has been the structure of the social security system. Incentives for men to stay in the labor force vary widely, with generous incentives to retire early being introduced in many countries. This was often done to reduce the labor supply, in the mistaken view that the problem of unemployment would consequently be resolved. So, with the exception of Spain, the Big Four and Belgium have exceptionally high inactivity rates among older men, on top of their exceptionally high unemployment rates.

Inactivity rates among women aged 25 to 54 also vary widely, with the Scandinavian countries showing the lowest rates in the OECD, and Italy and Spain the highest. While the majority of inactive women in this age group report themselves as looking after their family, Italy and Spain also have the lowest birth rates in the OECD. What is important here is the structure of the tax system, particularly the marginal tax rate facing wives whose husbands work,[3] and the existence of barriers to part-time work.

Finally, it is worth noting how unemployment in Italy, Spain, and to a lesser extent France is heavily concentrated among women and the younger working age population. This is partly due to employment protection laws that are generating barriers to employment for new entrants and partly due to the social mores on the need to make a living. For example, in Italy many young people, particularly if they are well educated, will live at home for many years without working but effectively queuing for the most desirable jobs and contributing to measured unemployment (although perhaps not to true unemployment). By contrast, the German apprenticeship system is very effective at managing the transition from school to work, so the levels of youth unemployment are relatively low.

Overall, it is clear that the unemployed are not the only relevant group when it comes to analyzing labor supply. In many countries there are significant flows into employment from the inactive groups that are as large as the flows from unemployment. Still, many more inactive than unemployed remain, so the probability each period that an unemployed person gets a job is generally several times higher than the probability each period that an inactive person gets a job. Thus the unemployed are the significant group of potential suppliers of labor because they are the group actively searching for and obtaining work at a substantial rate. In the remainder of what follows, this is the group that we will focus on.

2.3   Explaining Secular Shifts in Unemployment

Before turning to how we might explain the large unemployment changes over time, we start with a general picture of the period from 1960 presented in table 2.5. Note that in this table, the numbers for Germany refer to West Germany and the numbers for Italy have been subject to some correction described in the table. Both changes have been made in an attempt to ensure some consistency over time. Looking at the table, we see that unemployment was very low in the 1960s with the notable exceptions of Canada, Ireland, and the United States. Today there is only one country with unemployment lower than in the early 1960s. It is Ireland, although Austria, the Netherlands, Norway, Switzerland, and the United States have had very small increases. By contrast, the Big Four have unemployment today far in excess of its level in the early 1960s. Like most countries their unemployment rates took off in the late 1970s and early 1980s but unusually they have remained high ever since. So how might these patterns be explained?

Table 2.5
Unemployment (standardized rate, %)

	1960– 1964	1965– 1972	1973– 1979	1980– 1987	1988– 1995	1996– 1999	2000– 2001	2002
Australia	2.5	1.9	4.6	7.7	8.7	7.9	6.5	6.3
Austria	1.6	1.4	1.4	3.1	3.6	4.3	3.7	4.3
Belgium	2.3	2.3	5.8	11.2	8.4	9.2	6.8	7.3
Canada	5.5	4.7	6.9	9.7	9.5	8.7	7.0	7.7
Denmark	2.2	1.7	4.1	7.0	8.1	5.3	4.4	4.5
Finland	1.4	2.4	4.1	5.1	9.9	12.2	9.4	9.1
France	1.5	2.3	4.3	8.9	10.5	11.5	9.0	8.7
Germany (W)	0.8	0.8	2.9	6.1	5.6	7.4	6.4	6.8
Ireland	5.1	5.3	7.3	13.8	14.7	8.7	4.0	4.4
Italy	3.5	4.2	4.5	6.7	8.1	9.9	8.4	7.4
Japan	1.4	1.3	1.8	2.5	2.5	3.9	4.9	5.4
Netherlands	0.9	1.7	4.7	10.0	7.2	4.5	2.6	2.8
Norway	2.2	1.7	1.8	2.4	5.2	3.8	3.6	3.9
New Zealand	0.0	0.3	0.7	4.7	8.1	6.8	5.7	5.2
Portugal	2.3	2.5	5.5	7.8	5.4	6.0	4.1	5.1
Spain	2.4	2.7	4.9	17.6	19.6	19.4	13.5	
Spain[a]						15.8	11.0	11.4
Sweden	1.2	1.6	1.6	2.3	5.1	8.6	5.5	4.9
Switzerland	0.2	0.0	0.8	1.8	2.8	3.5	2.6	2.6
United Kingdom	2.6	3.1	4.8	10.5	8.8	6.8	5.2	5.1
United States	5.5	4.3	6.4	7.6	6.1	4.8	4.4	5.8

Notes: As far as possible, these numbers correspond to the OECD standardized rates and conform to the ILO definition. The exception here is Italy where I use the US Bureau of Labor Statistics "unemployment rates on US concepts." In particular, I use the correction to the OECD standardized rates made by the Bureau prior to 1993. This generates a rate that is 1.6 percentage points below the OECD standardized rate after 1993.
a. The rates for Spain refer to recently revised ILO rates. For earlier years I use the data reported in Layard et al. (1991).

2.3.1 Some Basic Analysis

The level of employment, and hence unemployment, is, at a given point in time, determined by aggregate demand.[4] This is influenced by many factors, mostly outside the direct control of policy makers. Monetary policy is, however, directly controlled by policy makers and has a significant impact on aggregate demand. These days, monetary policy tends to be set in order to stabilize inflation at relatively low levels. Suppose that as a result of adverse shocks, aggregate demand is low, unemployment is high, and the economy is in a recession. Then monetary policy will be loosened, aggregate demand will recover, and unemployment will start falling. At some point in this recovery the economy will run into labor shortages and inflationary pressure. In anticipation of inflation moving above target, monetary policy is then tightened. The key issue is how much unemployment remains before labor shortages become excessive and inflation starts to rise. This level of unemployment may be thought of as the equilibrium or sustainable rate at which there is no systematic tendency for inflation to rise or fall, (so it is also called the NAIRU, that is the nonaccelerating inflation rate of unemployment).

By and large, variations in this equilibrium rate of unemployment, over time and across countries, will lie behind the broad patterns of unemployment we observe in table 2.5. So explaining the equilibrium rate is the problem. Since aggregate demand determines unemployment, then variations in aggregate demand (relative to trend) should "explain" precisely the observed patterns of unemployment. But this is more of a tautology than an explanation. A country will suffer from persistently high unemployment and persistently "low" aggregate demand if its equilibrium level of unemployment is high. Because then, any attempt to raise aggregate demand and hence lower unemployment will run into the inflation constraint. For example, in the United Kingdom in the late 1980s, aggregate demand rose rapidly from 1986 and unemployment fell from 11.2 percent in that year to 8.6 percent in 1988 and 7.2 percent in 1989. Unfortunately, over the same period retail price inflation rose from 3.4 percent in 1986 to 4.9 percent in 1988 and 7.8 percent in 1989. Monetary policy was tightened dramatically and the short-term interest rate rose from around 8 percent in the spring of 1988 to 15 percent by the winter of 1989. Unemployment increased from its low point of 6.9 percent in 1990 to a high of 10.2 percent in 1993 as the direct consequence of this monetary tightening. It is clear from these data that equilibrium unemployment must have been well above the 1990 low point because inflation was rising quite rapidly well before this point was reached. By contrast, in the late 1990s, UK unemployment fell well below this 1990 low point with no inflationary consequences whatever, suggesting a significant decline in equilibrium unemployment.

A second interesting example is the eurozone in the late 1990s. The Eurozone is, of course, dominated in size by the big four continental economies, France, Germany, Italy, and Spain. A picture of events for

1994 to 2002 is set out in table 2.6. As a rule of thumb, monetary policy, as captured by short-term interest rates, affects demand with a lag of about a year and inflation in a further year. In the mid-1990s monetary policy was quite tight, domestic demand growth was relatively modest, unemployment was nearly 11 percent, and the inflation rate was falling. Monetary policy was eased in the late 1990s, domestic demand growth expanded, and unemployment started falling. However, by early 2000, inflation had started to move above 2 percent, the top of the ECB target range, even though unemployment was still above 8 percent. As a consequence monetary policy was tightened throughout 2000. Despite subsequent easing, particularly in late 2001, domestic demand fell rapidly from the second half of 2000, and unemployment started to rise from a low point of 7.9 percent in late 2001.[5] Despite this, inflation remains above the ECB target range. The lesson from this episode appears to be that in the Eurozone, the reduction in unemployment generated by monetary policy easing in the late 1990s hit the inflation constraint in 2000 and monetary policy had to be tightened to stop inflation rising further. This prevented Eurozone unemployment falling much below 8 percent. On the basis of this example, it is hard to see how average equilibrium unemployment in the eurozone can be below 8 percent, a relatively high level, particularly as unemployment in most of the small eurozone countries has been well below this level for many years.

2.3.2 Can Unemployment Deviate from its Equilibrium Level for Long Periods?

These are typical examples of how actual unemployment fluctuates around its equilibrium level. But it is not always like this. On some occasions countries may suffer from high levels of unemployment for long periods of time either because they experience an overwhelming adverse demand shock from which it takes a very long time to recover or because macroeconomic policy is persistently perverse. In the former case, we may observe unemployment well above its equilibrium rate, although falling back toward it. In this case inflation may not fall, although unemployment is above its equilibrium rate, because the very fact that unemployment is falling will itself typically generate upward inflationary pressure. This offsets the downward inflationary pressure produced by the high *level* of unemployment.[6] In the latter case, unemployment that is kept above its equilibrium rate will tend simply to

Table 2.6
Macroeconomic patterns in the eurozone, 1994 to 2003

	94	95	96	97	98	99	00 (i)	00 (ii)	00 (iii)	00 (iv)
Short-term interest rate (%)	5.3	4.5	3.3	3.3	3.5	3.0	3.5	4.3	4.7	5.0
Final domestic demand contribution to growth (annual %)	1.5	1.7	1.5	1.7	3.1	3.6	3.1	3.5	2.6	2.2
GDP growth (annual %)	2.4	2.2	1.4	2.3	2.9	2.8	3.8	4.2	3.2	2.7
Unemployment rate (%)	10.9	10.6	10.9	10.9	10.3	9.3	8.7	8.5	8.3	8.1
Inflation (CPI)	2.8	2.6	2.3	1.7	1.2	1.1	2.1	2.1	2.5	2.7

	01 (i)	01 (ii)	01 (iii)	01 (iv)	02 (i)	02 (ii)	02 (iii)	02 (iv)	03 (i)	03 (ii)	03 (iii)
Short-term interest rate (%)	4.8	4.6	4.3	3.4	3.4	3.4	3.4	3.1	2.7	2.4	2.1
Final domestic demand contribution to growth (annual %)	2.0	1.4	1.1	0.7	-0.2	-0.2	0.0	0.4	0.8	0.8	0.6
GDP growth (annual %)	2.4	1.5	1.3	0.5	0.5	0.9	1.0	1.1	0.7	0.1	0.3
Unemployment rate (%)	8.0	7.9	8.0	8.1	8.3	8.4	8.5	8.6	8.7	8.8	8.8
Inflation (CPI)	2.3	3.1	2.5	2.5	2.6	2.1	2.1	2.3	2.3	2.0	2.0

Source: Bank of England databank.
Note: The quarterly annual growth rates are based on the current quarter relative to the same quarter one year earlier. Final domestic demand is $C + I + G$ in obvious notation.

generate falling inflation. Good examples of these two cases are provided by Finland and Japan. In Finland, a combination of poor policy decisions including a mishandled deregulation of the financial sector produced a huge adverse demand shock in the early 1990s, which was reinforced by the collapse of trade with the Soviet Union. Consequently, as we can see in table 2.7, unemployment rose from 3.2 to 16.4 percent in three years. Starting in 1994, unemployment has fallen steadily without any serious inflationary consequences. This is a good example of unemployment being above the equilibrium rate for a decade but steadily falling back, simply as the consequence of an enormous adverse demand shock.

The example of Japan is different. From 1990 on, unemployment has been rising throughout and, with a brief hiccup, inflation has been falling, turning negative in 1999. This suggests that unemployment has been above the equilibrium rate for a long time, which equally suggests that something has gone wrong on the macro policy front.

Aside from these types of exceptions, the longer term patterns of unemployment tend to be dominated by shifts in the equilibrium rate. One way of checking on this is to look at two groups of European countries. In the first group are France, Germany, Italy, and Spain—the Big Four. In the second group are Denmark, Netherlands, and the United Kingdom. From table 2.5 we see that unemployment in the period 1973 to 1979 was much the same in all these countries. Then in the 1980s unemployment rose substantially, again in all these countries. But by 2000 to 2001, unemployment in the Big Four remained around twice as high as in the 1973 to 1979 period. By contrast, in the second group, unemployment was roughly the same in 2000 to 2001 as in 1973 to 1979. This suggests that equilibrium unemployment is much higher today in the Big Four than it was in 1973 to 1979 whereas, in the second group, equilibrium unemployment is today at roughly the same level as in the 1970s. We can see this clearly by looking at the relationship between unemployment and vacancies (the Beveridge curve). When vacancies are high, unemployment should be relatively low, because it is easy for unemployed people to find work. Yet, strikingly, in France, West Germany, and Spain vacancies in recent years have been extremely high by historical standards despite high unemployment. (There are no vacancy data for Italy.) It is this high level of vacancies that helped to generate increasing European inflation in 1999/2000, which led to higher interest rates and the end of the European recovery, as noted above. This situation is shown in figure 2.1. In

Table 2.7
Examples of unemployment and inflation patterns

	1987	1988	1989	1990	1991	1992	1993	1994	1995	1996	1997	1998	1999	2000	2001
Finland															
ILO unemployment rate	5.0	4.5	3.2	3.2	6.6	11.6	16.4	16.7	15.2	14.5	12.6	11.4	10.2	9.7	9.1
CPI inflation rate	3.6	4.7	6.5	6.1	4.1	2.6	2.2	1.0	1.0	0.6	1.2	1.4	1.2	3.4	2.5
Japan															
ILO unemployment rate	2.8	2.5	2.3	2.1	2.1	2.2	2.5	2.9	3.1	3.4	3.4	4.1	4.7	4.7	5.0
CPI inflation rate	0.1	0.7	2.3	3.1	3.2	1.8	1.2	0.7	-0.1	0.1	1.8	0.6	-0.3	-0.7	-0.7

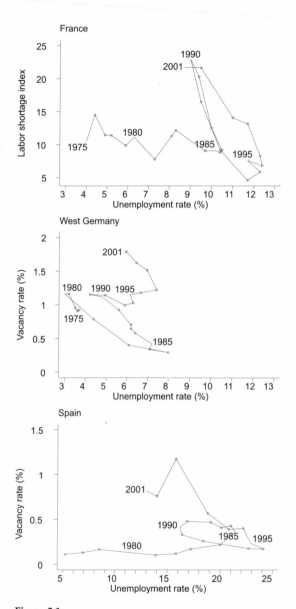

Figure 2.1
Unemployment/vacancy loci in France, Germany, and Spain.

all three countries vacancies in 2000/1 were far higher than in the late 1970s. One might have expected unemployment in 2000/1 to be lower. But, in fact, it was more than double, as we have already noted.

In the second group of countries shown in figure 2.2, we see that just as in the first group, unemployment rose significantly relative to vacancies in the 1980s. But, in the 1990s, in contrast to the Big Four, there was a backward shift in unemployment relative to vacancies so that by the end of the 1990s, the unemployment/vacancy loci were back at their 1975 positions.

So on the basis of these arguments we may conclude that aside from some notable exceptions, the secular shifts in unemployment were driven by shifts in the equilibrium rate, the major exceptions in the 1990s being Finland and Japan. So the next step is to discuss the factors that influence the equilibrium unemployment rate.

2.4   The Determinants of the Equilibrium Rate

There are innumerable detailed theories of unemployment in the long run. These may be divided into two broad groups, those based on flow models and those based on stock models. Pissarides (1990) and Mortensen and Pissarides (1999) provide good surveys of the former model type. Blanchard and Katz (1997) presents a general template for the latter models. Fundamentally, all the models have the same broad implications. The equilibrium level of unemployment is affected first, by any variable that influences the ease with which unemployed individuals can be matched to available job vacancies, and second, by any variable that tends to raise wages in a direct fashion despite excess supply in the labor market. There may be variables common to both sets. Finally both groups of variables will tend to move real wages in the same direction as they influence equilibrium unemployment, essentially because equilibrium labor demand, which is negatively related to wages, has to move in the opposite direction to equilibrium unemployment.

Before going on to consider these variables in more detail, it is worth noting that the first group of variables mentioned above will tend to affect the position of the unemployment/vacancy locus or Beveridge curve, whereas the second will not do so in any direct fashion. However, this division is not quite as clear-cut as it might appear at first sight (see below). What we can say, nevertheless, is that any variable that shifts the Beveridge curve to the right will increase equilibrium

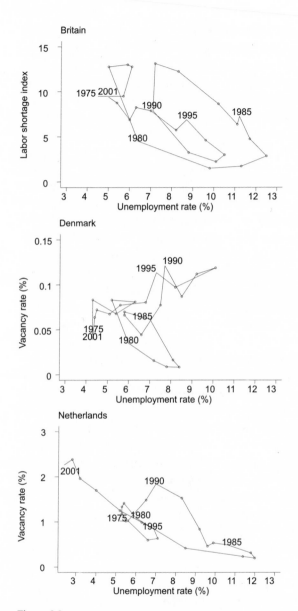

Figure 2.2
Unemployment/vacancy loci in Britain, Denmark, and the Netherlands.

unemployment. So a shift of the Beveridge curve is a sufficient but not necessary sign that equilibrium unemployment has changed.

We turn now to consider a series of variables that we might expect to influence equilibrium unemployment either because of their impact on the effectiveness with which the unemployed are matched to available jobs or because of their direct effect on wages. The *unemployment benefit system* directly affects the readiness of the unemployed to fill vacancies. Aspects of the system that are important are the level of benefits, their coverage, the length of time for which they are available, and the strictness with which the system is operated. Related to unemployment benefits is the availability of other resources to those without jobs. These include the returns on non–human wealth that may be increasing in the *real interest rate* (see Phelps 1994 for an extensive discussion). *Employment protection laws* may tend to make firms more cautious about filling vacancies, which slows the speed at which the unemployed move into work. This obviously reduces the efficiency of job matching. However, the mechanism here is not clear-cut. For example, the introduction of employment laws often leads to an increased professionalization of the personnel function within firms, as was the case in Britain in the 1970s (see Daniel and Stilgoe 1978). This can increase the efficiency of job matching. So, in terms of outflows from unemployment, the impact of employment protection laws can go either way. By contrast, it is clear that such laws will tend to reduce involuntary separations and hence lower inflows into unemployment. So the overall impact on the Beveridge curve, and hence on unemployment, is an empirical question. Furthermore employment law may also have a direct impact on pay, since it raises the job security of existing employees encouraging them to demand higher pay increases.

Anything which makes it easier to match the unemployed to the available vacancies will shift the Beveridge curve to the left and reduce equilibrium unemployment. Factors that operate in this way include the reduction of *barriers to mobility*, which may be geographical or occupational. Furthermore numerous government policies are concerned to increase the ability and willingness of the unemployed to take jobs. These are grouped under the heading of *active labor market policies*.

Turning now to those factors that have a direct impact on wages, the obvious place to start is the institutional structure of wage determination. Within every country there is a variety of structures. In some sectors, wages are determined more of less competitively, but in others, wages are bargained between employers and trade unions at the level of the establishment, firm or even industry. The overall outcome depends on *union power* in wage bargains, *union coverage*, and the degree of *coordination* of wage bargains. Generally, greater union power and coverage can be expected to exert upward pressure on wages, hence raising equilibrium unemployment. However, this can be offset if union wage setting across the economy is coordinated.

The final group of variables that directly affects wages falls under the heading of *real wage resistance*. The idea here is that workers attempt to sustain recent rates of real wage growth when the rate consistent with stable employment shifts unexpectedly. For example, when there is an adverse *shift in the terms of trade*, real consumption wages must fall if employment is not to decline. If workers persist in attempting to bargain for rates of real wage growth that take no account of the movement in the terms of trade, this will tend to raise unemployment. Exactly the same argument applies when there is an unexpected *fall in trend productivity growth* or an increase in *labor taxes*. For example, when labor taxes (payroll tax rates plus income tax rates plus consumption tax rates) go up, the real after-tax consumption wage must fall if real labor costs per employee facing firms are not to rise. Any resistance to this fall will lead to a rise in unemployment. This argument suggests that increases in real import prices, falls in trend productivity growth, or rises in the labor tax rate can lead to a temporary increase in unemployment.

Nevertheless, it may be argued that changes in labor taxes have a permanent impact on unemployment, depending on the extent to which the taxes are shifted onto labor. A key issue here is the extent to which benefits or the value of leisure adjust in proportion to after-tax earnings (e.g., see Pissarides 1998).

To summarize, the variables that we might expect to influence equilibrium unemployment include the unemployment benefit system, the real interest rate, employment protection laws, barriers to labor mobility, active labor market policies, union structures, and the extent of coordination in wage bargaining, labor taxes, and unexpected shifts in the terms of trade and trend productivity growth. So the interesting question is, To what extent can we explain the secular shifts in unemployment by changes in the mainly institutional variables noted above?

2.5   Labor Market Institutions and Unemployment Patterns

The purpose of this section is to consider whether it has proved possible to explain the unemployment patterns shown in table 2.5 by variations over time and across countries in the sort of labor market institutions discussed in the previous section. Cross-country variation in post-1980s unemployment is easy enough to explain by cross-country variation in labor market institutions (e.g., see Layard et al. 1991; Scarpetta 1996; Nickell 1997; Elmeskov et al. 1998; Nickell and Layard 1999). More interesting and more tricky is to explain the time-series variation since the 1960s.

There are several different approaches that have been used. First, there is a basic division between studies that use econometric techniques to fit the data and those that are calibrated typically distinguishing between a stylized "European" economy and a stylized "US" economy. Second there is a division between those that focus on changes in the institutions and those that consider "shocks" or baseline factors that shift over time and are typically interacted with average levels of institutional factors:

First among the panel data econometric models, which interact stable institutions with shocks or baseline variables, good examples include Layard et al. (1991, ch. 9), Blanchard and Wolfers (2000), Bertola et al. (2001), and Fitoussi et al. (2000). All these studies focus on the time-series variation in the data by including country dummies. Layard et al. (1991) present a dynamic model of unemployment based on annual data where the baseline variables include wage pressure (a dummy that takes the value one from 1970), the benefit replacement ratio, real import price changes, and monetary shocks. Their impact on unemployment differs across countries, since it depends on time-invariant institutions, with different sets of institutions affecting the degree of unemployment persistence, the impact of wage pressure variables including the replacement rate and import prices, and the effect of monetary shocks. The model explains the data better than individual country autoregressions with trends.

Blanchard and Wolfers (2000) use five-year averages to concentrate on long-run effects. The shocks or baseline variables consist of the level of TFP growth, the real interest rate, the change in inflation, and labor demand shifts (essentially the log of labor's share purged of the impact of factor prices). With the exception of the change in inflation, these "shocks" are not mean reverting, which is why we prefer the term baseline variables. These variables are driving unemployment, so that, for example, the fact that annual TFP growth is considerably higher in the 1960s than in the 1990s in most countries is an important reason why unemployment is typically higher in the latter period. Quite why this should be so is not wholly clear. Many mechanisms are discussed in Saint-Paul (1991), but there is no evidence that they are important or robust in Bean and Pissarides (1993), for example. Nevertheless, interacting these observed baseline variables with time-invariant institutional variables fits the data well. In an alternative investigation Blanchard and Wolfers replace the observed shock variables with unobserved common shocks represented by time dummies. When these are interacted with time-invariant institutions, the explanatory power of the model increases substantially.

The basic Blanchard and Wolfers model is extended in Bertola et al. (2001) who include an additional baseline variable, namely the share of young people (age 15–24) in the population over 15 years old. The model explains a substantial proportion of the divergence between US and other countries' unemployment rates (48 to 63 percent) over the period 1970 to 1995, although an even higher proportion is explained when the observed baseline variables are replaced by time dummies.

Fitoussi et al. (2000) proceed in a slightly different way. First they interact the baseline variables with country dummies and then investigate the cross-sectional relationship between these and labor market institutions. The baseline variables include nonwage support (income from private wealth plus social spending) relative to labor productivity and the real price of oil as well as two in common with Blanchard and Wolfers (2000), namely the real rate of interest and productivity growth. In all four papers the explanation of long-run changes in unemployment has the same structure. The changes depend on long-run shifts in a set of baseline variables, with the impact of these being much bigger and longer-lasting in some countries than others because of stable institutional differences. The persuasiveness of these explanations depends on whether the stories associated with the baseline variables are convincing. For example, the notion that a fall in trend productivity growth, a rise in the real price of oil, or a downward shift in the labour demand curve leads to a *permanent* rise in equilibrium unemployment is one that many might find unappealing.

An interesting alternative, still in the context of the institutions/ shocks framework is the calibration analysis discussed in Ljungqvist and Sargent (1998). The idea here is that in "Europe," benefits are high with a long duration of eligibility, whereas in the "United States," benefits are modest and of fixed duration. In a world where turbulence is low, the probability of large skill losses among the unemployed is low and the difference in the unemployment rates in "Europe" and the "United States" is minimal, because the chances of an unemployed person in "Europe" finding a job with wages exceeding the benefit level are high. In a world where turbulence is high, the probability of large skill losses among the unemployed is high. As a consequence the high level of benefits relative to past earnings and hence the high reservation wage in "Europe" now bites, and unemployment is much higher than in the "United States." So we have a situation where the relevant institution, namely the benefit system, remains stable but the consequences are very different in a world of high turbulence from those in a world of low turbulence.

While this model captures a particular feature of the situation, in order for it to be a persuasive explanation of recent history it must pass two tests. First, we need evidence that turbulence has indeed increased, and second, it must explain why many countries in Europe now have relatively low unemployment. Indeed the variation in unemployment (and employment) rates across European countries is far larger than the difference between Europe and the United States. To justify the assumption of increasing turbulence, Ljungqvist and Sargent point to the increasing variance of transitory earnings in the United States reported by Gottschalk and Moffitt (1994). There has also been a rise in the transitory variance in the United Kingdom, noted by Dickens (2000). However, these facts hardly add up to a full empirical test of the theory. For example, in Europe, TFP growth has been much lower since 1976 than it was in the earlier period, and we might expect TFP growth to be positively associated with turbulence. Indeed the *fall* in TFP growth is one of the main factors generating a rise in unemployment in Blanchard and Wolfers (2000). Furthermore there is no evidence of any significant changes in the rates of job creation and job destruction over the relevant period (see Davis and Haltiwanger 1999). Finally no evidence is presented that explains why the various European countries have such widely differing unemployment patterns. So, while the Lungqvist-Sargent model may capture an element of the story, it hardly comes close to a full explanation.

Turning now to studies that simply rely on changing institutions to explain unemployment patterns, notable examples include Belot and Van Ours (2000, 2001) and Nickell et al. (2002, 2005). The former papers provide a good explanation of changes in unemployment in eighteen OECD countries, although, in order to do so, they make extensive use of interactions among institutions, something that has a sound theoretical foundation (e.g., see Coe and Snower 1997). Their model is, however, static like that of Blanchard and Wolfers. The model developed in Nickell et al. (2002, 2005) uses annual data, and since they explain actual unemployment, they include in their model those factors that might explain the short-run deviations of unemployment from its equilibrium level. Following the discussion in Hoon and Phelps (1992) or Phelps (1994), these factors include aggregate demand shocks, productivity shocks, and wage shocks. More specifically, they include the following:

1. Money supply shocks, specifically changes in the rate of growth of the nominal money stock (i.e., the second difference of the log money supply).

2. Productivity shocks, measured by *changes* in TFP growth or deviations of TFP growth from trend.

3. Labor demand shocks, measured by the residuals from a simple labor demand model.

4. Real import price shocks, measured by proportional changes in real import prices weighted by the trade share.

5. The (ex post) real interest rate.

   With the exception of the real interest rate, these variables are genuine "shocks" in the sense that they are typically stationary and tend to revert to their mean quite rapidly. This distinguishes them from the "baseline variables" used in Blanchard and Wolfers (2000), for example. On top of these variables, Nickell et al. (2002) then use such time series of the institutional variables as are available, including employment protection, the benefit replacement rate, benefit duration, union density, coordination, and employment taxes. These variables are there to explain equilibrium unemployment. The time-series patterns of unemployment are well explained by a dynamic panel data model. Based on dynamic simulations keeping institutions fixed at their 1960s values, it is found that the institutional variables which are included explain about 55 percent of the individual country changes in unemployment from the 1960s to the early 1990s. This is reasonable, particularly as the early 1990s was a period of deep recession in much of Europe.

In Nickell et al. (2004) this model is extended to include time averages of the institutional variables interacted with time dummies in order to capture shocks/institutions interaction model of the Blanchard-Wolfers type. When these variables are entered alone, the results are much the same as in Blanchard and Wolfers (2000). When they are simply added to the institutions model presented in Nickell et al. (2002), the additional contribution of the shocks/institutions interaction terms to the explanation of unemployment patterns is nothing whatever. So we can perhaps conclude that variations in institutions alone can provide a reasonable explanation for the long-run changes in unemployment in the OECD reported in table 2.5.[7] As a final step, let us see how these institutional variables have changed over time and what these changes can tell us about why the European Big Four have performed less well than most other countries on the unemployment front in the 1990s.

2.6   Changes in Labor Market Institutions and Their Impact

In this section we look at changes in benefit systems, wage determination, employment protection, and labor taxes in the last decades of the twentieth century and see what they tell us.

2.6.1   The Unemployment Benefits System

There are four aspects of the unemployment benefits system for which there are good theoretical and empirical reasons to believe that they can influence equilibrium unemployment. These are, in turn, the level of benefits,[8] the duration of entitlement,[9] the coverage of the system,[10] and the strictness with which the system is operated.[11] Of these, only the first two are available as time series for the OECD countries. The OECD has collected systematic data on the unemployment benefit replacement ratio for three different family types (single, with dependent spouse, with spouse at work) in three different duration categories (first year, second and third years, fourth and fifth years) from 1961 to 1999 (every other year). (See OECD, 1994, tab. 8.1 for 1991 data.) From this we derive a measure of the benefit replacement ratio, equal to the average over family types in the first-year duration category and a measure of benefit duration equal to [0.6 (second- and third-year replacement ratio) + 0.4 (fourth- and fifth-year replacement ratio)] ÷ (first-year replacement ratio). So our measure of benefits duration is

Table 2.8
Unemployment benefit replacement ratios, 1960 to 1995

	1960–1964	1965–1972	1973–1979	1980–1987	1988–1995	1999
Australia	0.18	0.15	0.23	0.23	0.26	0.25
Austria	0.15	0.17	0.30	0.34	0.34	0.42
Belgium	0.37	0.40	0.55	0.50	0.48	0.46
Canada	0.39	0.43	0.59	0.57	0.58	0.49
Denmark	0.25	0.35	0.55	0.67	0.64	0.66
Finland	0.13	0.18	0.29	0.38	0.53	0.54
France	0.48	0.51	0.56	0.61	0.58	0.59
Germany (W)	0.43	0.41	0.39	0.38	0.37	0.37
Ireland	0.21	0.24	0.44	0.50	0.40	0.35
Italy	0.09	0.06	0.04	0.02	0.26	0.60[a]
Japan	0.36	0.38	0.31	0.29	0.30	0.37
Netherlands	0.39	0.64	0.65	0.67	0.70	0.70
Norway	0.12	0.13	0.28	0.56	0.62	0.62
New Zealand	0.37	0.30	0.27	0.30	0.29	0.30
Portugal	—	—	0.17	0.44	0.65	0.65
Spain	0.35	0.48	0.62	0.75	0.68	0.63
Sweden	0.11	0.16	0.57	0.70	0.72	0.74
Switzerland	0.04	0.02	0.21	0.48	0.61	0.74
United Kingdom	0.27	0.36	0.34	0.26	0.22	0.17
United States	0.22	0.23	0.28	0.30	0.26	0.29

Source: OECD.
Note: Based on the replacement ratio in the first year of an unemployment spell averaged over three family types. See OECD (1994), table 8.1 for an example.
a. This number refers to the "mobility" benefit, paid to those who become unemployed
as a result of a collective layoff. Most Italian unemployed do not fall under this category.

the level of benefits in the later years of the spell normalized on the
benefits in the first year of the spell. A summary of these data is presented in tables 2.8 and 2.9.

The key feature of these data is that in nearly all countries, benefits
replacement ratios have tended to become more generous from the
1960s to the late 1970s, the exceptions being Germany, Japan, and
New Zealand. Italy had no effective benefits system over this period
for the vast majority of the unemployed. After the late 1970s, countries
moved in different directions. Italy introduced a benefits system, and
the benefits in Finland, Portugal, and Switzerland became markedly
more generous. By contrast, benefits replacement ratios in Belgium,

Table 2.9
Unemployment benefit duration index, 1960 to 1995

	1960–1964	1965–1972	1973–1979	1980–1987	1988–1995	1999
Australia	1.02	1.02	1.02	1.02	1.02	1.00
Austria	0	0	0.69	0.75	0.74	0.68
Belgium	1.0	0.96	0.78	0.79	0.77	0.78
Canada	0.33	0.31	0.20	0.25	0.22	0.42
Denmark	0.63	0.66	0.66	0.62	0.84	1.00
Finland	0	0.14	0.72	0.61	0.53	0.63
France	0.28	0.23	0.19	0.37	0.49	0.47
Germany	0.57	0.57	0.61	0.61	0.61	0.75
Ireland	0.68	0.78	0.39	0.40	0.39	0.77
Italy	0	0	0	0	0.13	0
Japan	0	0	0	0	0	0
Netherlands	0.12	0.35	0.53	0.66	0.57	0.64
Norway	0	0.07	0.45	0.49	0.50	0.60
New Zealand	1.02	1.02	1.02	1.04	1.04	1.00
Portugal	—	—	0	0.11	0.35	0.58
Spain	0	0	0.01	0.21	0.27	0.29
Sweden	0	0	0.04	0.05	0.04	0.02
Switzerland	0	0	0	0	0.18	0.31
United Kingdom	0.87	0.59	0.54	0.71	0.70	0.96
United States	0.12	0.17	0.19	0.17	0.18	0.22

Source: OECD.
Note: Based on [0.06 (replacement ratio in second and third years of a spell) + 0.04 (replacement ratio in fourth and fifth year of a spell)] ÷ (replacement ratio in the first year of a spell).

Ireland, and the United Kingdom have fallen steadily since the late 1970s or early 1980s.

It is unfortunate that we have no comprehensive time-series data on the coverage of the system or on the strictness with which it is administered. This is particularly true in the case of benefits administration because the evidence we possess appears to indicate that this is of crucial importance in determining the extent to which a generous level of benefits will actually influence unemployment. For example, Denmark, which has very generous unemployment benefits (see tables 2.8, 2.9), totally reformed the operation of its benefits system through the 1990s with a view to tightening the criteria for benefit receipt and the enforcement of these criteria via a comprehensive system of sanctions. The Danish Ministry of Labor is convinced that this process has played

Table 2.10
Index of the strictness of work availability conditions, mid-1990s

Australia	3.6	Japan	—
Austria	2.3	Netherlands	3.7
Belgium	3.1	Norway	3.3
Canada	2.8	New Zealand	2.7
Denmark[a]	3.0	Portugal	2.8
Finland	2.7	Spain	—
France	2.7	Sweden	3.7
Germany	2.6	Switzerland	—
Ireland	1.7	United Kingdom	2.6
Italy	—	United States	3.3

Source: Danish Ministry of Finance (1999), *The Danish Economy Medium Term Economic Survey*, figure 2.4 d.
a. This refers to 1998. In the early 1990s, the corresponding number was 2.3.

a major role in allowing Danish unemployment to fall dramatically since the early 1990s without generating inflationary pressure (see Danish Ministry of Finance 1999, ch. 2). Just to see some of the ways in which systems of administration vary across country, in table 2.10 we present indexes of the strictness of the work availability conditions in various countries. These are based on eight subindicators, referring to the rules relating to the types of jobs that unemployed individuals must accept or incur some financial or other penalty. We can see that countries with notable lax systems in the mid-1990s include Austria, Finland, France, Germany, Ireland, and the United Kingdom, although Ireland and the United Kingdom have significantly tightened their benefits operations since that time.

A further aspect of the structure of the benefits system for which we do not have detailed data back to the 1960s are those policies grouped under the heading of active labor market policies (ALMP). We do, however, have data from 1985 which we present in table 2.11. The purpose of these is to provide active assistance to the unemployed which will improve their chances of obtaining work. Multi-country studies basically using cross-sectional information indicate that ALMPs do have a negative impact on unemployment (e.g., Scarpetta 1996; Nickell 1997; Elmeskov et al. 1998). This broad brush evidence is backed up by numbers of microeconometric studies (see Katz 1998, Martin 2000, or Martin and Grubb 2001 for useful surveys) that show that under some circumstances active labor market policies are effective. In particular, job search assistance tends to have consistently

Table 2.11
Expenditure on active labor market policies (%GDP)

	1985	1989	1993	1998
Australia	0.42 (0.051)	0.24 (0.039)	0.71 (0.065)	0.42 (0.053)
Austria	0.27 (0.075)	0.27 (0.084)	0.32 (0.080)	0.44 (0.098)
Belgium	1.31 (0.12)	1.26 (0.16)	1.24 (0.14)	1.42 (0.15)
Canada	0.64 (0.062)	0.51 (0.068)	0.66 (0.058)	0.50 (0.052)
Denmark	1.14 (0.13)	1.13 (0.12)	1.74 (0.17)	1.66 (0.32)
Finland	0.90 (0.18)	0.97 (0.26)	1.69 (0.10)	1.40 (0.12)
France	0.66 (0.065)	0.73 (0.078)	1.25 (0.11)	1.30 (0.11)
Germany	0.80 (0.11)	1.03 (0.18)	1.53 (0.19)	1.26 (0.14)
Ireland	1.52 (0.087)	1.41 (0.096)	1.54 (0.099)	1.54 (0.21)
Italy	—	—	1.36 (0.13)	1.12 (0.095)
Japan	0.17 (0.065)	0.16 (0.070)	0.09 (0.036)	0.09 (0.022)
Netherlands	1.16 (0.11)	1.25 (0.15)	1.59 (0.24)	1.74 (0.42)
Norway	0.61 (0.23)	0.81 (0.17)	1.15 (0.19)	0.90 (0.27)
New Zealand	0.90 (0.25)	0.93 (0.13)	0.79 (0.083)	0.63 (0.084)
Portugal	0.33	0.48	0.84 (0.15)	0.78 (0.15)
Spain	0.33 (0.015)	0.85 (0.050)	0.50 (0.022)	0.70 (0.037)
Sweden	2.10 (0.88)	1.54 (1.10)	2.97 (0.34)	1.97 (0.24)
Switzerland	0.19 (0.079)	0.21 (0.12)	0.38 (0.095)	0.77 (0.22)
United Kingdom	0.75 (0.067)	0.67 (0.093)	0.57 (0.054)	0.34 (0.054)
United States	0.25 (0.035)	0.23 (0.044)	0.21 (0.030)	0.17 (0.038)

Source: *OECD Employment Outlook 2001*, table 1.5.
Note: In brackets are the figures normalized on the percent unemployment rate.

positive outcomes, but other types of measures such as employment subsidies and labor market training must be well designed if they are to have a strong impact (see Martin 2000 for a detailed analysis).

Turning to the numbers, we see that by and large, the countries of Northern Europe and Scandinavia devote most resources to ALMPs. It might be hypothesized that they do this because high expenditure on ALMPs is required to offset their rather generous unemployment benefits systems and to push unemployed individuals into work. Such additional pressure on the unemployed is not required if benefits are very low relative to potential earnings in work.

2.6.2   Systems of Wage Determination

In most countries in the OECD, the majority of workers have their wages set by collective bargaining between employers and trade

Table 2.12
Collective bargaining coverage (%)

	1960	1965	1970	1975	1980	1985	1990	1994
Austria	na	na	na	na	na	na	99	99
Australia	85	85	85	85	85	85	80	80
Belgium	80	80	80	85	90	90	90	90
Canada	35	33	36	39	40	39	38	36
Denmark	67	68	68	70	72	74	69	69
Finland	95	95	95	95	95	95	95	95
France	na	na	na	na	85	na	92	95
Germany	90	90	90	90	91	90	90	92
Ireland	na	na	na	na	na	na	na	na
Italy	91	90	88	85	85	85	83	82
Japan	na	na	na	na	28	na	23	21
Netherlands	100	na	na	na	76	80	na	85
New Zealand	na	na	na	na	na	na	67	31
Norway	65	65	65	65	70	70	70	70
Portugal	na	na	na	na	70	na	79	71
Spain	na	na	na	na	68	70	76	78
Sweden	na	na	na	na	na	na	86	89
Switzerland	na	na	na	na	na	na	53	53
United Kingdom	67	67	68	72	70	64	54	40
United States	29	27	27	24	21	21	18	17

Source: These data were collected by Wolfgang Ochel. Further details may be found in Ochel (2001).

unions at the plant, firm, industry, or aggregate level. This is important for this discussion because there is some evidence that trade union power in wage setting has a large impact on unemployment.[12] Unfortunately, we do not have complete data on collective bargaining coverage (the proportion of employees covered by collective agreements), but the data presented in table 2.12 give a reasonable picture. Across most of continental Europe, including Scandinavia but excluding Switzerland, coverage is both high and stable. As we will see, this is either because most people belong to trade unions or because union agreements are extended by law to cover nonmembers in the same sector. In Switzerland and in the OECD countries outside continental Europe and Scandinavia, coverage is generally much lower, with the exception of Australia. In the United Kingdom, the United States, and New Zealand, coverage has declined with the fall in union density, there being no extension laws.

Table 2.13
Union density (%)

	1960–1964	1965–1972	1973–1979	1980–1987	1988–1995	1996–1998	Extension laws in place[a]
Australia	48	45	49	49	43	35	√
Austria	59	57	52	51	45	39	√
Belgium	40	42	52	52	52	—	√
Canada	27	29	35	37	36	36	×
Denmark	60	61	71	79	76	76	×
Finland	35	47	66	69	76	80	√
France	20	21	21	16	10	10	√
Germany (W)	34	32	35	34	31	27	√
Ireland	47	51	56	56	51	43	×
Italy	25	32	48	45	40	37	√
Japan	33	33	30	27	24	22	×
Netherlands	41	38	37	30	24	24	√
Norway	52	51	52	55	56	55	×
New Zealand	36	35	38	37	35	21	×
Portugal	61	61	61	57	34	25	√
Spain	9	9	9	11	16	18	√
Sweden	64	66	76	83	84	87	×
Switzerland	35	32	32	29	25	23	√[b]
United Kingdom	44	47	55	53	42	35	×
United States	27	26	25	20	16	14	×

Source: Ebbinghaus and Visser (2000).
Note: Union density = union members as a percentage of employees. In both Spain and Portugal, union membership in the 1960s and 1970s does not have the same implications as elsewhere because there was pervasive government intervention in wage determination during most of this period.
a. Effectively, bargained wages extended to non-union firms typically at the behest of one party to the bargain.
b. Extension only at the behest of both parties to a bargain. For details, see OECD (1994), table 5.11.

Table 2.13 presents the percentage of employees who are union members. Across most of Scandinavia, membership tends to be high. By contrast, in much of continental Europe and in Australia, union density tends to be less than 50 percent and is gradually declining. In these countries there is consequently a wide and widening gap between density and coverage, which it is the job of the extension laws to fill. This situation is most striking in France, which has the lowest union density in the OECD at around 10 percent but one of the highest levels of coverage (around 95 percent). Outside these regions both density and coverage tend to be relatively low, and both are declining at greater or lesser rates. The absence of complete coverage data means that we have to rely on the density variable to capture the impact of unionization on unemployment. As should be clear, this is only half the story, so we must treat any results we find in this area with some caution.

The other aspect of wage bargaining that appears to have a large impact on wages and unemployment is the extent to which bargaining is coordinated.[13] Roughly speaking, the evidence suggests that if bargaining is highly coordinated, this will completely offset the adverse effects of unionism on employment (e.g., see Nickell and Layard 1999). Coordination refers to mechanisms whereby the aggregate employment implications of wage determination are taken into account when wage bargains are struck. Coordination may be achieved if wage bargaining is highly centralized, as in Austria, or if there are institutions, such as employers' federations, that can assist bargainers to act in concert even when bargaining itself ostensibly occurs at the level of the firm or industry, as in Germany or Japan (see Soskice 1991). It is worth noting that coordination is not therefore the same as centralization, which refers simply to the level at which bargaining takes place (plant, firm, industry, or economywide). Table 2.14, presents coordination indexes for the OECD from the 1960s. The first index (coord 1) basically ignores transient changes, whereas the second (coord 2) tries to capture the various detailed nuances of the variations in the institutional structure. Notable changes are the increases in coordination in Ireland and the Netherlands toward the end of the period and the declines in coordination in Australia, New Zealand, and Sweden. Coordination also declines in the United Kingdom over the same period, but this simply reflects the sharp decline of unionism overall.

2.6.3 Employment Protection

Employment protection laws are thought by many to be a key factor in generating labor market inflexibility. Despite this, evidence that they have a decisive impact on overall rates of unemployment is mixed, at best.[14] Table 2.15 presents details of an employment protection index for the OECD countries. Features to note are the wide variation in the index across countries and the fact that, in some countries, the basic legislation was not introduced until the 1970s.

Table 2.14
Coordination indexes (range 1–3)

	1960–1964		1965–1972		1973–1979		1980–1987		1988–1995		1995–1999
	1	2	1	2	1	2	1	2	1	2	2
Australia	2.25	2	2.25	2	2.25	2.36	2.25	2.31	1.92	1.63	1.5
Austria	3	2.5	3	2.5	3	2.5	3	2.5	3	2.42	2
Belgium	2	2	2	2	2	2.1	2	2.55	2	2	2
Canada	1	1	1	1	1	1.63	1	1.08	1	1	1
Denmark	2.5	3	2.5	3	2.5	2.96	2.4	2.54	2.26	2.42	2
Finland	2.25	1.5	2.25	1.69	2.25	2	2.25	2	2.25	2.38	2.5
France	1.75	2	1.75	2	1.75	2	1.84	2	1.98	1.92	1.5
Germany (W)	3	2.5	3	2.5	3	2.5	3	2.5	3	2.5	2.5
Ireland	2	2	2	2.38	2	2.91	2	2.08	3	2.75	3
Italy	1.5	1.94	1.5	1.73	1.5	2	1.5	1.81	1.4	1.95	2.5
Japan	3	2.5	3	2.5	3	2.5	3	2.5	3	2.5	2.5
Netherlands	2	3	2	2.56	2	2	2	2.38	2	3	3
Norway	2.5	3	2.5	3	2.5	2.96	2.5	2.72	2.5	2.84	2
New Zealand	1.5	2.5	1.5	2.5	1.5	2.5	1.32	2.32	1	1.25	1
Portugal	1.75	3	1.75	3	1.75	2.56	1.84	1.58	2	1.88	2
Spain	2	3	2	3	2	2.64	2	2.3	2	2	2
Sweden	2.5	3	2.5	3	2.5	3	2.41	2.53	2.15	1.94	2
Switzerland	2.25	2	2.25	2	2.25	2	2.25	2	2.25	1.63	1.5
United Kingdom	1.5	1.56	1.5	1.77	1.5	1.77	1.41	1.08	1.15	1	1
United States	1	1	1	1	1	1	1	1	1	1	1

Notes: The first series (1) only moves in response to major changes; the second series (2) attempts to capture all the nuances. Coordination 1 was provided by Michèle Belot to whom much thanks (see Belot and van Ours 2000, for details). Coordination 2 is the work of Wolfgang Ochel, to whom I am most grateful (see Ochel 2000). Coordination 1 appears in all the subsequent regressions.

Table 2.15
Employment protection (index, 0–2)

	1960–1964	1965–1972	1973–1979	1980–1987	1988–1995	1998
Australia	0.50	0.50	0.50	0.50	0.50	0.50
Austria	0.65	0.65	0.84	1.27	1.30	1.10
Belgium	0.72	1.24	1.55	1.55	1.35	1.00
Canada	0.30	0.30	0.30	0.30	0.30	0.30
Denmark	0.90	0.98	1.10	1.10	0.90	0.70
Finland	1.20	1.20	1.20	1.20	1.13	1.00
France	0.37	0.68	1.21	1.30	1.41	1.40
Germany (W)	0.45	1.05	1.65	1.65	1.52	1.30
Ireland	0.02	0.19	0.45	0.50	0.52	0.50
Italy	1.92	1.99	2.00	2.00	1.89	1.50
Japan	1.40	1.40	1.40	1.40	1.40	1.40
Netherlands	1.35	1.35	1.35	1.35	1.28	1.10
Norway	1.55	1.55	1.55	1.55	1.46	1.30
New Zealand	0.80	0.80	0.80	0.80	0.80	0.80
Portugal	0.00	0.43	1.59	1.94	1.93	1.70
Spain	2.00	2.00	1.99	1.91	1.74	1.40
Sweden	0.00	0.23	1.46	1.80	1.53	1.10
Switzerland	0.55	0.55	0.55	0.55	0.55	0.55
United Kingdom	0.16	0.21	0.33	0.35	0.35	0.35
United States	0.10	0.10	0.10	0.10	0.10	0.10

Notes: These data are based on an interpolation of the variable used by Blanchard and Wolfers (2000). This variable is based on the series used by Lazear (1990) and that provided by the OECD for the late 1980s and 1990s. Since the Lazear index and the OECD index are not strictly comparable, the overall series is not completely reliable. The 1998 number is taken from Nicoletti et al. (2000), table A3.11 (first column rescaled).

2.6.4 Labor Taxes

The important labor taxes are those that form part of the wedge between the real product wage (labor costs per employee normalized on the output price) and the real consumption wage (after tax pay normalized on the consumer price index). These are payroll taxes, income taxes, and consumption taxes. Their combined impact on unemployment remains a subject of some debate despite the large number of empirical investigations. Indeed some studies indicate that employment taxes have no long-run impact on unemployment whatever, whereas others present results that imply that they can explain more or less all the rise in unemployment in most countries during the 1960 to 1985 period.[15] Table 2.16 presents the total tax rate on labor for the OECD

Table 2.16
Total taxes on labor, 1960 to 2000

	1960–1964	1965–1972	1973–1979	1980–1987	1988–1995	1996–2000
Australia	28	31	36	39	—	—
Austria	47	52	55	58	59	66
Belgium	38	43	44	46	49	51
Canada	31	39	41	42	50	53
Denmark	32	46	53	59	60	61
Finland	38	46	55	58	64	62
France	55	57	60	65	67	68
Germany (W)	43	44	48	50	52	50
Ireland	23	30	30	37	41	33
Italy	57	56	54	56	67	64
Japan	25	25	26	33	33	37
Netherlands	45	54	57	55	47	43
Norway	—	52	61	65	61	60
New Zealand	—	—	29	30	—	—
Portugal	20	25	26	33	41	39
Spain	19	23	29	40	46	45
Sweden	41	54	68	77	78	77
Switzerland	30	31	35	36	36	36
United Kingdom	34	43	45	51	47	44
United States	34	37	42	44	45	45

Source: Data are based on the London School of Economics, Centre for Economic Performance OECD dataset.
Note: Total tax rate (%) = Payroll tax rate + Income tax rate + Consumption tax rate.

countries. All countries exhibit a substantial increase over the period from the 1960s to the 1990s, although there are wide variations across countries. These mainly reflect the extent to which health, higher education, and pensions are publicly provided along with the all-round generosity of the social security system. Some countries have made significant attempts to reduce labor taxes in recent years, notably the Netherlands and the United Kingdom.

2.6.5 Labor Market Institutions and the Successes and Failures of the 1990s

Having looked at some of the key factors that the evidence suggests have some impact on equilibrium unemployment, let us see how changes in these variables over the last two decades can contribute to our understanding of unemployment changes over the same period. Table 2.17 provides a picture of changes in the relevant variables, with a tick referring to a significant move that can reduce unemployment and a cross for the reverse. Double ticks and crosses reflect really big moves. A dash implies no significant change. Of course, this is a pretty crude business without proper panel data analysis.[16] However, this way we are able to take account of variables where we are unable to obtain long time series. (Readers who prefer panel data analysis can consult the papers discussed in section 2.5.)

So we can ask the question, Do the ticks and crosses bear any relationship to the unemployment changes reported in the final columns of the table? If we regress the unemployment change on the number of ticks and crosses, we obtain

Unemployment change (%) = 0.25 − 1.25 ticks + 1.21 crosses,
(80/87 to 00/01)   (3.1)   (2.2)

$R^2 = 0.51,$
$N = 20,$

or, in restricted form,

Unemployment change (%) = −0.42 − 1.24 (ticks − crosses),
(80/87 to 00/01)   (4.3)

$R^2 = 0.51,$
$N = 20.$

The restriction is easily accepted. So the number of ticks and crosses explains about half the cross-country variation in unemployment changes from the early 1980s to the present day. We may reasonably conclude that the countries that had very high unemployment in the early 1980s and still have high unemployment today simply have too few ticks and/or too many crosses.

2.7   Summary and Conclusions

Average unemployment in Europe today is relatively high compared with OECD countries outside Europe. The majority of countries in Europe today have lower unemployment than any OECD country outside Europe, including the United States. These two facts are consistent

Table 2.17
"Policy" changes from the early 1980s to late 1990s

	Replace-ment rate	Benefit dura-tion	Benefit strict-ness	ALMP	Union coverage	Union density	Coordi-nation
Europe							
Austria	×	–	–	–	–	√	×
Belgium	√	–	–	–	–	–	×
Denmark	–	×	√	√√	–	–	×
Finland	×	–	–	–	–	×	√
France	–	×	–	√	×	–	×
Germany	–	×	–	√	–	–	–
Ireland	√	×	–	–	?	√	√
Italy	×	–	–	–	–	–	√
Netherlands	–	–	√	√	–	–	√
Norway	×	×	√	√	–	–	×
Portugal	×	×	–	√	–	√√	–
Spain	√	–	–	–	×	–	–
Sweden	×	–	–	–	–	–	×
Switzerland	××	×	–	√	–	–	×
United Kingdom	√	×	√	×	√√	√	–
Non-Europe							
Australia	–	–	√	√	–	√	×
Canada	√	×	–	–	–	–	–
Japan	×	–	–	–	–	–	–
New Zealand	–	–	–	×	√√	√	××
United States	–	–	√	–	–	–	–

Notes:
• √ implies "good" shift, × implies "bad" shift.
• See table 2.8. Replacement rate change (1980–87 to 1999) greater than 0.04 implies ×, less than −0.04 implies √. Double × or √ for changes in excess of 0.25. The latter does not apply to Italy because the figure in the 1999 column refers to so few people.
• See table 2.9. Duration index change (1980–87 to 1999) greater than 0.1 implies ×, less than −0.1 implies √. Double × or √ for changes in excess of 0.5.
• See table 2.10 and the discussion in OECD (2000), ch. 4. Author's judgment based on this information.
• See table 2.11. Change (1985–89 to 1993–98) greater than 0.2 implies √, less than −0.2 implies ×. Double √ or × for changes in excess of 0.5. Bracketed amount must move in the same direction by 0.05.

Table 2.17
(continued)

	Employment protection	Labor taxes	Total $\sqrt{}$	Total $\times$	Unemployment 1980–1987	Unemployment 2000–2001	Unemployment change
Europe							
Austria	−	×	1	3	3.1	3.7	0.6
Belgium	√	−	2	1	11.2	6.8	−4.4
Denmark	√	−	4	2	7.0	4.4	−2.6
Finland	√	−	2	2	5.1	9.4	4.3
France	×	−	1	4	8.9	9.0	0.1
Germany	√	−	2	1	6.1	6.4	0.3
Ireland	−	√	4	·1	13.8	4.0	−9.8
Italy	√	×	2	2	6.7	8.4	1.7
Netherlands	√	√	5	0	10.0	2.6	−7.4
Norway	√	−	3	3	2.4	3.6	1.2
Portugal	√	−	4	2	7.8	4.1	−3.7
Spain	√	−	2	1	17.6	13.5	−4.1
Sweden	√	−	1	2	2.3	5.5	3.2
Switzerland	−	−	1	4	1.8	2.6	0.8
United Kingdom	−	√	6	2	10.5	5.2	−5.3
Non-Europe							
Australia	−	?	3	1	7.7	6.5	−1.2
Canada	−	×	1	2	9.7	7.0	−2.7
Japan	−	−	0	1	2.5	4.9	2.4
New Zealand	−	?	3	3	4.7	5.7	1.0
United States	−	−	1	0	7.6	4.4	−3.2

• See table 2.12. Coverage change (1980 to 1994) greater than 0.1 implies ×, less than −0.1 implies √. Double × or √ for changes in excess of 0.3.
• See table 2.13. Density change (1980–87 to 1996–98) greater than 10 implies ×, less than −10 implies √. Double × or √ for changes in excess of 30.
• See table 2.14. Coordination (type 2) change (1980–87 to 1995–99) greater than 0.5 implies √, less than −0.5 implies ×. Double × or √ for changes in excess of 1.0.
• See table 2.15. Employment protection change (1980–87 to 1998) greater than 0.2 implies ×, less than −0.1 implies √.
• See table 2.16. Taxes change (1980–87 or 1988–95 to 1996–2000) greater than 0.07 implies ×, less than −0.07 implies √.

because the four largest countries in continental Western Europe, namely France, Germany, Italy, and Spain, (the Big Four), have very high unemployment and most of the rest have comparatively low unemployment. This variability is highly informative because the fifteen European countries that we consider have more or less independent labor markets in practice despite "free" movement of labor. Using this information, we see how changes in the structure of the various labor markets explain a substantial proportion of the secular fluctuations in unemployment in the various countries. In particular, we pin down some of the factors that enable us to understand why some European countries have been able fully to recover from the unemployment disasters of the early 1980s whereas some have not.

Notes

I would like to thank Ryan Banerjee and Luca Nunziata for their assistance in the preparation of this chapter and two anonymous referees for helpful comments. The data used may be found attached to CEP Discussion Paper 502 at http://cep.lse.ac.uk/papers/.

1. Australia, Canada, Japan, New Zealand, and the United States.

2. Most countries in the OECD are at similar stages in the cycle, gradually recovering from a relatively mild recession, so this is not causing significant distortions.

3. A key issue here is whether husbands and wives are taxed jointly or separately. See OECD (1990, tab. 6.3).

4. Clearly, there is some short-run slippage between aggregate demand and employment accounted for by variation in inventories and the intensity of work by employees. This is not germane to my main argument.

5. The US economy's downturn in 2001 would have had some additional impact on the eurozone. However, looking closely at the data, we see that in 2000/2, GDP growth exceeded the growth of final domestic demand in every quarter, indicating a positive contribution of net trade (plus inventories) throughout. Furthermore from the peak of GDP growth (2000: ii) to the trough (2002: i), GDP growth fell by 3.8 percentage points and the final domestic demand contribution fell by 3.5 percentage points. So the vast majority of the fall arises domestically.

6. This is a standard consequence of hysteresis in the unemployment process. There is a discussion on p. 382 of Layard et al. (1991).

7. Institutions are not always exogenous to the unemployment process but may reflect some kind of response to past shifts in unemployment. Such a response may be perverse, for example, when labor taxes are raised to pay for unemployment benefits as unemployment goes up. The existence of these responses does not invalidate the studies discussed here because the shifts in institutions usually occur well after the movements in unemployment. So the shifts are unlikely to create any problems of reverse causality in a time-series framework.

8. A good general reference is Holmlund (1998). A useful survey of micro studies can be found in OECD (1994, ch. 8). Micro evidence from policy changes is contained in Carling et al. (1999), Hunt (1995), and Harkman (1997). Cross-country macro evidence is available in Nickell and Layard (1999), Scarpetta (1996), and Elmeskov et al. (1998). The average of their results indicates a 1.11 percentage point rise in equilibrium unemployment for every 10 percentage point rise in the benefit replacement ratio.

9. There is fairly clear micro evidence that shorter benefits entitlement leads to shorter unemployment duration (see Ham and Rea 1987; Katz and Meyer 1990; and Carling et al. 1996).

10. Variations in the coverage of unemployment benefits are large (see OECD, 1994, tab. 8.4), and there is a strong positive correlation between coverage and the level of benefit (OECD, 1994, p. 190). Bover et al. (1998) present strong evidence for Spain and Portugal that the covered leave unemployment more slowly than the uncovered.

11. There is strong evidence that the strictness with which the benefits system is operated, at given levels of benefits, is an important determinant of unemployment duration. Micro evidence for the Netherlands may be found in Abbring et al. (1998) and Van Den Berg et al. (2004). Cross-country evidence is available in the Danish Ministry of Finance (1999, ch. 2) and in OECD (2000, ch. 4).

12. See the discussion in Nickell and Layard (1999, sec. 8) and Booth et al. (2000, particularly around tab. 6.2) for positive evidence.

13. See the discussion in Nickell and Layard (1999, sec. 8), Booth et al. (2000, particularly around tab. 6.1), and OECD (1997, ch. 3). One aspect of wage determination that I do not analyze in this chapter is minimum wages. This is for two reasons. First, the balance of the evidence suggests that minimum wages are generally low enough not to have much of an impact on employment except for young people. Second, only around half the OECD countries had statutory minimum wages over the period 1960 to 1995. Of course, trade unions may enforce "minimum wages," but this is only a minor part of their activities. This is already accounted for in my analysis of density, coverage, and coordination.

14. The results presented by Lazear (1990), Addison and Grosso (1996), Bentolila and Bertola (1990), Elmeskov et al. (1998), and Nickell and Layard (1999) do not add up to anything very decisive, although there is a clear positive relationship between employment protection and long-term unemployment.

15. A good example of a study in this latter group is Daveri and Tabellini (2000), whereas one in the former group is OECD (1990, annex 6). Extensive discussions may be found in Nickell and Layard (1999, sec. 6), Disney (2000), and Pissarides (1998).

16. It is also arguable that taking increased expenditure on active labor market policy as unambiguously good for unemployment is going a little too far, in the light of our discussion around table 2.10. If we omit this variable entirely from the analysis, the results are little changed.

References

Abbring, J. H., G. J. van den Berg, and J. C. van Ours. 1998. The effect of unemployment insurance sanctions on the transition rate from unemployment to employment. *Tinbergen Institute Discussion Paper* 96-132/3.

Addison, J. T., and J.-L. Grosso. 1996. Job security provisions and unemployment: Revised estimates. *Industrial Relations* 35: 585–603.

Bamber, G. J., and R. D. Lansbury, eds. 1998. *International and Comparative Employment Relations. A Study of Industrialised Market Economies.* Thousand Oaks, CA: Sage.

Bean, C., and C. A. Pissarides. 1993. Unemployment, consumption and growth. *European Economic Review* 37(4): 837–54.

Belot, M., and J. C. van Ours. 2000. Does the recent success of some OECD countries in lowering their unemployment rates lie in the clever design of their labour market reforms? *IZA Discussion Paper* 147.

Belot, M., and J. C. van Ours. 2001. Unemployment and labor market institutions: An empirical analysis. *Journal of Japanese and International Economics* 15: 1–16.

Bentolila, S., and G. Bertola. 1990. Firing costs and labour demand: How bad is euro sclerosis? *Review of Economic Studies* 57: 381–402.

Bertola, G., F. D. Blau, and L. M. Kahn. 2001. Comparative analysis of labor-market outcomes: Lessons for the United States from international long-run evidence. In A. Krueger and R. Solow, eds., *The Roaring Nineties: Can Full Employment be Sustained?* New York: Russell Sage Foundation.

Blanchard, O., and L. Katz. 1997. What we know and do not know about the natural rate of unemployment. *Journal of Economic Perspectives* 11: 51–72.

Blanchard, O., and J. Wolfers. 2000. The role of shocks and institutions in the rise of European unemployment: The aggregate evidence. *Economic Journal* 110: C1–C33.

Blondal, S., and S. Scarpetta. 1998. The retirement decision in OECD countries. *OECD Economics Department Working Paper* 202.

Booth, A., M. Burda, L. Calmfors, D. Checchi, R. Naylor, and J. Visser. 2000. *What Do Unions Do in Europe?* Milan: Fondazione Rodolfo DeBenedetti.

Bound, J., and R. V. Burkhauser. 1999. Economic analysis of transfer programs targeted on people with disabilities. In O. Ashenfelter and D. Card, eds., *Handbook of Labor Economics*, vol. 3C. Amsterdam: Elsevier/North Holland.

Bover, O., P. Garcia-Perea, and P. Portugal. 1998. A comparative study of the Portuguese and Spanish labour markets. Banco de Espana, mimeo.

Carling, K., P.-A. Edin, A. Harkman, and B. Holmlund. 1996. Unemployment duration, unemployment benefits and labor market programs in Sweden. *Journal of Public Economics* 59: 313–34.

Carling, K., B. Holmlund, and A. Vejsiu. 1999. Do benefit cuts boost job findings? Swedish evidence from the 1990s. Swedish Office of Labour Market Policy Evaluation. *Working Paper* 1999:8.

Coe, D. T., and D. J. Snower. 1997. Policy complementarities: The case for fundamental labour market reform. *CEPR Discussion Paper* 1585.

Daniel, W. W., and E. Stilgoe. 1978. *The Impact of Employment Protection Laws.* London: Policy Studies Institute.

Danish Ministry of Finance. 1999. *The Danish Economy: Medium Term Economic Survey.* Copenhagen: Ministry of Finance.

Daveri, F., and G. Tabellini. 2000. Unemployment, growth and taxation in industrial countries. *Economic Policy* 15(30): 47–104.

Davis, S., and J. Haltiwanger. 1999. Gross job flows. In O. Ashenfelter and D. Card, eds., *Handbook of Labor Economics*, vol. 3B. Amsterdam: Elsevier/North Holland.

Dickens, R. 2000. The earnings instability of men in the UK. *Economic Journal* 110: 27–49.

Disney, R. 2000. Fiscal policy and employment 1: A survey of macroeconomic models, methods and findings. IMF, mimeo.

Ebbinghaus, B., and J. Visser. 2000. *Trade Unions in Western Europe*. London: Macmillan.

Elmeskov, J., J. P. Martin, and S. Scarpetta. 1998. Key lessons for labour market reforms: Evidence from OECD countries' experiences. *Swedish Economic Policy Review* 5(2): 205–52.

Ferner, A., and R. Hyman, eds. 1998. *Changing Industrial Relations in Europe*, 2nd ed. Oxford: Malden.

Fitoussi, J.-P., D. Jestaz, E. S. Phelps, and G. Zoega. 2000. Roots of the recent recoveries: Labor reforms or private sector forces? *Brookings Papers on Economic Activity* 1: 237–91.

Gottschalk, P., and R. Moffitt. 1994. The growth of earnings instability in the US labor market. *Brookings Papers on Economic Activity* 2: 217–72.

Ham, J., and S. Rea. 1987. Unemployment insurance and male unemployment duration in Canada. *Journal of Labor Economics* 5: 325-53.

Harkman, A. 1997. Unemployment compensation and unemployment duration—What was the effect of the cut in the replacement rate from 90 to 80 percent? In A. Harkman, F. Jansson, K. Kallberg, and L. Öhrn, eds., *Unemployment Insurance and the Functioning of the Labour Market*. Stockholm: Swedish National Labour Market Board.

Holmlund, B. 1998. Unemployment insurance in theory and practice. *Scandinavian Journal of Economics* 100(1): 113–41.

Hoon, H. T., and E. S. Phelps. 1992. Macroeconomic shocks in a dynamized model of the natural rate of unemployment. *American Economic Review* 82: 889–900.

Hunt, J. 1995. The effect of unemployment compensation on unemployment duration in Germany. *Journal of Labor Economics* 13: 88–120.

Katz, L. F. 1998. Wage subsidies for the disadvantaged. In R. Freeman and P. Gottschalk, eds., *Generating Jobs*. New York: Russell Sage Foundation.

Katz, L., and B. Meyer. 1990. The impact of potential duration of unemployment benefits on the duration of unemployment. *Journal of Public Economics* 41: 45–72.

Layard, R., S. Nickell, and R. Jackman. 1991, *Unemployment: Macroeconomic Performance and the Labour Market*. Oxford: Oxford University Press.

Lazear, E. P. 1990. Job security provisions and employment. *Quarterly Journal of Economics* 105: 699–726.

Ljungqvist, L., and T. J. Sargent. 1998. The European unemployment dilemma. *Journal of Political Economy* 106(3): 514–50.

Martin, J. 2000. What works among active labour market policies? Evidence from OECD countries. *OECD Economic Studies* no. 30: 79–112.

Martin, J. P., and D. Grubb. 2001. What works and for whom: A review of OECD countries' experiences with active labour market policies. OECD, Paris, mimeo.

Mortensen, D. T., and C. A. Pissarides. 1999. New developments in models of search in the labor market. In O. Ashenfelter and D. Card, eds., *Handbook of Labor Economics*, vol. 3B. Amsterdam: Elsevier/North Holland.

Nicoletti, G., S. Scarpetta, and O. Boylaud. 2000. Summary indicators of product market regulation with an extension to employment protection legislation. *OECD Economics Department Working Paper* 226.

Nickell, S. J., and R. Layard. 1999. Labour market institutions and economic performance. In O. Ashenfelter and D. Card, eds., *Handbook of Labor Economics*, vol. 3C. Amsterdam: Elsevier/North Holland.

Nickell, S. J. 1997. Unemployment and labour market rigidities: Europe versus North America. *Journal of Economic Perspectives* 11(3): 55–74.

Nickell, S. J., L. Nunziata, W. Ochel, and G. Quintini. 2002. The Beveridge curve, unemployment and wages in the OECD from the 1960s to the 1990s. In P. Aghion, R. Frydman, J. Stiglitz, and M. Woodford, eds., *Knowledge, Information, and Expectations in Modern Macroeconomics: Essays in Honor of E. S. Phelps*. Princeton: Princeton University Press.

Nickell, S. J., L. Nunziata, and W. Ochel. 2005. Unemployment in the OECD: What do we know? *Economic Journal* 115: 1–27.

Ochel, W. 2000. Collective bargaining (centralization and co-ordination). Ifo Institute, Munich, mimeo.

Ochel, W. 2001. Collective bargaining coverage in the OECD from the 1960s to the 1990s. *CESifo Forum* 2(4): 62–65.

OECD. 1990. *Employment Outlook*. Paris: OECD.

OECD. 1994. *The OECD Jobs Study, Evidence and Explanations*, vols. 1 and 2. Paris: OECD.

OECD. 1997. *Employment Outlook*. Paris: OECD.

Phelps, E. S. 1994. *Structural Slumps: The Modern Equilibrium Theory of Unemployment, Interest and Assets*. Cambridge: Harvard University Press.

Pissarides, C. A. 1998. The impact of employment tax cuts on unemployment and wages; the role of unemployment benefits and tax structure. *European Economic Review* 47: 155–83.

Pissarides, C. A. 1990. *Equilibrium Unemployment Theory*. Oxford: Basil Blackwell.

Saint-Paul, G. 1991. Productivity growth and unemployment in OECD countries. *DELTA Working Paper* 91-09.

Scarpetta, S. 1996. Assessing the role of labour market policies and institutional settings on unemployment: A cross country study. *OECD Economic Studies* 26: 43–98.

Soskice, D. 1991. Wage determination: The changing role of institutions in advanced industrialised countries. *Oxford Review of Economic Policy* 6: 36–61.

Traxler, F. 1996. Collective bargaining and industrial change: A case of disorganization? A comparative analysis of eighteen OECD countries. *European Sociological Review* 12(3): 271–87.

Traxler, F., and B. Kittel. 1999. The bargaining system and performance: A comparison of 18 OECD countries. *Comparative Political Studies* 33: 1154–90.

Van den Berg, G., B. van der Klaauw, and J. C. van Ours. 2004. Punitive sanctions and the transition rate from welfare to work. *Journal of Labor Economics* 22: 211–41.

Visser, J. 1996. Unionisation trends: The OECD countries union membership file. University of Amsterdam, Centre for Research of European Societies and Labour Relations, mimeo.

Wallerstein, M. 1999. Wage-setting institutions and pay inequality in advanced industrial societies. *American Journal of Political Science* 43(3): 649–80.

Windmüller, J. P. 1987. *Collective Bargaining in Market Economics: A Reappraisal*. Geneva: ILO.

Zellner, A. 1962. An efficient method of estimating seemingly unrelated regression and tests for aggregation bias. *Journal of the American Statistical Association* 57: 348–68.

3

The Continent's High Unemployment: Possible Institutional Causes and Some Evidence

Edmund S. Phelps

(Europe, selected countries)

E 24

3.1 Introduction

Why is joblessness so relatively high in continental western Europe—the French and Italian unemployment rates 3 points higher than the rate in the United States and the rate in Western Germany, nearly 4 points higher than that in the United Kingdom?[1] How can this be explained when in the 1960s and even the 1970s joblessness on the Continent was markedly below that in the United States and below that in the United Kingdom as well?[2] In those years many economists inferred that in its deep parameters the continent's "model" had a hidden advantage over those two exemplars (relatively speaking) of capitalism and Anglo-Saxon culture.

That is the double-barreled question of this conference and it is my question here. Our answer is apt to shape our view of the remedy.

In addressing the question, I propose a broader perspective than I took in my earlier research. I believe that to understand the *intercountry differences* in unemployment as fully and deeply as possible, we economists have to widen our view beyond structural *shifts* and structural *swings*—beyond those market forces and policy parameters that have gone up or down and are natural to focus on when the question is the causes of the *changes* in the unemployment rate.[3] We must consider causal forces that have changed little or not at all in recent decades.

To generate such candidates to help explain high relative unemployment, I have taken a somewhat holistic approach to economic performance, of which employment is a part. My thought is that the main causal forces behind unemployment differences, thus the relatively high joblessness in much of continental Europe, are forces having systemic ill-effects on economic performance in general: on productivity, the rewards of work, participation rates, and so forth. For example, stifled entrepreneurship or an unsuitable financial sector might cause low productivity or low job satisfaction, which in turn might worsen employee conduct or loyalty and, in so doing, push up the natural, or equilibrium, path of unemployment. So my approach is to seek sources of high unemployment from among various suspected contributors to low performance in general.[4]

To begin, I review very briefly the newly developed economics of *swings* and *shifts* in the natural rate in order to defend my claim that this work has not helped us much to understand *differences* in unemployment.

3.2   The 1990s Theory: What It Did and Didn't Do

The macro paradigm built in the 1990s, a nonmonetary theory of equilibrium unemployment *paths*, focused on fluctuations in structural forces rather than in the "effective demand" and "effective supply" of monetary models. Developing the 1990s theory meant drawing back from the steps taken in the 1980s under the banner of hysteresis. The idea of hysteresis in my 1972 book was that if the aggregate demand schedule suffers a temporary drop, those who become unemployed will be losing their skills and that will tend to retard their re-employment; so joblessness will be found elevated even after demand fully recovers (Phelps 1972). The idea was taken to extreme in the 1980s with the strong hypothesis that those losing their jobs with such a demand shock will, absent a positive demand shock, never regain employment (Blanchard and Summers 1986; Lindbeck and Snower 1988)—at least in a European setting. Later statistical studies confirmed high *persistence* in the unemployment rate, which lent support to the basic idea—that some job losers may become employable only at lower real wages with attendant adjustment difficulties. However, to some extent it simply reflects rising marginal hiring costs, so employment cannot *jump* from one quasi–steady-state level to another.[5] In the end, studies testing the 1980s hypothesis of a unit root, one study by Bianchi and Zoega (1998) and the other by Papell, Murray, and Ghiblawi (2000), pretty decisively rejected the strong hysteresis thesis: mean reversion is found.[6] There is no support for the view that the relatively high-unemployment countries are mainly victims of relatively bad aggregate demand shocks decades ago.

The 1990s work on the role of *structural* forces as the drivers of the swings or shifts in unemployment began with a fascination for two single-cause "explanations." Neither proved remotely sufficient, though. One, the supply-side explanation, was that unemployment rose in continental Europe between the 1970s and the second half of the 1980s mainly as a result of rises in the taxation of wage incomes; unemployment rose less in the United States because income tax rates there generally rose less or not at all. But a scatter diagram presented by Phelps and Zoega showed little relationship between the rise of the unemployment rate among OECD economies over a three-decade span and the rise in the tax rate on labor: the fit was not good and the slope unimpressive (Phelps and Zoega 1998). True, statistical findings of mine and of others support the premise that an increase in the labor tax rate raises the unemployment rate, other things equal.[7] The reconciliation is that a proportional tax rate on labor income can be theoretically neutral in the *long run*. In my models and some others, if labor taxes are raised to finance increased government purchases (and they don't affect agents' preferences), which shifts down the demand–wage curve, the resulting cut in paychecks and jobs causes household wealth accumulation to slow, which gradually pulls down the wage curve. That decline may finally counterbalance the fall of the demand–wage, putting unemployment back where it started.[8]

Then there came the popular explanation that the replacement ratio provided by unemployment insurance benefits was so close to 100 percent in Europe that to lose one's job through no fault of one's own was to win life's jackpot. The disincentive to regain work made joblessness among experienced workers virtually permanent, thus raising the average unemployment rate in the affected (mostly European) countries. (The effect would be worse if the replacement of wages led employees to step up their shirking, but I stick here to the popular theory.) Judicious scholars have shown that the UIB ratio is statistically significant in combination with a whole battery of variables, at least in time-series analyses (Nickell et al. 2003). It is interesting, however, that a simple cross-sectional scatter plot of the unemployment rate against the UIB ratio in twenty countries appears to owe its coefficient solely to Spain's data point. In any case, the explanatory power of the UIB ratio for unemployment differences is pretty negligible (Baker et al. 2002).

The wave of new nonmonetary model building that several of us embarked on in the 1980s and tested with statistical analyses in the 1990s created a framework for analyzing unemployment (and other) effects of a great range of forces. The first in this line was actually Steven Salop's 1979 recasting of my 1968 turnover-training model of unemployment into a nonmonetary model.[9] I followed in a paper with Guillermo Calvo extending to general equilibrium the Phelps-Winter customer-market model (Calvo and Phelps 1983). Fitoussi and Phelps (1988) offered new ideas, though with money back in the models. Finally my *Structural Slumps* got the money out again and got *in* most of what I wanted, including actual/expected technical progress (Phelps 1994). Some earlier results on expected technical progress were obtained by Christopher Pissarides (1990) and some later results by Hoon and Phelps (1997).

In that work of mine and kindred work by others, the explanatory variables were largely the models' *private market forces*, such as households' accumulated private wealth (or the income therefrom), firms' stocks of business assets and the overseas real interest rate, as well as some familiar *policy parameters*, such as direct taxation rates and social wealth, or entitlement, also figuring in the models. The statistical findings laid the broad rise of unemployment in the West to the great productivity slowdown in the mid-1970s, the huge rise of social wealth (and cumulated tax forgiveness embodied in public debt) between the 1960s and the end of the 1980s, and the overseas forces pushing up world real interest rates in the early 1980s.[10] The steep rises in labor taxation in the 1960s and 1970s were seen as a powerful transient force.[11]

The findings also explained why some countries experienced a *greater rise* of unemployment than others did. First, because the great productivity slowdown circa 1974 was relatively severe on the continent, where catch-up growth had been spectacular in the 1950s and the 1960s, it drove unemployment up far more there, especially in Italy and France, than it did in the United States and the United Kingdom, where the slowdown was mild.[12] Second, findings that social-insurance wealth matters, as does private wealth, supported the thesis that as the continental nations regained in the postwar decades their long-run productivity paths, they responded with a huge increase in social insurance spending, mostly in the 1970s and even more strongly in the 1980s. The side-effect of this was a devaluation of work and a consequent rise in continental unemployment rates. In contrast, far more of the welfare state in the United States and the United Kingdom had already been built in earlier decades. Third, the significance of the world real interest rate variable gave support to the thesis that when the surge of military spending and tax cutting in the United States and later the investment boom in east Asia and China ended the era of a low world real interest rate, continental saving was pulled out to finance decreased saving in the United States and increased investment in east Asia, which squeezed continental investing in new plants, new customers, and new employees, lowering employment and real wages.[13]

The crucial point for this chapter, however, is that the forces that sufficed to explain why continental unemployment rates in the 1980s and 1990s are *higher than before* and *rose more* than they did elsewhere do not suffice to explain why those rates are now *higher than in the comparators,* the United States and the United Kingdom.[14] The fact that macroeconomic *changes* produced an unemployment rate *change* of 5.5 percentage points on the continent against a mere 2 percentage-point change in the United States and United Kingdom (averaged) does not rule out a large role for *institutions* in explaining *intercountry differences* in unemployment rates and other performance indicators. It is still logically possible that the continent labored from the beginning with *institutional disadvantages* the absence of which would permit continental rates of 1 or 2 or even 3 percentage points *lower* than they actually are now, and would have permitted rates 1 or 2 points *lower* than they were in the 1960s (without hitting zero). We are apt to overlook this possibility because unemployment rates on the continent were so extraordinarily low to begin with that we cannot easily imagine their being even lower with different institutions. But even if continental jobless rates had all been zero in the 1960s, that would not mean that institutions then could not have been better; it would only mean that better institutions had no room in that *temporary situation* to decrease unemployment further.

In proposing to address institutions I don't mean to re-invent what Layard, Nickell, and Jackman started doing with their 1991 book.[15] That approach sees certain institutions as amplifying bad shocks. A difficulty with it is that such an amplification would also apply to good shocks, and there was no shortage of good shocks in the 1990s. But I am not concerned with that difficulty. My thinking about institutions is not about amplification, and it has a different focus.

3.3 The Crucial Role of the Economic System's Institutions

Over the years I have come to hypothesize that many of the sharp differences among the advanced economies in their *institutions,* differences created by their histories or their understanding of how the

economy works or maybe their values, are important causes of disparities in these countries' *dynamism*; further that those disparities are
responsible for a large part of the variations in these countries' *economic
performance*. Three years of research on the Italian economy raised my
suspicions on this score and forced me to put my thoughts into what I
hope is a coherent (though not fully built) framework (Phelps 2002b).

What do these terms mean and where is unemployment in this
thesis? Economic performance has several dimensions, of course. For
me at any rate, the performance of an economy is better if, following
one or more sorts of structural, particularly institutional, changes, there
results increased *productivity* (thus wages), jobs with greater *stimulation
and challenge* (leading to greater job satisfaction and greater intellectual
development), broader *inclusion* (thus wider access to jobs), and finally,
more *robustness* against downside shocks (thus less severe downturns).

All these improvements, I would argue, act to lower unemployment.
A lift to (the path of) productivity, in normal cases, will tend to raise
wage rates and, in so doing, to shrink unemployment (as long as
wealth does not catch up). Greater job satisfaction will obviously boost
employees' loyalty—reduce their quitting, shirking, abstenteeism, and
other pathologies—and that presumably has a permanent effect on unemployment. Changes, such as policy measures, that widen inclusion
tend to reduce unemployment rates among those whose inclusion has
been only marginal, sporadic, or precarious. And reduced risk of deep
downturns, besides shaving off some of the peaks in the unemployment series, encourages firms to invest more in their employees and
workers to invest more in their own skills, both possibly reducing unemployment rates in good times.

Dynamism refers to vitality plus direction. "Greater dynamism"
means a greater volume of *well-directed innovation*—either more innovations (per unit time) to select among or better selection, or both. The
current growth rate is not the measure of this dynamism. At best the
economy's productivity growth under *current circumstances* is a sign of
how much dynamism there is. For example, while America's economy
is becalmed, that is not a reliable sign that America has somehow lost
its dynamism. While western continental Europe grew phenomenally
fast in the 1960s and 1970s, that does not signal the continent has
an extraordinarily dynamic system (and has been thwarted by current
market conditions).

On what grounds do I argue that such dynamism promotes economic performance? First, high performance consists of not just high

survival rates and low destitution rates but also, very important, people's intellectual development in the work, or projects, offered to them over their active ages—one of the satisfactions from work on which unemployment and participation rates depend in turn. (Even a dog wants to learn tricks and advanced zoos are beginning to engage apes in problem-solving.) Such intellectual development results if people's jobs enlist their minds and lead them to discover some of their talents and expand their capabilities: Henri Bergson's *becoming* versus *being*. We are doing well if and only if we are getting better. Second, such mental stimulation requires the challenge of *change*: new problems to be solved, new tasks to be mastered, new abilities to be acquired. And that is provided by an economy whose institutions generate economic dynamism, or what Schumpeter (1932) called economic development.[16]

It is widely thought that certain institutions of capitalism, if operable in the country in question, are best fitted to produce such dynamism. Schumpeter's early model is usually cited in which entrepreneurs enter with start-up firms to try out their ideas and drive out older firms, Darwinian style (see Schumpeter 1932). In the interwar years, though, it was claimed that socialism could do as well or better: state enterprises could have entrepreneurs and state banks could finance the best ideas. Corporatist systems of state and social-partner control without state ownership were instituted in Italy and elsewhere to harness the economy to the national interest.

The ensuing debate over systems stirred contributions by several European intellectuals toward a model in which dynamism is created by the interaction of certain institutions of capitalism. Mises (1922), sparking the property-rights school, said that the "motive force" of capitalism's entrepreneurs was their unfettered maximization of their own profits. This force socialism sought to do without and corporatism hampered with barriers to entry and political bargaining.[17] Hayek (1945) said that capitalism's entrepreneurs were not appointed or licensed: they were self-selected, inspired by their particular experience and emerging visions. Thus capitalism opened itself to the experience and knowledge of many participants, potentially all of them.[18] Mises also noted that the entrepreneurial project is not objectively valued until launched and tested in the market. The creative leaps of entrepreneurs involve what M. Polanyí called "personal knowledge," or tacit knowledge, which isn't in books and thus goes beyond what can be communicated or acquired in familiar terms.[19] For that reason, as Frydman et al. say, heads of socialism's state banks or corporatism's big banks, being accountable to the state or much of the nation's depositors, would not be comfortable accepting a relatively novel project for financing.[20] (If they took on such decisions, they could engage in self-dealing, claiming truthfully or not that the rejected applications were even more uncertain than the accepted one.) For the same reason even in capitalism a particular financier could not be counted on (contrary to Schumpeter's naïve view) to rank the economy's whole set of investment projects, since no one would have a general background. So it is crucial that an entrepreneur have access to a pluralism of financiers from which to seek financing, not just one source.[21] Similarly, by analogy, entrepreneurs must have access to a pluralism of managers from whom to pick the one most in tune and with the right background. In short, capitalism's entrepreneurs have the advantages of a high *incentive* to innovate but also of wide *access* to the product markets they wish to enter, to a pool of diverse financiers willing to bear the uncertainty of entrepreneurial projects and to a diverse pool of educated managers capable of coping with the new product or new market.

I find this perspective extremely suggestive. Yet a crude typology of monolithic capitalism, corporatism, and socialism would not be applicable. No real-life country uses only institutions of one system and none of the other two. Some capitalist institutions may be an evolutionary mistake, ineffective for generating dynamism or a hindrance. So we need to study individual institutions. But it is not only the economic institutions that matter. I suggest three *kinds* of institutions in a country as potentially important determinants of dynamism: (1) the *operating system* of the country's economy, with its mix of economic institutions—the focus of the early Interwar theorists; (2) the country's broad *social* policies and attendant institutions, such as entitlements legislation; (3) the country's *cultural attitudes*.

3.3.1 The Operating System

The market economies of the OECD do not all have the same sort of operating system. The predominance of *private ownership* is universal but the degree of private *control* is limited in varying ways. At the *capitalist* end we don't find Smithian capitalism—an ideal construct of atomistic self-financing firms, atomistic workers, and a government that has only to establish and enforce property rights and to administer justice to violators. Modern systems of finance-capitalism have corporations too big to be controlled by a single person through a large block of shares and so have to be public companies. Such systems, recognizing information-based moral hazards to shareowners preventing their full corporate control, include extensive regulations against fraud and theft (called "tunneling"). Recognizing the hazards to investors from managers' self-dealing, misjudgments, or negligence, these systems also include regulatory standards of disclosure, transparency, accounting, and board membership. These un-Smithian systems still leave *uncoordinated* entrepreneurs with relatively unobstructed opportunities to compete for external financing of proposed innovative projects by *uncoordinated* stock market investors and venture-capital funds counting on selling the shares they acquire through an initial public offering to the stock market.[22]

The present-day operating system of continental Western Europe, for all of its capitalist elements and vestiges, is more corporatist. The *classic* corporatist model was pioneered on the continent in the 1920s in the name of mediating conflicts between interest groups, particularly labor and capital. It took the form of a tripartite system of big corporations, big industrial unions, and big banks, all presided over by a big bureaucracy that could negotiate with their the leaders (of the corporations and so forth), control economic change through barriers to entry, licenses, and standards, exert influence over big banks, and, in some countries, wield power of some companies through government share-holdings. A familiar instrument of corporatist control effectively taxes the monopoly profits of the domestic banks or provides state loan guarantees to finance reduced-cost loans for favored investment projects or favored enterprises.

The core of corporatist systems is that they are run by elites who hold authority in the government, the large corporations, and the large unions. These elites impede or block new firms, new unions, and new banks from entering to compete with incumbents. Big changes require consensus among these elites.

In other dimensions the thrust of corporatism is flexible. Prewar corporatism actually weakened labor unions in some European countries, even outlawing strikes and reducing (probably inflated) wages. Then postwar corporatism empowered unions through Italian *concertazione*, German co-determination (*mit Spreche*), workers councils, and an unqualified right to strike. On the other hand, the Netherlands, with the Wasenaar pact, apparently used the corporatist scaffolding to negotiate increased employment. "Coordination" of a country's workers and of its firms in wage setting is still widely used as a *sign* of the "degree" of its corporatism.

A *decentralized* instrument of control in a somewhat corporatist spirit surrounds each corporation with a set of "stakeholders," such as community representatives and local labor leaders. They may be able to block the opening of a new plant or the closing of an old one.

This corporatism was seen by its theoreticians as a market economy that is both more efficient and more humane than the disorganized, and therefore wasteful, inequitable, and unstable system that capitalism was held to be. The presence of these benefits needs to be tested. They could be large. But the costs could be larger.[23]

One cost of corporatism, which has received much emphasis, is that it lends itself to cronyism and corruption, in which contracts are won and resources allocated on the basis of connections and bribes rather than price competition. This is both inefficient and inequitable. Another of its costs is its tendency to stimulate wasteful rent-seeking from the bureaucracies.

What may be the worst cost by far, however, is that corporatism may cost the economy a great deal of its potential dynamism. In operating almost intentionally to slow or to resist change except when there is a consensus for it, corporatism is very poor at providing the adventure, the mental stimulus, and the succession of challenges at work on which business people will depend for their intellectual development and personal growth. And if jobs are less compelling and engaging as a result, there may result collateral damage in reduced labor force participation and diminished employee morale, leading to increased unemployment. In a very literal sense, corporatism prevents the economy from being as *developed* as it would be under an operating system hospitable to innovation. The corporatist economy is stultifying.

The prime modus operandi here is the many permissions and licenses that are required in order to be allowed to start up a new firm. If every new firm has to run this gauntlet, quite a few applicants will not make it through the process. And if every new firm has to have such wide approval, many entrepreneurs will not even try to start up a new company. (Yet perhaps some of the Continent's social policies are also at fault here.)

3.3.2 Social Policy

Social policy in western continental Europe has institutional features not found in the United States and even the United Kingdom. Everyone knows that Europe's social insurance and social assistance system tends to be more massive and more comprehensive than the one in the United States. Europe's personal income tax is generally more progressive than the American one too.[24]

Regarding social insurance, it is pretty clear that the provision of so many benefits is a kind of wealth (I call it social wealth) that may very well weaken employees' attachment to their jobs and thus raise the unemployment rate. However, it is not at all clear that this social wealth discourages entrepreneurship and thus dynamism. At the dawning of the welfare state, in fact, social theorists such as William Beveridge saw social insurance and assistance programs as fostering resilience, versatility, and self-confidence. (On the other hand, self-employed entrepreneurs in most European countries gain little here, being ineligible for several of the social insurance benefits that employees can obtain.)

Progressive income taxation, that is, high tax rates on upper incomes, were originally seen (and perhaps still are) as a way to boost after-tax wages and employee morale at the low end and midrange of the labor force; such effects might possibly reduce the unemployment rate. However, it is plausible that such income-leveling may cost the economy some loss of dynamism (in which case the progressivity may be harmful on balance to productivity, to job satisfaction, and to other aspects of economic performance). Conservative economists in America argue that entrepreneurs must invest money of their own in order to obtain the rest of the money from the venture capitalists, and if the tax rates on their incomes are high (because they have high incomes), they will be unable to start up new companies.

For dynamism, the most problematic part of continental social policy is something quite different. In the name of "social protection," meaning protection from "the market," continental social policy is quite interventionist toward the market in several ways. Employment protection legislation aims to protect employees from dismissal by exacting large penalties on employers for dismissing their workers. The *exception culturelle*, which is not confined to France, protects vested interests in the entertainment sector from overseas competition through quotas on TV programming and subsidies to established domestic producers.

On close examination this social protection is selective in such a way as to hinder new entrepreneurs and thus to reduce dynamism. As a collaborator of mine, David Jestaz, points out, the French subsidies to the arts seldom if ever go to *new* producers to help them to enter the market with new domestic product—new filmmakers, new musicians, and so forth. Since the same entrenched producers and artists get each year's subsidies, potential new producers find it all the more difficult to break into the field. As another young economist, Rainer Fehn, points out, there is an inverse relation among European economies between protection of investors and entrepreneurs on the one hand and protection of employees (Fehn and Meier 2001).

Marco Buti and colleagues have observed that generous employment protection is a low-cost substitute from the standpoint of government finances for generous unemployment insurance benefits: in general, some countries use one; others use the other (Buti, Pench, and Sestito 1998). But from society's standpoint it is not at all clear that these are close substitutes, with one as bad or as good as the other, since entrepreneurs contemplating a start-up firm may be scared off by the probabilistic costs of having to downsize in the event that the new venture has disappointing sales.

3.3.3 Cultural Attitudes

Another distinguishing feature of the setting in which continental European economies operate is their culture, which appears to contrast mightily with America's ethos of ambition, competition, self-help, and initiative. We commonly give little attention to economic culture for the good reason that we cannot be sure it is a cause, not just an effect. But we can still recognize it.

In Europe there is still an antipathy toward money-grubbing, though not as strong, it appears, as it once was. As Hans-Werner Sinn remarked to me, a German would rather say he had inherited his wealth than have to say he made it himself. A theme in recent papers by Mark Roe is that in Europe there is relatively poor acceptance of outsize profits from successful investment projects, with the result that political structures arise to determine and stabilize the division among the social partners (Roe 2002). Investors receive little protection and gain little corporate control because there is little competition in product markets, so giving increased weight to shareowner rights would lead to increased markups and output contraction. The bottom line is that entrepreneurs weighing entry would expect to have to hand over an appreciable share of the profit in the event that their venture succeeded while they could expect nothing in the event it failed.

European children do not grow up with the same experiences as American children. In contrast to most children in Germany, France, and Italy, American children generally begin babysitting for money at an early age, progress to summer jobs as waitresses and cashiers, and some reach more sophisticated jobs as camp counsellors, musicians, and interns before they are out of their teens. This way they learn what is involved in work—the value of money (how hard it may be to earn it) and work's demands (the importance of discipline and teamwork)—and the gratification from earning one's own way. Europeans' sheltering their children from such early experience could inadvertently channel them away from business.

Another cultural difference is that American children leave home at 18, some earlier; the same is true in the United Kingdom. They are largely self-supporting after that age, except for emergencies and college tuition. Continental offspring expect family support for as long as desired. A recent court case in Italy cites full and indefinite support as a legal right. An explanation of economists is that the European housing market does not permit the youth to move out. In any case, most Europeans see this continuing family support as healthy. It does appear true that European youth have a lower incidence of alcoholism and drug addiction than American youth. Critics of this dependency think it breeds an unduly large share of young people who have little sense of independence and who are unwilling to strike out on their own.

If some or all of these things are true, the continental European countries, especially the Big Three, which have done so badly in the past decade, would do well to attempt some changes—not a wholesale revolution but selected changes, in some cases incremental changes—in the hope of sharply boosting the dynamism of their economies. If I am right, higher employment would be one of a whole range of benefits that would result.

3.4   A Glance at Some Evidence

I will discuss in the small remaining space some evidence in favor of elements of my thesis on the sources of dynamism and its benefits for performance.

Part of the evidence is simply an imaginative reading of recent history, which is perfectly legitimate though not sufficient to convince. The continent enjoyed rapid growth when it could exploit the yawning gap that had opened up between its technological practice and the best practice in the world—generally US practice but later also Japan's practice in some of its export industries. This gave a misleading impression that its economy was structured for dynamism somehow. In

fact the dearth of dynamism became apparent once the gap had nar-
rowed to such an extent that investing of all kinds—in new employees,
new plants, and so forth—was no longer at the elevated levels necessi-
tated in the catch-up phase. Then unemployment rates crept up inexo-
rably to much *higher* levels than the range in which the rates fluctuated
in the United States and the United Kingdom. It is pretty compelling
that what the continent needs to spark higher levels of activity is a return to higher rates of such investing, though of course it will not be
possible to get back to the rates of the 1960s. Yet it is fair to say that
this recent experience is inspiration for my thesis, not a test of it.

What then are the thesis's testable implications? Here is one set of
tests. Corporatist systems tend to inflate the share of gross income
going to capital rather than labor by suppressing competition among
incumbent firms and by controlling and impeding entry of new start-
ups innovators. This same monopolization plus the costs of the bureaucratic red tape and the unanimity-seeking required by investment
projects tend also to depress the value (per unit) put by CEOs on all
or most of the various business assets (plant, equipment, job-ready
employees, customers) in which firms must invest in order to make
profits. The result, in turn, of this weakness in business-asset values is
diminished investment in these assets by the business sector and thus
weakness in real wages, employment, and entrepreneurship. Are these
predictions borne out by the data? It seems to me that they are. Capital's share is far bigger on the continent, I believe, than in the United
States and United Kingdom, and share prices are, I believe, more
depressed. And this has been the pattern for a decade.

Some novel ideas for empirical tests began arising in the course of a
paper on investment booms, which I wrote with Gylfi Zoega a couple
of years ago following a preliminary piece in the *Financial Times*.[25] The
background to this research was the record-breaking investment boom
in the United States over the second half of the 1990s that was not
explained by existing models (at least not models that tie the expected
growth rate of productivity to recent growth). My modeling of the
boom was based on the theory, given an intuitive expression by
Spiethoff and Cassel, that asset values and thus investment activity
jump *off* their accustomed saddlepaths and *onto* (explosive) boom tra-
jectories when there is the sudden expectation of new uses for capital
(at normal rates of return)—in some new method, new product, or
new region—*at some future date*. These effects are apt to be "signaled"
by the value of the *stock market* per basket of business assets or per unit

of GDP. (In the unemployment equation studied in the 2001 piece this "normalized market cap" variable performed very well.) Thus market economies are excited by visions of future lifts to productivity. At least the more entrepreneurial ones are.

It also came to me that investment booms may be generally good (on balance) and are a sign of dynamism. A productively creative economy has the occasional investment boom followed by a spell of tidying up, learning by doing and the occasional research just as a productively creative person has the occasional rush of energy and focus, then returns to a relaxed and ruminative state.[26]

These thoughts led to a question: If some economies are more capable of responding to the prospects driving a boom than others, was there evidence that the countries having the strongest booms in the late 1990s had more entrepreneurial economies? More of certain capitalist institutions and fewer of certain corporatist ones? Yes. Some countries were clear boomers—the United States, United Kingdom, and the Netherlands, with Canada, Australia, and Sweden less so, others nonboomers—Germany, Italy, and Belgium, with Spain, Austria, and France showing more life. And the endowment of institutions among the former differed markedly from that of the latter (see table 3.1).

The data tend to confirm that a country was more likely to have seized the boom if it had capital markets providing entrepreneurs with access to venture capital and stock exchanges offering liquidity and transparency, product markets open to start-ups and to new entrants generally, and labor markets offering opportunities to hire and boss and fire employees without large and uncertain penalties and restrictions. The ranking of countries by strength of the boom correlates well with several institutional indicators: notably the OECD index of bureaucratic red tape and the OECD employment protection index. It is also weakly correlated with that strange "index of corporatism" sometimes used, the degree of employer- and union-coordination in wage setting. (These good results are not regularly obtained.)

Two much more original results are, for me, most arresting. The proportion of the labor force having a university or college degree turned out to be strongly correlated with a country's ranking by strength of the boom. The inspiration to try this indicator came from the Nelson and Phelps (1966) paper. That simple model of the diffusion of innovations emphasizes the facilitating role of advanced education in an entrepreneurial economy: managers have to use their education to

Table 3.1
The 1990s investment boom: Measures and some sources

	Mean annual growth rate			Stock market capital-ization (%GDP)	Red tape index	Union and em-ployer coord'n	Univer-sity degree (%LF)
	Fixed invest-ment	Real exchange rate	Labor's share				
Strong general investment boom in evidence							
United Kingdom	10.8%	8.5%	2.0%	80	0.5	2	21
United States	10.6%	4.3%	0.6%	50	1.3	2	33
Canada	11.6%	−2.2%	1.3%	45	—	2	37
Holland (1997)	7.6%	0.9%	0.3%	40	1.4	4	22
Sweden (1997)	9.1%	−2.4%	2.1%	50	1.8	6	28
Australia (1995)	8.5%	−0.2%	−0.4	50	—	—	24
Few signs of investment boom driving the expansion (if any)							
Austria	8.7%	−1.4%	0.1%	13	—	6	8
Spain	8.8%	−1.3%	−0.7%	25	1.8	3	16
France	6.2%	−1.9%	−0.3%	25	2.7	4	19
Belgium	6.0%	−1.9%	−1.1%	42	2.6	4	25
Italy	4.0%	0.3%	−0.7%	18	2.7	4	8
Germany	3.6%	−2.2%	−0.1%	22	2.1	5	23
Euro zone	5.7%	−1.5%	−0.5%	—	—	—	—

Source: OECD, *Economic Outlook* (June 2000, app. and ch. VII).
Notes: Mean growth rate is the mean of the annual growth rates up to 1999 from 1996 or the start date given in parentheses. Investment is real gross private nonresidential fixed capital formation. Compensation per employee is real total labor cost per person employed in the business sector. Labor's share is compensation per employee to output per employee in the business sector; only the growth rates from 1996 are available. The exchange rate is an index of trade-weighted nominal rates deflated by consumer price indices. Market capitalization figures from Morgan Stanley Capital International are for 1988. The OECD red tape index is from *The Economist*, July 1999. Proportion of labor force with university degrees is from the OECD.

solve the many problems that new ideas pose. A corollary I would add here is that *without* such problem-solving capacity in others, innovations will be few and far between. Entrepreneurs will innovate fewer intermediate products and new consumer goods if their diffusion would be slowed or permanently limited by the dearth of sophistication among the managers, employees, or households on whom adoption and use would depend. Furthermore entrepreneurs, who may themselves not be of sterling educational attainment, can't design and launch commercial innovations without well-educated managers to address legal, technical, financial, and even cultural problems that come up.

Another unexpected result was the stunning predictive power of the proxy for the prior development of the stock market—stock market capitalization in 1988 normalized by the GDP. There are three reasons for its importance, I believe. First, innovators often want a stock market for their financing or require a venture capitalist who will in future need to sell their shares to that market. Second, the listing of a firm's shares in a stock exchange is like a seal of approval that boosts the price of the shares, since to gain listing the firm has to meet requirements for financial accounting—transparency, frequency, prompt disclosure—that the exchange finds advantageous to impose. Finally the stock market establishes benchmarks indicating what various kinds of enterprises are worth, which helps investors in the private equity market.

The last exercise has been to examine how the *levels* of the various performance indicators, such as the unemployment rate and labor productivity, correlate across the (large) OECD economies with these institutional data. This work is in its infancy. An initial look at the data is provided in some recent reflections (Phelps 2003). I look at these levels in a relatively normal year, namely 1995, just before the upheaval of the investment boom in several of our twelve economies—as if the economies were in a steady state that year. No purpose would be served by repeating here the exposition of those results. Suffice it to say that they are favorable to my thesis that institutions fostering dynamism correlate positively with performance level and institutions blocking or inhibiting dynamism correlate negatively with performance.

Let me conclude. It seems to me reasonable to surmise from this evidence, in conjunction with the few precious theoretical insights we have so far about dynamism, that *economic* institutions—not just the political/legal institutions and the social institutions that have received so much attention in recent years—are deeply involved in determining a country's economic performance in general and its employment (both participation rates and unemployment rates) in particular.

Notes

1. In the latest data, the US rate is between 5.7 and 5.9 percent, the UK rate 5.2, but the west German rate is close to 8 percent; the French and Italian rates at or above 9.

2. In the 1960s, the jobless rate in West Germany averaged 0.7 percent, in France 1.7, while in the United States it averaged 4.7, in the United Kingdom 2.6. By 1979, the Continent still held its lead: the rate had risen about 2 points in West Germany, about 3 in France, yet the United States rate had also risen about 2 points and the United Kingdom rate also by about 3; Italy's rate had risen hardly at all.

3. A clear example of that line of work is Phelps (1994); see also my subsequent papers.

4. Such explanatory forces would have some tendency to make one country a better (or worse) performer in all dimensions than another country. For possible evidence of such an effect, see Phelps (2002a).

5. For example, Phelps (1994).

6. See also Aberg (2000). They conclude that the equilibrium path itself—the natural rate path, so to speak—is occasionally disturbed by a large and sudden structural shift bringing a new mean level of the unemployment rate. (In my view, that path is displaced every day by one or more permanent nonstationary shocks.)

7. See Phelps (1994, ch. 17) and also Bianchi, Gudmundsson, and Zoega (2001).

8. Findings of mine and others support the premise that private (as well as social) wealth adds to unemployment. See, for example, Fitoussi et al. (2000) and Olivier Blanchard's discussion (Blanchard and Katz 1999).

9. Salop (1979). A shirking model was introduced the same year in Calvo (1979). See also the analytical device of the wage curve in Shapiro and Stiglitz (1984). Labor unions were introduced in Layard and Nickell (1986).

10. These are the main results of a series of statistical studies starting from my own *Structural Slumps* (ch. 17) through Phelps and Zoega (1998) to Fitoussi et al. (2000, especially the first part, pp. 237–53).

11. Recent analyses by Blanchard and Wolfers (2000) and by Nickell et al. (2003) also find these forces at work and add others: for Nickell and colleagues, the upward trend is in the replacement ratio and the influence of unions; for Blanchard and Wolfers, the movement is in factor shares.

12. There are two channels: The ensuing expectation of slower trend growth of productivity operated like a rise in expected real interest rates, as first shown in Pissarides (1990), and touched on here and there in *Structural Slumps*. Second, with productivity and hence wages growing more slowly, workers' asset holdings began to rise toward a higher level as a ratio to the wage; theoretically, the income or services from all these riches weakened workers' incentives not to quit or shirk at the drop of a hat. The benefits offered by social entitlements likewise rose as a ratio to the slowed-down wage, with the same effects.

13. Later we found that demographics helped greatly in lowering the United States unemployment rate through a steep upward trend in the proportion of US workers with some college and in the proportion with a college degree—groups relatively immune to joblessness. In the high school dropout group, unemployment in the 1980s was nearly double the rate in the 1970s, and it did not get out of "double digits" until the mid-1990s, as if it were a country on the continent.

14. Had those rates been at zero in the 1960s and had their increase caught up with the *initial* level in the United States and United Kingdom *plus* the subsequent increase there, one would have to work harder to explain why the *rise* does not explain the new *differential*.

15. Layard, Nickell, and Jackman (1991). See also Blanchard and Wolfers (2000).

16. He speaks of new and discontinuous changes in uses of labor (p. 95).

17. He denied making the criticism that pricing is too complex a matter for socialism to administer, crediting it instead to the eclectic Hayek.

18. A standard citation is Hayek (1945). More central is Hayek (1968).

19. Polanyí (1962). A forerunner was the "animal spirits" of the entrepreneurs in Keynes's *General Theory*.

20. Frydman, Hessel, and Rapaczinsky (2001). Accountability was a major theme in the conference volume on mass privatization in eastern Europe (*Rivista di Politica Economica*, 1981).

21. A state investment bank or the sort of big bank characteristic of corporatism would tend to reject the greatly innovative proposals, since it couldn't handle the greater ambiguity of the evidence on behalf of these.

22. Some features of regulatory law serve to protect entrepreneurs: bankruptcy laws, for example.

23. A proponent of postwar corporatism was Tarantelli (1986). An early critic was Giersch (1993).

24. The United States also has a social welfare system—in a medical emergency those without insurance or documents are issued at once a temporary Medicaid card—but not as comprehensive and, in general, not as generous, though there are exceptions. The main lacuna in the American system is that low-wage employees are ineligible for Medicaid yet typically lack other medical insurance, since their employers, whom the system offers a tax incentive to provide their employees with medical insurance, find it too expensive to extend that insurance to their low-productivity employees. The states insist on a uniform insurance program for all employees and pile up insurance protections that the politicians believe their middle-income voters want.

25. Phelps and Zoega (2001). See also Phelps (2000a).

26. Phelps and Zoega (2001, sec. 5). See also Phelps (2000b).

References

Aberg, R. 2000. Equilibrium unemployment, search behavior and unemployment persistency. Umea University, mimeo.

Baker, D., A. Glyn, D. Howell, and J. Schmitt. 2002. Labour market institutions and unemployment. New School University, New York, mimeo.

Bianchi, M., B. Gudmundsson, and G. Zoega. 2001. An Icelandic natural experiment in supply-side economics. *American Economic Review* 91: 1564–79.

Bianchi, M., and G. Zoega. 1998. Unemployment persistence: Does the size of the shock matter? *Journal of Applied Econometrics* 13: 283–304.

Blanchard, O., and L. Katz. 1999. Wage dynamics: Reconciling theory and evidence. *American Economic Review Papers and Proceedings* 89: 69–74.

Blanchard, O., and L. Summers. 1986. Hysteresis and the European unemployment problem. In S. Fischer, ed., *NBER Macroeconomics Annual*. Cambridge: MIT Press.

Blanchard, O., and J. Wolfers. 2000. The role of shocks and institutions in the rise of European unemployment: The aggregate evidence. *Economic Journal* 110: C1–C33.

Buti, M., L. R. Pench, and P. Sestito. 1998. European unemployment: Contending theories and institutional complexities. *European Investment Bank Report* 98/01.

Calvo, G. 1979. Quasi-Walrasian models of unemployment. *American Economic Review* 69: 102–108.

Calvo, G., and E. S. Phelps. 1983. A model of non-Walrasian general equilibrium. In J. Tobin, ed., *Macroeconomics, Prices and Quantities*. Washington, DC: Brookings Institution.

Fehn, R., and C.-P. Meier. 2001. The positive economics of labor market rigidities and investor protection. *CESifo Working Paper* 456.

Fitoussi, J.-P., D. Jestaz, E. S. Phelps, and G. Zoega. 2000. Roots of the recent recoveries: Labor reforms or private sector forces? *Brookings Papers on Economic Activity* 1/2000: 237–311.

Fitoussi, J.-P., and E. S. Phelps. 1988. *The Slump in Europe: Open-Economy Theory Reconstructed*. Oxford: Basil Blackwell.

Frydman, R., M. Hessel, and A. Rapaczinsky. 2001. Why ownership matters. In M. Fox and M. Heller, eds., *Corporate Governance Lessons from Transition Economy Reforms*. Princeton: Princeton University Press.

Giersch, H. 1993. *Openness for Prosperity*. Cambridge: MIT Press.

Hayek, F. A. von 1945. The use of knowledge in society. *American Economic Review* 35: 519–30.

Hayek, F. A. von 1968. Competition as a discovery procedure. In F. A. von Hayek, *New Studies in Philosophy, Politics, Economics and the History of Ideas*. Chicago: University of Chicago Press, pp. 179–90.

Hoon, H. T. and E. S. Phelps. 1997. Growth, wealth and the natural rate: Is Europe's jobs crisis a growth crisis? *European Economic Review* 41: 549–57.

Layard, R., and S. Nickell. 1986. Unemployment in Britain. *Economica* 53: S121–S169.

Layard, R., S. Nickell, and R. Jackman. 1991. *Unemployment: Macroeconomic Peformance the Labour Market*. Oxford: Oxford University Press.

Lindbeck, A., and D. J. Snower. 1988. *The Insider-Outsider Theory of Employment and Unemployment*. Cambridge: MIT Press.

Mises, L. von 1932 (first published: 1922). *Die Gemeinwirtschaft*. 2nd ed. Jena: Fischer (trans. J. Kahane, 1936, *Socialism*, London: Jonathan Cape).

Nelson, R., and E. S. Phelps. 1966. Investment in humans, technological diffusion and economic growth. *American Economic Review* 61: 69–75.

Nickell, S., L. Nunziata, W. Ochel, and G. Quintini. 2003. The Beveridge curve, unemployment and wages in the OECD from the 1960s to the 1990s. In P. Aghion, R. Frydman, J. Stglitz, and M. Woodford, eds., *Knowledge, Information and Expectations in Modern Macroeconomics: In Honor of Edmund S. Phelps*. Princeton: Princeton University Press.

Papell, D. H., C. J. Murray, and H. Ghiblawi. 2000. The structure of unemployment. *Review of Economics and Statistics* 82: 309–15.

Phelps, E. S. 1972. *Inflation Policy and Unemployment Theory*. New York: Norton.

Phelps, E. S. 1994. *Structural Slumps: The Modern Equilibrium Theory of Unemployment, Interest and Assets*. Cambridge: Harvard University Press.

Phelps, E. S. 2000a. Europe's stony ground for the seeds of growth. *Financial Times*, August 9, 2000.

Phelps, E. S. 2000b. IMF seems to have lost sight of rationale for capitalism. *Financial Times*, April 25, 2000.

Phelps, E. S. 2002a. European myths, European realities. Project Syndicate, November 2002.

Phelps, E. S. 2002b. *Enterprise and Inclusion in Italy*. Dordrecht: Kluwer Academic.

Phelps, E. S. 2003. Reflections II. In P. Aghion, R. Frydman, J. Stiglitz, and M. Woodford, eds., *Knowledge, Information and Expectations in Modern Macroeconomics: In Honor of Edmund Phelps*. Princeton: Princeton University Press.

Phelps, E. S., and G. Zoega. 1998. Natural rate theory and OECD unemployment. *Economic Journal* 108: 782–801.

Phelps, E. S., and G. Zoega. 2001. Structural booms: Productivity expectations and asset valuations. *Economic Policy* 32: 85–126.

Pissarides, C. 1990. *Equilibrium Unemployment*. Oxford: Blackwell.

Polanyí, M. 1962. *Personal Knowledge*. Chicago: University of Chicago Press.

Roe, M. J. 2002. Corporate law's limits. *Journal of Legal Studies* 31: 233–71.

Salop, S. 1979. A model of the natural rate of unemployment. *American Economic Review* 69: 117–25.

Schumpeter, J. A. 1932 (first published: 1911). *Theory of Economic Development*. Cambridge: Harvard University Press.

Shapiro, C., and J. Stiglitz. 1984. Equilibrium unemployment as a worker discipline device. *American Economic Review* 74: 433–44.

Tarantelli, E. 1986. *Economia Politica del Lavoro*. Torino: UTET.

4

From Excess to Shortage—
Recent Developments in
the Danish Labor Market

Torben M. Andersen

4.1 Introduction

The Danish labor market underwent a remarkable change during the 1990s. At the start of the decade the policy debate was still dominated by the concern of how to adapt to long-lasting unemployment, and policy initiatives were mainly passive in nature, based on the view that there was an excess of labor supply relative to the job creation potential of the economy. By the turn of the century the debate is focused on how to expand labor supply so as to prevent overheating of the labor market and to prepare for the demographic changes, which in the absence of reforms will lead to a decline in labor supply. The current policy debate is thus dominated by reform proposals to strengthen the incentives underlying labor supply in all its dimensions (hours, participation, retirement, etc.).

Like many European countries Denmark experienced an increase in unemployment in the mid-1970s. The tendency to increasing unemployment was interrupted in the mid-1980s during an upswing in the Danish economy, but it began to pick up again in the latter half of the 1980s. The unemployment problem has thus been persistent, and the registered unemployment rate peaked at 12 percent in 1993. Subsequently it has been steadily decreasing, and currently the rate has been stable for a couple of years at a level slightly below 5 percent; see figure 4.1. In early 2003 there is some tendency to an increase in unemployment, reflecting a less favorable business-cycle situation.

The rise of unemployment took place against the background of different levels of nominal wage and price inflation; see figure 4.2. During the late 1970s and the early 1980s inflation was high, but a disinflationary policy initiated by the re-launch in 1982 of a fixed exchange rate policy combined with a tight income policy brought inflation down. In

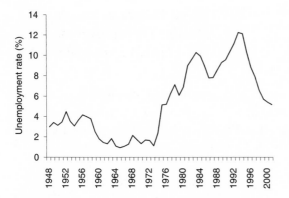

Figure 4.1
Unemployment rate in 1948 to 2001. Note the number of unemployed as a percentage of
the labor force. Source: ADAM-databank, Statistics Denmark.

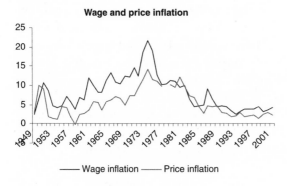

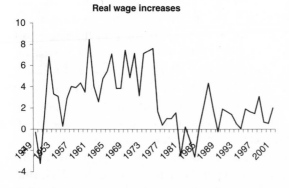

Figure 4.2
Wage and price increases. Source: ADAM-databank, Statistics Denmark.

recent years inflation has been stable at a level around 2 to 3 percent. It is particularly noteworthy (see figure 4.2) that nominal wage increases have been stable over the period in which unemployment has been reduced.

Despite the substantial differences in nominal wage increases over the past decades, real wages development has been fairly steady, and the period since 1970 can, in terms of real wage growth, be divided into three periods. The period 1960 to 1975 had a real wage growth of 5.5 percent, from 1976 to 1992 it was only 0.8 percent, and over the period 1993 to 2001 it was 1.9 percent. It is worth noting that inequality in Denmark has remained roughly unchanged over the period in which the unemployment rate has varied substantially (see Det Økonomiske Råd 2001). This can both be taken as a reflection of how the Danish welfare model works and the political constraints that were imposed on the policies pursued.

The aim of this chapter is to consider the reason for the sharp reduction in unemployment, and the fact that it has been possible to maintain a lower unemployment rate without inducing wage increases. To set the scene for the subsequent discussion of changes in the Danish labor market during the 1990s, it is useful to put the development in perspective by briefly reviewing the developments and policy views prevailing in the past. From practically full employment during the 1960s, unemployment rose to double-digit figures in the mid-1970s, and this situation turned out to be very persistent (see figure 4.1). Various measures were launched in the late 1970s and early 1980s, including devaluations and a twist strategy for aggregate demand management aiming at curtailing private demand and expanding public demand to direct demand toward domestic producers and thereby improving both unemployment and the current account situation. However, this line of policy did not succeed in reducing the unemployment problem (nor any other major macroeconomic policy concern). During the early 1980s there was a shift toward a fixed exchange rate policy accompanied by income policy and a tight fiscal policy (see Andersen 1994). A hike in domestic demand initiated a boom, which also brought unemployment down (see figure 4.1). However, a wage hike in 1987 (see figure 4.2a) suggested that structural problems prevented a lasting reduction in the unemployment rate, and subsequently the unemployment rate rose again. This started a seven-year period with low growth and high and increasing unemployment, which was terminated by the policy shift in 1993 to 1994 (see below).

Throughout there has been broad political support for the view that the unemployment problem should not be solved by a retrenchment of welfare policies via reductions in unemployment benefits and social assistance. On the contrary, various policy initiatives have been taken to ensure income maintenance for the unemployed. As a consequence the rules for benefit duration were extended, and participation in various so-called job-offer schemes could be used to re-qualify for unemployment benefits. Other measures were introduced to reduce labor supply, most important was the early retirement scheme launched in 1979. In the late 1980s and early 1990s an increasingly dominating view in the public debate was that "we have to learn to live with an excess of labor."

After a change in government in 1992 a new policy was launched, which in retrospect can be interpreted as having followed a two-handed approach, although the policy strategy developed over time. Part of the shift was an expansionary fiscal policy to boost growth and pave the way for a reduction in unemployment. The other part was a shift in labor market policy, which implied that more passive policies pursued in the past were changed in a more active direction. In particular, the incentive structure was changed, although there have been few direct cuts in transfer payments and the like (see below).

Against this background, the chapter provides an overview of the developments in the Danish labor market during the 1990s. It reviews the major policy shifts during the 1990s, and discusses possible explanations of the remarkable reduction in unemployment.

The chapter is organized as follows: Section 4.2 provides a few facts on labor market developments in Denmark, and section 4.3 turns to a discussion of the role of business cycle and structural factors for unemployment. Section 4.4 offers a detailed discussion of labor market policies with particular focus on the implications of the shifts from passive to more active measures. Wage formation is addressed in section 4.5, which also considers the roles of decentralization, mismatch, and taxation. The implications of aging and integration of immigrants for labor supply are briefly discussed in section 3.6, and section 3.7 gives a few concluding remarks.

4.2   A Few Facts

The Danish labor market is characterized by a relatively high labor force participation rate (76 percent in 2001), and especially the partici-

Table 4.1
Key labor market facts, 1970 to 2000

	1970	1975	1980	1985	1990	1995	2000
Registered unemployment rate[a]	1.2	5.0	6.8	9.1	9.7	10.4	5.4
Youth unemployment rate[b]	4.0	16.2	10.6	10.2	10.6	8.5	3.1
Female unemployment rate	0.5	3.9	7.5	11.0	11.3	12.0	6.3
Long-term unemployment[c]	na	na	28	32	35	35	250

Source: Danmarks Statistik.
a. Registered unemployed as share of labor force.
b. Age group 16 to 24 years.
c. Fraction of unemployed being unemployed for at least 80 percent of the working year.

pation rate for women is high by international standards (71 percent in 2001). There has been a trend decline in the participation rate for men (it was 95 percent in 1950), and a trend increase for women until the early 1990s (reaching 72 percent in 1990). Over the years there has been a trend decline in working hours (average working hours were above 2,300 hours per year in 1950, and below 1,700 in 2001), and the retirement age has also dropped (currently the average retirement age is about 61 years, whereas the official pension age is 65).

Some summary statistics on the developments in the Danish labor market are given in table 4.1. It is seen that female and youth unemployment went up during the high-unemployment period, which also had an increase in long-term unemployment, in particular, for the unskilled. The reduction in unemployment has reversed these trends.

In an extended welfare state like the Danish with strong universal elements in welfare policies, it is important to consider the unemployment problem from two angles, namely the number of people effectively available for the labor market and the number of people relying on income transfers from the public. The two need not coincide, since the use of passive measures in labor market policies may imply that those qualifying for welfare payments of one form or another are not necessarily available for the labor market. Figure 4.3 shows that this distinction is not trivial for Denmark, since there has been a large and systematic difference between the two. The figure plots the registered unemployment rate as well as a measure for search unemployment (those actively searching for jobs and ready to work; see ILO definition) and a gross measure for unemployment (unemployed plus people in activation and early retirement schemes from unemployment). The figure brings out two important features. First, search unemployment

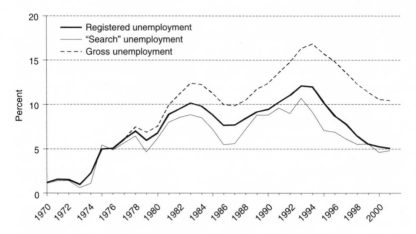

Figure 4.3
Search and gross unemployment. Source: Det Økonomiske Råd.

has generally been below the registered unemployment rate, suggesting that the latter does not provide a reliable indicator of the slack in
the labor market and that some are claiming unemployment benefits
without being actively searching for jobs. Second, the gross unemployment rate is much larger than the registered rate, indicating that the
implications of unemployment for public finances are much larger
than the official unemployment figures suggest.

4.3 Business Cycle versus Structural Components

The development in the labor market during the 1990s was accompanied by a business-cycle upturn. The average growth rate for GDP in
the period 1993 to 2001 was 2.5 percent compared to only 0.25 percent
for the period 1987 to 1993. The level of unemployment prevailing in
the early part of the 1990s undoubtedly had a nontrivial business-cycle
component, that is, it was to be expected that a turn in the business-
cycle would be able to reduce unemployment.

  However, structural improvements are also important. To see this, it
is interesting to compare the developments during the 1980s and the
1990s, which get close to a controlled experiment of the effects of substantial increases in aggregate demand.[1] In the first part of the 1980s
there was also a business-cycle upturn, growth rates soared and unemployment started to fall. However, the upturn was constrained by
labor shortage in specific areas, and wage increases reached almost 9

percent in 1987, which was well beyond the level consistent with the fixed exchange rate policy. Since growth in domestic demand was high, there is no doubt that various supply constraints played a role. This is directly seen from the fact that import growth peaked, and the current account turned into a record deficit of 5.3 percent of GDP in 1986. This suggested binding structural problems in the labor market preventing unemployment from falling below a level of 8 to 9 percent. However, during the recent upswing it has been possible to bring unemployment below this level without igniting wage increases. This indicates that structural unemployment was reduced in the 1990s.

It is very difficult to disentangle the business cycle and the structural component in the reduction in unemployment for several reasons. First, the policy changes over the period can be interpreted as following a two-handed strategy involving both demand and supply measures. Initially the period was kicked off by an expansionary fiscal policy,[2] and subsequently, when unemployment started to decrease, the labor market policy was tightened in several steps (see below). In political economy terms there is no doubt that these changes in labor market policy were only possible because unemployment was falling. The measures were motivated by the fact that it was possible to do something about the unemployment problem and that it was important not to repeat the experience from the mid-1980s.

Various measures of the structural unemployment rate have been made (e.g., see Finansministeriet 2002a). These measures suggest that structural unemployment peaked at 11 percent in 1993 and subsequently fell to a level of 5 to 6 percent.

A recent estimate (Det Økonomiske Råd 2002) suggests that the reduction in unemployment from 1993 to 2001 of 7 percentage points can be decomposed into 1 to 1.5 percentage points, due to passive measures transferring unemployed to other schemes (early retirement, paid leave schemes, etc.), 2 to 3 percentage points can be attributed to the business-cycle component, and 2 to 3 percentage points to structural improvements.

However, it should be noted that measures of structural unemployment can be difficult to interpret. First, the estimated structural unemployment rates follow a smoothened version of the actual unemployment rate and do not relate the changes to underlying structural variables; that is, the changes in the structural unemployment rate are basically unaccounted for. Second, it is very hard to envision structural changes of such strength that the structural unemployment rate went up by several percentage points from 1987 to 1990. The only possible candidate seems to be a depreciation of human capital, but it is hard to reconcile this explanation with the subsequent sharp reduction in unemployment.

The presence of substantial business-cycle components in the reduction in unemployment and the fact that unemployment has been persistently high suggest that the self-equilibrating mechanisms in the labor market work very sluggishly. Attempts to identify the persistence of generation mechanisms suggest substantial inertia in the adjustment process (e.g., see Andersen and Hylleberg 2000). Both nominal and real sources of inertia are found to be important, but the former seems to be quantitatively more important. However, the adjustment failures are not strong enough to support the interpretation that the deteriorating labor market performance is due to a sequence of adverse shocks in combination with substantial inertia.

Accordingly, to account for the persistence of unemployment, it is necessary to take structural factors into account. A pertinent question is whether the extended arrangements of the welfare state have been successful in ensuring a very high degree of income insurance (reflected in inequality being unaffected by the rise in unemployment), but at the cost of a worsening of the incentive structure so as to cause an increase in the structural unemployment rate.

4.4   Labor Market Policies

During the 1990s a number of labor market reforms were initiated. Whereas the initial phase was characterized by a continuation of passive policies via, for example, a paid leave scheme (later abolished), the policy gradually changed to put more emphasis on active measures with the specific aim of reducing the possibilities of passively claiming unemployment benefits, and to enhance the possibilities for unemployed to find regular jobs.

4.4.1   Unemployment Benefits

The Danish unemployment insurance scheme is by international standards fairly generous. The average replacement ratio is some 60 percent, and the entitlement period has in the past—despite various statutory limits—effectively been open-ended, so eligibility could easily be obtained (via education or work for six months). The benefits are calculated as 90 percent of previous earnings, but there is a maximum benefit level (currently constituting about 50 percent of the average pay for ordinary wage earners). This implies that the replacement rate is highest for low-wage groups and declines with wage income. Membership of an unemployment insurance scheme is voluntary, and members pay a fixed contribution. Membership is therefore closely correlated with unemployment risk (see Parsons et al. 2002). Marginal expenses in the unemployment insurance system are covered by the public sector, implying that in periods with high unemployment the public financial contribution has been large. In the past there has been no severance pay in the Danish system. Denmark has therefore had an internationally high rate of short-term unemployment. Hiring and firing rules are flexible (Nicoletti et al. 2000).

A key political premise underlying the labor market reforms during the 1990s has been that there should be no direct reductions in transfer payments. The political constraint has therefore been to improve the incentive structure without undertaking a retrenchment of key welfare state arrangements. Still the unemployment scheme has been tightened substantially, and the Danish case is thus an interesting example of a possible route for labor market reforms that do not jeopardize basic welfare state objectives.

The duration of the entitlement period for unemployment benefits has been radically reduced. In 1993 the duration period was officially seven years (although in practice it could be prolonged by participation in job-offer schemes), and in a sequence of reforms it is now reduced to four years; see figure 4.4. At the same time passive collection of unemployment benefits is no longer possible. The current policy[3] is based on a "rights and obligations" principle, implying that individuals have a right to compensation for loss of income but also an obligation to take action. At the same time society has an obligation to improve the situation of the individual, and therefore a right to impose certain requirements for entitlement for benefits. The current scheme implies that the "passive" period on unemployment benefits cannot exceed one year, and that the "activation period" should be initiated no later than one year after unemployment sets in. While maintaining the unemployment benefits unchanged, the introduction of such mandatory activation schemes has effectively influenced the incentives to search for regular jobs, and introduced obstacles to reduce misuse of the system (e.g., by voluntary unemployed or people working in the shadow economy).

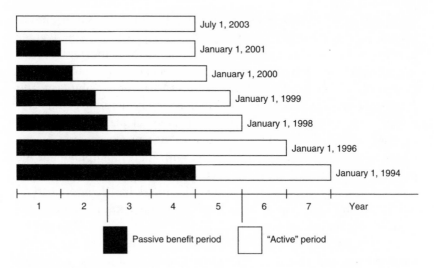

Figure 4.4
Changes in the unemployment system: benefit and "activation" period. The "right and obligation principle" in the "active" period was introduced in 1995. As of 2003 there is no distinction between the passive benefit period and the activation period. Sources: Finansministeriet (1999), Arbejdsministeriet (2000), and Beskæftigelsesministeriet (2002).

Entitlement to unemployment benefits now requires regular work of a duration of one year within the last three years (previously six months within the last three years). Importantly, participation in activation schemes does not qualify (since 1994) for renewed entitlement to unemployment benefits. If the benefit period expires before a regular job is found, the person will have to rely on social assistance (means tested on the basis of among other things the family situation). While the unemployment benefits are flat during the unemployment period, the combination of the unemployment benefit scheme and social assistance implies that the individual faces a stepwise profile of compensation as illustrated in figure 4.5. As of 1998 the "right and obligations" principle has also been extended to the social benefit scheme. It is readily seen from figure 4.5 that the economic incentives for low-income groups moving from unemployment to work are small (regardless of whether unemployment benefits or social benefits are claimed), whereas the incentive for higher income groups is larger. Several studies have confirmed that for low-income groups the economic incentive to work can be small or even absent (taking into account transport costs and child care), which is the net result of the

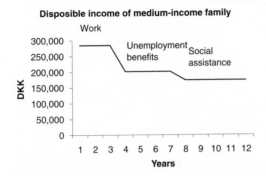

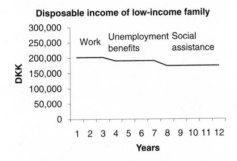

Figure 4.5
Duration dependence: Unemployment benefits and social assistance. The calculations are
for families with one child. Source: Det Økonomiske Råd (2002).

taxation system (see below) and the design of the welfare system (see
Finansministeriet 2002b and Pedersen and Smith 2002).

Despite unchanged statutory benefit levels the unemployment insurance scheme has thus been tightened substantially. It is difficult to
summarize the many dimensions and changes of the system in a single
measure, but figure 4.6 gives an indication of the changes made by
considering the development in the replacement rate for an average
worker with and without the reforms. Two things are noteworthy.
First, there is a trend decline in the replacement rate for the average
worker due to the upper limit on unemployment benefits (which has
not been fully adjusted to average wage increases following the trend
in average pay). Second, the shortening of the duration period and the
fact that entitlement cannot be regained by participation in activation
measures have implied a substantial decrease in the effective replacement rate.

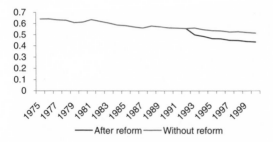

── After reform ── Without reform

Figure 4.6
Benefit replacement ratio. The figures show the replacement ratio for an average worker
as the present value of unemployment benefits and social assistance over a twenty-year
horizon, that is, the option value of unemployment benefits and social assistance relative
to the present value of average pay. Source: Det Økonomiske Råd (2002).

Since 1995 firms have been obliged to pay unemployment benefits
for the first two days of an unemployment spell. The system with
low hiring and firing costs gave firms and workers an incentive to exploit the unemployment insurance scheme in cases with short-run variations in labor demand. It is a fact that the incidence of short spells
of unemployment is particularly high in Denmark, and that the re-
employment propensity is high. Of those becoming unemployed in
1998 more than 40 percent were rehired by the same employer within
26 weeks (Det Økonomiske Råd 2002). This suggests that employers
can use the unemployment insurance system as a buffer to cope with
temporary variations in the need for workers.

There is one important exception to the rule that statutory benefit
levels have not been changed, namely the so-called youth package
implemented in 1996. The reform was targeted at persons below 25
and restricted the period for which unemployment benefits could be
claimed to six months. This was a significant tightening, since it previously was fairly easy to enter the unemployment insurance scheme
by working six months, and the unemployment compensation would
exceed study support and wages in apprenticeships by a wide margin.
The reform implies that an unemployed youth after the six-month
period would have to accept an education offer at 50 percent of unemployment benefits (equivalent to a study grant; this scheme has
been partially extended to everyone below 30 in the sense that in education activation they are entitled to a study grant and not unemployment benefits). One outstanding fact concerning the development in
unemployment is that youth unemployment has come down from a

peak level of 16 percent to about 3 percent. The reform has undoubtedly contributed to this development.

4.4.2 Activation

An essential ingredient of the labor market policy has been a collection of
so-called activation measures. Whereas such measures have been part
of the labor market policy since 1978, the main purpose in the past has
effectively been to provide a scheme to make it possible to regain the
right to unemployment benefits. With the labor market reforms in the
mid-1990s the activation schemes became an integral part of the "right
and obligation" principle (society offers income compensation, and the
individual has the obligation to participate in activation schemes) to
prevent passive collection of unemployment benefits. As noted above,
an important part of the reform was that participation in an activation
activity would not qualify for a new spell on unemployment benefits.

In principle, one can think of various effects of activation. There is an
incentive effect, since the value of unemployment benefits decreases
when time-consuming obligations are part of the package. This may induce some to search more actively for regular work (or give up work
in the shadow economy), or leave the labor force because their value
on leisure is high. This is a sorting effect, implying that unemployment
benefits become more targeted to those in real need. In principle, the
incentive or sorting effect could be achieved with any mandatory time-
consuming activity.[4] However, if the job prospects of unemployed can
be improved by participation in activation, this is a potentially important additional effect. The job activation program could work via both
a motivation effect (participating in activities motivating people to get
back to regular work, or give them the habit of regular activities and
the self-confidence needed) and a qualification effect (providing skills
needed to improve employment chances). However, participation in
activation could also have a negative effect on job search, since people
may search less actively while participating in such activities, and this
may create lock-in effects. Moreover participation in such schemes
may affect the reservation requirements, such as by narrowing job
search to jobs very closely linked to the type of training received during activation.

The activation instrument has been extensively used since the policy
reform made it an obligation to offer such activation at a predeter-
mined time (see above). The volume of activation has also been

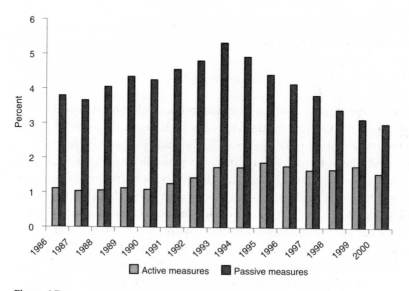

Figure 4.7
Expenses for labor market programs as share of GDP. Passive measures include expenses
for unemployment benefits. Active measures include administrative expenses. Source:
OECD (2002).

affected by the shortening of the "passive" unemployment benefit period, which implies a forward move of the stock of people to be offered
activation. Denmark has thus in international comparison used a substantial amount of resources on active labor market policies; see figure
4.7. Expenses for active measures thus amount to about 1.5 percent of
GDP, and total expenses on labor market policies peaked at almost
7 percent of GDP in 1993.

The types of activation used basically fall in three categories: private
job offers, public job offers, and educational activities. On average less
than 10 percent of those in activation have been in private job offers,
between 15 and 20 percent have been in public job offers, and the
remaining in various forms of educational and training activation. A
number of analyses have recently been made of the effects of these various activation schemes (for an overview see Det Økonomiske Råd
2002). There is evidence in support of some motivational effect (the
sorting effect is difficult to analyze empirically). However, for those being activated, the improvements in labor market prospects are very
small or even negative. Private job training improves job market prospects in general if employment can be gained at the workplace in

which activation is taking place, but outside the specific firm this form of activation does not seem to improve labor market prospects. Public job training has been found to have a substantial lock-in effect, and no or even a negative qualification effect (possibly by affecting the reservation demands of unemployed). Educational activities have therefore implied some improvement in qualifications for women, skilled, and older workers, but with substantial lock-in effects.

The dismal effects of activation can have several causes. First, given the increased emphasis on activation and the forward shift in activation, the system has been overloaded, and "quantity" may have come to dominate "quality"; that is, activation has become a routine and not a genuine attempt to identify adequately the needs of each person. Second, although the empirical methods are designed to account for sorting problems, it may empirically be difficult to fully control for sorting mechanisms working before the mandatory activation period is initiated; that is to say, if those ending up in activation do so because they have low qualifications, it is not surprising that their labor market prospects are also weak after activation.

Another issue is the way that the activation policies, and in particular, the educational activities, have been implemented. Problems of low labor market qualification are unlikely to be solved by participation in educational activities for which almost 40 percent have a duration of maximum eight weeks. In net terms, the activation scheme as it has been implemented offers relatively little value for money, and there is thus a need to reform the activation system (see Det Økonomiske Råd 2002).

4.5   Wage Formation

The most visible indication that structural changes have taken place during the 1990s is the fact that unemployment has been reduced substantially without inducing a wage hike (see figure 4.1). Accordingly, all macro-wage models have had difficulties explaining wage developments during the latter part of the 1990s, and they all predict wage increases in excess of what has actually been observed. Figure 4.8 shows this for a simple Phillips-curve, but the wage equations used in macroeconomic forecasting[5] (see Det Økonomiske Råd 2002) all share this feature.

Re-estimations extending the sample period thus tend to imply a reduction in the sensitivity of wages to unemployment, which is

Figure 4.8
Actual and estimated wage increases. The wage relation is a traditional Phillips curve estimated for the period 1960 to 2001.

paradoxical since it should be expected that structural reforms would have implied the opposite. This finding may be the result of missing structural variables in such macro-wage equations, and thus a transitional phenomenon in a sample period in which wage increases are moderate and unemployment falling due to structural changes in the labor market. Recent work (Det Økonomiske Råd 2002) has shown that a wage equation where the registered unemployment rate is replaced by an unemployment measure more directly related to the number of people actively searching for jobs (and also foreign wages) does a much better job accounting for the wage developments. Importantly, this wage equation implies that passive measures withdrawing unemployed from active search will have detrimental effects on employment in the long run.

The Danish labor market is well organized (more than 70 percent of the work force belong to a trade union), and traditionally the wage bargaining has been fairly centralized.

The 1990s also saw important changes in the institutional structure of the labor market with a shift from centralized towards more decentralized bargaining structures. Boeri et al. (2001) report an index[6] for centralization/coordination of the bargaining system taking both horizontal and vertical elements into account and find that for Denmark it has dropped from 0.64 for the period 1973 to 1977, to 0.47 for 1983 to 1987 and 0.34 for 1993 to 1997.

The developments in the Danish labor market during the 1990s are, however, a challenge to the literature on the relation between centralization/decentralization and labour market performance (for a survey and references, see Boeri et al. 2001). According to the centralization index, Denmark was ranked fourth in the 1970s and ninth in the 1990s for the fifteen countries included in the study. Hence Denmark has moved from centralized/coordinated bargaining to an intermediate position. According to empirical estimates reported in Boeri et al. (2001), this should imply an increase in the unemployment rate between 3.4 and 6.8 percentage points. If Denmark instead is interpreted as moving from an intermediate position to low centralization/coordination, the unemployment effect should be in the interval spanned by an increase of 3.2 percentage points and a decrease of 1.9 percentage points. Even this interpretation leaves some margin to the actual change in unemployment.

A further puzzle in recent developments is that decentralization of wage formation should be expected to enhance the sensitivity of wages to short-run fluctuations in activity, but empirical evidence shows that this has not been the case (see above). One explanation may be that the simultaneous shift in labor market policies has reduced the outside option of workers, and therefore induced wage moderation (e.g., see figure 4.6). Empirically it is difficult to distinguish this trend shift in market power from the change in cyclical sensitivity over a short sample period.

With the increased decentralization of wage formation, it is natural that there has been changes in wage systems in the labor market in the sense that more workers are now employed under a wage system, allowing local and individual variations in wages, and fewer workers are employed under the traditional wage system, implying a centrally stipulated wage. The traditional wage system in Denmark has been the so-called standard pay system (*normallønssystem*) that fixes the wage for different categories of workers in the labor market for the contract period (usually two years). Historically this system has dominated the labor market for unskilled workers. Various other wage systems[7] allow for a larger decentralized element in wage formation, which either makes room for personal allowances related to observable facts like job functions, experience, and qualifications or leaves the

Table 4.2
Wage systems in the Danish labor market

Contract form	1989	1991	1993	1995	1997	2000
Standard wage	34	19	16	16	16	15
Wage systems with decentralized wage setting	66	81	84	84	84	85
Sum	100	100	100	100	100	100

Source: Dansk Arbejdsgiverforening (2002).
Note: Wage systems with decentralized wage setting include *minimalløn* (minimum wage), *mindstebetaling* (minimum pay), and *uden lønsats* (without statutory wage rate).

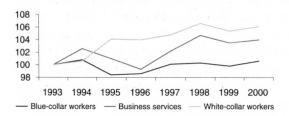

Figure 4.9
Wage dispersion for job functions in 1993 to 2000. Source: Dansk Arbejdsgiverforening (2001).

wage for local negotiation between employer and employee subject to certain minimum levels.

Table 4.2 shows the development in the use of the various wage systems during the 1990s, and there is a clear trend toward the use of wage systems with more flexible and decentralized wage determination. Note that central bargaining still determines the wage for workers on the standard wage contract. In the past local elements in wage determination have appeared in the form of wage drift.

Another noteworthy feature of the development during the 1990s is an increase in wage dispersion for workers with job functions at a high and intermediate level within firms, and also within business services, while no increases in wage dispersion have been observed among ordinary workers; see figure 4.9.

With a move from centralized toward a more decentralized system of wage determination it is natural to expect that firm-specific factors come to play a larger role for wage formation. The Danish labor market has historically been characterized by a fairly equal wage distribution, and therefore firm-specific factors have previously played a minor role (despite variation across firms). Bingley and Westergaard-Nielsen (2002) include tenure among standard explanatory variables in estimations of individual (annual) wage equations, and they use the estimated coefficient to construct a measure of the return to firm-specific human capital. While the return to firm-specific human capital is moderate, it is found that it has been increasing in recent years.[8] One interpretation is that this is the outcome of the decentralization process making it possible for firms to use wage incentives to protect investments in firm-specific human capital.

Another indirect approach by which to assess the importance of decentralization of wage formation is to exploit that wage formation is affected differently by taxation, depending on whether the market is competitive or imperfectly competitive. While average taxes unambiguously increase wages under imperfect competition, they have an ambiguous effect in competitive markets (income vs. substitution effects). Marginal taxes would under standard assumptions increase wage demands in competitive markets and reduce them in imperfectly competitive markets. Using this insight, Pedersen and Smith (1999) and Pedersen, Rasmussen, and Clemmensen (2002) study wage formation for various groups in the labor market, taking explicit account of the more decentralized wage formation by allowing a larger role for individual effects on wages. Interestingly they find that relative to earlier studies, a sample including the first part of the 1990s yields results on the effects of taxation more in line with competitive models. They take this as evidence that wage formation effectively has become more decentralized.

In sum, wage formation has become more decentralized, but the Danish experience during the 1990s cannot simply be explained by decentralization of wage formation. This does not mean that decentralization is unimportant but that it may be interacting with other important changes.

4.6 Mismatch

The extent to which aggregate unemployment is driven by mismatches along dimensions like qualification and geography is usually addressed by considered so-called Beveridge curves. However, vacancy data for Denmark are only available from business surveys, and the data indicate that mismatch problems increased during the 1970s and 1980s, since there was an increase in both vacancies and unemployment; see

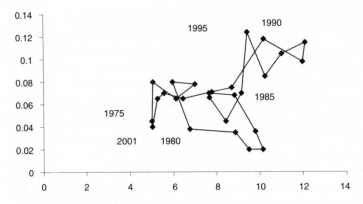

Figure 4.10
Vacancies and unemployment. Vacancies are calculated from survey data as 0.5 (proportion of firms reporting shortage of skilled workers + proportion of firms reporting shortage of other labor). Source: Unemployment as in figure 4.1. Statistics Denmark.

figure 4.10. Judged by these data, it seems that mismatch problems were reduced during the 1990s.

Both skill and geographical aspects seem to have been of importance for mismatch problems in the labor market. Despite a period with high overall unemployment there have been substantial differences in unemployment across skill groups. In particular, it does not seem that skill differences are lower at present than during the high-unemployment period. Regular differences in unemployment rates for various skill groups are thus no smaller today than in the early 1990s, and, if anything, they have tended to increase.

There is also evidence that shifts in relative labor demand have been skill biased in favor of highly skilled. Fosgerau et al. (2001) find the relative demand shift (skilled relative to unskilled) over the period 1980 to 1998 to have been above 4 percent. Still the relative wage structure between skilled and unskilled has remained practically unchanged (the ratio of unskilled wages to the average was 90 percent in 1980 and 89.4 percent in 1998), and the unemployment rate for unskilled has not increased either. Hence, although the skill bias has been as large in Denmark as in many other countries, the consequences have been less dramatic, since the relative shift in the skill composition of labor demand has been matched by an almost identical change in the skill composition of labor supply (see Fosgerau et al. 2001).

Whereas there are substantial differences in unemployment rates across geographical areas (in 2001 the unemployment rate across counties varied between 3 and 7 percent), various analyses have had difficulties relating geographical mobility to economic variables. Hence mobility does not seem to play an important role in eliminating geographical differences in unemployment. Even if disaggregated at skill levels, there is no indication that geographical differences were reduced during the recent period with falling unemployment (Det Økonomiske Råd 2002).

In the international debate it has been proposed that housing may be an impediment to mobility and therefore contribute to persistent unemployment problems (see Oswald 1996). However, since the share of homeowners is high (above 50 percent), Denmark should be a country where housing contributes to a high unemployment rate. However, empirical studies fail to find support for this hypothesis, if anything homeowners seem to return more quickly to work than others. Still, the fact that homeowners tend to be less geographically mobile than tenants could be interpreted as evidence either of a sorting effect of entrance into homeownership or that homeowners more quickly lower their reservation demands due to their financial obligations.

4.7 Taxation

The average tax burden in Denmark is high (in 2001, 55 percent of GDP), and the tax structure is such that the bulk of revenue accrues from direct income taxation and indirect taxes (VAT). The total tax wedge on labor income may be a better indicator than the gross tax burden for the effects of taxation for the labor market. For an average worker the tax wedge is 60 percent, which is among the highest in Europe (Skatteministeriet 2002). Progressive elements in the taxation system imply that the tax burden is increasing in income. A recurrent theme has been the disincentive effects of taxation for the labor market. This issue is complicated because the effects depend both on the institutional structure of the labor market as well as possibly counteracting substitution and income effects. In recent years focus has been on the possibility of reducing marginal tax rates on labor income with the aim of improving incentives for work including mobility in all its dimensions.

Since about 40 percent of full-time employed pay the top marginal tax rate, it has been a concern for tax reforms how to reduce marginal tax rates. A number of tax reforms have taken place in recent years,

Table 4.3
Marginal tax-rates by personal income

Income level[a]	1986	1993	1998[b]	2002[b]
Low	48.0	50.6	45.2	44.2
Medium	62.4	58.2	50.7	49.7
High	73.2	68.7	62.0	63.3

Source: Andersen et al. (2001).
a. Income level is defined for the income levels applying to payment of *bundskat* (low bracket income tax), *mellemskat* (medium bracket income tax), and *topskat* (top bracket income tax).
b. Inclusive labor market contributions. For 2002 low income would apply for incomes below DKK 191,200, and high income for incomes above 285,200.

aiming at broadening the tax base and reducing marginal tax rates on labor income. Table 4.3 summarizes the development in marginal tax rates. As is seen, marginal tax rates have been reduced, but they are still high.

A number of recent empirical studies have considered the determinants of labor supply. It is, in general, found that the income effect is negative, and the substitution effect positive. While the income effect is approximately equal for men and women, the substitution elasticity (both the compensated and the uncompensated) is larger for women than for men by a factor of 2 to 3. Given this, it is possible within the existing tax system to propose tax reforms that would increase labor supply and have a nontrivial self-financing element (e.g., see Frederiksen and Hansen 2002 and references therein).

Taxation, and in particular, marginal taxes, may affect the labor market through other routes than the quantity of labor supply. High marginal taxes may reduce the incentive for mobility both across the geographical and the skill dimension, since the private return of such mobility is reduced. Moreover taxation may affect wage formation and lead to higher wages. This relation depends critically on the institutional arrangements concerning wage formation, since centralized wage-setting institutions can internalize tax externalities (see Summers et al. 1993). However, this is not the case in a labor market with a more decentralized system of wage formation. Since Denmark has moved from a fairly centralized to a more decentralized system of wage formation (see above), the distortionary consequences of taxation on wage formation should increase. Empirical evidence already indicates that such a change is taking place (see Pedersen et al. 2002).

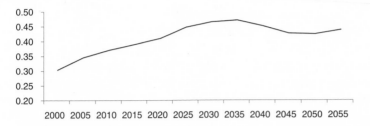

Figure 4.11
Demographic shifts. Over 62 age group relative to 17 to 61 age group. Source: Det Økonomiske Råd (Autumn 2002).

The need for tax reform is thus a recurrent theme, and the possibility of shifting some of the tax burden from labor to internationally less mobile tax objects like houses and natural resources is often debated.

4.8   Labor Shortage?

Demographic changes are also going to affect the Danish labor market. Figure 4.11 shows the relation between the number of people aged 62 and over relative to those between 17 and 61, and it is seen that the demographic changes are fairly substantial within the next 30 years. Recent projections suggest that the labor supply will be reduced by about 2.5 percent from 2000 to 2010 as a result of demographic changes. At the same time a number of strong trends are reducing the labor supply, namely the trend decline in working hours (over the week and the year), lower labor market participation for prime age groups, and early retirement. The early retirement problem is particularly problematic, since it is induced by a scheme subsidizing early retirement. Although the scheme was originally intended to provide an escape route for those who for physical or mental reasons have difficulty coping with an ordinary job, it has become quite popular for large groups in the labor market as a means to enjoy more leisure, meaning early retirement has become a welfare item. A recent analysis shows that 7 out of 10 in the scheme enter from regular work, and that 8 out of 10 have chosen early retirement voluntarily. The number of persons in the scheme by 2002 amounts to more than 5 percent of the labor force. The popularity of the scheme has made it difficult to reform, although there was a minor reform in 1998.

The demographic changes thus pose a challenge to the labor market, and there has been wide concern that shortage of labor will arise, which in turn will make it difficult to maintain wage developments on a path consistent with the overall macroeconomic policy strategy.

A further challenge arises from the fact that the demographic shifts have substantial consequences for public finances given the way the Danish welfare model is organized. Various projections indicate that public finances would be significantly affected if current standards and systems are to be maintained (Finansministeriet 2002a; Det Økonomiske Råd 2002; L. H. Pedersen 2002).

Another key issue in the Danish labor market is the poor integration of immigrants. For men the labor force participation rate is about 20 percentage points lower than that of Danes, and for women it is close to 40 percentage points lower (P. Pedersen 2002). However, analyses have documented that when controlling the labor force participation for various background variables, the difference in labor force participation can mainly be attributed to lower average qualifications for immigrants (Det Økonomiske Råd 2002). Accordingly, improved labor market integration would have to go via more education, training, and so forth, which raises new demands for labor market policy.

4.9   Concluding Remarks

The labor market developments in Denmark during the 1990s were unique relative to historical experience. The development cannot only be attributed to favorable macroeconomic conditions and a successful stabilization policy, important institutional changes as well as structural policies have played an important role.

The Danish labor market is adapting to a number of international trends including the consequences of technological developments and international integration. A skill bias in labor demand has had quantitatively strong effects also on the Danish labor market, but the consequences have been less visible since it has been accompanied by a quantitatively similar change in relative labor supply. The latter can partly be attributed to passive measures reducing labor supply, and the fact that a larger share of young generations have labor market-relevant qualifications. International integration may make employment more sensitive to wages, and it may change the outside options determining bargaining power in the labor market. These effects are more difficult to identify empirically, but the changes in wage formation and the more decentralized wage-setting institutions can be interpreted as a response to the challenges arising from international integration.

The unique Danish aspect has been how to combine extended welfare arrangements with an incentive structure in the labor market that does not induce rigidities and persistent high unemployment. Whereas policies in the past have been passive in nature with focus on income maintenance, a number of reforms during the 1990s led to a more active approach. The reforms basically respected the political constraint that transfer incomes could not be reduced but changed the incentive structure by reducing the possibilities for passively claiming benefits (stricter eligibility rules, short benefit periods, etc.). Also, via the so-called activation policies, they attached obligations to claiming unemployment and social benefits. It is very difficult to precisely quantify the contribution of the many elements in the policy reforms. From an overall assessment there is no doubt that labor market structures have been changed, and this is an important reason for the large reduction in unemployment. However, business-cycle developments have also played a role.

Despite the reforms, incentive problems remain. In a forward-looking perspective an important objective would be to increase labor force participation (to counteract the effects of demographic shifts, and reduce the burden on public finances) along two dimensions, namely better integration of immigrants into the labor market and incentives for later retirement (where the current policies encourage early retirement). Since immigrant groups have hitherto had a more marginal attachment to the labor market, the challenge is large. The political constraints on early retirement are also very tight, since the early retirement scheme has become very popular. So the overall tax burden and the structure of taxation will increasingly become an important issue in the future. By international standards the tax burden and marginal taxes are high in Denmark, and it is an open question how robust this situation is to further international integration.

Notes

Comments and suggestions from participants, the discussant Jan van Ours and an anonymous referee at the CESifo/Yrjö Jansson Foundation conference on Unemployment in Europe, December 6–7, 2002, as well as from Jan V. Hansen are gratefully acknowledged.

1. Both periods were characterized by substantial increases in domestic demand. The aggregate demand increase in the 1980s boom was slightly more rapid and stronger than

the increase in the 1990s. However, the two periods also differ in a number of other respects including the current account position, public deficits, inflation etc.

2. Estimates of the expansionary effects of discretionary fiscal policy changes show that it added about 0.7 percentage points to growth in 1993 and 1994 (Finansministeriet 2000).

3. After a recent reform, interpretation of the rules will be more flexible as of July 2003; see also figure 4.4.

4. It could be argued that the incentive effect could be strengthened by making the activation activities demanding but meaningless. However, this would not be possible given the political constraint of decency in the treatment of people.

5. This includes the wage equations in the ADAM model used by the Ministry of Finance, the MONA model used in the central bank, and the SMEC model used by the Economic Council.

6. Defined to belong to the unit interval. A value of 1 corresponds to fully centralized, and 0 to fully decentralized bargaining.

7. The two major systems are the standard pay system (*normallønssystemet*) and the minimum wage system (*minimallønssystemet*). Note that the latter is not to be confused with the minimum wage. The minimum wage is determined through negotiation and gives an absolute floor below for wage determination.

8. Firm-specific returns play a less important role than in, for example, the United States.

References

Andersen, T. M. 1994. Disinflationary stabilization policy—Denmark in the 1980s. In J. Åkerhold and A. Giovannini, eds., *Exchange Rate Policies in the Nordic Countries*. London: CEPR.

Andersen, T. M., and S. Hylleberg. 2000. Source of persistence in employment adjustment. *Oxford Economic Papers* 52: 72–95.

Andersen, T. M., B. Dallum, H. Linderoth, V. Smith, and N. Westergård-Nielsen. 2001. *The Danish Economy—An International Perspective*. Copenhagen: DJØF Publishing.

Arbejdsministeriet. 2000. *Effekter af aktiveringsindsatsen*. Copenhagen: Arbejdsministeriet.

Beskæftigelsesministeriet. 2002. *Flere i arbejde*. Copenhagen: Beskæftigelsesministeriet.

Bingley, P., and N. Westergaard-Nielsen. 2002. Tenure and firm-specific capital. Aarhus School of Business, *Working Paper*.

Boeri, T., A. Brugiavini, and L. Calmfors, eds. 2001. *The Role of Unions in the Twenty-First Century*. Oxford: Oxford University Press.

Dansk Arbejdsgiverforening. 2001. *Arbejdsmarkedsrapport 2001*. Copenhagen: DA Forlag (www.da.dk).

Dansk Arbejdsgiverforening. 2002. *Arbejdsmarkedsrapport 2002*. Copenhagen: DA Forlag (www.da.dk).

Det Økonomiske Råd. 2001. *Dansk Økonomi Efteråret 2001*. Copenhagen: Det Økonomiske Råd (www.dors.dk).

Det Økonomiske Råd. 2002. *Dansk Økonomi Efteråret 2002*. Copenhagen: Det Økonomiske Råd (www.dors.dk).

Finansministeriet. 1999. *Finansredegørelsen 98/99*. Copenhagen: Finansministeriet (www .fm.dk).

Finansministeriet. 2000. *Finansredegørelsen 2000*. Copenhagen: Finansministeriet (www .fm.dk).

Finansministeriet. 2002. *Finansredegørelsen 2002*. Copenhagen: Finansministeriet (www .fm.dk).

Finansministeriet. 2002. *Fordeling og Incitamenter*. Copenhagen: Finansministeriet.

Fosgerau, M., S. E. H. Jensen, and A. Sørensen. 2001. Relative demand shifts for educated labour. *CEBR Discussion Paper* 2000-11.

Frederiksen, A., and J. V. Hansen. 2002. Skattereformer: Dynamiske effekter og fordeling-skonsekvenser. *Nationaløkonomisk Tidsskrift* 2: 112–28.

Nicoletti, G., S. Scarpetta, and O. Boylaud. 2000. Summary of indicators of product market regulation with an extension of employment protection legislation. *OECD Economics Department Working Paper* 226.

Oswald, A. J. 1996. A conjecture on the explanation for high unemployment in industrialized nations: Part I. University of Warwick, *Working Paper*.

OECD. 2002. *Employment Outlook 2002*. Paris: OECD.

Parsons, D. O., T. Tranæs, and H. B. Lilleør. 2002. Voluntary public unemployment insurance. University of Copenhagen, *Working Paper*.

Pedersen, L. H. 2002. *Befolkningsudvikling, integration og økonomiske politik* (Danish Rational Economic Agents Model, DREAM, www.dream.dk).

Pedersen, L. H, J. H. Rasmussen, and K. Clemmensen. 2002. Individual wage formation and minimum wages: Theoretical and empirical effects of progressive taxation. University of Copenhagen, *Working Paper*.

Pedersen, L. H., N. Smith, and P. Stephensen. 1999. Minimum wage contracts and individual wage formation: Theory and evidence from Danish panel data. In T. M. Andersen, S. E. Hougård-Jensen, and O. Risager, eds., *Macroeconomic Perspectives on the Danish Economy*. Basingstoke: Macmillan.

Pedersen, P. J. 2002. Arbejdsmarkedsintegration, arbejdsmarkedspolitik og overførsel-sindkomster—Forskningsmæssig viden om immigration fra mindre udviklede lande siden 1980. *AMID Working Paper* 7/2002.

Pedersen, P. J., and N. Smith. 2002. Unemployment traps: Do financial disincentives matter? *European Sociological Review* 18: 271–88.

Skatteministeriet. 2002. *Skat—Beskatning af arbejdskraft*. Copenhagen: Skatteministeriet.

Summers, L., J. Gruber, and R. Vergara. 1993. Taxation and the structure of labor markets: The case of corporatism. *Quarterly Journal of Economics* 108: 385–411.

5   The Rise and Fall of Swedish Unemployment

Bertil Holmlund

5.1 Introduction

During the 1980s Swedish labor market performance was widely appreciated as a remarkable success story. Whereas unemployment in Western Europe climbed to double-digit figures, the Swedish unemployment rate remained exceptionally low by international standards. The average unemployment rate during the 1980s was around 2 percent, and by the end of the decade it had fallen to 1.5 percent. Employment-to-population rates were also exceptionally high by international standards. In 1990, total employment had risen to 83 percent of the working age population, whereas the average European figure was 61 percent and the OECD average 65 percent.

The rosy picture of outstanding Swedish labor market performance did not fare well during the 1990s, however. Between 1990 and 1993, unemployment increased from 1.6 percent to 8.2 percent, and total employment declined to 73 percent of working age population. For five successive years in the mid-1990s, official unemployment was stuck at around 8 percent, and extended measures of unemployment reached double-digit figures. The Swedish performance seemed to have converged the European average.

Although the prospects for a sustained labor market improvement appeared remote in the mid-1990s, a strong recovery was in fact around the corner. From 1997 and onward, employment exhibited a marked increase and unemployment fell precipitously. By the end of 2000, unemployment had reached 4 percent of the labor force, and it remained fairly constant at this level during 2001 and 2002.

Why did Swedish unemployment rise so sharply in the early 1990s, and why did it decline during the end of the decade? Those are the issues discussed in this chapter. It is argued that the steep increase in unemployment in the early 1990s was mainly the result of a series of adverse macroeconomic shocks, partly self-inflicted by bad policies and partly caused by unfavorable international developments. Even if macroeconomic shocks explain most of the steep rise in unemployment, other factors have caused some rise in the Swedish NAIRU since the 1960s and throughout the 1980s. A trend increase in the generosity of unemployment insurance is a case in point. During the 1990s, however, unemployment insurance became less generous. Other factors, such as product market deregulations and innovations in wage bargaining, may also have contributed to some decline in equilibrium unemployment in recent years.

I begin in section 5.2 by describing the evolution of unemployment and its structure. In section 5.3, I discuss the causes of the increase in unemployment in the early 1990s, and in section 5.4, the fall in unemployment during the late 1990s. In section 5.5, I offer some concluding observations.

5.2 The Evolution of Unemployment

5.2.1 The Aggregate Picture

The Swedish unemployment rate displayed modest fluctuations around an average level of 2 percent during the 1960s, the 1970s, and the 1980s.[1] A weak trend increase in unemployment could be identified, however. The recession of the early 1970s entailed higher unemployment than what was observed during the 1960s. Likewise the early 1980s witnessed a recession where unemployment approached 4 percent, a level considered as exceptionally high by the standards of the 1960s and the 1970s. However, by the end of the 1980s the unemployment rate had reached a decade low of close to 1 percent.

The three decades from the early 1960s to the late 1980s also involved sharply rising female participation rates. In 1965, female participation in the labor force stood at 54 percent; by 1989, it had risen to 82 percent. Male participation rates fell only modestly—from 89 to 86 percent between 1965 and 1989—and the aggregate labor force participation rate thus rose dramatically. Employment increased in tandem with the increase in participation.

The slump of the early 1990s involved a fall in GDP from peak to trough by 6 percent and produced an unprecedented increase in unemployment. Between 1990 and 1993, unemployment rose from 1.5 to

8.2 percent. The increase in unemployment was accompanied by a sharp decline in labor force participation for both men and women. The total decline in employment in the early 1990s amounted to a fall in the employment-to-population rate from 83 percent in 1990 to 73 percent in 1993. Over the period 1993 to 1997, the unemployment rate hovered around 8 percent, whereas employment fell slightly (reaching 70.7 percent of population in 1997). However, a strong rebound began in 1997 and involved a rise in GDP growth, a substantial fall in unemployment and a rise in employment. By 2001, the unemployment rate had fallen to 4 percent, and the employment-to-population rate had risen to 75 percent.

The evolution of unemployment is displayed in figure 5.1. The gap between ILO unemployment and official unemployment consists of full-time students searching for a job. Students are classified as unemployed according to the conventions of the International Labour Organisation (ILO) but as nonparticipants in the Swedish national statistics. The ILO rate hit 10 percent in 1996 and 1997 and fell to 5 percent in 2001. An extended measure of unemployment includes also jobless "latent job seekers" who are "willing and able" to work but do not meet the criteria for being classified as unemployed.[2] This extended unemployment rate hit 12 to 13 percent in the mid-1990s and fell below 7 percent by 2001.

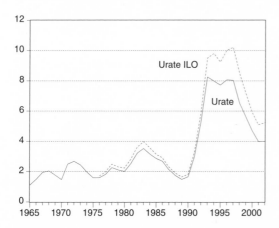

Figure 5.1
Official unemployment (Urate) and ILO unemployment in 1965 to 2002 as percentage of labor force. The ILO unemployment rate is based on a labor force measure that includes full-time students engaged in job search. Source: Labor force surveys, Statistics Sweden.

5.2.2 The Structure of Unemployment

The aggregate figures presented above hide considerable diversity in labor market outcomes across demographic and occupational groups. However, a basic similarity across groups is that they were all affected by the slump: unemployment rose for all groups, albeit more for some groups than for others.

Age and Gender
Table 5.1 presents unemployment rates by age and gender for some selected years. Also presented are nonemployment rates, defined as the number of nonemployed (unemployed plus nonparticipants) divided by the relevant population size. The unemployment rate for youths aged 16 to 24 increased from less than 4 percent to over 15 percent during the first half of the 1990s. In terms of percentage points this increase was clearly much higher than the average increase. In proportional terms, however, the differences across age groups were fairly small. Roughly speaking, the slump brought about a rise in unemployment for all age groups by a factor of four to five. Turning to nonemployment, the development for youths stands out with a rise by over 20 percentage points between 1990 and 1995. This reflects to a large extent participation in labor market programs as well as increased enrollment in (general) education. The increases in nonemployment among prime age and older individuals are of fairly similar magnitudes. The recovery has led to a fall in unemployment and nonemployment for all groups.

Rising unemployment is clearly only one part of the increase in nonemployment, the other being rising nonparticipation. Table 5.2 provides a decomposition of nonemployment into a few major (self-reported) categories. Of the increase in total nonemployment between 1990 and 1995, amounting to 10.9 percentage points, rising unemployment accounts for 4.6 percentage points or 42 percent. Unemployment accounts for around half of the total increase in nonemployment among prime age and older people, whereas it only accounts for about 20 percent of the increase in youth nonemployment. Activities classified as studies, which include various active labor market programs in addition to general education, account for about 20 percent of the increase in youth nonemployment. The 1990s have seen a marked increase in enrollment in higher education, which accounts for part of the increase nonemployment. Between 1993 and 1999, the number of

Table 5.1
Unemployment and nonemployment rates by age and gender (%)

	1980		1985		1990		1995		2001	
	Unemployed	Nonemployed	Unemployed	Nonemployed	Unemployed	Nonemployed	Unemployed	Nonemployed	Unemployed	Nonemployed
Total										
16–24	5.1	32.7	5.8	37.8	3.7	34.0	15.3	57.6	8.0	52.1
25–54	1.4	11.9	1.9	9.7	1.2	8.4	6.6	17.4	3.3	15.4
55–64	1.6	34.3	4.0	35.0	1.5	30.6	7.4	38.1	4.2	33.0
16–64	2.0	20.1	2.8	19.7	1.6	16.9	7.7	27.8	4.0	24.7
Men										
16–24	4.5	31.7	5.8	38.2	3.8	33.9	16.7	58.2	9.1	52.7
25–54	1.1	5.7	2.0	6.7	1.3	6.5	7.2	16.0	3.5	13.3
55–64	1.6	22.6	3.5	26.7	1.3	25.6	8.4	35.6	4.6	30.4
16–64	1.7	13.8	2.8	16.4	1.7	14.8	8.5	26.5	4.3	23.0
Women										
16–24	5.6	33.8	5.7	37.4	3.6	34.1	14.0	57.1	6.8	51.5
25–54	1.6	18.4	1.9	12.8	1.2	10.3	5.9	18.9	3.0	17.5
55–64	1.6	45.6	4.6	42.9	1.6	35.2	6.3	40.5	3.8	35.7
16–64	2.3	26.6	2.9	23.1	1.6	19.0	6.9	29.2	3.6	26.5

Source: Labor force surveys, *Statistics Sweden.*
Note: The unemployment rate is measured relative to the labor force; the nonemployment rate relative to population.

Table 5.2
Nonemployment by type of (in)activity (% of population)

	1990 age group				1995 age group				2001 age group			
	16–24	25–54	55–64	16–64	16–24	25–54	55–64	16–64	16–24	25–54	55–64	16–64
Unemployed	2.5	1.1	1.0	1.4	7.7	5.8	4.9	6.0	4.2	2.9	3.0	3.1
Students	26.3	1.9	0.1	6.4	39.5	3.3	0.3	9.3	37.2	4.1	0.8	8.9
Household work	1.1	1.8	5.3	2.2	1.1	1.6	2.4	1.6	0.7	1.0	0.8	0.9
Other[a]	4.1	3.6	24.2	6.9	9.3	6.7	30.5	10.8	10.0	7.4	28.5	11.7
Total nonemployment	34.0	8.4	30.6	16.9	57.6	17.4	38.1	27.8	52.1	15.4	33.0	24.7

Source: Labor force surveys, *Statistics Sweden*.
a. Includes individuals receiving early retirement pensions and other pensions as well as people in long term sickness.

undergraduate students rose by 25 percent, and a major educational drive for low-educated adults (*Kunskapslyftet*) was initiated in 1997, encompassing 2 percent of the working age population by the end of that year.

A significant fraction of nonparticipation involves "inactivity" associated with early retirement, receipt of disability pensions and long-term sickness. There is strong evidence that nonparticipation for various disability and sickness-related reasons has increased over the 1990s. The residual category "other" includes, inter alia, persons in long-term sickness and persons receiving disability pensions. This category rose by 4 percentage points between 1990 and 1995 and accounts for over a third of the increase in total nonemployment. For older workers the category accounts for over 80 percent of the increase.

Education and Citizenship
Unemployment rates for those with low education are roughly two to three times as high as unemployment among those with university education. The increase in unemployment during the early 1990s affected all education groups. Unemployment rates increased for all education categories by a factor of five to six (table 5.3). Unemployment among immigrants is generally higher, sometimes dramatically higher, than unemployment among native Swedes. Table 5.4 gives some data on unemployment and nonemployment rates for foreigners and for the whole labor force. Unemployment and nonemployment among immigrants vary tremendously by country of origin. Among non-Nordic citizens the unemployment rate rose from 5 to 30 percent between 1990 and 1995, whereas nonemployment rose from 34 to 64 percent during the same period.

5.2.3 Active Labor Market Policies

Internationally Sweden stands out as a country that spends large resources on active labor market policy (ALMP). In addition to job broking measures, ALMP has involved skills training as well as various forms of subsidized employment. The latter have traditionally taken the form of "relief jobs" (temporary public jobs). In recent years relief jobs have disappeared, and other recruitment subsidies have been introduced. For example, subsidies are paid to employers that hire long-term unemployed (with the going wage paid to those hired).

Table 5.3
Unemployment and nonemployment by education, age 25 to 54 (%)

	1980		1985		1990		1995		2001	
	Unem-ployed	Nonem-ployed	Unem-ployed	Nonem-ployed	Unem-ployed	Nonem-ployed	Unem-ployed	Nonem-ployed	Unem-ployed	Nonem-ployed
Compulsory	2.0	16.0	3.1	15.5	1.5	9.4	8.7	18.7	4.7	24.1
High school	1.2	9.6	2.0	9.1	1.3	6.4	7.5	15.5	3.6	14.7
University	0.7	6.1	1.0	4.2	0.8	4.6	3.7	10.0	2.2	11.6

Source: Labor force surveys, *Statistics Sweden.*
Note: The unemployment rate is measured relative to the labor force; the nonemployment rate relative to population.

Table 5.4
Unemployment and nonemployment among foreign citizens

	1990		1995		2001	
	Unem-ployed	Nonem-ployed	Unem-ployed	Nonem-ployed	Unem-ployed	Nonem-ployed
Nordic	2.5	21.2	12.2	37.3	6.6	35.6
Other	5.0	33.8	30.0	64.2	13.0	46.3
Total foreign	3.9	28.5	22.7	55.3	10.6	42.6
Total population	1.6	16.9	7.7	27.8	4.0	24.7

Source: Labor force surveys, *Statistics Sweden.*
Note: The unemployment rate is measured relative to the labor force; the nonemployment rate relative to population.

ALMP volumes have been gradually expanded from the early 1960s and onward. By the late 1970s, the number of participants in ALMPs had increased to 2 percent relative to the labor force.[3] ALMPs were markedly countercyclical, rising in recessions and falling in booms. In the 1990s, there emerged a large number of new programs, often targeted at unemployed youths. The slump in the early 1990s was initially met by a steep increase in the volume of training programs, later to be followed by an expansion of subsidized employment and "youth practice" programs. In the mid-1990s, ALMPs stood at 5 percent relative to the labor force. The labor market rebound in the late 1990s involved a fall in the number of program participants by roughly 50 percent.

5.3 Why Did Unemployment Rise?

What caused the dramatic increase in unemployment in the early 1990s? The exposition that follows provides a partly chronological account of the events that led to skyrocketing unemployment. We begin by discussing the shocks that hit the economy, some of them largely self-inflicted and others more exogenous to domestic policies.

5.3.1 The Shocks That Hit

Stabilization Policy in Turmoil[4]
For most of the twentieth century, Sweden pursued a fixed exchange rate policy. A crucial requirement for the feasibility of the fixed exchange regime was, of course, that domestic inflation was kept in line with inflation abroad. This turned out to become increasingly difficult,

and a series of devaluations took place in the late 1970s and the early 1980s. These devaluations resulted in temporary improvements in competitiveness that counteracted the adverse employment effects of unsustainable inflation. The large devaluations in the early 1980s paved the way for an employment expansion that lasted throughout the decade, reinforced by an international upswing as well as expansionary domestic policies. However, the expansionary domestic policies during the 1980s carried the seeds that ultimately led to a complete regime shift in stabilization policy in the early 1990s.

The credit market was one important source of domestic demand expansion. By the end of 1985, Swedish financial markets had been largely deregulated. Restrictions on household loans in commercial banks and credit institutions had been lifted, which set in motion a rapid increase in bank loans to the household sector. This change took place during a period when marginal tax rates were generally high and when mortgage payments were deductible in income taxation. The interaction of financial deregulation, progressive taxes, and generous rules for deducting interest payments created the preconditions for a strong credit expansion. The consumption boom that followed involved a fall in the household saving rate to minus 5 percent of disposable income in 1988 and a gradual buildup of household debt. By the end of the 1980s, unemployment was approaching 1 percent of the labor force. Monetary policy was tied to defending the fixed exchange rate and fiscal policy was too lax to prevent the rise in inflationary pressure.

During the late 1980s, a government committee developed a far-reaching proposal for reform of the Swedish tax system. Key elements were lower marginal tax rates on labor earnings and the introduction of a dual system of income taxation with a 30 percent tax rate on income from capital. Mortgage payments could then be deducted at 30 percent. These reforms were put into practice in 1990 and 1991 and caused a marked increase in after-tax real interest rates. The demand for owner-occupied housing fell predictably; between 1990 and 1993, the fall in real prices amounted to 30 percent. On top of this, the household saving rate rose from minus 5 percent in 1988 to plus 7 percent in 1992. The rise in saving reflected households' attempts to bring down a debt-to-income ratio that had shown a marked increase over the 1980s, especially during the second half of the decade.

In this environment Swedish stabilization policy took close to a U-turn. The prime objective for decades had been full employment, although the desirability of low inflation was recognized in words. In practice, this has led governments to undertake several devaluations in the late 1970s and the early 1980s so as to restore competitiveness that had been eroded by high inflation and fixed exchange rates. In the early 1990s the government declared that low inflation was the prime objective of stabilization policy. A unilateral affiliation of the krona to the ECU was declared in May 1991.

In addition to self-inflicted wounds Swedish policy making was hit by bad luck in the early 1990s. An international recession struck during the first years of the decade. Industrial production declined between 1990 and 1993 by 4 to 5 percent in the EU area and by over 6 percent in Germany. The general weakening of major Swedish export markets added to the falling demand for Swedish exports and reinforced the sharp decline in GDP.

During the fall of 1992, the krona was put under a number of speculative attacks, and it became increasingly doubtful whether the fixed exchange rate was sustainable. In November 1992, the fixed exchange regime had to be abandoned and the krona was floating. A new monetary regime was established, including an inflationary target (from early 1993) and a more independent central bank (from the late 1990s).

The chronological tale told so far emphasizes two main policy failures. First, it is clear that fiscal policy was too lax in the second half of the 1980s. Unemployment reached levels well below available estimates of the NAIRU.[5] The fixed exchange rate target had tied the hands of monetary policy and only fiscal policy tools were available to combat rising inflationary pressure. Second, it is also clear that the timing of financial deregulation and tax reform was less than optimal. Under more ideal circumstances the tax reform should have preceded financial liberalization rather than the other way around. Had the financial liberalization taken place in an environment with less favorable conditions for household loans, the effects on credit demand and private consumption would have been smaller.

Climbing Real Interest Rates
The rise in real after-tax interest rates in the early 1990s had essentially three sources, namely the international rise in interest rates, the tax reform that raised after-tax rates, and the steep fall in inflation. These developments triggered a decline in aggregate demand in general and housing demand in particular. However, higher real interest rates can also have "supply-side" effects via firms' behavior. In the matching

model of Pissarides (2000), for example, a higher real interest rate effectively works as a tax on new hires.

Swedish real interest rates exhibited a marked increase over the period 1989 to 1992. According to one measure, the rates went up from 4 percent to double-digit figures.[6] However, interest rates fell sharply when the fixed exchange rate regime was abandoned in November 1992. Although it is difficult to assess quantitatively how the interest rate shocks affected employment, it is safe to argue that the interest rate hikes reinforced other adverse shocks that hit the Swedish economy in the early 1990s. Some back-of-envelope calculations in Edin and Holmund (1997) suggest that the rise in the real interest rate that took place could translate into a nonnegligible increase in equilibrium unemployment.

Falling Public Sector Employment

Public sector employment in Sweden expanded rapidly from the early 1960s to the late 1980s, most of it in local governments. By the end of the 1980s, the number of public sector employees accounted for 40 percent of the total wage and salary employment. In the early 1990s, however, the rise in public employment came to a sharp halt. In fact, between 1990 and 1994, the number of public sector employees declined by 15 percent which was equivalent to a decline in employment relative to population of 5 percentage points. This apparently dramatic fall in public sector employment may overstate the amount of job destruction that actually took place. During the 1990s, there was much organizational restructuring and privatization, and some of the decline in public sector employment reflects these organizational changes rather than job destruction. However, the organizational changes that took place may also have increased competitive pressure and involved some initial shakeout of labor.

To assess the impact of public sector employment on unemployment, one has to distinguish between the short run and the long run. The short-run effect almost certainly contributed to the rise in unemployment. An assessment of the long-run effect is more difficult. Clearly, a rise in public employment financed by taxes can induce some crowding out of private sector employment. Theoretical models in this area include papers by Holmlund (1993, 1997) and Algan et al. (2002). A plausible benchmark case is where the long-run unemployment effect of public sector expansion is zero. In a standard model of decentralized bargaining between unions and employers, this long-run neutrality result holds if the bargaining power of unions does not differ between private and public sectors.

Empirical studies in this area encounter the difficult problem of identifying the causal effects of public employment on unemployment. The studies are few and the results are mixed. For example, Edin and Holmlund (1997) could not find any long-run effect, although they did find a negative and significant effect in the short run. Algan et al. (2002) report results that are somewhat sensitive to the exact specification; their preferred estimates suggest that an expansion of public employment would actually increase unemployment in the long run.

Summing up, in the early 1990s there were a number of adverse shocks to employment. In addition to the shocks affecting private sector employment, there was also a marked decline in public sector labor demand. Although the long-run effect of public sector contraction may well be negligible, the short-run impact almost certainly reinforced the steep rise in unemployment.

5.3.2   Work Hours, Absenteeism, and Cyclical Unemployment

Flexible work hours can to a degree function as an adjustment margin that reduces fluctuations in employment. In Sweden, however, average hours per worker are countercyclical. One factor of importance is markedly pro-cyclical absence rates. In 1990, the fraction of employed absent from work during a whole week was on average close to 18 percent. In the mid-1990s, absenteeism had fallen to 14 percent; see figure 5.2.

Pro-cyclical absenteeism reinforces the negative employment effects of adverse shocks to labor demand. It reinforces symmetrically the positive employment effects of favorable shocks. The magnitude of the potential employment effect is nontrivial. As shown in figure 5.3, there is a marked rise in hours per employed worker during the early 1990s. The rise of about 4 percent can be taken as a rough indication of the magnitude of the potential employment effect. If hours and workers were perfect substitutes in production, and absent fixed costs per worker, a rise in work hours by 4 percent would translate into a decline in employment by 4 percent. Of course, the actual effect is lower because of fixed costs and (perhaps) imperfect substitutability. However, the magnitude of the potential effect is substantial.

To conclude, it is clear that movements of work hours do not tend to offset the employment effects of adverse shocks to labor demand.

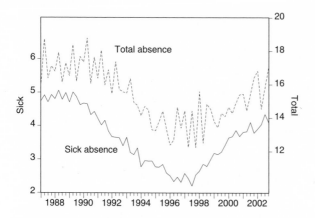

Figure 5.2
Absenteeism among employed workers in 1987 to 2002, using seasonally adjusted quarterly data. The measures refer to absences over an entire week as percentages of all employed workers. Source: Labor force surveys, Statistics Sweden.

Figure 5.3
Average hours of work per week in 1987 to 2002, using seasonally adjusted quarterly data. The data have been smoothed by a three-quarter moving average. Source: Labor force surveys, Statistics Sweden.

By contrast, countercyclical work hours tend to reinforce the adverse effects on employment. In all likelihood, the decline in absenteeism, and associated rise in work hours, contributed to the rise in unemployment in the early 1990s.[7]

5.3.3 Other Suspects

We have emphasized macroeconomic shocks as main explanations of why unemployment rose so sharply in the 1990s. For completeness, a few other candidate explanations need to be briefly discussed. They belong to the group of usual suspects when one considers determinants of equilibrium unemployment.

Unions and Wage Bargaining
The shocks that kicked Sweden into a major slump had nothing to do with a sudden surge in union density. In fact union density declined slightly—from 82 to 80 percent—between 1987 and 1990 (Kjellberg 2001). An arguably more promising explanation focuses on changes in wage-bargaining systems. The heydays of centralized wage bargaining in Sweden were the period 1956 to 1983, which involved nationwide negotiations between the peak employee and employer organizations. A significant step toward more decentralized wage bargaining came in 1983, when the metalworkers' union and their employer counterpart sidestepped the national negotiations and opted for an industry agreement. Wage negotiations after 1983 have mainly taken place at the industry level.

It is possible that the breakdown of centralized bargaining contributed to some increase in wage pressure and made it more difficult to curtail inflation in the late 1980s. It seems unlikely, however, that the impact was strong, and econometric work has not confirmed such an effect. In fact it is noteworthy that recent evidence reveals a remarkable stability of Swedish wage-setting relationships (Forslund and Kolm 2000; Holden and Nymoen 2002; Nymoen and Rødseth 2003).

Unemployment Insurance and Matching
Sweden has a generous UI system. Before-tax replacement rates for eligible workers have reached 90 percent during some years. The development of average replacement rates has shown a trend increase from the early 1960s to the 1980s (Björklund and Holmlund 1991; Forslund and Kolm 2000). In the late 1980s average replacement rates hovered

around 85 to 90 percent. This increase in the generosity of UI is a prime candidate explanation of the trend increase in the duration of unemployment that can be observed between 1960s and the 1980s. It is difficult, however, to identify specific sharp UI changes around 1990 that can explain the rise in unemployment in the early 1990s. It might perhaps be argued that the existence of a generous benefit system reinforced the rise in unemployment, even if the rise was ultimately caused by adverse macroeconomic shocks (see Blanchard and Wolfers 2000). However, generous benefits should also strengthen the automatic stabilizers in the economy, thus reducing the adverse employment effects of recessionary shocks.

Was the rise in unemployment driven by a general deterioration in matching efficiency or by a fall in search effort? If any of these changes were important, we should observe outward shifts of the Beveridge curve. Of course, an outward shift of the Beveridge curve may be ultimately caused by more generous UI that reduced search effort. Figure 5.4 shows Beveridge scatter-plots for unemployment and vacancy rates. The rise in unemployment seems to be best characterized as a movement along a convex Beveridge curve rather than as a shift of the curve.[8] All in all, the rise in unemployment in the early 1990s cannot easily be attributed to deteriorating matching efficiency or to a sudden fall in search effort, since it is hard to identify sharp adverse changes in the incentive structure.

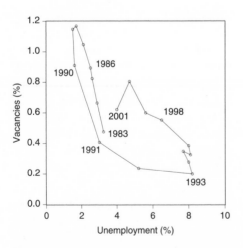

Figure 5.4
Beveridge curve for Sweden in 1983 to 2001, as percentage of labor force. Sources: Statistics Sweden (unemployment) and the National Labour Market Board (vacancies).

Taxes

The period from the early 1960s to the late 1980s exhibited an almost monotonic rise in the total tax pressure. The total tax wedge, including direct and indirect taxes on workers and payroll taxes on employers, increased by over 50 percent over this period.[9] The fact that unemployment remained low strongly suggests that most of these tax increases were borne by labor in the form of slower growth of real take-home pay. A marked trend reversal took place in the early 1990s and involved base broadening and lower marginal tax rates. It was certainly not a sharp rise in the tax wedge that threw Sweden into mass unemployment in the early 1990s.

Demographic Changes

Did changes in the age composition of the labor force contribute to the rise in unemployment? If a group with a high "natural" unemployment rate becomes relatively larger, there is a presumption that overall unemployment will increase. A simple shift share analysis reveals that the age structure tended to increase nonemployment during the 1980s, whereas it tended to reduce nonemployment during the second half of the 1990s. The maximum effects in both directions amount to one percentage point. The age structure effect is negligible during the early 1990s. During the second half of the 1990s, the relative size of the youth cohorts declined. It is safe to conclude that the causes of the steep rise in nonemployment in the early 1990s had little to do with demographic changes.

A Rise in Equilibrium Unemployment?

What do empirical studies suggest regarding the equilibrium unemployment rate in Sweden? Almost all attempts to estimate the NAIRU arrive at series that can be described as smoothed versions of the actual unemployment rate. The estimates in Holmlund (1993) indicated a trend rise in NAIRU since the mid-1960s and a NAIRU close to 3 percent around 1990. Forslund (1995) estimated wage- and price-setting schedules and solved for the equilibrium unemployment rate; this turned out to be around 4 to 6 percent in the early 1990s. Elmeskov et al. (1998) reported estimates according to which NAIRU had risen by 4 percentage points between the late 1980s and the mid-1990s. Apel and Jansson (1999) presented system estimates of potential output and the NAIRU with results that differed depending on the exact specifications. Some specifications indicated a marked rise in the NAIRU over the 1990s, whereas others indicated only marginal changes. Recent estimates reported by Konjunkturinstitutet (2002) suggest that the NAIRU was around 2 percent during the 1980s but hit 5 percent in the mid-1990s.

To reiterate what has been argued above, it is difficult to identify sharp changes in the usual structural suspects—benefits, labor market institutions, taxes, and so forth—that could explain the huge rise in unemployment. Climbing real interest rates probably added to some increase in the NAIRU in the early 1990s but cannot explain the persistence of high unemployment during the mid-1990s. The steep rise in unemployment is thus best understood as being mainly the result of a series of adverse macroeconomic shocks. It should be recognized, however, that the shocks hit when unemployment in all likelihood was well below the NAIRU, so part of the rise reflected an adjustment toward a more sustainable level of unemployment.

5.4   Why Did Unemployment Fall?

In the mid-1990s unemployment hovered around 8 percent and employment was stagnant or even falling. The sustained labor market recovery from 1997 and onward reflects favorable macroeconomic conditions but also "structural" factors that may have reduced the equilibrium unemployment rate. I discuss these factors in turn.

5.4.1   Monetary and Fiscal Policy

When the krona was left to float in November 1992, it depreciated immediately, and by the end of 1992 it had fallen by 15 percent against the ECU. Competitiveness was restored to a level comparable to the situation after the devaluation in 1982. The improved competitiveness as well as stronger market growth allowed a rise in export. Between 1993 and 1995 manufacturing output increased by over 20 percent and manufacturing employment by around 15 percent. Despite this marked rebound the overall effect on employment and unemployment was initially negligible because of negative contributions to growth from private and public consumption.

In early 1993 the central bank announced a strategy of inflation targeting. The goal of monetary policy should be to stabilize annual (consumer price) inflation at 2 percent, with a margin of tolerance of ± 1

percentage point. A new amendment to the central bank legislation, in force from 1999, gave the central bank greater independence from direct political influence. By and large, the new framework for monetary policy has been successful in achieving its main goal. Inflation has stayed within the tolerable band for most of the time and a credible low inflation regime seems to have been established. Has this also been good for employment? There are pros and cons.

On the pros side, it can be argued that a more independent central bank strengthens incentives for wage moderation. This argument presupposes a strategic interaction between wage setters and the central bank and is relevant only if wage setting takes place in a coordinated fashion; wage setters would then recognize that their decisions would affect monetary policy. A more independent ("conservative") central bank works as a deterrent to wage increases (Rantala 2001). As we will see, Swedish wage setting took a turn toward enhanced coordination in the second half of the 1990s. The interaction of a more independent central bank and more coordinated wage-bargaining arrangements has arguably been good for employment.

The cons side in this matter concerns the level of the inflation target. As emphasized by Akerlof et al. (1996, 2000) and others, it is plausible that an ambitious inflation target in the presence of nominal rigidities can be bad for employment. Indeed, the choice of a positive inflation target reflects in part the presumption that nominal wages are rigid. Some recent empirical studies have tried to pin down the role of nominal rigidities for the long-run Phillips curve. These contributions include Akerlof (1996, 2000) for the United States and Lundborg and Sacklén (2001) for Sweden. The results suggest that the long-run Phillips curve is negatively sloped at low inflation rates. Taking the estimates in Lundborg and Sacklén at face values, the inflation rate that minimizes Swedish unemployment would be around 4 percent.

The bottom line here is that we can be reasonably sure about the existence of nominal rigidities. It is much more difficult to ascertain how these rigidities affect unemployment–inflation trade-offs. It may well be the case that a less ambitious Swedish inflation target could have boosted faster employment growth over the 1990s, but it takes an act of faith to pin down the magnitude of this effect.

During 1993 the consolidated public sector's budget deficit stood at 12 percent of GDP. The government's debt-to-GDP ratio amounted to 76 percent by the end of the year. The need to bring government finances under control became a top priority for the new (social democratic) government in 1994. The following years involved a major effort to stabilize government debt and to reduce the budget deficit. The program entailed expenditure cuts, especially concerning transfers, as well as tax increases. The policies were resoundingly successful in terms of the stated objectives: by the end of the decade the government's budget deficit was eliminated, and the debt-to-GDP ratio had declined to 60 percent.

The generally contractive fiscal policy is one reason why unemployment remained stubbornly high in the mid-1990s. However, the fiscal consolidation added credibility to the anti-inflationary stance of macroeconomic policy. Fiscal policies were eased to support growth of private and public consumption as the budgetary goals were met and absent any visible threat to the low inflation target.

5.4.2 Collective Bargaining

In the summer of 1996 several blue-collar unions in manufacturing industry launched an important initiative that eventually materialized as the so-called Industrial Agreement (IA) of 1997 (Elvander 2002). The agreement was struck by the blue- and white-collar unions as well as employer organizations in the industrial sector and was mainly concerned with procedural "rules of the game." It represented an attempt to establish consensus around timetables for negotiations, the role of mediators, and rules for conflict resolution. A group of "impartial chairs" have been appointed, and the agreement states rules for when and how these chairs could intervene in the negotiation process. For example, they can order a delay of industrial action for up to two weeks. The Industrial Agreement has served as a model for similar agreements in the public sector (and also in parts of the service sector). As of 2002, over 50 percent of the labor force is covered by IA-type agreements.

The IA innovations that emerged in the late 1990s represent a move toward informal coordination in wage bargaining. The new rules of the game and the efforts to build consensus on wage developments consistent with low inflation and high employment seem to have borne some fruit in terms of wage moderation. The reforms pertaining to monetary policy discussed above seem to have reinforced the incentives for wage moderation. It is difficult, however, to assess quantitatively how important this effect has been.

5.4.3   Employment Regulations and Temporary Work

Fixed-Term Contracts
The Swedish legislation on employment protection presumes that unless otherwise stipulated, an employment contract is valid until further notice. When terminating the contract, the employer must provide a valid reason and advance notice. Compared to many other OECD countries, the periods of notice are lengthy but no redundancy pay is stipulated. The grounds for collective redundancies are liberal, although they have to proceed in accordance with seniority. During the 1990s there were no significant reforms of the employment protection legislation concerning the termination of open-ended contracts. There have, however, been several changes concerning the regulation of fixed-term contracts.

In January 1994 the maximum permitted duration for probationary contracts and those motivated by a temporary increase in labor demand were prolonged from six to twelve months. However, this was immediately repealed in January 1995. A new law in 1997 introduced the opportunity to strike collective agreements on derogations from statutory law regarding fixed-term contracts at the local level, provided that the parties had a central agreement on other matters. Prior to 1997 these agreements could only be made at the central (usually national) level. The 1997 legislation also opened up for fixed-term contracts without specified reasons.

From the early 1990s and during most of the rest of the decade there was a remarkable increase in fixed-term contracts. Measured relative to total wage and salary employment, the number of temporary workers rose from 10 to 16 percent; see figure 5.5. Holmlund and Storrie (2002) discuss this development and conclude that legislative changes are unlikely to be important. At least a partial explanation focuses on the consequences of adverse macroeconomic conditions. A recession is associated with relatively more hirings on temporary contracts, presumably reflecting stronger incentives on part of firms to offer short-term jobs when workers are easier to find as well as an increased willingness on part of workers to accept temporary work when, in general, job offers are in short supply.

The effects of a rising number of fixed-term contracts on flows into unemployment are obvious, at least in an accounting sense: the higher the share of fixed-term contracts, the larger the inflow to unemployment as these contracts entail substantially higher unemployment risks

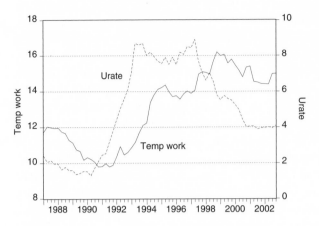

Figure 5.5
Temporary work as percentage of total wage and salary employment and unemployment as percentage of the labor force in 1987 to 2002, using seasonally adjusted quarterly data. Source: Labor force surveys, Statistics Sweden.

than open-ended contracts. In fact there was a marked rise in unemployment inflow over the 1990s, and roughly 50 percent of this rise in inflow can be accounted for by higher inflow from temporary jobs. To the extent that there has been a trend rise in temporary work that will prevail also in favorable macroeconomic conditions, it is conceivable that it has contributed to some increase in equilibrium unemployment through higher job separation rates. On the other hand, there may be offsetting effects on unemployment duration, as firms are likely to perceive fixed-term contracts as less risky than open-ended ones. Korpi and Levin (2001) find some evidence that participation in temporary employment in Sweden may reduce subsequent unemployment.

Temporary Work Agencies
Employment intermediaries in the form of temporary agency work have been on the rise in most OECD countries in recent years (Storrie 2002). Since 1993 Sweden has one of the most liberal statutory TWA regulations in the OECD. Most EU countries have some specific regulations concerning TWAs. Sweden, on the other hand, has essentially no special regulation. The TWA sector was virtually illegal and therefore nonexistent in Sweden before 1993. It is still small and accounts for less than 1 percent of the labor force. However, the sector is presumably much more important if measured relative to the number of new hires.

There is so far only scanty empirical knowledge about the TWA sector and its labor market impact. It is plausible that TWAs can have favorable impact on overall recruitments by effectively reducing hiring costs. These effects may conceivably be stronger in an economy with stringent employment protection, namely high costs of hiring and firing. Emerging evidence from the United States suggests that TWAs can serve to screen prospective employees and thereby perhaps improve matching between workers and vacancies (Katz and Krueger 1999).

In summary, the 1990s have seen notable changes concerning employment contracts in the Swedish labor market. The steep rise in the number of fixed-term contracts appear to be an endogenous response to macroeconomic and presumably also structural (but not well-understood) factors. The fast growth of employment intermediaries is clearly due to a major reform in the early 1990s. The growth of fixed-term contracts appear to have contributed to some rise in unemployment through more frequent worker separations. The growth of the temporary work agencies should have improved matching efficiency. On balance, the total effect on unemployment is probably small.

5.4.4   Deregulations in Product Markets

The 1990s have seen a general trend toward increased competition in Swedish product markets. The areas of deregulation include public procurement, telecommunications, energy, domestic air-traffic, railway transport, and taxi. The share of household consumption that is directed at markets exposed to competitive forces increased between 1991 and 1999 by 7 percentage points (Braunerhjelm et al. 2002). A new competition law was put in place in 1993 that involves tougher sanctions against noncompetitive behavior in product markets. In addition there has been some rise in competitive pressure coming from Sweden's participation in the European economic integration.

Standard theory predicts that more competitive product markets are conducive to low unemployment, at least in the long run. More intense competition brings about increased output and employment at given wage costs. It should also foster wage moderation by raising the costs to unions of aggressive wage demands. Nicoletti et al. (2001) have tried to obtain quantitative estimates of the impact of product market regulations on employment by exploiting information on regulatory reform in OECD countries since the late 1970s. Taken at face value, the estimated effects are quantitatively nontrivial. The results for Sweden imply that regulatory reform over the 1980s and the 1990s have added 2 percentage points to private sector employment relative to population (OECD 2002). Although such an estimate should be taken with at least the usual caution, it suggests that the regulatory reforms in conjunction with intensified international competition have led to some decline in the Swedish NAIRU.

5.4.5 Unemployment Insurance

The fiscal crisis in the early 1990s induced a sequence of decisions to make the UI system less generous and less expensive. The statutory replacement rate was reduced from 90 to 80 percent on July 1, 1993, and was further reduced to 75 percent on January 1, 1996. In the wake of fiscal consolidation in the late 1990s, a decision was taken to raise the UI replacement rate to 80 percent from September 1997.

The presence of a ceiling on the benefit level implies that the effective replacement rate will be lower than the statutory one for workers with above-average earnings. The ceiling was reduced in 1993 and remained constant in nominal terms until 1998 when a rise was undertaken. However, the increase was small and did not even restore the nominal value of the pre-1993 ceiling. (The next adjustments of the ceiling came in 2001 and 2002.) The combination of a slightly declining benefit ceiling and continuous nominal wage growth led to a substantial fall in replacement rates for workers with above-average earnings. Figure 5.6 shows replacement rates by wage percentiles of the overall wage distribution. For workers in the first quartile (P25) of the wage distribution, the fall in replacement rates between 1992 and 2000 amount to 10 percentage points. The fall amounts to 20 percentage points for a median-wage worker (P50) and to 25 percentage points or more for workers in the top quarter (P75) of the wage distribution.

Available empirical studies indicate that the benefit cuts of 1993 and 1996 led to a fall in the duration of unemployment. Harkman (1997) examined the effects of the 1993 reform and found that it had some positive effect on job finding. He also identified a fairly large positive effect on the exit rate to nonparticipation. Carling et al. (2001) investigated the effects of the 1996 benefit cut and estimated a positive job finding effect but found no effects on labor force exits.

Received theory suggests that higher replacement rates should raise wage pressure so there is a presumption that the benefit cuts have

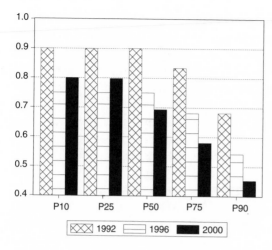

Figure 5.6
Replacement rates in unemployment insurance by wage percentiles. Source: Computations based on benefit data from the insurance unit of the National Labour Market Board and wage data from the statistical yearbooks of wages and salaries from Statistics Sweden.

caused wage moderation. Unfortunately, it has been notoriously difficult to pin down precisely how UI benefits affect wage determination. Two recent studies report somewhat conflicting results. Forslund and Kolm (2000) find some evidence supporting the conventional hypothesis, but the results are sensitive to the exact specifications. Nymoen and Rødseth (2003) cannot confirm that replacement rates matter for Swedish wage setting.

In summary, the UI system around the year 2000 was less generous than in the early 1990s. There is some evidence that the benefit cuts during the 1990s reduced the duration of unemployment and presumably therefore also reduced the NAIRU. If these effects were quantitatively important, they should also reveal themselves in aggregate data on job findings and possibly as a leftward shift of the Beveridge curve. However, such effects do not speak loudly in the data. This suggests that whatever effects there were, they were probably quantitatively modest.

5.4.6 Active Labor Market Policy

In the 1990s Sweden experienced not only an increase in various ALMP measures but also a marked growth in the number of

evaluation studies. Is there any evidence that the intensive use of
ALMPs has had beneficial employment effects? By and large, such positive evidence is rather hard to find. There is fairly clear evidence
that subsidized employment has had large crowding-out effects. Similar crowding-out effects are not found for training programs. The experiences of youth programs are largely negative: it has been difficult to
find positive effects on earnings or employment.[10] On the positive
side, however, there is some evidence that the policies have encouraged labor force participation, which may have facilitated the employment rebound in the late 1990s (Johansson 2001).

All in all, it is plausible that the intensive use of ALMP has resulted
in lower open unemployment than otherwise would have prevailed.
It is less clear, however, whether the policies have had much positive
effect on total employment.

5.4.7 Other Suspects

It remains to briefly consider other factors that could have contributed
to the fall in unemployment. Among the possible suspects, the tax
system is not a plausible one because there were few changes in the
system. Concerning demographic changes, a declining relative size of
youth cohorts has produced some "mechanical" decline in nonemployment in the late 1990s and early 2000s. The evolution of public-sector
employment in recent years has also added to the overall rise in employment. Finally, it is remarkable that absenteeism has risen sharply
since the mid-1990s (figure 5.2). A mirror image of this development is
a marked decline in average work hours among the employed (figure
5.3). This decline in average work hours should have raised the demand for workers compared to an alternative with constant absenteeism and work hours.

5.5 Concluding Remarks

In the chapter I have argued that adverse macroeconomic shocks were
mainly responsible for the steep rise in Swedish unemployment in the
early 1990s. These shocks had both domestic and foreign origins,
where the domestic shocks can be seen as the outcome of major policy
failures. The timing of financial liberalization and the "tax reform of the
century" was certainly not well designed. The consumption boom that
emerged in the late 1980s, involving gradually rising inflation as well

as falling unemployment, could have been curtailed by fiscal policy. However, fiscal policy was generally too lax, and the hands of monetary policy makers were tied to the defense of the fixed exchange rate. When macroeconomic policy finally took a firm anti-inflationary stand, the economy was already edging toward recession. The depth of the recession was reinforced by the international recession of the early 1990s and by generally rising real interest rates.

The strong recovery in the late 1990s has moderated fears that the high unemployment should become persistent. In many respects the labor market rebound from 1997 and onward indicates that the Swedish labor market has worked reasonably well. Inflation has been largely under control, job-finding rates have risen, and there is little evidence of worsening matching problems.

Several policy changes may have contributed to some decline in the NAIRU over the 1990s. Unemployment benefits became less generous, the labor market was opened for employment intermediaries, and regulatory reforms enhanced competition in product markets. Innovations in collective bargaining arrangements facilitated informal coordination of wage negotiations.

Although there are grounds for a generally positive rating of recent Swedish labor market performance, there are also grounds for a less sanguine verdict. The problems become evident as one redirects attention from unemployment to nonemployment. The overall nonemployment rate among prime age individuals increased from 8.4 percent in 1990 to 17.4 percent in 1995 and declined to 15.4 percent in 2001. This development of nonemployment is mirrored by a sharp fall in labor force participation during the early 1990s. Some of the rise in nonparticipation is probably socially beneficial. For example, it reflects, in part, increasing enrollment in higher education. However, there is also a trend toward more "inactivity" in the form of long-term sickness and early retirement. In fact the overall labor force participation rate is roughly the same in 2001 as in 1995, and lower for prime age individuals. To the extent that there are important interaction effects between shocks and institutions, as discussed by Blanchard and Wolfers (2000), they have probably mainly operated by reducing participation as a result of generous schemes favoring nonparticipation.

Swedish labor market policies have traditionally focused on open unemployment and been less concerned with employment. There are signs that policies are changing towards more emphasis on employment.[11] This is a welcome reorientation, not the least in light of future demographic developments. This reorientation toward enhancing employment needs to address several routes to "inactivity," including long-term sick absence and early retirements. A unified approach to unemployment, employment, and nonparticipation also needs to take seriously the evidence that suggests that incentives for nonwork activities arise in rules pertaining to early retirement and sickness insurance as much as in rules for unemployment insurance.

Notes

I thank Rainer Fehn and conference participants for useful comments. Valuable comments from Nils Elvander, Ingemar Hansson, Jens Henriksson, Oskar Nordström Skans, Henry Ohlsson, and Donald Storrie are also acknowledged. A longer and more detailed working paper version is available at the Web site of CESifo and at http://www.nek.uu.se/faculty/holmlund/index.html.

1. The unemployment figures refer unless stated otherwise to labor force survey data and national definitions. The working age population is generally confined to those aged 16 to 64.

2. The latent job seeker category comprises also full-time students (including persons in labor market training) that search for employment.

3. Most program participants are classified as being outside the labor force, but I follow the common practice of measuring ALMP relative to the labor force (as measured by the labor force surveys).

4. The section draws on a variety of sources, including material from Konjunkturinstitutet (the National Institute of Economic Research) and OECD Economic Surveys.

5. Estimates in Holmlund (1993a) indicated a trend increase in the Swedish NAIRU since the mid-1960s. According to these estimates, NAIRU was close to 3 percent around 1990, about twice as large as actual unemployment during 1989 to 1990.

6. The figures are based on nominal interest rates for three-months treasury bills and the producer price index.

7. As is well known, some types of working time changes can influence wage determination (Hunt 1999; Nordström Skans 2002). In the short run, however, one can reasonably take hourly wages as given.

8. The increasing unemployment in the early 1990s was associated with a sharp increase in the inflow to unemployment that produces an outward shift of the Beveridge curve. The outward loop in figure 5.4 would be much less marked if the rise in inflow were controlled for. See the working paper version of this chapter.

9. The measure of the total tax wedge is $\theta = (1 + s)(1 + vat)/(1 - t)$, where s is the payroll tax rate (levied on firms), vat is the value-added tax, and t is the income tax paid by workers. See Forslund and Kolm (2000) for more information about the evolution of the tax wedge.

10. Calmfors et al. (2001) present a comprehensive survey of Swedish experiences of active labor market policies. Larsson (2002) presents evaluations of youth programs. Fre-

driksson and Johansson (2003) examine how program participation affects reemployment rates among prime age individuals. Martin and Grubb (2001) present evidence for a number of OECD countries.

11. The government's "employment goal" states that 80 percent of the population aged 20 to 64 should be employed in 2004.

References

Akerlof, G., W. Dickens, and G. Perry. 1996. The Macroeconomics of Low Inflation. *Brookings Papers on Economic Activity* 1: 1–59.

Akerlof, G., W. Dickens, and G. Perry. 2000. Near-rational wage and price setting and the long run Phillips curve. *Brookings Papers on Economic Activity* 1: 1–44.

Algan, Y., P. Cahuc, and A. Zylberberg. 2002. Public employment and labour market performance. *Economic Policy* 34: 9–64.

Apel, M., and P. Jansson. 1999. System estimates of potential output and the NAIRU. *Empirical Economics* 24: 373–88.

Björklund, A., and B. Holmlund. 1991. The economics of unemployment insurance: The case of Sweden. In A. Björklund, R. Haveman, R. Hollister, and B. Holmlund, eds., *Labour Market Policy and Unemployment Insurance*. Oxford: Oxford University Press.

Blanchard, O., and J. Wolfers. 2000. The role of shocks and institutions in the rise of European unemployment: The aggregate evidence. *Economic Journal* 110: 1–33.

Braunerhjelm, P., ed. 2002. *Gränslös konkurrens*. Stockholm: SNS Förlag.

Calmfors, L., A. Forslund, and M. Hemström. 2001. Does active labour market policy work? Lessons from the Swedish experiences. *Swedish Economic Policy Review* 8: 61–124.

Carling, K., B. Holmlund, and A. Vejsiu. 2001. Do benefit cuts boost job finding? Swedish evidence from the 1990s. *Economic Journal* 111: 766–90.

Edin, P.-A., and B. Holmlund. 1997. Sectoral structural change and the state of the labor market in Sweden. In H. Siebert, ed., *Structural Change and Labor Market Flexibility*. Tübingen: Mohr Siebeck.

Elmeskov, J., J. P. Martin, and S. Scarpetta. 1998. Key lessons for labour market reforms: Evidence from OECD countries' experiences. *Swedish Economic Policy Review* 5: 205–52.

Elvander, N. 2002. The new Swedish regime for collective bargaining and conflict resolution: A comparative perspective. *European Journal of Industrial Relations* 8: 197–216.

Forslund, A. 1995. Unemployment—Is Sweden still different? *Swedish Economic Policy Review* 2: 25–58.

Forslund, A., and A.-S. Kolm. 2000. Active labour market policies and real wage determination. Institute for Labour Market Policy Evaluation (IFAU), *Working Paper* 2002: 7.

Harkman, A. 1997. Arbetslöshetsersättning och arbetslöshetstid—Vilken effekt hade sänkningen från 90 till 80 procents ersättningsnivå? In A. Harkman, F. Jansson, K. Källberg, and L. Öhrn, eds., *Arbetslöshetsersättningen och arbetsmarknadens funktionssätt*. Stockholm: Swedish National Labour Market Board.

Holmlund, B. 1993a. Arbetslöshetskrisen—Konjunkturfenomen eller systemfel? In SOU 1993: 16 *Nya villkor för ekonomi och politik* (Bilagedel 1). Stockholm: Allmänna Förlaget.

Holmlund, B. 1993b. Wage setting in private and public sectors in a model with endogenous government behavior. *European Journal of Political Economy* 9: 149–62.

Holmlund, B. 1997. Macroeconomic implications of cash limits in the public sector. *Economica* 64: 49–62.

Holmlund, B., and D. Storrie. 2002. Temporary jobs in turbulent times: The Swedish experience. *Economic Journal* 112: F245–69.

Hunt, J. 1999. Has work sharing worked in Germany? *Quarterly Journal of Economics* 114: 117–48.

Johansson, K. 2001. Do labor market programs affect labor force participation? *Swedish Economic Policy Review* 8: 215–34.

Katz, L., and A. Krueger. 1999. The high-pressure U.S. labor market of the 1990s. *Brookings Papers on Economic Activity* 1: 1–65.

Kjellberg, A. 2001. *Fackliga organisationer och medlemmar i dagens Sverige.* Lund: Arkiv förlag.

Konjunkturinstitutet. 2002. *Konjunkturläget* (December 2002). Stockholm: Konjunkturinstitutet.

Korpi, T., and H. Levin. 2001. Precarious footing: Temporary employment as a stepping stone out of unemployment in Sweden. *Work, Employment and Society* 15: 127–48.

Larsson, L. 2002. Evaluating social programs: Active labor market policies and social insurance. PhD thesis. Department of Economics, Uppsala University.

Lundborg, P., and H. Sacklén. 2002. Is there a long run unemployment–inflation tradeoff in Sweden? Trade Union Institute for Economic Research (FIEF), *Working Paper* 173.

Martin, J. P., and D. Grubb. 2001. What works and for whom: A review of OECD countries' experiences with active labour market policies. *Swedish Economic Policy Review* 8: 9–56.

Nicoletti, G., A. Bassanini, E. Ernst, S. Jean, P. Santiago, and P. Swaim. 2001. Product and labour markets interactions in OECD countries. *OECD Economics Department Working Paper* 312.

Nordström Skans, O. 2002. Labour market effects of working time reductions and demographic changes. PhD thesis. Department of Economics, Uppsala University.

Nymoen, R., and A. Rødseth. 2003. Explaining unemployment: Some lessons from Nordic wage formation. *Labour Economics* 10: 1–29.

OECD. 2001. *Employment Outlook 2001.* Paris: OECD.

OECD. 2002. *Employment Outlook 2002.* Paris: OECD.

Pissarides, C. A. 2000. *Equilibrium Unemployment Theory.* Cambridge: MIT Press.

Rantala, A. 2001. Does monetary union reduce employment? *Bank of Finland Discussion Papers* 2001/7.

Storrie, D. 2002. *Temporary Agency Work in the European Union.* Dublin: European Foundation for the Improvement of Living and Working Conditions.

6

Rising Unemployment at the Start of the Twenty-first Century: Has the Dutch Miracle Come to an End?

Jan C. van Ours

6.1 Introduction

In the early 1980s the Dutch labor market was in such bad shape that it was derided as the Dutch disease. While unemployment rates in the 1960s and 1970s were below the European average, in 1982 to 1983 unemployment suddenly hit 12 percent, well above the European average. Surprisingly over the past decade the Dutch labor market experienced a rapid decline in unemployment. The still high unemployment rate of 8 percent in 1992, came down to 1.8 percent in 2001, and was hailed a "Dutch miracle." Recently, however, the unemployment rate has gone up to a level of 4.0 percent as of the end of 2003. Figure 6.1 shows more precisely these recent events.[1] Unemployment has remained quite low. Nevertheless, the shifts are striking. In the spring of 2001 unemployment went down a bit, and it did not go down at all in the spring of 2002; unemployment continued to rise throughout 2003, but remained constant throughout 2004.

In this chapter, I assess the current situation in the Dutch labor market and attempt to answer whether the Dutch miracle has ended.[2] The chapter is organized as follows. Section 6.2 contains a general overview of the Dutch labor market focusing on unemployment, employment, vacancies, productivity, and wages. Section 6.3 provides details on unions and wage bargaining, unemployment benefits, active labor market policies and disability insurance. Section 6.4 brings the pieces of the Dutch puzzle together. Section 6.5 concludes.

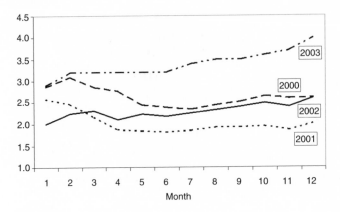

Figure 6.1
Monthly unemployment rates in 2000 to 2003 as percentage of labor force.

6.2   The Dutch Labor Market

6.2.1   General Overview

In the Dutch labor market, several major changes can be distinguished (e.g., see Hartog 1999; Nickell and Van Ours 2000). In the 1960s came the establishment of the welfare state. In 1963 the Law on Child Allowances was introduced, in 1965 the General Social Assistance Law, in 1966 the Law on Sickness Benefits, and in 1967 the Law on Disability Benefits. The first big shock to the Dutch labor market was that of the oil crisis of 1973. Unemployment started to rise as a result. The Dutch government introduced expansionary measures, financed by the abundant revenues from natural gas. The 1970s is the decade of the Dutch disease, characterized by inflation, expanding government expenditures, and sharply declining profits. The second oil crisis of 1979 fueled a deterioration of the Dutch labor market, and unemployment rose at an unprecedented speed. The year 1982 is considered by many to be a turning point. In that year, under the pressure of the seemingly endless rise in unemployment, a Central Agreement was reached between the labor unions and the employers' federation. This agreement was reached in Wassenaar, a village near The Hague, at the home of the chairman of the employers' federation. In this so-called Wassenaar agreement employers agreed to reduce work time and unions gave up on price indexation of wages and to moderate wage claims (see the appendix for the full text of the agreement). It was also agreed that obstacles to temporary work would be removed. Persons with part-time jobs would get full social security coverage (including after six months the accumulation of pension rights), while their wages would depend on the amount of work they actually provide. More specific unions agreed that working time reduction and part-time labor should not increase labor cost or reduce operating hours of firms. Although the agreement was bilateral between unions and employers, at the same time the government agreed to get its budget under control and reform social security.

The Wassenaar agreement marks a change in labor relations, from a period of frictions and ideological differences of opinion toward a more consensus approach in labor relations. Although the actual meaning is sometimes questioned in hindsight, the Wassenaar agreement is sometimes considered the start of the period of the Dutch miracle. Many detailed agreements between unions and employers were established on training, the functioning of the labor market, and the labor market position of specific groups. In the Wassenaar agreement and other agreements that were established at the same time, there were arrangements concerning wage restraint, reduction in working hours, restoration of profit levels of firms, labor market flexibility, early retirement, and the creation of jobs. Also the government agreed to get its budget under control, reform social security, and reduce taxes. In the course of the 1980s many of these agreements were implemented. In the next sections these developments will be discussed more fully.

6.2.2 Unemployment

Long-term developments in the unemployment rate in the Netherlands are shown in figure 6.2. Note that unemployment rate in the 1960s is 1 to 2 percent and increases to about 6 percent at the end of the 1970s. At the beginning of the 1980s the unemployment rate doubles within a time span of a couple of years to 12 percent in 1984. Then, apart from 1995, there is a steady decrease in unemployment to a low 2 percent in 2001 and an increase to 4.2 percent in 2004.[3]

Table 6.1 shows the developments in the unemployment rates by sex, age group, and education. Note that unemployment for men in the Netherlands has always been lower than for women but the difference becomes smaller over time. In 1979 the difference was 5.8 percentage points, in 2000 it was 0.7 percentage points. For older males (55+ years) unemployment rates in the 1990 and 1995 were lower than the

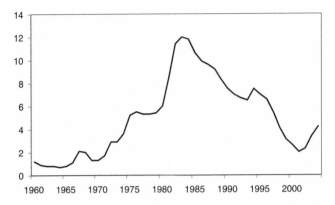

Figure 6.2
Unemployment rates in 1960 to 2003, as percentage of labor force.

unemployment rates of prime age workers (25–54 years), whereas in 2000 the difference was very small with prime age males workers having an unemployment rate just below that of older workers. For females the same age pattern emerges except for the year 2000 where the unemployment rate of prime age workers is just above the unemployment rate of older workers. For both males and females there is a clear inverse relationship between unemployment rate and level of education. This relationship is stable over time. While in 1985 higher educated male workers had an unemployment rate of about 5 percent, male workers with only primary education had an unemployment rate of almost 23 percent. In the year 2000 the unemployment rate of higher educated male workers was down to 1.4 percent, while the unemployment rate of males with only primary education was still 7.4 percent. For females a similar pattern is shown in table 6.1.

Unemployment rates are very important, but international comparisons may not tell the whole story because some countries systematically shift people out of unemployment into other nonworking categories, notably disability and early retirement. This suggests that we should also look at nonemployment rates that refer to the percentage of the population of working age who are not employed. These figures basically capture unemployment, disability, early retirement, full-time education, and other elements of nonparticipation, notably married women involved in childcare. Also note that of the nonemployment rates by sex, age group, and education in table 6.1, average nonemployment rate in the Netherlands went down from 48

Table 6.1
Unemployment rates and nonemployment rates

		Unemployment rates (%)					Nonemployment rates (%)				
		1979	1985	1990	1995	2000	1979	1985	1990	1995	2000
Total		6.2	12.8	5.9	6.9	2.5	46.1	47.7	44.8	40.6	34.4
Age	25–54	4.7	10.8	5.6	6.8	2.6	38.1	37.2	33.9	30.2	23.5
	55–64	6.6	13.2	3.2	3.4	2.9	64.8	72.6	74.2	74.2	66.0
Education	Higher	3.2	6.3	4.2	4.7	1.6	16.5	18.4	22.8	24.4	18.3
	Intermediate	3.7	7.6	3.6	5.5	1.9	23.4	27.4	35.5	33.6	28.3
	Lower	5.0	14.0	6.8	9.0	3.6	39.3	44.6	53.0	53.1	46.9
	Primary	9.1	24.1	15.2	17.2	7.6	56.7	63.6	68.5	68.5	62.0
Male		4.5	11.2	5.4	6.3	2.2	24.5	31.3	28.9	28.5	24.3
Age	25–54	3.2	9.2	5.2	6.2	2.2	8.7	15.0	12.9	12.8	9.1
	55–64	5.9	13.1	3.1	3.1	2.8	39.9	55.2	58.4	61.2	52.0
Education	Higher	2.2	4.8	3.3	4.1	1.4	4.9	8.9	13.4	17.9	12.9
	Intermediate	2.3	6.2	3.0	4.5	1.5	6.4	12.2	23.1	22.1	17.9
	Lower	3.4	12.6	5.9	8.0	2.7	10.2	20.6	33.3	34.6	29.2
	Primary	7.5	22.7	15.7	16.2	7.4	24.3	40.7	51.1	52.6	46.6
Female		10.3	15.7	6.8	7.9	2.9	68.3	64.4	61.2	53.2	44.9
Age	25–54	8.8	14.3	6.6	8.0	3.2	68.8	60.5	55.9	48.2	38.3
	55–64	9.5	13.6	3.6	4.0	3.1	87.5	88.4	89.1	87.0	80.1
Education	Higher	5.9	9.1	5.7	5.6	1.8	37.5	31.9	35.0	32.9	24.8
	Intermediate	7.1	10.2	4.7	7.0	2.5	48.6	45.9	50.3	46.5	39.5
	Lower	6.1	16.3	8.3	10.6	4.8	63.5	63.3	69.5	68.4	62.4
	Primary	13.3	27.0	13.7	19.6	8.1	80.2	80.1	83.2	82.5	75.9

Source: Central Bureau of Statistics.
Notes: The unemployment definition changed in 1987. The figures before and after 1987 are not fully comparable. Nonemployment figures differ from OECD numbers because the Dutch employment definition is referring to jobs of at least 12 hours of work per week (OECD: 1 hour per week). In 1979 and 1985 in the population outside the labor force there are many persons of which the educational level is unknown.

percent in 1985 to 34 percent in 2000. This decline is largely due to the decline in the nonemployment rate among females. Whereas the non-employment rate among males in 1979 with 24.5 percent was very similar to the nonemployment rate in 2000 with 24.3 percent among females, there was a decline over the same period from 68 to 45 percent. It is mainly the increase in part-time employment, which will be discussed in more detail below, that is responsible for this decline.

The activity in the nonemployment rates is mostly in the prime age category, since among older workers nothing much happens between 1985 and 1995. As in many countries nonemployment rates for older males are high because of early retirement and disability, while they are low for older females because of a cohort effect. Only in the period 1995 to 2000 was there a remarkable decline in nonemployment rates of older workers among males (61 to 52 percent) as well as among females (87 to 80 percent). This decline in nonemployment rate can be related to the shift from the pay-as-you-go early retirement schemes (VUT) to capital-funded schemes (pre-pensions), which increased the retirement age.[4]

There is also an inverse relationship between nonemployment rates and level of education. Whereas among males the nonemployment rate of higher educated workers is 13 percent, it is 47 percent among workers with only primary education. For females this is 25 percent for higher educated workers and 76 percent for workers with only primary education.

Finally the labor market position of immigrants has improved.[5] The immigration of the past decades originates from two rather different processes: the de-colonization and the hiring of immigrant workers because of cyclical labor shortages (Van Ours and Veenman 2005). Current labor market problems are to some extent related to the shift in immigration from a business-cycle phenomenon to a structural process. In the 1960s immigrant workers were hired because the Dutch labor market was booming. The immigrant workers got jobs in industries with low paid labor. Since these industries were particularly hit by the economic recession of the 1980s, many immigrant workers lost their jobs to become long-term unemployed. The labor market position of many immigrant workers is weak because of their low educational level and lack of Dutch language skills. Therefore it is remarkable that the unemployment rate among immigrant groups has also gone down substantially since 1995. The unemployment rate among for example Turks went down from 31 percent in 1995 to 8 percent in 2001, the unemployment rate of Moroccans went down from 32 percent in 1995 to 10 percent in 2001. Also in terms of nonemployment rates there was a substantial improvement of the labor market position of immigrants. The nonemployment rates among Turks went down from 70 percent in 1995 to 52 percent in 2001, while for Moroccans these numbers are 71 and 52 percent. Although there is still a distance both in terms of unemployment rates and nonemployment rates among native Dutch and immigrants, it is clear that immigrants have benefited a lot from the Dutch miracle.

6.2.3 Employment

Employment can be measured in different ways: the number of jobs, the number of labor years where part-time jobs are expressed in terms of full-time equivalents, and the number of working hours. As shown in table 6.2, the total number of jobs has increased a lot over the past decades. The increase in the number of jobs was lowest in the 1980s with 393,000 and highest in the 1990s when employment increased with 1.6 million jobs. To a large extent the increase in employment was in the part-time jobs. In the 1980s, for example, the number of full-time jobs decreased by 66,000 while the number of part-time jobs increased by more than 700,000. Over the 1990s, 900,000 additional part-time jobs were created, but also the number of full-time jobs increased close to 500,000.

Because the increase in the number of jobs is mainly due to part-time jobs, the evolution of the number of labor years is less spectacular, but even in terms of labor years employment increased with almost 1 million in the 1990s. Table 6.2 also shows that the number of working hours of a standard full-time job has decreased substantially over the past decades. Whereas the number of annual working hours for a full-time job was 2,240 in 1960 it was 1,740 by 1990. This decline is due to an increase in the length of the holidays and the introduction of so-called shorter work-hours days, which are nonwork days the worker can choose to have throughout the year. Of course, the sharp decline in the number of work hours per full-time equivalent also implies that the total number of individuals working in the Netherlands did not increase as spectacularly as the numbers of jobs or labor years. As figure 6.3 shows that the total number of work hours increased in the 1960s but declined afterward to reach a level of 7.4 billion in 1984, which was the same number of hours as in 1958. After 1984 there is an almost

Table 6.2
Employment

	Old				New					
	1960	1970	1980	1990	1990	2000	1960–1970	1970–1980	1980–1990	1990–2000
Jobs (1,000)										
Part-time employment	—	854	1,225	1,934	2,250	3,150	—	371	709	900
Full-time employment	—	3,742	3,846	3,780	3,648	4,134	—	104	−66	486
All employees	—	4,596	5,071	5,714	5,898	7,284	—	475	643	1,386
All workers	4,506	5,469	5,862	6,559	7,017	8,582	963	393	697	1,565
Labor years (1,000)										
Employees	3,403	4,115	4,383	4,702	4,779	5,665	712	268	319	886
All workers	4,155	4,763	4,932	5,257	5,441	6,426	608	169	325	985
Working time (hours)										
Full-time year	2,241	2,007	1,839	1,741	1,741	1,723	−234	−168	−98	−18
Working hours (million)	7,626	8,257	8,061	8,185	—	9,846	631	−196	124	1,386

Source: Central Bureau of Statistics.
Notes: In 1995 there was a revision of the employment numbers. This revision was also applied to earlier years. Therefore there are two numbers for 1990. For the total number of working hours the new 1990 number is unavailable. For 1995 the old number was 8,405, and the new number is 8,680. This difference has been taken into account when calculating the change over the period 1990 to 2000. See also figure 6.3.

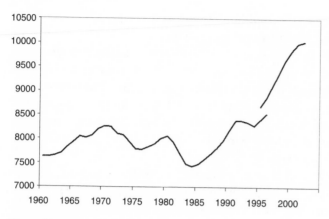

Figure 6.3
Number of working hours in 1960 to 2002 mil.

steady increase in the total number of work hours, but it lasted until 1987 before the 7.6 billion work hours of 1960 was reached. This pattern lasted until 1991 until the 8.3 billion work hours of 1970 was reached. In 2001 a level of almost 10 billion work hours was reached.

The huge increase of part-time labor is due to several combined developments. For a long time labor market participation of Dutch females had been low compared to other European countries. The increase in female participation is partly a catch-up effect. Furthermore barriers for part-time employment were removed. Until the Wassenaar agreement part-time jobs were clearly inferior to full-time jobs in terms of employment rights and benefits. After the unions gave up their resistance to part-time jobs there was a positive relation between supply and demand.[6] For employers part-time jobs are useful because they have flexibility then to allocate more labor toward weekly peak hours in production (e.g., in retailing) and because it attracts new labor supply. Females that withdrew from the labor market for family reasons return to take up part-time jobs, and females that would otherwise have left the labor market are now staying in part-time jobs. So the effective labor supply has increased. For females part-time jobs are valuable because they allow them to combine paid work with childcare.

In the aftermath of the Wassenaar agreement shorter work hours were introduced in ways different from part-time labor: shorter work weeks, extra holidays, and early retirement. Growth of part-time jobs was also encouraged by laws that made part-time work more attractive. In 1993 the statutory exemption of jobs of less than one-third of the normal work week from application of the legal minimum wage and related social security entitlements were abolished. Currently most taxes are neutral and social security benefits are usually pro rata. Also since 1993 unions and employers representatives have recommended that employers grant workers' requests to work part-time unless there are compelling business reasons to avoid this. In 1995 unions and employers signed the first formal collective agreement for temporary workers. In 2000 a right to part-time work law was introduced (see Tijdens 2002 for details).

The increase in part-time jobs has had a positive effect on employment growth. Because labor supply effectively increased, many firms could expand their business. Part-time labor is not just a redistribution of a fixed amount of labor over a larger number of workers (the "lump-of-labor fallacy") as is shown in figure 6.3 and affirmed in a study by Van Lomwel and Van Ours (2005) in which it is argued that the growth of part-time labor even had positive effects on the growth of full-time labor.

6.2.4   The Beveridge Curve

The relationship between unemployment and vacancies—the Beveridge curve—is shown in figure 6.4. The data are for the third quarter of every year in the period 1988 to 2004. Note that the number of unemployed in the third quarter of 1988 was equal to 440,000 with 70,000 vacancies. Up to 1991 there was an increase in the number of vacancies

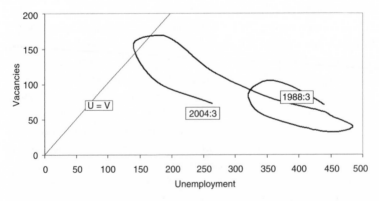

Figure 6.4
Beveridge curve for 1988 to 2004, using third-quarter data.

and a decrease in the number of unemployed. Then between 1991 and 1994 there was a decline in the number of vacancies. From 1995 onward the number of vacancies increased to a maximum of 170,000 in the third quarter of 2000, while the unemployment declined to 140,000 in 2001. In the third quarter of 2003 the number of vacancies had fallen to 73,000 while the number of unemployed had increased to 264,000. In 2004 unemployment increased to 315,000, while the number of vacancies increased to 100,000. The Beveridge curve shows two full counterclockwise loops. Overall, the clear inward shift of the Beveridge curve indicates that the functioning of the Dutch labor market has improved.[7]

6.2.5 Productivity and Wages

Table 6.3 shows the evolution of productivity since 1960 in terms of GDP per hour worked. Whereas in the 1960s and 1970s there was a substantial productivity growth, respectively at 4.4 percent per year and 2.5 percent per year, in the 1980s and 1990s the average increase of GDP per hour was only about 1 percent per year. Conditional on GDP per hour data, the evolution of GDP per capita depends on changes in work time and changes in employment–population rates. In the 1960s and 1970s the increase in employment-participation rate was not sufficient to balance the reduction in work time. In the 1980s and 1990s the increase in the employment–population rates was substantially larger than the reduction of work time. As a result the increase in GDP per capita in the 1980s was about the same as in the 1970s, while the increase in GDP per capita in the 1990s was a 0.5 percentage point per year larger than it was in the 1970s.[8]

Table 6.3
GDP growth and growth of real wages, 1963 to 2000 (%/yr)

	1960–1973	1973–1980	1980–1990	1990–2000
GDP per hour	4.4	2.5	0.9	1.1
Change in working time	−1.2	−1.2	−1.0	−0.5
Change in participation	0.3	0.4	1.8	1.6
GDP per capita	3.5	1.7	1.6	2.2
Gross real wage	—	2.7	0.5	0.6

Sources: Authors' calculations on the basis of the Groningen Growth and Development Center (GGDC) Total Economy Database (GDP) and CPB Netherlands Bureau for Economic Policy Analysis (real wage).

The real wage in the Netherlands increased about 50 percent in the 1970s. In the 1980s there is hardly any increase. More precisely, in the first half of the 1980s there was a clear decline. This was due to the disappearance of the cost-of-living clauses in the Wassenaar agreement. In the second half of the 1990s the real wage increases again. As table 6.3 shows, on average in the 1980s and 1990s real wages increased with only about 0.5 percent per year.[9]

6.3   The Pieces of the Puzzle

6.3.1   Unions and Wage Bargaining

In 2000 there were about 2 million union members in the Netherlands, with union density about 27 percent.[10] As shown in table 6.4, union density has declined over the past decades from around 35 percent in 1980. The most common opinion about the improvement of labor market performance in the Netherlands is that it has to do with the cooperative nature of the unions.[11] As Hartog (1999, p. 484) puts it: "If there is anything like a Dutch model, it is the Dutch brand of corporatism, with consultation, coordination and bargaining over all important issues of socioeconomic policy between union federations, employer federations and the government. The Dutch example shows that corporatist institutions are not synonymous with suffocating rigidity." The cooperative

Table 6.4
Labor market institutions, 1970 to 2000

	1970	1980	1990	2000
Union density (%)	33.2	35.3	28.9	27.1
Employment protection (index)	1.35	1.35	1.25	1.10
Replacement rate (%)	72.0	70.7	61.0	55.9
Labor taxes (% of labor costs)	33.6	42.5	41.9	40.0
Minimum wages (% of average wage)	58	61	52	47
Active labor market policies				
Expenditures (% of GDP)	—	—	1.3	1.6
Participant inflow (% of labor force)	—	—	3.1	6.9

Sources: Union density: Central Bureau of Statistics (CBS); replacement rate, labor taxes: CPB Netherlands Bureau for Economic Policy Analysis (see Stegeman 2002); minimum wage: OECD; active labor market policies: OECD, Employment Outlooks; employment protection: Nickell (2003).
Note: The employment protection number for 2000 refers to 1998.

nature of Dutch unions is also present in the changing laws concerning employment protection. In 1996 unions and employers agreed on a relaxation of statutory dismissal protection for regular employment contracts in exchange for an improvement of the rights of temporary workers. New legislation removing constraints on shop-opening hours, business licenses, temporary job agencies, working time, dismissal, and so on, consolidated and promoted flexibility. As table 6.4 shows, the index indicating employment protection has decreased in strictness since 1980. A new law on work hours permits longer work hours and weekend and evening work hours, if agreed between employers and their workers (Visser and Hemerijck 1997).

The economic downturn in 1993 was mild and the recovery much stronger than in the rest of Europe. This is probably also why unions were modest and passive. As discussed before, there was wage moderation. This too could have been related to the restructuring of the benefit system. The wage moderation could also have been responsible for the boost in part-time employment. Average earnings per family increased much more than wages did.

6.3.2 Unemployment Benefits and Labor Taxes

The current unemployment law dates from January 1, 1987. Workers losing their jobs in the Netherlands are entitled to unemployment benefits, provided some conditions are fulfilled. Those who fulfill these conditions are entitled to initial benefits of 70 percent of the wage in the last job before unemployment. The maximum duration of these benefits ranges from six months to five years, depending on the employment history of the unemployed.[12] If, after the expiration of the unemployment insurance benefits, the unemployed individual has not found a job, the individual may receive social assistance benefits, which are means-tested and related to what is considered to be the social minimum income.

Table 5.4 shows that the average unemployment benefit replacement rate has gone down in the past decades from about 71 percent in 1980 to 56 percent in 2000. The decline in replacement rate had a clear effect on unemployment. Broersma, Koeman, and Teulings (2000), for example, find that the lowering of the replacement rate since the mid-1980s has contributed to the decline in unemployment both directly through its effect on search behavior and indirectly through its effect on wages. Broer, Draper, and Huizinga (1999) also find that the replacement rate (in addition to tax rate and the real interest rate) is a major determinant of the Dutch unemployment rate.

Although average replacement rates have gone down, many unemployed workers face an incentive problem. Unemployed with high unemployment benefits (those with well-paid jobs before unemployment) would lose by taking up a job that pays the minimum wage. A single unemployed worker who would accept a job at the minimum wage level would loose on average 225 euros per year (Ministerie van Sociale Zaken en Werkgelegenheid 2002). A single individual that would accept a job at the minimum wage level would have lost 7 percent of its net income in 2000 (2 percent in 2001). A single earner that would accept a job at 130 percent of the minimum wage would have lost 5 percent of the net income in 2000 (1 percent in 2001).

In August 1996 a new law on benefit sanctions was introduced. Under this law people who receive benefits may get a reduction of their benefits if they don't follow the rules related to the benefits (not giving proper information, lack of effort of keeping a job, refusing job offers, etc.). Sometimes people have to pay back (part of) their benefits if they got them for the wrong reasons. Sometimes people have to pay a penalty. Figure 6.5 shows the evolution of unemployment benefits and benefit sanctions as a percentage of unemployment benefits. For many years the sanction percentage was between 10 and 15 percent. Since 1996 this number increased to about 35 percent to go down from 1999 onwards.

From recent micro studies on the effect of benefit sanctions in the Dutch labor market we know that a reduction of unemployment bene-

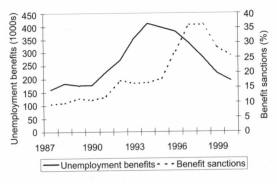

Figure 6.5
Unemployment benefits and sanctions in 1987 to 2000.

fits can have a substantial effect on the outflow from unemployment to a job.[13] In addition to that, the presence of a system of benefit sanctions may stimulate workers to search more intensive even before they get a benefit sanction imposed (Boone and Van Ours 2005). Therefore the restructuring of the benefit system, including the introduction of a system of benefit sanctions, may be one of the main policy measures responsible for the Dutch miracle.

In 2002 there was another reform of the social security system. The collecting of social security contributions and the payment of benefits is still under public control but the reintegration of unemployed and disabled workers is privatized.

As shown in table 6.4 other work incentives increased too. Labor taxes as a percentage of labor costs have gone down since 1980. The minimum wage as a percentage of average wage has gone down from 61 percent in 1980 to 47 percent in 2000. Note that this decrease in the minimum wage is also an incentive for job creation.

6.3.3   Active Labor Market Programs

Table 6.4 indicates that in the course of the 1990s active labor market programs have expanded. The expenditures as a percentage of GDP increased from 1.3 to 1.6; the inflow into the programs as a percentage of the labor force increased from 3.1 to 6.9. By the end of the 1990s there were a variety of programs ranging from limited subsidies to sheltered jobs.

Among the limited subsidy schemes there was a scheme intended to help long-term unemployed workers to find a job through lowering their costs at and just above the minimum wage. The maximum subsidy for employers was 2,215 euros per year for maximum four years. Another scheme targeted low-skilled workers. Employers could get a maximum fiscal allowance of 1,924 euros per year for workers that did not earn more than 115 percent of the minimum wage (in a job of 36 hours per week).

Among the larger wage subsidies was a subsidy that targeted the creation of jobs for long-term unemployed through the mediation of the municipality or through subsidizing of temporary jobs at regular firms. In 2000 about 40,000 of these subsidies were provided 8,485 euros for a maximum of one year. There were also so-called inflow–outflow jobs that targeted creating employment for long-term unemployed in the nonprofit sector and supplying useful public services.

These jobs were administered by local municipalities and with pay up to 130 percent of the minimum wage. The average subsidy was between 16,790 and 20,875 euros. In 2000 about 45,000 jobs were created under this scheme.

Finally there are the sheltered jobs for people who, for physical or mental reasons, cannot work in regular jobs. In 2001 there were about 90,000 workers in these sheltered jobs.

Although wage subsidies were successful in bringing back long-term unemployed to work, their success in bringing back these long-term unemployed to regular jobs is doubted. In a recent evaluation study it was concluded that workers tend to get locked into subsidized jobs, so there is insufficient outflow from subsidized job to regular jobs (IBO 2001).

6.3.4 Disability

The use of disability benefits in the Netherlands is remarkably high. In 2003 almost 1 million individuals collected disability benefits.[14] The story of increasing disability starts in 1967 when the comprehensive disability insurance for employees (WAO) was introduced. Under the terms of this law workers were insured against wage loss due to long-term disability. From then on, any worker that became ill was allowed to claim a benefit under the illness scheme for a maximum period of one year. After that the worker could claim a disability benefit. Workers were entitled to disability benefits after a so-called disability examination, which consisted not only of a medical examination but also of an investigation of the labor market position of the worker. Workers could be considered disabled if there were no suitable jobs for them at their educational levels in their previous occupations. Furthermore unemployment was "internalized," which means that those workers who were considered to be partially (more than 15 percent) disabled could collect full disability benefits because it was assumed that partially disabled were doomed to remain unemployed. The benefit had a maximum of 80 percent of the wage in the last job. Disability benefits could be collected until age 65. Since the introduction of comprehensive disability insurance, the number of workers collecting disability benefits has increased massively. This huge increase in the numbers on disability benefits induced the government to adjust some elements of the disability benefit system on several occasions. In 1985 the maximum replacement rate was reduced from 80 to 70 percent. In

1987 there was a major restructuring of the disability benefit system, of which the main objective was to reduce the inflow into disability. The most important change was the abolition of the "internalization of unemployment" rules. Partially disabled workers were considered as such and were expected to find a job or claim unemployment benefits for their remaining work capacity. The reform of the disability insurance was very important. Empirical studies find that before the 1987 reform of the disability benefit system up to 50 percent of the disability enrollment was related to redundancy of workers. Hassink, Van Ours, and Ridder (1997) show that at the end of the 1980s employers still used disability enrollment as an alternative to dismissals. They find that about 10 percent of the transitions into disability are due to redundancy of the worker. An implication of this result is that even after the social security reform of 1987, some employers and employees used disability enrollment to avoid dismissals.

In the early 1990s there were some further changes. The disability insurance premium was experience rated, the disability examination no longer took the availability of suitable jobs with respect to education and previous occupation into consideration, the duration of the benefit was limited to five years after which a re-examination had to take place, and all disabled workers younger than 50 years had to be re-examined.

Table 6.5 shows the numbers of disability benefits distinguished by age and gender. As shown most of the people collecting disability benefits are above age 44. Nevertheless, there is a substantial number below age 45 as well. In the age range 15 to 24 years, there are 30,000 individuals collecting disability benefits; in the age range 25 to 34 years, there are 100,000 individuals collecting disability benefits, a number that is 175,000 for the age group 35 to 44 years. In the lower age categories, more females than males collect disability benefits. From 45 years onward, the number of male disability benefit recipients is larger than the number of female disability benefit recipients. In the age group 55 to 64, 15 percent of all females collects disability benefits while 30 percent of all males in this age group collects disability benefits.

In 2002 the so-called gatekeeper model in which employers and workers carry more responsibility was extended. Now the employer has to provide a plan for re-integration within thirteen weeks after his worker became ill. This has to be done to make sure that workers and their employers try to prevent abuse of the disability benefit system. If

Table 6.5
Benefits by age groups and gender, June 2001

	Females			Males		
	Social assistance	Unem- ployment benefits	Disability benefits	Social assistance	Unem- ployment benefits	Disability benefits
Age (1,000)						
15–24	16	4	15	10	3	16
25–34	45	18	62	30	12	41
35–44	52	18	91	37	15	84
45–54	42	17	122	32	17	168
55–64	36	19	124	27	48	241
Total	191	76	414	136	95	550
Age (% of population)						
15–24	1.7	0.4	1.6	1.1	0.3	1.7
25–34	3.7	1.5	5.2	2.5	1.0	3.4
35–44	4.1	1.4	7.2	2.9	1.2	6.7
45–54	3.7	1.5	10.7	2.8	1.5	14.7
55–64	4.5	2.4	15.4	3.4	6.0	29.9
Total	3.6	1.4	7.7	2.5	1.8	10.3

Source: Central Bureau of Statistics.

an application is made for a disability benefit, a re-integration report has to be submitted. If there is insufficient proof of re-integration activities, the worker may not get disability benefits after one year of illness. In that case the employer may be obliged to pay the wages for another year, and the worker faces the risk of receiving a lower disability benefits or no disability benefits at all. At the present moment there is insufficient information available for an effective assessment of the gatekeeper model. Nevertheless, as figure 6.6 shows, for the first time since the mid-1990s, in 2003 the inflow into disability was smaller than the outflow from disability.

6.4 Bringing the Pieces of the Puzzle Together

Now that the pieces of the puzzle are presented they can be brought together. There are several explanations for the recent events in the Dutch labor market. As the OECD (1998) puts it: "Confronted with a deeper crisis than most other European countries, the Netherlands started its reform process earlier, with a greater scope for improve-

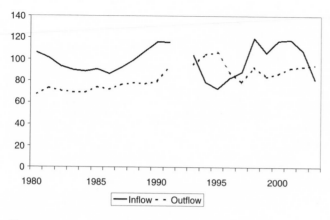

Figure 6.6
Inflow and outflow of disability in 1980 to 2003, in thousands.

ment." According to Visser and Hemerijck (1997) three policy shifts are responsible for the Dutch miracle. First, there was wage moderation that started in the early 1980s and was concluded in negotiations between unions and employers in 1982. Because of this the competitiveness of the Dutch industry increased a lot. Second, there was of reform of the social security system, starting with a freezing of benefits in 1983 and an overhaul of unemployment insurance in 1987. The major reforms in social security took place in the early 1990s when disability insurance and sickness leave schemes were reformed. The third policy shift concerns the innovation of labor market policies and the emphasis on activating measures of various kinds. Nickell and Van Ours (2000) conclude that the unemployment rate in the Netherlands went down because of a significant reduction of the equilibrium unemployment rate since the early 1980s. Responsible for this are wage moderation, the popularity of part-time work, and the re-enforcement of financial incentives for work for unemployed workers collecting benefits.

In assessing the current situation in the Dutch labor market, I hold changes in labor market institutions to be the main determinants of the Dutch labor market success.[15] Based on the discussion in the previous sections, table 6.6 gives a summary representation of the main policy changes and their effects on the unemployment rate and the employment population rate. There are three major and three minor changes in labor market institutions that generated the employment miracle. The three major changes are the removal of the barriers for part-time labor, changing incentives with respect to unemployment benefits, and

Table 6.6
Bringing the pieces of the puzzle together

Topic	Policy 1980s–1990s	Unemployment rate	Employment rate	Remarks
Part-time labor	Barriers removed	−	++	Also legal barriers
Unemployment benefits				
Replacement rate	Reduced	−	+	For some groups still no incentives to look for a job
Entitlement period	Experience rated	−	+	
Benefits sanctions	Introduced	−	+	
Wage negotiations	Central agreements	−	+	Cooperative unions
Employment protection	More flexibility	0	+	
Disability insurance	Attempts to reform	−	−	No political consensus
ALMPs				
Subsidized jobs	Increased	−	0	Locked-in effects
Sheltered labor	Mild expansion	−	0	
Matching	Reorganizations	−	+	Privatizations

the cooperative relations between employers and unions. The three (relatively) minor changes concern employment protection, disability insurance, and active labor market policies.

The first component of the Dutch success story is part-time labor. The main institutional change here is the removal of institutional barriers. After the barriers were removed, part-time jobs were no longer inferior in terms of taxes and social security benefits and part-time employment grew very rapidly. This increased employment not only in terms of jobs but also in terms of overall work hours. Rather than being created at the expense of full-time jobs, they stimulated the creation of full-time jobs. So the creation of part-time jobs both reduced unemployment and stimulated employment.

The second component concerns the changes in the system of unemployment benefits. Incentives to search and find a job were improved by lowering of replacement rates, by relating entitlement periods to past employment experience, and by introducing a system of benefit sanctions. These changes reduced unemployment, and because effective labor supply increased, the changes also stimulated employment.

The third component concerns the structure of wage bargaining. The Wassenaar agreement was the central agreement between unions and employers' organizations that triggered a number of other central agreements that stimulated wage moderation. Wage moderation is not only due to the structure of wage bargaining but also related to the decline of the benefit replacement rates. Furthermore the growth of part-time labor stimulated effective labor supply, which supported wage moderation. So part-time labor stimulated total employment both directly and indirectly. The central agreements stimulated employment and as a result reduced unemployment.

Besides the three main institutional changes there are three smaller changes that brought improvement to the functioning of the Dutch labor market. Reduced employment protection created a more flexible labor market. This did not have a negative effect on employment but rather stimulated employment. Reforms of the disability insurance system changed incentives but largely failed to bring down the number claiming disability. If anything the disability benefit policy has been one of muddling through. Perhaps the new gatekeeper model will improve matters, but it is too early to draw any conclusions. Therefore both unemployment and employment have been negatively affected. Finally a number of active labor market policies were introduced, or expanded, and the organization of the public employment services was changed with a negative effect on the unemployment rate.

When assessing the current situation in the Dutch labor market, it is necessary to distinguish between actual unemployment and equilibrium unemployment. The inward shift of the Beveridge curve shows that in the 1990s the functioning of the labor market improved. Equilibrium unemployment went down due to changes in labor market institutions. Nevertheless, in the late 1990s actual unemployment fell below the equilibrium unemployment, causing wages to rise and unemployment to increase. So part of the recent rise in unemployment has to do with an equilibrium adjustment. Another part of the recent rise may be related to the business cycle. All in all, there does not seem to be a lot of reason to worry a lot about the recent rise in unemployment. That does not mean that all labor market problems are solved. The main problems facing the Netherlands in the near future are the large number of workers collecting disability benefits and the low employment rate among elderly workers. Since the first problem is around for decades and the second problem is a consequence of 1980s policy that intended to reduce unemployment through early retirement, it will not be easy to find solutions. Usually the labor market can be expected to depend more or less on the political arena. However, because the Netherlands is a coalition country where there is never one party in power, no big changes should occur. Nevertheless, coalitions of the same parties that were responsible first for the Dutch disease and then for the Dutch miracle are still in power at the start of the twenty-first century.[16]

6.5   Conclusions

Over the past decades unemployment in the Netherlands has declined substantially. Mainly responsible for this decline are the growth of part-time labor, reform of the benefit system, and wage moderation. In recent years, however, the unemployment rate in the Netherlands has started to rise. The increase is partly a response to the low unemployment rate and the accompanying rise in wages and partly business-cycle related, that is, affected by the recession that has hit many European countries. Since the huge decline in unemployment was due to structural improvements in the functioning of the labor market, there is not a lot of reason to worry about the recent increase. The current structure of the labor market is a lot "healthier" than it was in the early 1980s. Therefore the unemployment rise is bound to be a mild one.

Appendix: "Wassenaar" Agreement

The national employers' associations and trade union confederations, represented in the Labor Foundation, considering that

• the following factors are essential for the structural improvement of employment: recovery of economic growth, stable price levels, improved competitiveness of enterprises and, in connection therewith, improved returns;

• a long-term social and economic policy, intended to achieve the above, is necessary;

• even if economic growth recovers, it will not be possible in the medium term to assist the entire existing labor force and the growth in the labor force in finding paid employment in the near future;

• in connection with the aforementioned policy, it would be advisable to introduce a long-term approach aimed at re-distributing existing employment more effectively; i.e., an approach which encompasses several methods of re-distributing employment, such as working time reduction, part-time work, and efforts to reduce unemployment among young people;

• in connection with the agreements to be made by the collective bargaining partners regarding the form, phasing and employment effects, one of the premises must be that—in view of the weak financial position of enterprises—a better distribution of existing employment should not result in higher costs, and

• efforts must be made to make a start with the implementation of this policy in 1983, with the collective bargaining partners having the exclusive right to re-negotiate between them wage agreements already set out in collective bargaining agreements;

I. call upon the collective bargaining partners to create the conditions required to introduce a policy along these lines as quickly as possible;

II. give it as their view that there are also reasons to have consultations with one another in the Labor Foundation on a number of aspects related to the re-distribution of work and efforts to reduce unemployment among young people, in order to arrive at a set of recommendations on these issues before 1 January 1983;

III. express the desirability—while respecting one another's opinions and feelings regarding the new Cabinet's policy intentions—that the collective bargaining rounds for 1983 will start shortly in enterprises and sectors of industry, based on the considerations and policy intentions described above, and urge the Cabinet to do everything possible to enable the collective bargaining partners to negotiate freely with one another on the basis of the above recommendations. They declare their willingness in that regard to inform the Cabinet about the actual developments and results of the collective bargaining rounds in the Spring of 1983.

The Hague, 24 November 1982.

Notes

The author would like to thank participants of the December 2002 CESifo-YJS conference in München on "Unemployment in Europe: Reasons and Remedies" for helpful suggestions and remarks.

1. The source of all data is the Netherlands Central Bureau of Statistics.

2. The term "miracle" may be somewhat misleading, since it implies events that cannot be explained rationally. There are in fact clear explanations for the decline in Dutch unemployment.

3. The numbers refer to registered unemployment, thus representing the numbers of individuals registered at a public employment office who do not work or work for less than 12 hours per week and who are available to work 12 hours per week or more. For example, in 2003 there were, on average, 255,000 registered unemployed workers. However, in 2003 there were, on average, 248,000 workers collecting unemployment benefits.

4. The number of workers on the early retirement plan fell from 152,000 in 1995 to 113,000 in 2000. In the same period the number of workers on a pre-pension plan increased from 23,000 to 66,000.

5. As of the beginning of the new millennium, about 2.7 million people live in the Netherlands who by their own birthplace or that of at least one of their parents are considered to be immigrants. Together they comprise about 17 percent of the total population. Among the larger groups of immigrants are Turks (300,000), Surinamese (300,000), Moroccan (250,000), Antilleans (100,000), and people from (former) Yugoslavia (65,000). About 90,000 immigrants from the southern European countries are comprised of people of different nationalities. Even more diversity of nationality is found among the political refugees, who comprise about 180,000 people. As of January 1, 2002, there were 1.4 million second-generation immigrants, that is, children of immigrants.

6. In 1981 the main federation of unions (FNV) decried the inferiority of employment rights, wages, fringe benefits, and career prospects in part-time jobs and the declining union membership. The federation did not want a secondary job market created and demanded an improvement in statutory protection for part-time workers (Visser and Hemerijck 1997).

7. Note that over the period presented the labor force increased substantially. A Beveridge curve with unemployment and vacancies as a percentage of the labor force could show an even larger inward shift.

8. Also in international perspective the increase in the Dutch employment–population rate was an important component of GDP per capita growth. From Scarpetta et al. (2000) it appears, for example, that in relation to the EU average, the GDP per work hour in the Netherlands has declined. The 1985 GDP per hour worked was 19 percent higher than the EU average, but in 1998 this was reduced to a difference of 10 percent. In contrast, the GDP per capita in the Netherlands was only 4 percent higher than the EU average in 1985 and rose to 11 percent higher than the EU average in 1998.

9. Wage moderation had an important effect on the relative labor costs of Dutch industry as compared to, for example, the German industry. If the ratio of real labor costs of Netherlands and Germany are indexed to 100 in 1980, this index is 62 in 1995 and 75 in 2000 (these calculations are on the basis of CPB Netherlands Bureau for Economic Policy Analysis).

10. Of the union members almost 350,000 were not employed, and about 200,000 of these were older than 65 years. Visser and Hemerijck (1997) present an excellent overview of the Dutch miracle and the peculiarities of Dutch industrial relations. See Checci and Lucifora (2002) for a recent overview of the way labor unions affect the functioning of labor markets.

11. In 2000 there were about 200 industry-specific collective agreements and about 800 firm-specific collective agreements.

12. Depending on their work history some workers were entitled to two years of extended benefits, equal to 70 percent of the minimum wage. This benefit extension was abolished August 2003.

13. Abbring, Van den Berg and Van Ours (2005) study the effect of financial incentives by comparing the unemployment duration of individuals that have faced a benefit reduction with similar individuals that have not been penalized. They find that the job-finding rates double after a sanction has been imposed. Van den Berg, Van der Klaauw, and Van Ours (2004) perform a similar study for welfare recipients in the city of Rotterdam. Although this group of unemployed has a labor market position that is often considered to be very weak, they too find that the job-finding rate doubles at the imposition of a sanction.

14. Note that persons collecting disability benefits may be part-time disabled; that is, they are capable of holding a (part-time) job. For example, in July 2002 there were 975,000 persons collecting disability benefits of which 245,000 had a part-time job and 730,000 did not.

15. See Layard and Nickell (1999) for an overview of the relationship between institutions and labor market performance and Nickell (2004) for a recent application. See also Belot and Van Ours (2004) for a cross-country comparison of the effects of labor market institutions on unemployment.

16. The three main political parties responsible for the change in institutions in the 1980s and 1990s are the Christen Democrats (CDA), the liberals (VVD), and the Social Democrats (PvdA). They have ruled the Netherlands in various combinations. There was a shock to the political system when the leader of a new political party—Pim Fortuyn— was killed just before the elections of May 2002. In the aftermath of the assassination, Fortuyn's party won many seats in Dutch parliament. A coalition with Fortuyn's new party that started August 2002 had already collapsed by October 2002. In January 2003 there were new elections as a result of which an old-style coalition was again in power.

References

Abbring, J. H., G. J. van den Berg, and J. C. van Ours. 2005. The effect of unemployment insurance sanctions on the transition rate from unemployment to employment. *Economic Journal* 115: 602–30.

Belot, M. V. K., and J. C. van Ours. 2004. Does the recent success of some OECD countries in lowering their unemployment rates lie in the clever design of their labor market reforms? *Oxford Economic Papers* 56: 621–42.

Boone, J., and J. C. van Ours. 2005. Modeling financial incentives to get unemployed back to work. *Journal of Institutional and Theoretical Economics*, forthcoming.

Broer, P., N. Draper, and F. Huizinga. 1999. The equilibrium rate of unemployment in the Netherlands. Netherlands Bureau for Economic Policy Analysis, The Hague, Research memorandum.

Broersma, L., J. Koeman, and C. Teulings. 2000. Labor supply, the natural rate, and the welfare state in the Netherlands: The wrong institutions at the wrong point in time. *Oxford Economic Papers* 52: 96–118.

Checchi, D., and C. Lucifora. 2002. Unions and labor market institutions in Europe. *Economic Policy* 35: 361–408.

Hartog, J. 1999. Whither Dutch corporatism? Two decades of employment policies and welfare reforms. *Scottish Journal of Political Economy* 46: 458–87.

Hemerijck, A., and J. Visser. 2002. Het "Nederlandse mirakel" revisited. *Tijdschrift voor Arbeidsvraagstukken* 18(4): 291–305.

Hassink, W. J. H., J. C. van Ours, and G. Ridder. 1997. Dismissal through disability. *De Economist* 145: 29–46.

IBO (Interdepartementaal Beleidsonderzoek 2001). *Aan de slag*. The Hague: Ministerie van Sociale Zaken en Werkgelegenheid.

Ministerie van Sociale Zaken en Werkgelegenheid (2002). *Sociale Nota 2003*. The Hague: Sdu Uitgevers.

Nickell, S. J., and R. Layard. 1999. Labor Market Institutions and Economic Performance. In O. Ashenfelter and D. Card, eds., *Handbook of Labor Economics*, vol. 3C. Amsterdam: Elsevier/North Holland.

Nickell, S. J., and J. C. van Ours. 2000. Falling unemployment; the Dutch and British cases. *Economic Policy* 30: 137–80.

OECD. 1998. *OECD Economic Surveys: Netherlands 1997/98*. Paris: OECD.

Scarpetta, S. 1996. Assessing the role of labor market policies and institutional settings on unemployment: A cross-country study. *OECD Economic Studies* 2(26): 43–82.

Stegeman, H. 2002. Lange reeksen voor replacement rates en wiggen. CPB Netherlands Bureau for Economic Policy Analysis. The Hague, CPB memorandum.

Tijdens, K. G. 2002. Arbeidsduurverkorting en het Akkoord van Wassenaar. *Tijdschrift voor Arbeidsvraagstukken* 18(4): 309–18.

Van den Berg, G. J., B. van der Klaauw, and J. C. van Ours. 2004. Punitive sanctions and the transition from welfare to work. *Journal of Labor Economics* 22: 211–41.

Van Lomwel, A. G. C., and J. C. van Ours. 2005. On the employment effects of part-time labor. *De Economist*, forthcoming.

Van Ours, J. C., and J. Veenman. 2005. The Netherlands; old emigrants–young immigrant country. In K. Zimmermann, ed., *European Migration: What Do We Know?* Oxford: Oxford University Press, pp. 173–96.

Visser, J., and A. Hemerijck. 1997. *A Dutch Miracle, Job Growth, Welfare Reform and Corporatism in the Netherlands*. Amsterdam: Amsterdam University Press.

7 (Finland)

The Un-intended Convergence: How the Finnish Unemployment Reached the European Level

Erkki Koskela and Roope Uusitalo

7.1 Overview

The rise of unemployment in Finland during the 1990s was an exceptional episode in the modern Finnish economic history. For most of the 1980s the unemployment rate was around 5 percent, close to that of the other Scandinavian countries but much lower than in the continental Europe. In just four years, beginning in 1991, the unemployment rate shot up to close to 20 percent. Increases of this magnitude within such a short period had not occurred in the OECD countries after the Second World War.

The recovery was almost equally remarkable. The average growth rate of the Finnish economy during the period 1994 to 2001 was 3.3, the second highest in the EU countries after Ireland. Despite the fast growth the unemployment rate remained high when compared to the pre-recession level. The latest figures at the time of writing of this chapter show that the seasonally adjusted unemployment rate was 9.0 percent in January 2003.

The Finnish economy had experienced several adverse economic shocks in the early 1990s. These shocks were largely unavoidable international developments, namely the collapse of exports to the Soviet Union, the fall in the terms of trade, and the rise in the interest rates in Europe after the German unification. However, domestic economic policies also contributed. Real interest rose to close to 15 percent and real asset prices fell, creating problems first to the highly indebted private sector firms and eventually to the banking sector. Due to adverse macroeconomic shocks job destruction was rapid during the first years in the 1990s. The inflow to unemployment rose by 60 percent compared to the pre-recession level.

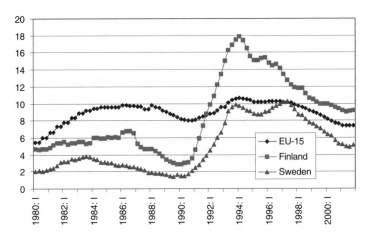

Figure 7.1
Standardized unemployment rates in Finland, Sweden, and EU-15. Source: OECD Main
Economic Indicators. Before 1988 EU-12 from OECD Employment Outlook.

The recession in the 1990s was also associated with a rapid restructuring of the economy. The recovery in the sectors with largest
declines in employment during the recession was slow compared with
the rapid growth in some new service sectors. This created a large mismatch problem in the labor market. As we will argue later, the labor
market institutions cannot be blamed for the decline in employment
in the early 1990s, but some institutional features, particularly the unemployment benefits system, clearly slowed the adjustment by lessen-
ing the incentives for regional and occupational mobility. The benefits
system may partially account for the increase in the duration of unemployment during the 1990s.

It is useful to start by putting the Finnish unemployment in perspective, by comparing the Finnish unemployment rates to the EU average
and to other neighbor countries.

Figure 7.1 presents the seasonally adjusted standardized unemployment rates for Finland, Sweden, and the EU-15 since 1980. Note that
the Finnish (and Swedish) unemployment rates are much below the
European average for most of the 1980s. The low unemployment rate
in Scandinavian countries is often cited as evidence of the success of
Scandinavian corporatist wage-setting model. For example, Layard,
Nickell, and Jackman (1991) argue that coordinated bargaining moderates wage growth and decreases unemployment by internalizing
the employment effects of wage bargains. But as seen in figure 7.1,

the Scandinavian model appears to have worked less well during the 1990s. Unemployment rates increased rapidly in both Finland and Sweden, and followed very similar time pattern in the late 1980s and early 1990s. In Finland the unemployment rate started to increase in 1991, reached the peak of 18 percent in 1994, and then began a rapid decline that lasted until 2001.

In this chapter we provide a full description of the events, and offer some explanation for the exceptional rise and fall of unemployment. The rest of the chapter is organized as follows: In section 7.2, we describe the macroeconomic conditions that led to the crisis of the early 1990s. In section 7.3, we analyze the structural changes during the recession. In section 7.4, we begin the second, more micro-oriented part of our analyses, looking first at the effects of various labor market institutions on the level of unemployment. In section 7.5, we examine the changes in the duration of unemployment. Finally in section 7.6, we summarize our findings.

7.2 Economic Crisis in the Early 1990s

The record high increase in unemployment in the early 1990s was caused by large macroeconomic shocks, both international and domestic. The roots of the 1990s crisis can be traced to the overheating period in the late 1980s, so we first characterize the changes that occurred in the late 1980s.

7.2.1 The 1980s Boom[1]

In the first half of the 1980s the performance of the Finnish economy, measured in terms of economic growth, was relatively smooth with an average growth rate slightly above the OECD-European rate. This smooth development changed around 1986 to 1987. Growth accelerated significantly. The rate of unemployment declined from the approximately 4 percent of the first half of the decade to about 2.5 to 3 percent at the end of 1989. Several factors were behind this change. Without trying to quantify their relative significance, these can be summarized as follows: (1) financial market deregulation, including deregulation of domestic bank lending rates and the lifting of restrictions on private borrowing from abroad, which led to an explosion of bank credit and large capital inflows; (2) a sharp increase in the terms of trade as a result of the fall in energy prices and the rise in world market prices of forest products; (3) the failure of fiscal policy to restrain excess demand.

The deregulation of financial institutions in the second half of the 1980s was problematic. Its timing coincided with the upswing of the business cycle. The rules and practices in prudential regulation and bank supervision were left unchanged. Also the tax system, which had favored debt financing of investments, was not reformed. When monetary policy tried to maintain some tightness in the wake of the boom, both the real and nominal interest rates increased. In the late 1980s nominal interest rates were on average 6 percent higher in Finland than, for example, in Germany. This, and the investors' belief in the fixed exchange rate, contributed to the capital inflow in foreign currency terms.

7.2.2   Big Negative Shocks

The end of the boom came in 1990; then the rapid process toward bust started. Economic activity, as measured by the growth rate of the real GDP, declined extremely sharply from a positive growth of 5.4 percent in 1989 to a negative growth of 6.5 percent in 1991. Thereafter the decline continued but at a slower pace through 1992 and most of 1993. While all domestic components of aggregate demand contributed to the decline in economic activity, a particularly important feature was the large decline in investment activity. Also price inflation slowed down significantly. The banks suffered large credit losses when the number of bankruptcies increased and the collateral values had decreased because of the rapid fall in the asset values (see figure 7.2). This led to a banking crises that forced the government to provide public monies to support the banks. The banking crises had major financial consequences and strongly contributed to the fall in aggregate demand.

The international and domestic factors behind the onset of the crisis can be classified as "bad luck and bad policies." The Finnish exports to the market economies declined as a result of slow international growth, loss in the price competitiveness of the Finnish industry, and the fall in the terms of trade. With the collapse of the Soviet Union in 1991, the Finnish exports to Russia dropped by 70 percent almost overnight. Interest rates rose in the whole Europe because of the loose fiscal and tight monetary policy in Germany after German unification. High real

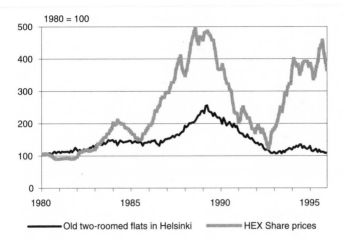

Figure 7.2
Real asset prices.

interest rates caused a large negative shock to the highly indebted private sector. Finnish monetary policy had already turned very restrictive in early 1989 after the revaluation of the Finnish markka. The defense of the markka against speculative attacks increased nominal interest rates, and when the inflation rate decreased at the beginning of the recession, the real interest rate increased dramatically (see figure 7.3). The fixed exchange rate was eventually abandoned with the devaluation of the Finnish markka in November 1991 and its floating in September 1992. Depreciation of the currency improved the price competitiveness of the export sector, but the companies that had large debts in foreign currency suffered large losses.

7.2.3   Resumed Growth

The Finnish economy turned around in late 1993. Initially this recovery was mostly concentrated in the export industries that benefited from the depreciation of the Finnish markka. Despite rapid growth, inflation remained low and external competitiveness increased rapidly (see figure 7.4).

The low inflation and strong external competitiveness were the result of two other political changes: First, the European new architecture of inflation targeting altered the relationship between economic growth and inflation. Second, the centralized wage bargaining,

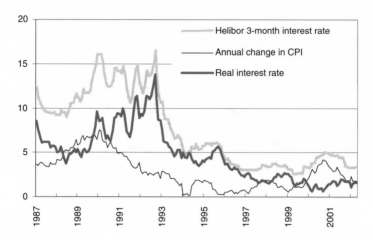

Figure 7.3
Real interest rate.

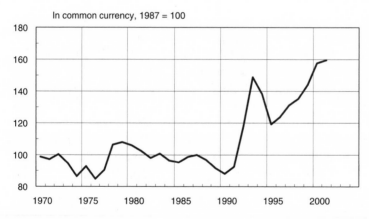

Figure 7.4
Relative unit labor costs in fourteen competitor countries and Finland. Source: Bank of Finland.

prevailing in most years, moderated wage formation and, thereby, contributed to higher competitiveness of the manufacturing sector. Moreover in Spring 1995 a new government was formed, and from the start it formulated a program of fiscal consolidation that lasted its whole term in office.

In the end, by the mid-1990s, inflation targeting, centralized bargaining, and a systematic program of fiscal consolidation had turned around the Finnish economy and economic growth in Finland was resumed.

7.3   Structural Changes after Recession

During just four years of the economic crisis, 450,000 jobs were lost. Total employment declined by 18 percent from its 1990 level. In the first quarter of 1994, employment was slightly below 2 million, which is its lowest level since 1949. After 1994, employment grew steadily, by approximately 2 percentage points each year. By 2001, total employment has grown by 313,000, that is, by about two-thirds of the decline in the early 1990s.

During the recession some sectors suffered much more than others. The construction industry was hit particularly hard; half of the jobs in construction disappeared between 1990 and 1994. Employment declined by approximately 25 percent also in manufacturing, retail trade, hotels and restaurants, and financial services. Figure 7.5 shows the contributions of the sectors to the decline in employment.

Total employment increased rapidly during the recovery after 1994. The largest increases in employment occurred in the business services and in the manufacturing of equipment. The electronics industry was responsible for most of the growth in manufacturing; other manufacturing sectors experienced only modest employment increases. The service sector, particularly business services, education, and social services, grew rapidly. After 1994 employment declined substantially only in agriculture and financial services. Decline in the agriculture continues a long trend that had begun already in the 1960s. Decline in bank financing was mostly due to the restructuring of the banking sector after the financial crisis.

As figure 7.5 shows, the newly created jobs were different from the jobs lost in the early 1990s. The most rapidly growing service sectors had only experienced small employment declines during the recession.

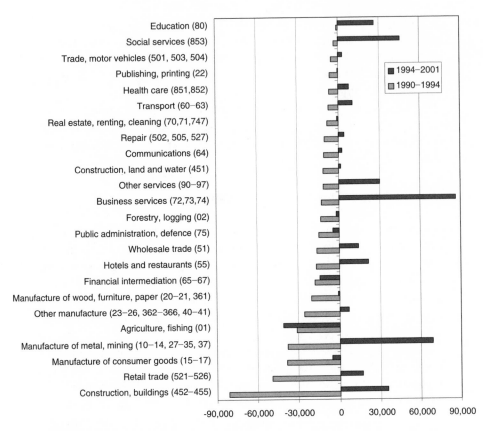

Figure 7.5
Change in employment by industry during the recession and recovery. Source: Calculations based on data from the Labour Force Survey. Industry classification according to ISIC 2–3 digit classification as used in the LFS.

Of the sectors that experienced large job losses during the recession, employment returned close to the pre-recession level only in the manufacturing of equipment. Less than half of the employment decline in construction and only a third of the employment decline in retail trade were matched by subsequent employment growth after 1994.

The rapid structural change in employment created an increasing mismatch problem in the labor market. Unemployed construction workers were poorly equipped to find jobs in the growing service sector. Since skill requirements were often higher than the education level of the unemployed, the differences in unemployment rates across groups with different levels of education grew rapidly. The unemploy-

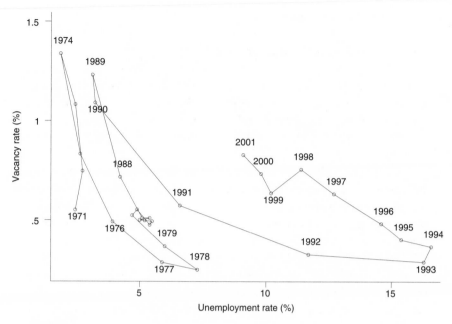

Figure 7.6
Beveridge curve. Source: *Finnish Labour Review* (1/2002).

ment rate for those with only compulsory education exceeded 20 percent, while the unemployment rate for those with university education remained around 3 to 4 percent. Uneven regional development also contributed to the mismatch problem. After the recession the employment growth was rapid in the capital region and southern Finland, and much slower in the high-unemployment regions in northern and eastern Finland.

The clearest indication of growing mismatch is the Beveridge curve, which shows the relationship between the unemployment rate and open vacancies in the employment offices. Figure 7.6 shows the Beveridge curve for the period 1971 to 2001. Note how most of the variation in the unemployment rate is related to business cycle (movements along the curve in northwest to southeast direction). However, the curve has also clearly moved outward. Of the two clear outward shifts in the curve, the first occurred in late 1970s and the other much larger shift in the early 1990s. By the year 2000 the vacancy rate is back to its level in 1988, but the unemployment rate is about 6 percentage points higher.

7.4   Labor Market Institutions

7.4.1   Labor Market Institutions and Unemployment

It is often said that the low unemployment rates in the United States are due to dynamic and flexible job markets, and the high European unemployment rates to rigid and inflexible markets. So the important question is: Which features of labor markets generate unemployment and which do not matter?

Nickell (1997) classifies labor market institutions into the following categories: (1) employment protection and labor standards, (2) benefit replacement ratio and benefit duration, (3) active labor market policies, (4) union density and coverage of bargaining agreements, (5) coordination of wage bargaining, and (6) the tax wedge. In our working paper (Koskela and Uusitalo 2003) we examine these institutions in detail. However, many institutional features in Finland are similar to those in many other European countries. For example, taxes or job protection may have something to do with unemployment, but the effects are likely the same in many other European countries. We have little to add to the discussion on the effects of these institutions, and refer the reader to chapter 2 by Nickell in this volume. Here we concentrate on the institutions that differ from the other European countries and that we believe are most important for the Finnish case. Therefore we start with a description of the unemployment benefits, continue by discussing wage-bargaining system, and conclude with some remarks on the active labor market polices.

7.4.2   Unemployment Benefits and Unemployment

The Current Benefits System
Unemployment benefits in Finland consist of labor market subsidies and unemployment allowances. Unemployment allowances can be further classified as the basic allowances paid by the state through the Social Insurance Institution (UA) and the earnings-related allowances paid by the unemployment funds (UI).

To qualify for an unemployment allowance the unemployed must have been employed for 43 weeks during the past two years. The earnings-related allowance also requires the unemployed worker to have been a member of an unemployment insurance fund for 10 months prior to unemployment.

Unemployment allowance can be received for 500 days. An exception is made for the unemployed who turn 57 before the benefits expire. These unemployed are entitled for an extension of benefits until the age of 60. The age limit for the benefit extension was 55 up to 1997 and was raised to 59 in 2005. The extended duration of unemployment benefits for the older workers is popularly known as unemployment pension tunnel. The unemployed who lose their jobs after age of 55 can receive unemployment and unemployment pension benefits up to the retirement age. These unemployed have minimal incentives to search for work, and consequently a job loss after age of 55 most often leads to a permanent exit from the labor market (Hakola and Uusitalo 2001).

Those unemployed who do not meet the employment condition, or who have already received an unemployment allowance for 500 days, can receive a labor market subsidy from the state. The labor market subsidy is paid, subject to the means test, for an unlimited period. Both the labor market subsidy and the basic allowance are currently 23.24 euros a day (2005). Dependent children increase the benefits. The earnings-related unemployment allowance consists of a basic amount equal to the basic allowance, and of an earnings-related part, which is 45 percent of the difference between previous daily earnings and the basic allowance. There is no ceiling on the unemployment benefits, but the earnings exceeding 2,091 euros (2005) per month increase the allowance by only 20 percent of the exceeded amount. In practice, this implies that for the median income earner (2,142 €/month), the gross replacement rate is 55 percent. Since benefits increase by only a fraction of the previous earnings, replacement rate decreases with earnings. For someone earning twice the median income, the gross replacement rate is 38 percent.[2]

Unemployment benefits are taxable income, just as wages and salaries. Due to the progressive taxation, net replacement rates are higher than gross replacement rates. Accounting for the effect of the income taxes increases the replacement rate for the median earner from 55 to 64 percent. Other earnings-related benefits such as housing allowance further increase net replacement rates.

Evidence on the Employment Effects of Unemployment Benefits
The effect of the unemployment benefits on re-employment has been subject to a number of studies during the past ten years. Below we survey a selective sample of the Finnish studies.

Kettunen (1993) uses data from the Ministry of Labour by drawing a random sample of 2,077 unemployed from the flow into unemployment during 1985. He finds that a higher replacement ratio lowers the exit hazard and that the effect is larger for the nonmembers of the UI funds. He also finds that there was a peak in the hazard rates after twenty weeks of unemployment when unemployment benefits were reduced by 20 percent. Another early study worth mentioning is by Lilja (1993). She estimates competing risk models of exit from unemployment based on data from Finnish Labour Force Surveys of 1984 to 1987. She does not calculate the replacement rates but estimates the model separately for the recipients of unemployment insurance (UI) and basic unemployment allowance (UA). The hazard rate for the UI recipients is twice as high as for the otherwise similar UA recipients. As the UI recipients have generally much higher replacement rates, this suggests that other factors vary considerably across the two groups.

Holm, Kyyrä, and Rantala (1999) attempt to improve the estimates by using forward-looking measures of replacement rates. As unemployment periods are often associated with significant wage decreases, the replacement rates based on the previous earnings may overstate the gains from re-employment. They estimate expected post-unemployment wages based on data on those who exit from employment and show that the expected gain of employment increases considerably the likelihood of employment.

A common problem in the existing Finnish studies is the lack of convincingly exogenous variation in the replacement rates. The variation in the replacement rates is driven by the variation in previous earnings and is hence correlated with a number of factors that may influence the re-employment probabilities.

Evidence on the effect of the duration of unemployment benefits is somewhat more convincing. Rantala (2002) studies the effect of the change in the age limit of the "unemployment pension tunnel" in 1997. The change effectively reduced the maximum benefit duration to 500 days for workers who were between 53 and 54 years old. Prior to the reform they could keep receiving unemployment benefits up to the retirement age. According to figure 7.7, which shows the "transition rates" to unemployment by age between 1995 and 1999, the unemployment risk increases considerably at the beginning of the unemployment tunnel. Before the reform, the unemployment risk doubled from 3 to 6 percent when the workers turned 53. After the reform, the un-

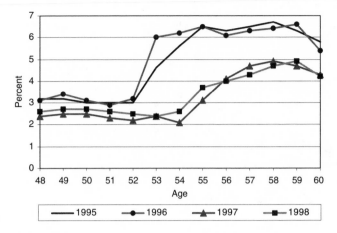

Figure 7.7
Transitions to unemployment by age. Source: Rantala (2002).

employment risk for the 53- to 54-year-olds was similar to that for the younger workers. In 1997 and 1998 the unemployment risk increased only after the workers turned 55, and met the new age criteria.

There are important interactions between unemployment benefits and economic shocks. Hakola and Uusitalo (2001) show that the incentives created by the generous unemployment benefits for the older unemployed had little effect on the unemployment rates before the recession. As seen in figure 7.8, the unemployment rates for the 55- to 59-year-olds were close to the unemployment rates of the younger groups up to the early 1990s. The generosity of benefits suddenly started to matter during the recession. The unemployment rates of 55- to 59-year-olds increased to over 20 percent, twice as high as the rates for the younger age groups. Similar interaction effects between shocks and institutions can be found also in micro cross-sectional data. Using a linked worker–firm panel, Hakola and Uusitalo (2001) show that the effect of the unemployment tunnel eligibility on displacement probability is much larger when the firm faces a negative demand shock.

Extended unemployment benefits for the older workers are responsible for a large share of aggregate unemployment. In 2000 one-third of all registered unemployed (including those on unemployment pension) were over 55. The effect on long-term unemployment was even larger; in 2000 two-thirds of long-term unemployed were over 55.

A number of studies on the effect of the benefit duration focus on the hazard of employment around the benefit exhaustion date. For

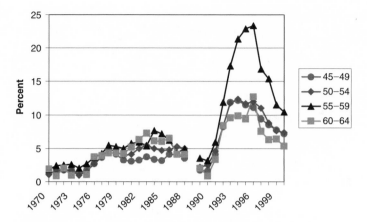

Figure 7.8
Unemployment rates by age. Source: Hakola and Uusitalo (2001).

example, Meyer (1990) and Katz and Meyer (1990) note that in the
United States the probability of leaving unemployment rises just prior
to when the benefits elapse. Carling et al. (1996) find a similar but
smaller effect using Swedish data. They also note that the exit rates to
various training programs rise dramatically around the time of the
benefit exhaustion.

To examine the question, we constructed a data of all unemployment spells experienced by 350,000 individuals drawn from the Employment Statistics of Statistics Finland.[3] We selected all new entrants
to unemployment between 1995 and 1998. Of the 104,358 unemployment spells, 57 percent ended in re-employment. Some 30 percent of
the unemployed entered training programs or subsidized jobs, and 9
percent moved out of the labor force.

In figure 7.9 we show the empirical hazard rates separately by the
exit route, treating other exits as censored observations. The top left
corner includes exits to all destinations, with two clear spikes in the
hazard rate. The first is at 360 days, and the second right after the maximum duration of the benefits at 500 days. However, when we look
only at the exits to the open employment, these spikes disappear altogether. The hazard to the open employment shows negative duration
dependence but no effects of the benefit exhaustion. There is no clear
pattern in the exits from the labor force. Finally the lower right corner
provides an explanation for the spikes in the hazard. Most labor
market programs are targeted to the long-term unemployed who have

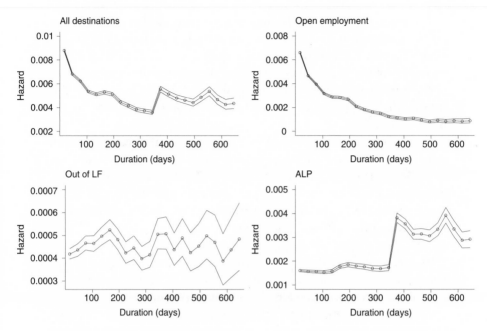

Figure 7.9
Hazard of exit from unemployment. All destinations, open employment, out of LF, ALP.

been unemployed for over a year. This explains the big increase in the hazard at 360 days. The hazard of entering labor market programs also grows around the benefit expiration date.

7.4.3   Unions and Wage Formation

As in other Scandinavian countries the union density is high in Finland. Union density increased rather steadily from the 1960s to the early 1990s. Pehkonen and Tanninen (1997) report that the union density was 22 percent in 1960 and has since then increased, reaching 82 percent in 1992. According to the Working Life Barometer the union density peaked at 86 percent in 1995 and has slightly declined during the latter half of the 1990s, to 83 percent in 2001. One of the main reasons for increased union density is the increase in unemployment. Under a "Gent-system" the unemployment insurance is organized around UI funds administered by the unions and subsidized by the government. Membership is voluntary, and the increase in the unemployment risk encourages workers to seek membership in the UI funds. In most cases this is easiest to do by joining a union.

The wage bargains—containing an agreement on the general wage increase applied to all wages—are negotiated at the industry level between the worker and the employer organizations. Collective agreements cover also nonunion members in the sectors where at least half of the employers belong to an employer organization. In practice, this implies that 95 percent of the workers in Finland are covered by the union contracts.

Most bargaining rounds start with negotiations between confederations of employer and employee unions, creating a high degree of coordination in the individual union contracts. The union bargains are then negotiated based on the agreed wage increases in the central agreement. There can be considerable variation in the degree of centralization between the different bargaining rounds. During the period 1969 to 2002, there were seven bargaining rounds (1973, 1980, 1983, 1988, 1994, 1995, and 2000) when no central bargain was reached and bargaining occurred at the industry level. Also even in the years when a central bargain was reached, not all unions accepted it.

Coordination in the union bargaining may moderate wage increases by internalizing the cost of unemployment due to extensive wage increases. Calmfors (2001) summarizes the results of recent studies, which indicate that unemployment is lowest in countries where bargaining is most centralized. Given the variation in the degree of centralization between the different bargaining rounds, we can extend the previous analyses by examining the effects of the year-to-year differences in bargaining regimes within a country. With our data it is more natural to examine the effects of centralization on wage growth than on unemployment, and we report these results below.

As shown in the table 7.1, the average bargained wage increases have been 1.8 percentage points lower during the centralized bargaining rounds. The difference between centralized bargains with wide coverage (almost all unions accepting the central agreement) and decentralized bargains is even greater, 4 percent. Controlling for the difference in unemployment and inflation at the time of wage negotiations does not alter the picture. The difference between central bargains and industry-level bargains is 3.3 percent and the difference between centralized bargains with wide coverage and decentralized bargains is 4.1 percent.

Wage drift, meaning average wage growth that exceeds the bargained wage increases, may offset the wage moderating effects of centralized bargaining. According to figures in the rightmost column of

Table 7.1
Nominal wage increases by the level of wage bargaining

	Number of cases	Bargained wage increase	Nominal wage growth
Raw averages			
Decentralized bargaining	7	6.5	10.1
Centralized bargaining (all)	27	4.7	8.9
Degree of centralization			
No coverage (decentralized)	7	6.5	10.1
Low coverage	3	8.4	13.3
Medium coverage	10	6.6	12.0
Wide coverage	14	2.5	5.1
Controlling for unemployment and inflation			
Decentralized bargaining	7	7.7	12.2
Centralized bargaining (all)	27	4.4	8.1
Degree of centralization			
No coverage (decentralized)	7	7.3	11.8
Low coverage	3	7.1	10.6
Medium coverage	10	5.5	9.5
Wide coverage	14	3.2	6.7

Sources: Data on the degree of centralization, the bargained wage increases, and the nominal wage growth are from Marjanen (2002). Unemployment and inflation rates are from Labour Force Survey and Consumer Price Index of Statistics Finland.
Notes: The numbers in the lower section of the table are based on a regression model of bargained wage increase (and nominal wage growth) on lagged unemployment and inflation rates and the dummies for the different bargaining regimes. Estimation period is 1969 to 2002 for the bargained wage increases and 1969 to 2000 for the nominal wage growth. In all estimated equations unemployment had a significant negative effect on both the bargained and the actual wage increases. The dummy variables for different bargaining regimes were highly significant in all estimated equations.

table 7.1, this has not been the case in Finland. On average, the nominal wage increases have exceeded the bargained wage increases by 4 percentage points, but the differences in nominal wage increases between the centralized and the industry-level bargains are approximately as large as the differences in the bargained wage increases.

To conclude, the results using Finnish data are in conformity with findings from cross-country data. Centralized bargaining moderates wage increases and thereby helps decrease the equilibrium unemployment. Prime examples from the 1990s include national bargains in the recession years 1992 and 1993 when the wages were not increased at all. On the other hand, different rates of economic recoveries across industries lead to industry-level bargaining and somewhat higher wage increases in 1994 and 1995.

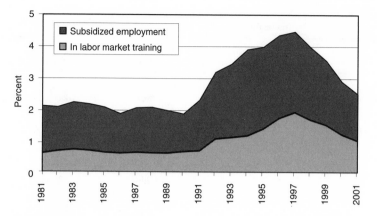

Figure 7.10
Share of the labor force in active labor market programs. Source: *Finnish Labour Review* (1/2002).

7.4.4   Active Labor Market Policies

Figure 7.10 shows how the size of the active labor market programs has evolved over the past twenty years. In the 1980s the vast majority of programs were placements to subsidized jobs in the public sector. In the 1990s the share of labor market training increased. The total number of individuals in the different programs was highest in 1997 when more than 100,000 persons, or more than 4 percent of the labor force, were placed in active labor market programs. Simply adding the individuals in programs to open unemployment would increase the unemployment rate by 4 percent, but the calculation is not quite as simple because some of these individuals are already classified as unemployed in the Labour Force Surveys.

Most empirical Finnish studies on the effects of ALMPs have concentrated in estimating the employment effects of different programs using micro-level data. The results indicate that participation in training programs has, in general, improved labor market prospects. Hämäläinen (1999) finds that training programs have been beneficial for 80 to 90 percent of the participants, and Tuomala (2002) reports that labor market training has increased postprogram employment probability and shortened the duration of unemployment. The results on the subsidized job programs are less encouraging. Tuomala (2002) finds that program participation has even reduced the probability of finding a job from open labor markets. Also Hämäläinen (1999) reports that subsidized jobs have been less effective than other labor market programs, but notes that placements to the private sector improve labor market opportunities more than placements to the public sector.

7.5 On the Duration of Unemployment

For most of the 1980s long-term unemployment was not much of the problem in Finland. Average duration of ongoing unemployment spells was around 25 weeks, and the proportion of the long-term unemployed (unemployed for more than a year) slightly over 10 percent. This was partly due to favorable employment situation and partly to legislation enacted in 1987 (abolished in 1992) that required employment offices to place long-term unemployed to subsidized jobs.

During the recession in the early 1990s this favorable picture changed completely. First the average duration declined, and the fraction of the long-term unemployed fell to 3 percent. Then the fraction of the long-term unemployed grew, in sync with the unemployment rate, until 1995. By then almost a third of the unemployed were classified as long-term unemployed. Long-term unemployment remained high also after 1995, even though the unemployment rate had started to decline. The average duration of the ongoing unemployment spells has been approximately 52 weeks since 1995.

Long-term unemployment displays counterclockwise loops and lags behind the unemployment rate (figure 7.11). The same effect is observed by Machin and Manning (1999) in a number of other European countries. Variation in the inflow rates is partly responsible for these loops. It is also possible that the outflow rates for the long-term unemployed fall more in a recession because employers have a larger pool of unemployed to choose from. In the ranking model by Blanchard and Diamond (1994), employers always choose to hire the workers with the shortest unemployment duration. The ranking model therefore implies that the duration dependence increases during a recession.

To look at the issues more closely, we performed some empirical calculations using administrative data from the unemployment offices. We used a sample containing all recorded unemployment spells experienced by 350,000 individuals, drawn randomly from the *Employment Statistics*. We collected information on the dates of entry into unemployment and exit out of unemployment for the period 1987 to 1999. After discarding cases where individuals had missing dates,

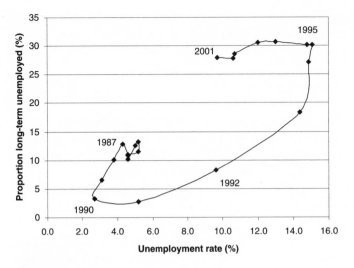

Figure 7.11
Proportion of long-term unemployed in 1981 to 2001. Source: *Finnish Labour Review*
(1/2002).

we were left with 664,000 unemployment spells. Given the long time
period, we could examine the changes in the re-employment hazard
and duration dependence over the whole business cycle.

First, in table 7.2, we show the calculated exit rates from unemployment to the active labor market programs, open employment, and out
of the labor force. We find that only less than half of the unemployment spells end by an exit to open employment. The fraction of exits
to open employment varies across the cycle, and account for only a
quarter of exits during the worst years of recession. Opposite cyclical
movements can be observed in the exits to the active labor market programs and out of the labor force. A high fraction of the unknown destinations, particularly in the early 1990s, may have an effect on these
estimates.

Below, we focus on the exits to the open employment (including
recalls from layoffs) and treat all other exits as censored observations.
In table 7.3 we report results from fitting a simple parametric Weibull
model to the duration data. In the first column we include no covariates except the year dummies (entry year). The results are reported
as hazard ratios restricting the year 1990 to one.

The estimation results show that hazard rates are clearly countercyclical. During the boom in the late 1980s, the employment hazards

Table 7.2
Reasons for ending unemployment (%)

Year	ALP	Employed	Out of labor force	Recall	Unknown	Total
1987	5.32	60.58	9.55	1.93	22.62	28,383
1988	4.54	57.42	8.04	8.28	21.73	29,838
1989	4.44	57.43	8.44	8.12	21.56	28,194
1990	8.80	41.76	9.04	7.72	32.69	31,192
1991	15.05	24.89	12.97	3.09	44.01	57,309
1992	18.57	24.25	16.12	4.32	36.74	66,016
1993	24.35	23.47	15.96	9.12	27.11	67,613
1994	27.12	37.73	16.31	5.33	13.51	64,585
1995	28.63	38.55	15.50	4.69	12.63	64,395
1996	28.69	39.27	13.81	4.46	13.77	66,027
1997	27.88	40.38	12.71	4.51	14.52	57,162
1998	25.97	42.48	11.14	4.77	15.64	53,554
1999	21.26	45.66	10.26	6.49	16.33	49,094
Total	21.13	37.77	13.23	5.44	22.43	664,082

were about 50 percent higher than in 1990. In contrast, during the recession, 1992 to 1993, the hazard was only third of the 1990 level. Toward the end of the 1990s, the hazard rates are increasing but are still below the pre-recession level. The duration dependence is documented by the Weibull coefficient p at the base of the table. For the exponential model with constant hazard the p is equal to one. Value 0.67 shows strong negative duration dependence. Probability of exit decreases rapidly with the spell duration.

The changes in the hazard rates over the cycle could be explained by the compositional effects. If groups that typically can expect relatively longer durations enter unemployment in proportionally greater numbers during the recession, the aggregate average duration will display countercyclical variation.

We examine the composition effects in column 2 of table 7.3. We add covariates measuring age, education, and sex to the duration model. To capture the regional differences, we include a measure of the regional unemployment rate. We also add an indicator on whether an unemployed has been classified mentally or physically disabled by the employment offices. These additional covariates have a large impact on the hazard rates. As expected, the hazard rates increase with education and decrease with age. Females have a slightly higher hazard, and a

Table 7.3
Duration model for employment hazards

	(1)	(2)	(3)
Year (base 1990)			
1987	1.160	1.143	0.952
	(0.013)**	(0.013)**	(0.017)**
1988	1.434	1.424	1.313
	(0.016)**	(0.016)**	(0.023)**
1989	1.570	1.587	1.523
	(0.018)**	(0.018)**	(0.027)**
1991	0.426	0.415	0.291
	(0.005)**	(0.005)**	(0.005)**
1992	0.343	0.331	0.214
	(0.004)**	(0.004)**	(0.004)**
1993	0.389	0.374	0.239
	(0.004)**	(0.005)**	(0.005)**
1994	0.556	0.531	0.402
	(0.006)**	(0.006)**	(0.007)**
1995	0.594	0.567	0.438
	(0.006)**	(0.007)**	(0.008)**
1996	0.639	0.616	0.484
	(0.006)**	(0.007)**	(0.009)**
1997	0.693	0.674	0.546
	(0.007)**	(0.008)**	(0.009)**
1998	0.746	0.697	0.554
	(0.008)**	(0.008)**	(0.009)**
1999	0.915	0.850	0.668
	(0.010)**	(0.010)**	(0.011)**
Age (base 35–44)			
15–24		1.113	1.017
		(0.006)**	(0.008)*
25–34		1.070	1.038
		(0.006)**	(0.008)**
45–54		0.913	0.932
		(0.006)**	(0.009)**
55–64		0.417	0.344
		(0.005)**	(0.005)**
Education (base primary)			
Secondary		1.150	1.219
		(0.010)**	(0.015)**
Vocational		1.413	1.641
		(0.007)**	(0.011)**
Higher		1.544	1.800
		(0.009)**	(0.017)**
University		1.733	1.949
		(0.021)**	(0.036)**

Table 7.3
(continued)

	(1)	(2)	(3)
Female		1.028	1.077
		(0.004)**	(0.006)**
Disabled		0.487	0.370
		(0.006)**	(0.006)**
Local unemployment rate		0.999	0.999
		(0.000)**	(0.001)*
Observations	664082	663692	663692
P	0.67	0.70	0.94
Frailty			1.61

Notes: Reported coefficients are hazard ratios. P is a parameter describing the direction dependence. Standard errors are in parentheses; *significant at 5% level; **significant at 1% level.

higher regional unemployment lowers the hazard rates. Having been classified as disabled almost halves the re-employment hazard. However, adding all these covariates has little effect on the time pattern of the hazard rates. Hence, according to estimation results, the changes in the hazard rates over the cycle are not driven by the composition of the unemployed.

In the third column we generalize the model to allow for unobserved heterogeneity. We make a standard assumption that the unobserved heterogeneity is multiplicative, and follows a gamma distribution. The main impact of allowing for the unobserved heterogeneity is that our estimate of duration dependence declines. We also estimated the model allowing the duration dependence differ across the years (not reported in the table). The results were quite interesting. Negative duration dependence was strongest in the years 1992 to 1994, when the expected durations (and the unemployment rates) were at their highest level. The results are consistent with the ranking model by Blanchard and Diamond (1994).

7.6 Conclusions

What are the lessons that can be drawn from the Finnish unemployment experience over the last twenty years? First one might observe that today the Finnish unemployment rates are close to the European average, both in terms of the level and the duration. The interesting question is why the unemployment rate remained so low until the late

1980s. One explanation is that the Finnish economy experienced much smaller shocks than the countries in continental Europe.

During the 1980s the Finnish economy was relatively isolated from the rest of the Europe. In the absence of free international capital movements the central bank could set the interest rates freely, and the devaluations of the Finnish markka could be used to adjust the price level to maintain the competitiveness of the export sector. Bilateral trade with the former Soviet Union contributed to the stability. Because of the bilateral trade agreements, an increase in oil prices led automatically to an increase in the export demand. Therefore trade with the Soviet Union effectively isolated Finland from the oil price shocks that are often at least partly blamed for the increased unemployment in Europe in the 1970s. The liberalization of the financial markets at the end of the 1980s and the end of the bilateral trade agreements opened the Finnish economy to the outside shocks. However, the deregulation of the financial markets was incomplete. The exchange rate of the Finnish markka remained fixed and the business sector incurred large debts both domestically and in foreign currency terms. The high real interest rate and depreciation of the Finnish markka thus constituted large adverse shocks to a highly debt-ridden business sector.

While the economic shocks may sufficiently explain the rapid increase in the unemployment in the early 1990s, these shocks cannot explain the persistency of unemployment during the strong recovery period in the later part of 1990s.

If not the shocks, then perhaps the institutions were partially to blame. However, the labor market institutions have not changed much since the 1980s. The main features of the unemployment insurance system are the same. Union density has increased, but the union coverage has remained roughly constant. The main features of the wage-bargaining system are also unchanged. The changes to the tax system and the active labor market policies should probably be seen as the consequences and not as the causes for the changes in unemployment. Also empirically the effects of these changes on employment appear to have been relatively small. These institutions did not create high unemployment rates in the 1980s. Nickell (1999) calculates the change in the equilibrium unemployment rate from 1980s to 1990s in Finland based on the coefficients from cross-country regressions of unemployment on institutional features. He concludes that the changes in the institutions only explain the rise in equilibrium unemployment from 5.7 to 6.1 percent.

When the major shocks hit the economy in the early 1990s, the institutional rigidities started to matter. Therefore the interactions between institutions and shocks, à la Blanchard and Wolfers (2000), might provide the better explanation for persistent unemployment. The main example is the unemployment tunnel that guarantees elderly unemployed benefits until retirement. The policy was introduced when the unemployment rates were low, and long-term unemployment rare. The extended benefits did not appear to have much effect then. But when the recession created a need to cut the workforce, the better benefits for the older unemployed workers induced the firms to target the layoffs to the older workers. As these workers had small incentives to search for jobs the duration of unemployment increased.

Notes

We thank Brendan Walsh as well as other conference participants for useful comments. We also thank the seminar participants at the Institute for Labour Market Policy Analysis (IFAU) in Uppsala, at the Trade Union Institute for Economic Research (FIEF) in Stockholm, and at the Bank of Finland for their comments on an earlier draft, and Kari Hämäläinen, Juhana Hukkinen, and Juha Tuomala for comments and advice on data questions. Koskela thanks *The Research Unit of Economic Structures and Growth (RUESG)* at the University of Helsinki for financial support and *the Bank of Finland* for its hospitality.

1. See Honkapohja and Koskela (1999) for a detailed description of the overheating and the onset of the crisis.

2. According to the original Unemployment Security Act of 1984, earnings-related unemployment benefits were reduced by 20 percent after 100 days of unemployment. In 1987, the rule was changed so that the benefits would be reduced by 12.5 percent after 200 days. In 1989, the paragraph was excised, and since then the earnings related benefits have been paid without a reduction up to 500 days.

3. *Employment Statistics* contain information from various registers and covers the entire Finnish population. The information on unemployment periods is based on administrative records showing the dates when the unemployed were registered at the employment offices. In order to concentrate on the unemployed who risk losing their benefits after 500 days, we restrict the sample to the unemployed who are under 53 at the start of the unemployment spell, and who receive earnings-related unemployment benefits. Information on the benefits is based on tax records and was available for 1995 to 1998. We excluded some 10 percent of the unemployment spells because the reason the spell ended was unknown. The spells that continued beyond the end of 1999 we regarded as censored.

References

Blanchard, O., and P. Diamond. 1994. Ranking, unemployment duration and wages. *Review of Economic Studies* 61: 417–34.

Blanchard, O., and J. Wolfers. 2000. The role of shocks and institutions in the rise of European unemployment: The aggregate evidence. *Economic Journal* 110: C1–C33.

Calmfors, L. 2001. Wages and wage bargaining institutions in the EMU—A survey of the issues. *Empirica* 28: 325–51.

Carling, K., P.-A. Edin, H. Anders, and B. Holmlund. 1996. Unemployment duration, unemployment benefits and labour market programs in Sweden. *Journal of Public Economics* 59: 313–34.

Hakola, T., and R. Uusitalo. 2001. Let's make a deal: The impact of social security provisions and firm liabilities on early retirement. Government Institute for Economic Research, *Discussion Paper* 260.

Holm, P., T. Kyyrä, and J. Rantala. 1999. Household economic incentives, the unemployment trap and the probability of finding a job. *International Tax and Public Finance* 6: 361–78.

Honkapohja, S., and E. Koskela. 1999. Finland's depression in the 1990s: A tale of bad luck and bad policies. *Economic Policy* 29: 399–436.

Hämäläinen, K. 1999. Aktiivinen työvoimapolitiikka ja työllistyminen avoimille työmarkkinoille. The Research Institute of the Finnish Economy, Series B 151. Helsinki: ETLA.

Katz, L., and B. Meyer. 1990. The impact of potential duration of unemployment benefits on the duration of unemployment. *Journal of Public Economics* 41: 45–72.

Kettunen, J. 1993. Increasing incentives for reemployment. *Finnish Economic Papers* 6: 51–60.

Koskela, E., and R. Uusitalo. 2003. The un-intended convergence: How the Finnish unemployment reached the European level. *CESifo Working Paper* 878.

Layard, R., S. Nickell, and R. Jackman. 1991. *Unemployment: Macroeconomic Performance and the Labour Market.* Oxford: Oxford University Press.

Lilja, R. 1993. Unemployment benefit system and unemployment duration in Finland. *Finnish Economic Papers* 6: 25–37.

Lundqvist, B. 1996. Työttömyys ja työeläke. Central Pension Security Institute, Helsinki, *Papers* 1996.

Machin, S., and A. Manning. 1999. The causes and consequences of long term unemployment in Europe. In O. Ashenfelter and D. Card, eds., *Handbook of Labour Economics*, vol. 3C. Amsterdam: Elsevier/North Holland.

Marjanen, R. 2002. Palkkaratkaisujen sisältö ja toteutuminen tulopolitiikan aikakaudella. The Research Institute of the Finnish Economy, Series B 188. Helsinki: ETLA.

Meyer, B. 1990. Unemployment insurance and unemployment spells. *Econometrica* 58: 757–82.

Nickell, S. J. 1997. Unemployment and labour market rigidities: Europe versus North America. *Journal of Economic Perspectives* 11: 55–74.

Nickell, S. J. 1999. Finnish unemployment: A view from outside. *Finnish Economic Papers* 12: 62–81.

Pehkonen, J., and H. Tanninen. 1997. Institutions, incentives and trade union membership. *Labour* 11: 580–98.

Rantala, J. 2002. Ikääntyvien työttömyys ja työttömyyseläke. *Central Pension Security Institute Report* 2002:28.

Tuomala, J. 2002. Työvoimakoulutuksen vaikutus työttömien työllistymiseen. *Government Institute for Economic Research, Research Report* 85.

8 When Unemployment Disappears: Ireland in the 1990s

Brendan Walsh

8.1 Introduction

In the 1980s Ireland's labor market was one of the worst performing in Europe. The unemployment rate rose from 7 percent in 1979 to 17 percent in 1986, and two-thirds of the unemployed had been out of work for six months or more, almost half for over a year. An already low labor force participation rate fell further. At the end of the decade net emigration more than offset the rate of natural increase, leading to population decline. An influential comparative study of unemployment in OECD countries estimated that the Irish equilibrium or natural unemployment rate had risen from 9 percent over the period 1969 to 1979 to 13.1 percent between 1980 and 1988 (Layard, Nickell, and Jackman 1991).

The employment picture was transformed in the 1990s. The labor market situation improved, slowly at first but then at a pace that took commentators by surprise. Between the trough in 1986 to 1987 and 2002 total employment grew by 62 percent, nonagricultural employment by over 78 percent, and private sector employment even faster. By 2000 the unemployment rate had fallen below 4 percent, long-term unemployment had virtually disappeared, labor force participation rates had risen to the European average, and the age-old Irish problems of emigration and population decline had given way to the highest rate of net immigration and the fastest growing population in the European Union. There was general agreement that full employment had been reached—if not surpassed. Ireland's success over this period compares favorably with what has been labeled the US "employment miracle" (Krueger and Pischke 1997). Even at the time of writing, more than two years since the economy came off the boil, the Irish unemployment rate remains under 5 percent and the annual rate of net immigration is still over 1 percent of the population.

This chapter examines and interprets these developments. Section 8.2 contains a detailed description of what happened. Section 8.3 looks at the factors that may be invoked to explain the very favourable Irish experience. Section 8.4 concludes with a brief discussion of what lessons, if any, may be drawn for other countries.

8.2   The Record[1]

Ireland was for long a case study of a labor-surplus economy. The famines of the 1840s triggered large-scale emigration and a decline in the national population that continued until the 1960s. Even then subsistence farmers and unskilled workers predominated in the employed labor force, employment opportunities in industry and services were limited, and emigration remained significant. During the 1960s there was a slight increase in the population and numbers at work, but these modest gains were dissipated in the recessions of the 1970s.

Overt unemployment was kept in check by the continued operation of the safety valve of emigration, now mainly to the United Kingdom. Any widening of the Irish–UK unemployment rate differential was quickly closed by higher outflows. This ensured that the Irish unemployment rate was typically only 3 or 4 percentage points above the EU average for most of the 1960s and into the 1970s (figure 8.1). It rose more steeply than in other OECD countries during the first oil-price recession of the early 1970s but fell back fairly quickly later in the decade. The rapid reduction in unemployment was partly due to an inappropriate fiscal stimulus in 1977 that yielded a short-lived growth

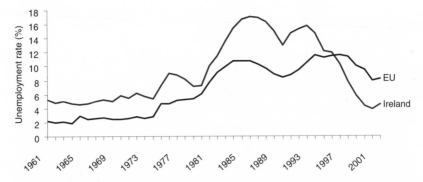

Figure 8.1
Irish and EU unemployment rates.

spurt but launched the economy on an unsustainable debt-to-GDP trajectory. A pro-cyclical fiscal correction intensified the effects of the global recession in the early 1980s. This painful correction lasted well into the second half of the decade.

The effects of this long recession on the Irish labor force were devastating. The unemployment rate reached record levels—peaking at 17 percent in 1986–87—the labor force participation rate declined, the employment-to-population ratio fell sharply, and large-scale emigration resumed as soon as employment opportunities presented themselves abroad. The numbers employed in the productive sectors of the economy fell over these years, while the numbers in all the dependent categories (except children) increased. Despite the falling birth rate, the ratio of inactive to employed in the total population rose from an already exceptionally high 200 percent in 1981 to a peak of 224 percent in 1986. It fell back to 213 percent in 1991 but only because of the resumption of emigration and the continuing decline in the birth rate.

The historic link between Irish and British labor markets broke down in the 1980s, possibly due to the severity of the recession in the United Kingdom and the collapse in that country's demand for unskilled workers in construction and industry. In the second half of the decade the gap between the Irish and UK unemployment rates was over 6 percentage points—higher than ever previously recorded. The closure of the traditional safety valve of emigration was seen at the time as a severe adverse shock to the Irish economy, although its longer run repercussions on wage bargaining and domestic employment growth were benign (see below). Once recovery got underway in Britain it was to be expected that the pent-up tide of Irish emigrants would flow out. And in fact the initial easing of the labor market problem came in the form of renewed emigration to the United Kingdom and United States as these economies emerged from recession sooner than Ireland.

Renewed emigration helped stabilize the Irish unemployment rate in the late 1980s, but its continued rapid fall in the 1990s was increasingly due to the domestic employment boom, as the change in the country's economic fortunes that began in the late 1980s transformed the labour market situation. Figures 8.2 through 8.4 show the dramatic improvement in Ireland's labor market indexes during the 1990s.[2] The falling unemployment rate and rising participation rate resulted in a steep rise in the employment-to-population ratio.[3] The rise in the labor force participation rate was due mainly to the retention of more married women in the labor force. By 2002, 62 percent of married women

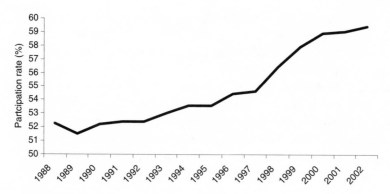

Figure 8.2
Participation rate, population aged 15 and over.

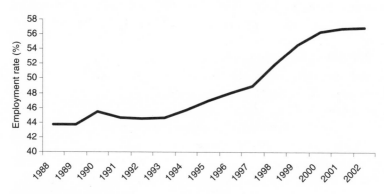

Figure 8.3
Employment rate, population aged 15 and over.

aged 35 to 44 were economically active on ILO definitions, compared with only 29 percent in 1988. The availability of affordable childcare rather than of job opportunities became the binding constraint on higher participation rates among women with children. The long-term unemployment rate fell even faster than the overall rate, reaching 1.2 percent in 2000. The short-term unemployment rate—usually a more cyclically sensitive measure of labour market conditions—fell to 2.5 percent. Broader measures of the potential labour force that take account of various measures of "discouraged workers" also support the view that very little labor market slack remained by the end of the decade. The proportion of industrial firms reporting that labor shortages were a constraint on increased production reached almost 10 percent, supporting the general perception that unemployment had ceased to

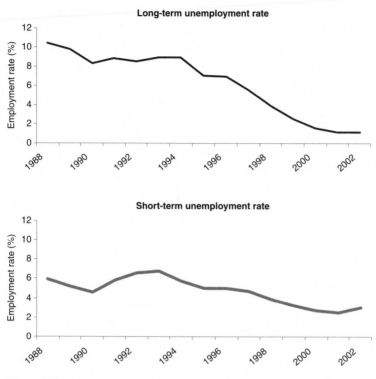

Figure 8.4
Long-term and short-term unemployment rates.

be a general problem. Indeed, labor shortages, unfilled vacancies, and the issues raised by substantial immigration replaced unemployment and emigration as concerns.

In most OECD countries part-time contracts contributed more than half of employment growth in the 1990s. The extreme example was the Netherlands, where women working part-time in the service sector accounted for over half the total increase in employment between 1983 and 1997 (Garibaldi and Mauro 2002). In contrast, the Irish employment boom was biased toward full-time jobs. Women working part-time accounted for only 26 percent of the total growth in employment between 1988 and 2002. While the share of part-time working among women rose from 16.5 to 30.4 percent, the proportion of these declaring themselves "underemployed" was only 0.7 percent. Nor was the growth in the numbers at work or the decline in unemployment unduly dependent on the expansion of public sector employment schemes designed to provide work for the long-term unemployed and other hard-to-employ categories. The employment boom started during a period of fiscal austerity when the numbers at work in the core areas of public administration were reduced and employment in public services such as health and education were held in check. However, several special employment schemes were introduced during the 1980s and 1990s to alleviate unemployment. These comprised a mixture of (1) subsidies to regular employment in the private sector, (2) support for unemployed persons starting enterprises, and (3) direct employment on special schemes. The numbers employed on the largest of these—the Community Employment Scheme—rose from about 1 percent of the labor force in the late 1980s to a peak of 2.8 percent in 1995, falling back to 2 percent by 2001.[4] It has been estimated that about half of those leaving these schemes return to unemployment, so they may be credited with taking about one percentage point off the total unemployment rate. But since many participants churn through the system, interrupting spells of unemployment with spells on schemes, the impact on the long-term unemployment rate has been greater (O'Connell 2000). Nonetheless, the low short-term unemployment rate suggests that the displacement from long-term to short-term unemployment was not significant. However, because so few participants move on to regular paid employment, these schemes have come to be viewed as part of the problem of structural adjustment rather than part of the solution. At a time when work permits are being issued to non–EU immigrants to take low-paid jobs in the private sector at a rate equaling about 2 percent of the labor force each year, the rationale for public sector schemes to provide work for the hard-to-employ is being queried. As a result, and bearing in mind the deterioration in the public finances, the provision for these schemes in 2003 has been reduced by about a quarter.

The social welfare system has also been used to encourage some of the unemployed to reclassify as retired or disabled. During the 1980s the system was modified to encourage people approaching retirement age (65) to change their unemployment allowance into a "pre-retirement allowance" on condition that they withdraw from the labor force. The numbers on this scheme reached 15,000 (less than 1 percent of the labor force) in the early 1990s but fell to less than 12,000 in 2001. The labor force participation rate among men aged 60 to 64—the principal category affected by these measures—dropped from 60.6 percent in 1988 to 55.6 percent in 2002. Some of this reduction was due to the changes in the social welfare code, but other factors, such as improved private sector pension provision and the declining number of farmers, also contributed. Despite these trends the Irish participation rate among older males remains considerably above the average for OECD–Europe.

In summary, the fall in the Irish unemployment rate cannot be dismissed as artifacts of make-work schemes or policies designed to disguise unemployment. While there has been a growth in part-time employment of women, this appears to be voluntary and under-employment among them is very low. While special employment schemes absorbed an increased proportion of the labor force in the 1990s, by the end of the decade their impact on the aggregate labor market statistics was modest. The same is true of social welfare induce-ments to early retirement. The broadest measure of potential labor supply, which includes those with only a marginal interest in employ-ment, has fallen as rapidly as the conventional unemployment rate.

8.3   Accounting for the Transformation[5]

We have seen that Irish unemployment rose sharply during the global recession of the 1970s. Domestic fiscal stimulus provided only short-term relief and created macroeconomic imbalances that deepened and prolonged the recession of the 1980s. At the same time the rise in UK unemployment shut off the traditional safety valve of emigration, with the result that the Irish unemployment rate reached unprecedented levels. All these factors went into reverse in the late 1980s and 1990s. Unemployment was stabilized as the Lawson boom in the United Kingdom re-opened the safety valve of emigration. But by the end of 1980s, the Irish economy had begun to outperform the European Union, and in the 1990s, truly exceptional output growth rates were achieved. Between 1993 and 2000, the real GNP growth rate averaged 8 percent.[6] Since there was no marked change in the rate of increase in (labor) productivity, this output boom was accompanied by a very rapid increase in the numbers at work and eventually a sharp reduc-tion in the unemployment rate.

8.3.1   Macroeconomic Developments

The foundations for the Irish economic boom of the 1990s were laid down in earlier decades. The economy had been gradually opened up to international trade and investment during the 1960s and especially by accession to the European Economy Community in 1973 and the implementation of the Single European Act by 1992. The economy's adjustment to free trade was assisted by increased inflows of "structural funds" from Europe; these funds have been proportionately more important in Ireland than in any other member state. Since joining the European Union in the 1970s, Ireland has benefited disproportionately from the Common Agricultural Policy. The country enjoyed additional aid on joining the European Monetary System in 1979 and—of more immediate relevance to an understanding of the boom in the 1990s— more money flowed in from the Cohesion, Regional, and Social Funds in the late 1980s to help the economy adjust to the full rigors of free trade and the single market. This last infusion helped insulate Ireland from the global recession of the early 1990s and helped fund a resumption of public capital spending that had been pared down as part of the fiscal adjustment. The substantial transfers from the European Union are estimated to have lifted the *level* of Irish output on a sustained basis by as much as 4 percent. Although not trivial, this boost is dwarfed by the exceptional growth rates recorded in the 1990s—for example, between 1992 and 2001 the level of real GNP doubled.

The resort to an expansionary fiscal policy in the late 1970s provided only a temporary boost to the main macroeconomic indicators and eventually demanded a severe correction that dampened aggregate demand for much of the earlier part of the 1980s. As the economy improved some authors (Giavazzi and Pagano 1990; McAleese 1990) pointed to the dramatic fiscal correction as an important part of the explanation of Ireland's altered fortunes, arguing that this was an example of an "expansionary fiscal contraction." Subsequent work (Barry and Devereux 1994) cast doubt on the mechanisms proposed, pointing instead to the fact that exports led consumption, which in turn led investment in the recovery. Yet the fiscal correction was undoubtedly a necessary precondition for restoring confidence and the subsequent improved performance.

Several additional favorable macroeconomic developments may also be invoked to explain the timing of the boom. During the period of the European Monetary System, real interest rates were relatively high due to the risk premium attached to Ireland's participation in this adjustable peg. Following the virtual collapse of the EMS in 1993, Irish growth was further fueled by the fall in Irish real interest rates during the period of generalized exchange rate floating that followed and as

Irish nominal rates converged on German rates when the adoption of the euro became credible. By 1999 Irish real interest rates had become negative, while the Irish pound depreciated relative to sterling and the US dollar as the exchange for entry to the single currency were finalized. By then the Irish economy had become "supercompetitive." While a soft currency can hardly be credited with the sustained increase in the Irish growth trajectory, the timing of the depreciations of the Irish exchange rate between 1986 and 1999 should be included among the catalysts that initiated the period of faster growth.

Further external stimulus came through the effects of rapid US and UK growth on the large traded sector of the Irish economy. In particular, the Irish boom coincided with the strongest expansion in the US economy since the Second World War. The buoyancy of the global economy spilled over to Ireland through the increased flow of FDI from the United States, as well as through strong demand in exports markets in Britain, Europe, and the United States. Having redressed the imbalances that emerged in the domestic economy in the late 1970s and offering a low corporation tax regime and selective grant assistance to manufacturing firms, the Irish economy was well positioned to benefit from these favorable external developments. By the early 1990s the economy was fully integration into the European economy and offered a suitable export platform for subsidiaries of US firms.

The inflow of FDI to Ireland has attracted considerable international attention and tends to be given much of the credit for the boom. Commenting on Ireland's success a recent study claimed that "the exogenous driving force was a well-thought out strategy to attract foreign direct investment" (Garibaldi and Mauro 2002, p. 73).[7] But this interpretation ignores the fact that the Irish inducements to FDI had been in place for many years and were in fact scaled back over the 1990s.[8] There are three possible explanations for the increased effectiveness of the Irish incentives to FDI during the 1990s. The first is that as they were scaled back, the incentives became better targeted. The Irish development agencies claim credit for attracting some flagship companies in key sectors to Ireland.[9] Second, it can be argued that international capital flows became more sensitive to fiscal considerations during the 1990s. Finally, the attractiveness of Ireland as a location was greatly enhanced by its full integration into the European economy.

However, the "high-tech" manufacturing sectors where MNCs predominate directly accounted for only about 13 percent of the total employment growth since the late 1980s. This should be compared with the growth of employment in "marketed services"—everything from international financial services to tourism—which contributed over 40 percent of the total employment growth.[10] But it is true that the growth of industrial employment in Ireland over this period bucked the general downward trend in OECD countries and raised its share of total employment to close to 20 percent in 2000.

8.3.2 The Supply of Labor

It would not have been possible for real GNP to grow by 8 percent a year over the period 1993 to 2000 without a very elastic labor supply. Since the initial high level of unemployment contributed to this elasticity, the rate of growth of output was not a purely exogenous variable that can be used to explain the fall in unemployment.[11] Despite the rise in the participation rate and the reversal of migration flows, the link between the growth of GNP and the fall in the unemployment rate during the 1990s was similar to that estimated over earlier periods (Walsh 2000). The correlation between these variables remained high ($\bar{R}^2 = 0.70$) and the implied steady-state GNP growth rate of 4.5 percent is much the same as earlier estimates (figure 8.5).

In addition to the high initial level of unemployment, the factors that contributed to the elastic labor supply included:

• A high rate of natural increase of the working-age population, as the baby-boom generation of the 1960s and 1970s came on the labor market. Increased expenditure on education in earlier years assured that the labor force entrants were well qualified.

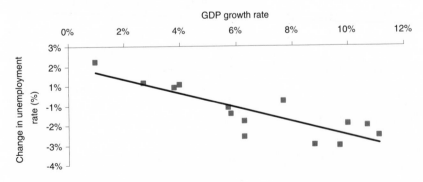

Figure 8.5
Okun's law, Ireland 1988 to 2002.

• The low initial labor force participation rates, especially among married women.

• The openness of the labor market to migration flows. The initial inflows contained a significant proportion of returning emigrants, but in later years non-Irish immigrants predominated.

In the early phase of the expansion, the growing demand for labor could be met from the natural growth of the labor force and returning emigrants. The impact on the nonemployed population lagged, giving rise to concerns about "jobless growth." As late as 1997 the OECD survey of the Irish economy noted that "despite rapid employment growth the unemployment rate remains high, participation rates are low, and net emigration has been substantial,"[12] but by then this was already changing dramatically.

An elastic labor supply was not a new phenomenon in Ireland. However, success in absorbing the potential growth of the labor force into employment—rather than dissipating it in emigration, unemployment, and nonparticipation—was. An immediate reason for this change was improved wage competitiveness, which made the country a more attractive location for investment (Honohan and Walsh 2002). Figure 8.6 shows Irish wages[13] in a common currency relative to a weighted average of our trading partners. This series deteriorated until the mid-1980s and then reversed trend in 1987—a pattern that is closely correlated with the pattern of employment. The improvement in competitiveness was, in turn, due to several developments. The devaluation of the Irish pound in 1986 and 1993 played a part. While a

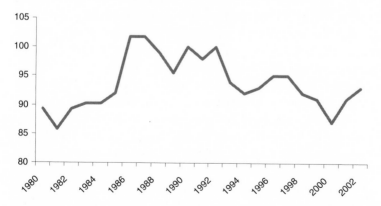

Figure 8.6
Relative wage costs in a common currency.

weaker currency is not likely to bestow a permanent advantage, it did provide temporary boosts at key junctures in the recovery. Higher productivity may also be invoked, but this was partly endogenous— reflecting the dramatic impact of new industries on the aggregate figures. There was no marked jump in the rate of improvement of productivity in existing firms. The main factor that needs to be considered—and the one that receives the lion's share of the credit from many Irish and foreign commentators—is the return to central wage bargaining or "social partnership" in 1987.

8.3.3   The Return to Centalized Wage Bargaining

The disastrous labor market trends of the 1980s hit the Irish trade union movement very hard. Union membership, which had been growing rapidly from the 1960s, peaked in 1980 and declined steadily until the 1990s. Union density declined even more rapidly and did not recover, as most of the new jobs created in the booming economy were in union-free workplaces. However, there was no explicit government agenda to curb union power, along Thatcherite lines. On the contrary, the role of unions was strengthened by the revival and deepening of a centralized bargaining process that went beyond wages to cover taxation and other aspects of economic policy.

In 1987 a new centralized agreement was negotiated in very altered circumstances from Ireland's earlier—and unsuccessful—experimentation with corporatism at the end of the 1970s. The much-weakened unions were glad of the lifeline thrown to them by social partnership. The unprecedented high unemployment rate—attributable not only to the economy's poor performance but also to the exogenous shock of high British unemployment—led to a widespread consensus that generalized belt-tightening was needed. The first National Wage Agreement was followed by four others. These agreements, negotiated over successive three- or four-year horizons extending from 1988 to 2003, and each exceeding the previous in its ambition and scope. The range of objectives was extended far beyond the basic goal of promoting industrial peace and keeping the economy competitive to objectives like "bringing about a fairer and more inclusive Ireland" and "promoting an entrepreneurial culture." (Some details of the wage agreements are provided in an appendix to this chapter.) Growing scepticism as to the benefits of the approach was evident during the negotiations for a sixth agreement; nonetheless, a new agreement on "Sustaining Prosperity" was reached in February 2003. This program provides for a 7 percent increase in wages over an 18-month period. Several large firms in the exposed sectors have warned that they will not follow this guideline.

Admirers of the partnership approach, with its use of income tax concessions to win moderate nominal pay increases, claim that because it eliminated local disputes over pay bargaining and moderated real wage growth, it deserves much of the credit for the exceptional employment growth in the 1990s. The strike rate fell to a much lower level after the new wage-bargaining system was launched, and by the end of the decade industrial disputes had ceased to be a general problem (although militancy has recently increased among public sector unions). However, econometric research on the underlying dynamics of Irish wage inflation has yielded inconclusive results. Much of the short-term fluctuation in the relative position is attributable to autonomous exchange rate changes involving the sterling and the US dollar. In fact, once these are allowed for, it is hard to identify a statistically significant role for the domestic unemployment rate, let alone the pay-bargaining regime (Curtis and FitzGerald 1996; Walsh 2000). But exchange rate movements are not a plausible explanation for the sustained reversal of trend. Although econometric proof is lacking, the coincidence of the improvement in competitiveness with the new approach to pay bargaining is widely accepted as evidence that it did pay dividends.

A key feature of the national wage agreements was the lowering of the burden of taxation on employees. Reductions in tax rates were implicit in the negotiation of each agreement, with government promising income tax "concessions" in return for pay moderation. Because of the rapidly falling top marginal tax rates, the income tax thresholds were raised sharply in real terms, taking more and more of the lower-paid out of the income tax net. But this was a somewhat Faustian bargain in that the process of lowering tax rates had a natural limit influenced by public perceptions of the adequacy of the provision of public services. Indeed, targeted improvements to public services became part of the later pay bargains. And these debates were overtaken by the rapid deterioration in the public finances after 2000. By 2002, tax increases were needed to contain the emerging fiscal deficit.

Moreover by 1998 there was considerable drift in actual private sector wage rates above what was agreed in the national agreements. The era of wage restraint seemed nearing its end. The weakness of the euro between 1999 and 2001 helped keep Irish labor competitive despite accelerating nominal wage increases, but its recovery in 2002 and 2003 amplified the effects of relatively high wage inflation. Finally tax cuts could have been implemented outside centralized wage agreements. On the key issue of whether they moderated wage the jury is still out.

In summary, while centralized wage bargaining did not deliver much long-run wage moderation, it has played some role in the timing of the economic recovery and the subsequent employment boom through its impact on external competitiveness.

8.3.4   Removing Structural Rigidities

The point of departure in the 1980s was a social welfare system that was not unduly generous and relatively market-friendly labor market policies by continental European standards. However, serious disincentives and anomalies, as well as a lax attitude toward eligibility for benefits and assistance, existed and were invoked as reasons for the persistence of high unemployment. As the unemployment rate soared, the fact that unemployment assistance could be collected more or less indefinitely without any evidence of active job search received growing critical attention. The growing gap between the survey-based measure of unemployment, based on ILO definitions, and the larger number registered as unemployed pointed to the need for stricter enforcement of job search criterion for eligibility for unemployment benefits.

The Irish case is a useful study of the validity of the emphasis in the OECD *Jobs Strategy* on reforms in the tax and benefit systems and increased labor market flexibility as preconditions for improved labor market outcomes. It is hard to imagine more favorable circumstance for implementing such reforms than during the buoyant labor market conditions that prevailed in Ireland in the 1990s. The OECD itself reviewed progress on these fronts in its *Economic Surveys* of Ireland in 1997 and 1999. It recognized that Ireland made progress in many areas, notably as follows:

• *Preventative approach to long-term unemployment.* Since September 1998 all those who have been unemployed for six months are called for interview to assess whether they are apt for an existing vacancy or in need of training. To cite the OECD, "a surprisingly high share of these can be dealt with in this fashion: nearly half either failed to attend the interview or refused intervention, and 28 percent were struck off the rolls ..." (OECD 1999, p. 127). This helped close the very large gap that had emerged between registered unemployment and ILO unemployment. There was a fall in the long-term unemployment rate after 1988, but the major reductions did not occur until much later (see figure 8.4a).

• *Active labor market policies.* A plethora of special employment schemes and other active labor market initiatives was introduced and spending on them reached 1.5 percent of GDP in the late 1980s. The most costly measure was the Community Employment scheme, which was discussed above. OECD data reveal that Ireland moved well up the league table on spending on active labor market policies between 1985 and 1997, which increased from 14 percent of average industrial earnings per person unemployed in 1985 to 29 percent in 1997, when only rates observed in the Netherlands and the Scandinavian countries were higher. This level of spending has proved controversial. Although there is some microeconometric evidence to suggest that the increased emphasis on "back to work" measures did help to improve the functioning of the labor market in the 1990s, its role should not be exaggerated (Martin 2000). This expenditure has come under closer scrutiny in current more constrained budgetary context and is likely to be significantly reduced and rationalized.[14]

• *Reducing the work disincentives in the benefit system.* Higher replacement ratios were blamed for about half the rise in the Irish structural unemployment rate between the 1970s and the mid-1990s (Scarpetta 1996), but the disincentive effects that have been uncovered appear to be small compared to those reported in the international literature and the largest effects are reported among relatively advantaged unemployed groups and not the long-term unemployed who constitute such a large proportion of the core unemployment problem in Europe (Layte and Callan 2001). Net replacement ratios—which were roughly in the middle European range in the 1980s—stabilized and in some cases declined in the 1990s. This was due to changes in the income tax code and in the social welfare system. The rate of increase in basic benefits did not keep pace with the rise in after-tax pay, especially among the lower-paid. A significant innovation was the introduction of a "back to work allowance" in 1993, which permits the long-term unemployed to hold on to 75 percent of their social welfare payments in the first year of employment, 50 percent in the second, and 25 percent in the third. At its peak in 2000, there were 39,000 participants on this scheme, but by 2002, numbers had fallen to 25,000 and further reductions are planned in 2003. In the 1980s a Family Income Supplement was introduced to raise the take-home pay of those on low earnings. This too was a form of in-work benefit.

• *Burden of taxation.* Changes in the income tax system increased the incentives to accepting paid employment. The marginal income tax rate (including social security charges) facing an unmarried industrial worker on average wages peaked at 68.5 percent in 1984. By 2002 this had fallen to 48 percent. The marginal tax rates facing other categories of workers were lower and also declined, although less dramatically. Many low-paid workers were completely removed from the income net by progressively raising the tax threshold, which for an unmarried worker reached half average industrial earnings in 2002. The introduction of "individualization" in the income tax code greatly increased the after-tax returns to a second income earner in a household. Certain benefits such as rent supplements are no longer withdrawn on taking up employment, and child benefits have been increased and uncoupled from unemployment benefits. But while moving in the right direction, these changes were hardly sufficient to account for much of the dramatic fall in unemployment and rise in employment.

• *Increased real wage flexibility?* Greater wage flexibility could also have contributed to the improved labor market performance. Low inflation and a falling tax burden reinforced nominal wage moderation even as the unemployment rate plummeted in the second half of the 1990s. But as the unemployment rate fell to unprecedented levels, wage inflation pressures built up. Numerous groups in the public sector clamored for large pay increases in order to participate in the country's newfound prosperity. However, when the global slowdown in the technology sectors hit Ireland in 2001 and 2002, anecdotal evidence and the behavior of income tax receipts[15] suggest that wages and salaries have adjusted through the nonpayment of bonuses in sectors where employment is at risk.

But not all policy changes went in the direction of greater labor market flexibility. Employers and many commentators viewed the introduction of a statutory national minimum wage at about 55 percent of average industrial earnings in 2000 with some apprehension. The minimum wage has since been increased to keep pace with wage inflation but its effects on employment levels have been small (Nolan, O'Neill, and Williams 2002).

In view of the less than radical nature of the structural reforms that have been implemented, it is safe to conclude that although their cumulative effect on unemployment claims could have been significant, not much of Ireland's "employment miracle" should be attributed to them.

8.4 Conclusion

During the 1990s the Irish economy grew at an exceptional rate. This rapid output generated an unprecedented employment boom, which reduced the unemployment rate, raised participation rates, and reversed the outflow of population from the country. Employment grew much more rapidly that the population and the rise in the employment-to-population ratio played a large part in Ireland's belated, but very rapid, catch-up in living standards with the leading economies.

This chapter explores the factors that contributed to the transformations of the Irish economy and labor market over the period. It is argued that once the Irish economy had recovered from the effects of the policy errors of the 1970s and the protracted recession of the 1980s, it responded strongly to several favorable demand-side shocks. These took the form of increased inflows of aid from the European Union, falling real interest rates, the weakness of the Irish pound relative to the dollar and sterling, and the booming US and UK economies. Attracted by a favorable tax regime, an elastic labor supply and Ireland's integration into the European economy, the inflow of FDI to the country accelerated. The elastic labor supply reflected the high initial level of unemployment and low participation rates, the pool of recently emigrated young people interest in returning to the country, and the high rate of natural increase of the labor force.

The Irish example shows the importance for the labor market of achieving rapid economic growth. It is a case study of how an output boom turned one of Europe's worst performing labor markets into one of the best in the course of a decade. While the causation also ran in the other direction—such exceptional output growth rates could not have been achieved without a very elastic labor supply—an excess supply of labor had not in the past triggered an economic boom. The catalyst that did so in the 1990s was a reversal of the deteriorating trend in wage competitiveness. Favorable exchange rate developments played their part, but pride of place is usually given to the modest nominal

wage settlements negotiated under the central wage agreements reintroduced in 1987. However, even if the return to "social partnership"
and the government's commitment to easing the income tax burden
are given credit for the improved wage bargaining outcomes, we
should not lose sight of the contribution of the unprecedented unemployment rate and the reduced strength of the trade union movement
to the new sense of realism that prevailed in wage negotiations. That
Irish unemployment rose so high in the mid-1980s was due to the level
of unemployment reached in the United Kingdom and the lack of
opportunities for Irish emigrants. Paradoxically, in light of the eventual
impact on Irish wage bargaining, this factor too can be regarded as a
favorable external shock.

The exceptional performance of the Irish labor market during the
1990s was not triggered by radical structural reforms. True, the disincentives to paid employment were reduced, the administration of the
social welfare system became more rigorous, and a plethora of active
labor market measures was launched, but these were not sufficiently
far-reaching or effective to account for the initial drop in the unemployment rate, much less the spectacular rise in the numbers in employment. However, they undoubtedly helped maintain the momentum
toward lower unemployment created by the favorable macroeconomic
developments.

Many of the factors behind the Irish success story are not likely to
be replicated in other European economies. Some of the policies
pursued had a "beggar-my-neighbor" component. For example, it is
not possible for all countries to improve their competitiveness by simultaneous devaluations! Some would also argue that there is a
beggar-my-neighbor element in the use of a low corporation tax regime to attract a larger share of FDI—Ireland's low profits tax rate has
provoked accusations of "unfair tax competition" in EU forums. But a
favorable environment for investment, a low tax burden, moderate
growth in wage costs, and a cooperative approach to industrial relations are policies that other countries might with benefit emulate.

After 2002 Irish economic growth slowed and unemployment
increased. However, by past standards the recent rise in unemployment has been modest. It is likely that the structural changes documented in this chapter have lowered the equilibrium unemployment
rate and that the calamitous unemployment rates of the 1980s will not
recur.

Appendix: Social Partnership in Ireland

In 1979 the first National Understanding for Economic and Social Development was negotiated against a backdrop of disastrous industrial strife. While this Agreement achieved a reduction in the level of strikes, a second Agreement collapsed in 1982 and there followed a five-year period of decentralised collective bargaining, characterized by high wage inflation and considerable industrial unrest. In 1987 a new centralized wage deal was negotiated. This national wage agreement was called the Programme for National Recovery and was the first of six whose ambition and scope have grown. Recent negotiations involved a very wide range of organizations, representative of a variety of pressure groups and sectoral interest, and the objectives have extended far beyond the basic goal of promoting industrial peace and

Table 8.1
Chronology of Irish corporatism

Title of national agreement/program	Period
Programme for National Recovery	1988–1990
Programme for Economic and Social Progress	1991–1993
Programme for Competitiveness and Work	1994–1997
Partnership 2000 for Inclusion, Employment and Competitiveness	1997–2000
Programme for Prosperity and Fairness	2000–2003
Sustaining Progress	2003–2004

Notes: The parties to the Programme for Prosperity and Fairness included the government, the national employers' federation, the trade unions, the farmers and the community and voluntary sector. The following is a list of the participants:
Irish Business and Employers' Confederation (IBEC)
Irish Congress of Trade Unions (ICTU), Construction Industry Federation (CIF)
Irish Farmers' Association (IFA), Irish Creamery Milk Suppliers' Association (ICMSA)
Irish Co-operative Organisation Society Ltd. (ICOS)
Macra na Feirme, Irish National Organisation of the Unemployed (INOU)
Congress Centres for the Unemployed
The Community Platform
Conference of Religious of Ireland (CORI)
National Women's' Council of Ireland (NWCI)
National Youth Council of Ireland (NYCI)
Society of Saint Vincent de Paul
Protestant Aid
Small Firms' Association (SFA)
Irish Exporters' Association (IEA)
Irish Tourist Industry Confederation (ITIC)
Chambers of Commerce of Ireland (CCI)

keeping the economy competitive to include, for example, "bringing about a fairer and more inclusive Ireland" and "promoting an entrepreneurial culture."[1] As many as 68 committees were established to discuss these issues!

With the advent of full employment in 2000, and the increasing drift between the terms of the agreement and actual wage inflation, employers became increasingly sceptical of the appropriateness of negotiating a new deal for after the present one expires.

Notes

I am grateful to Mark Berger, David Grubb, John Martin, Cormac Ó Gráda, Philip O'Connell, Frank Walsh, and two anonymous referees for helpful comments.

1. For an extended account of Ireland's economic fortunes since the 1960s, see Honohan and Walsh (2002).

2. The definitions of labor force status used in the chapter are mainly based on the ILO classification, derived from household surveys since 1988. Earlier measures are reasonably consistent with this. The first Labour Force Survey (LFS) was conducted in 1977. A Quarterly National Household Survey (QNHS) was introduced in September 1997. The introduction of a new questionnaire in 1998 may have raised the numbers recorded as "employed"—note the kink at 1998 in figure 8.2.

3. The continued fall in the number of children in the population further contributed to reversing the rise in the dependency ratio, which had fallen to 121 percent by 2002.

4. These figures are from special tabulations of the QNHS furnished by the Central Statistics Office. They refer to those reported as employed on "government schemes" at the time of the Survey. The flow through the schemes in the course of a year is higher. Many of the supported jobs are part-time.

5. This draws heavily on the section headed "Output growth and productivity" in Honohan and Walsh (2002).

6. GNP is a better measure than GDP of Irish living standards. The gap between GDP and GNP grew rapidly in the 1990s, to the point where GDP is now 20 percent higher than GNP. This is mainly due to the importance of MNCs in the economy and their propensity to generate profits in Ireland that are subsequently remitted abroad. This issue is discussed at length by Honohan and Walsh (2002).

7. The main incentives to invest in Ireland were a low corporation tax rate and various fixed asset grants.

8. However, at this time the Irish incentives became better targeted and international capital flows became more sensitive to fiscal considerations.

9. The decision by Intel to invest in Ireland in 1985 is often cited as an example. The company now employs over 4,500 near Dublin.

10. But we should not overlook the fact that the preferential 10 percent corporation tax rate was extended to internationally traded financial services located in a designated area of Dublin during the 1980s, where over 8,000 people are now employed.

11. See Walsh (2000) for a more technical discussion of this point.

12. These were subheadings in the section on the "Labour market and economic performance" in the OECD *Economic Survey of Ireland* 1997.

13. That is, average hourly earnings, not including employer's taxes and social charges.

14. Recent newspaper accounts suggest that places on the various training and special placement scheme exceed the numbers unemployed.

15. Tax revenue fell much more rapidly than the numbers at work, and one explanation offered has been the collapse of bonuses and performance-related pay. Recent changes in the structure of income taxation have made revenue more sensitive to levels of pay among the highest paid.

References

Barry, F., and M. Devereux. 1994. The macroeconomics of government budget cuts: Can fiscal contractions be expansionary? In W. B. Robson and W. M. Scarth, eds., *Deficit Reduction: What Pain, What Gain?* Toronto: C. D. Howe Institute.

Curtis, J., and J. Fitzgerald. 1996. Real wage convergence in an open labour market. *Economic and Social Review* 27 (4): 321–40.

Giavazzi, F., and M. Pagano. 1990. Can severe fiscal contractions be expansionary? Tales of two small European countries. In O. J. Blanchard and S. Fischer, eds., *NBER Macroeconomics Annual*. Cambridge: MIT Press.

Honohan, P., and B. Walsh. 2002. Catching up with the leaders: The Irish hare. *Brookings Papers on Economic Activity* 1: 1–78.

Krueger, A., and J.-S. Pischke. 1998. Observations and conjectures on the U.S. employment miracle. In German-American Academic Council, ed., *Third Public GAAC Symposium: Labor Markets in the USA and Germany*. Bonn: GAAC.

Layard, R., S. Nickell, and R. Jackman. 1991. *Unemployment: Macroeconomic Performance and the Labour Market*. Oxford: Oxford University Press.

Layte, R., and T. Callan. 2001. Unemployment, welfare benefits and the financial incentive to work. *Economic and Social Review* 32 (2): 103–30.

Martin, J. 2000. What works among active labour market policies? Evidence from OECD countries' experiences. In OECD, ed., *Policies towards Full Employment*. Paris: OECD.

McAleese, D. 1990. Ireland's economic recovery. *Irish Banking Review* (summer): 18–32.

Murphy, A., and B. Walsh. 1996. The incidence of male non-employment in Ireland. *Economic and Social Review* 25 (5): 467–90.

Nolan, B., B. Gannon, R. Layte, D. Watson, C. T. Whelan, and J. Williams. 2002. Monitoring poverty trends in Ireland: Results from the 2000 Living in Ireland Survey. Economic and Social Research Institute, Dublin. *ESRI Policy Research Series 45*.

Nolan, B., D. O'Neill, and J. Williams. 2002. The impact of the minimum wage on Irish firms. Economic and Social Research Institute, Dublin. *ESRI Policy Research Series 44*.

O'Connell, P. J. 2000. The dynamics of the Irish labour market in historical perspective. In B. Nolan, P. O'Connell, and C. Whelan, eds., *Bust to Boom? The Irish Experience of Growth and Inequality*. Dublin: Institute of Public Administration.

OECD. 1997. *Economic Surveys: Ireland*. Paris: OECD.

OECD. 1999. *Economic Surveys: Ireland*. Paris: OECD.

Scarpetta, S. 1996. Assessing the role of labour market policies and institutional settings on unemployment: A cross-country study. *OECD Economic Studies* 26: 43–98.

Walsh, B. M. 2000. Cyclical and structural influences on Irish unemployment. *Oxford Economic Papers* 12 (3): 119–45.

9   Unemployment in Britain: A European Success Story

Christopher A. Pissarides

(UK)

E24   J63

E31   J65

9.1   Introduction

The decline in unemployment in Britain is one of Europe's success stories. Starting in 1993, when it stood at 10.3 percent of the labor force, it came down to 5.1 percent in 2002. The beneficiary was employment. The percentage of the working-age population employed since 1993 has risen every year from 70.4 percent in 1993 to 74.7 percent in 2001. The labor force changed very little, from 78.5 percent of the working-age population in 1993 to 78.7 percent in 2001. Moreover men and women of all ages participated in this employment gain. This chapter documents this success story and discusses the factors behind it.

In section 9.2, I review the evidence and show how the big swings of the 1980s gave way to a long expansion of employment in the 1990s. What appeared like a permanent rise in unemployment in the first half of the 1980s was reversed in the second half of the 1990s. In section 9.3, I discuss the British Beveridge curve, with a view to establishing shifts in the curve that indicate a structural break. I argue, somewhat unconventionally, that there is only one convincing structural shift, in the second half of the 1970s. The long swings of the 1980s, which appear like long-term shifts, should be attributed to cyclical shifts. In section 9.4, I do the same for the Phillips curve, and find the clue to the British success story. Whereas in the past a prolonged fall in unemployment led to inflationary pressures and contraction, in the 1990s inflation did not materialize. The economy's expansion was not halted by policy because the inflation constraint did not bind. I argue that the key to this change is the combination of the decline of trade union power and the credible reform of the monetary policy regime, taking place first in 1993, when the exchange rate target was abandoned in favor of an inflation target, and strengthened in 1997, when the Bank of England was given operational independence.

In section 9.5, I review some of the institutional features of the British labor market. I argue that the reforms to the unemployment insurance system are not likely to have contributed much to the fall in unemployment. But the decline of trade union power almost certainly did, in combination with the change in the monetary policy regime. Trade union power reached its peak in Britain in the late 1970s and its trough in the 1990s (for reasons that we do not yet fully understand). The fact that unions did not have the power to push for wage rises when unemployment was falling in the 1990s reinforced the low-inflation credentials of the monetary policy regime, and helped sustain the fall of unemployment.

In section 9.6, I change the theme and report growth accounting results to show whether the expansion of employment associated with the fall in unemployment was autonomously induced by institutional change or by exogenous output shocks. If unemployment falls because of institutional change total factor productivity (TFP) progress and labor productivity should be less important and employment a more important cause of output growth. If, on the other hand, the reason for the fall is an exogenous output shock, TFP should be the main driving force of the output growth. I show that in the two big employment expansions, in the late 1980s and in the period since 1993, employment played a bigger role in output growth than in other periods. But although the evidence points to a slightly more important role for employment in the more recent period, it is on the whole unconvincing.

Britain has always been a liberal economy when compared with continental Europe. Employment protection legislation has never been very strong and product market regulation, in the form of start-up costs for new businesses and ongoing business regulation, have been weak (except for a large public sector, which was privatized in the 1980s). So two questions need to be answered to establish our claim that the reform of the monetary policy regime was behind the British success story. First, why was unemployment so low up to the mid-1970s, well before the monetary policy reforms? Second, why did continental Europe, with even stronger anti-inflationary credentials than Britain, not experience a similar success story?

The answer to the first question lies in the nature of the shocks that have hit the British economy. In the period before 1974 the shocks that drove output growth were almost entirely productivity shocks, and there was hardly any employment growth. When productivity growth slowed down in the 1970s wage demands did not follow suit, and inflation became a constraint to maintaining high employment. The answer to the second question lies in the institutional structure of the labor market. The continental European countries with the anti-inflation credentials have restrictive labor market institutions, which Britain does not have. With the exception of trade union power, where Britain was firmly in the European arena until the second half of the 1980s, British institutions have always been closer to US institutions than to continental European ones. The constraint that stopped Britain short of achieving US-style success in the 1970s and 1980s was the wage pressure and subsequent inflation that each fall in unemployment caused. Once trade unions lost their power and the Bank of England established its anti-inflation credentials, the inflation constraint eased and the British labor market took the transition path from continental Europe to the United States.

9.2   Unemployment Trends

Figure 9.1 shows the recorded rate of unemployment in Great Britain since 1970 and a rate that is smoothed for short-term fluctuations. Most of the rise in unemployment from the low values of 2 to 3 percent before 1973 to nearly 12 percent in 1986 is clearly due to a rise in the smoothed rate. Commentators have concluded from this that the

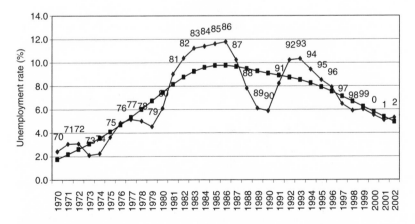

Figure 9.1
Actual and smoothed unemployment rates.

rise in British unemployment is a rise in the "natural rate," namely in the underlying unemployment rate that cannot be reduced by expansionary aggregate demand management.[1] Equally, the fall in unemployment since then, to about 5 percent of the workforce, is a fall in the natural rate. Currently (2002) aggregate demand policy is neither expansionary nor contractionary, something confirmed by the stability of inflation over the last few years.

Whether the smoothed rate shown in figure 9.1 is the natural rate and the deviation between the smoothed rate and the actual rate is the cyclical component is open to question. One thing that we can say is that the deviation between the two rates shown in figure 9.1 is not the only component of cyclical unemployment. Cyclical shocks can be real and the natural rate as defined in the preceding paragraph is a cyclical variable. It is certainly true to say, however, that changes in unemployment due to unanticipated monetary policy are not interesting in the British context.

The series shown in figure 9.1, which is based on the labor force based ILO definition of unemployment, rises fast between 1979 and 1983 and then falls fast again after 1986. This is a feature of other definitions of unemployment in the 1980s, but whether the peak year is 1983, 1984, or 1986 varies according to definition. The underlying feature of unemployment in the 1980s (the "stylized fact") is a fast rise in 1979 to 1983, a plateau in 1983 to 1986, and a fast decline in 1986 to 1990. The plateau took place at a time when the economy and labor productivity were growing fast, and it is the feature that gave rise to the "hysteresis" view of unemployment. Namely, why did the rise in the actual rate of unemployment persist well into the recovery?[2]

In order to shed more light onto what was really happening to unemployment during this period we turn to employment data. The employment series shown in figure 9.2 shows a fast decline between 1979 and 1983, and then a fast recovery between 1983 and 1989, meaning there is no plateau. Naturally this is reflected in the labor force series. Adding together the employment and unemployment series gives the participation rate shown in figure 9.2. Participation rises between 1965 and 1980, falls sharply between 1980 and 1983, and rises again between 1983 and 1986. The "hysteresis" years of 1983 to 1986 appear to be years of rising employment but not falling unemployment. In figure 9.3, I correct for the temporary changes in the participation rate, which is a reflection of "discouraged" workers who were obviously prepared to come back into employment when the opportunities presented

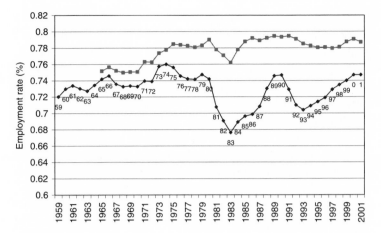

Figure 9.2
Participation and employment rates as percentage of working age population.

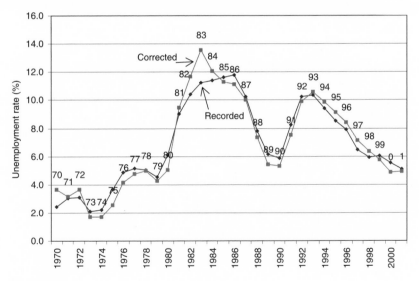

Figure 9.3
Corrected and recorded unemployment rates.

themselves. The participation rate was put through an HP filter and the difference between the filtered participation series and the actual employment series plotted against the recorded unemployment series. The two series track each other very closely, except for the period 1983 to 1986. The plateau disappears, and the constructed unemployment series shows a steep cycle that peaks in 1983 and falls when the economy begins its recovery in that year. It would appear that on this interpretation, the "mystery" that taxed the minds of labor economists at the time—why is unemployment apparently immune to what is happening elsewhere in the economy—is a peculiarity of the statistical definition of unemployment. Namely it ignores discouraged workers who are available to take up work but are not searching when the number of vacancies is very low.

The duration of unemployment in the recent expansion has been relatively unaffected until 1997, when the ratio of long-term unemployment (over 52 weeks) to the total declined sharply, and the ratio of under 26 weeks increased sharply (figure 9.4). This is consistent with the view that in expansion the main vehicle for changes in the long-term unemployment rate is the inflow from short-term unemployment and not the outflow. Namely, when the expansion started, the long-term unemployed did not initially benefit more from it than the short-

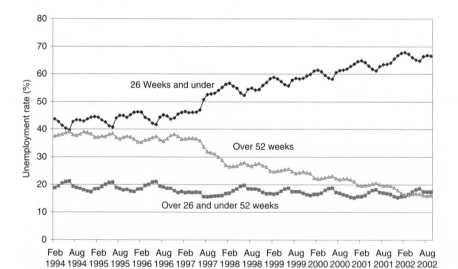

Figure 9.4
Duration of unemployment.

term unemployed did, but their numbers declined because as more of the short-term unemployed found jobs fewer entered long-term unemployment.

The number of new jobs created in the 1990s have mostly been full-time regular jobs. Figures 9.5 and 9.6 show the proportion of part-time and temporary jobs for men and women separately. The proportion of temporary jobs grew slightly for both sexes in the 1990s, but only by about 1 percentage point in total. Temporary jobs are below 8 percent for both sexes and not an important ingredient of British labor markets, perhaps because employers do not have much difficulty hiring and firing employees as needs arise.

Part-time jobs, however, are a different proposition altogether, especially for women. Part-time jobs are an important element in the female labor market, accounting for about 45 percent of total employment. Surprisingly this proportion has been fairly constant during the recent cycles in employment. Survey evidence shows that far from employers using part-time jobs for women to smooth fluctuations, or to get around labor restrictions, they are jobs that are in demand by women and used by employers in their normal operations.[3]

Part-time jobs for men account for a much smaller fraction of employment, but this fraction has grown by some 3 percentage points

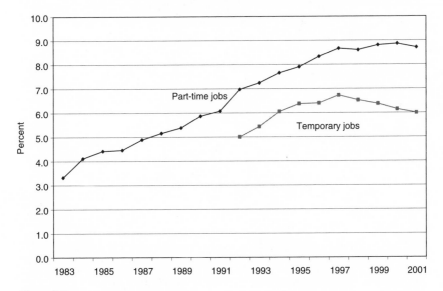

Figure 9.5
Part-time and temporary jobs held by men as a percentage of employment.

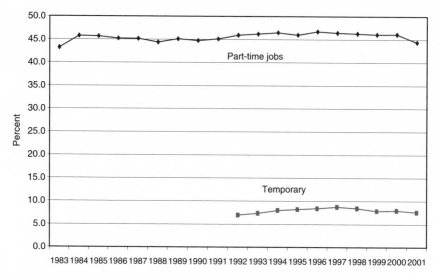

Figure 9.6
Part-time and temporary jobs held by women as a percentage of employment.

during the recent employment expansion. The fastest growth, however, took place during the employment contraction of 1989 to 1993, and it continued in the subsequent expansion, especially in 1993 to 1997. This goes against any argument that the fall in male unemployment after 1993 is due to the expansion of part-time jobs. More work is needed on the role of part-time jobs in the male labor force, as more Labour Force Survey data become available and part-time jobs are acquiring an increasing role in it.[4]

9.3   The British Beveridge Curve

Beveridge curves have become important tools for identifying the causes of changes in unemployment. Their interpretation, however, is still open to question. Recent theoretical advances show that both the cycle and structural changes can shift the Beveridge curve, although the shift due to the business cycle should reverse when the cycle reverses.

The position of the Beveridge curve depends on the rate of job destruction in the economy (the ratio of jobs destroyed to the stock of employment), the incentives that unemployed workers have to look for a job and on mismatch. The Beveridge curve should be further away from the origin in recession than in recovery. One reason for this claim is the higher job destruction that takes place in recession. Another is connected with the search disincentives that workers have in recession. Search disincentives are likely to be higher in recession partly because nonmarket returns, including the real level of unemployment benefits, are likely to be less cyclical than market returns, and partly because during recession the average duration of unemployment lengthens and discouragement builds up. The traditional classification of shocks as cyclical when they cause a movement along the curve and structural when they shift the curve needs to be modified to take into account large departures of the economy from the underlying curve that may appear as shifts to the econometrician, although they are temporary deviations due to the cycle.

Generally, a structural shift in the Beveridge curve is one that does not reverse itself when the cycle returns to the point where it was when the curve started its shift. One that reverses is a cyclical one. The problem with identifying some shifts is that the cycle may be long, and the temporary shift in the Beveridge curve associated with it may last sufficiently long to appear as a structural one.

The British Beveridge curve, shown in figure 9.7, is consequently open to more than one interpretation, depending on how one views the apparent shifts in the curve. My interpretation of some of the observations on this curve is unconventional. A "textbook" interpretation is provided by the experience of the 1970s. In 1974 vacancies were falling sharply and unemployment was rising, so one would expect to see a counterclockwise loop and the 1975 observation to be to the left of the 1972 one. This is not the case in figure 9.7, so this would normally be evidence of a small shift. But, if instead of actual unemployment we use the corrected unemployment series of figure 9.3, this shift disappears: the 1975 observation in the corrected series is to the left of the 1972 one. So it is not clear if a shift occurred between 1974 and 1975. A much clearer shift in the curve took place between 1975 and 1978. The key to a structural shift at this time lies in the fact that when vacancies recovered in 1978 and 1979, they recovered at some 2 percentage points of unemployment above the level that the observations from the early 1970s would lead one to expect. Between 1970 and 1981 there are two Beveridge curves in Britain, each broadly associated with a growth cycle. The curve traced by the 1978 to 1981 observations is clearly to the right of the one traced by the 1970 to 1974 observations. The shift in the curve in the second half of the 1970s was probably due

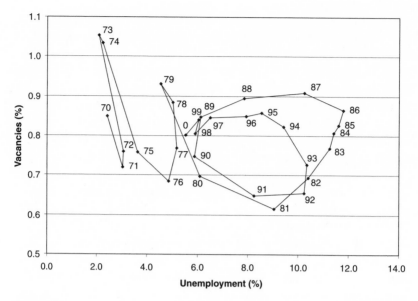

Figure 9.7
UK Beveridge curve.

to the sharp realignment of relative input prices that took place in 1974 and 1975, and the mismatches that it created in the labor market.

An apparently uncontroversial interpretation of what happens next is that between 1981 and 1983 the curve shifted out, because of its northeastern movement. But my interpretation is that this shift is temporary and is associated with an unusually long cycle. The outward shift in the early 1980s was due to two events, the big structural change that took place in the British economy in the early 1980s, with the associated fast decline of manufacturing, and the buildup of long-term unemployment, which followed the unusually deep recession in 1981. Both these events eventually corrected themselves, in the recovery phase of the cycle. The rate of growth of GDP increased in the United Kingdom in every year between 1980 and 1988 (except for 1984), the rate in 1988 being the highest observed since 1973. Growth was still positive in 1990. The deep recession of 1981 was succeeded by the long recovery of 1981 to 1990. Because the recession in the early 1980s was so deep, the shift in the curve associated with the cycle was bigger than in previous cycles. The return path was also longer and slower than previously. The buildup of long-term unemployment and the discouragement that it precipitated are key to the slow reversal of the shift. The observations from 1980 to 1989 trace an unusually large counterclockwise loop, with 1983 to 1986 the deepest points of the recession in the labor market.

The increase in long-term unemployment in the 1980s led to the introduction of active labor market policies. ALMPs shift the Beveridge curve toward the origin, and Britain had some moderate success with these, especially with the restart programme for the long-term unemployed (see Jackman et al. 1990; OECD 1993). At best, however, these programs accelerated the self-correcting mechanism that took place during recovery. It is doubtful whether the active labor market policy measures of the late 1980s had a permanent effect on the position of the Beveridge curve.

The year 1989 appears to be a turning point in the labor market. Growth was at 2 percent, unemployment down to 6 percent, and vacancies high. In 1990 growth and vacancies fell sharply, but unemployment continued for a while its downward path. A doubt that may be raised about the cyclical interpretation of the shift in the 1980s is the question, Why did unemployment not fall more before recession came in 1990? The recession of the early 1990s, however, was policy induced. Monetary policy in Britain changed at this time, first shadowing the deutchemark and then entering the ERM, and the 1989 inflation rate of 7.5 percent was unsustainable (the Chancellor of the Exchequer expressed "surprise" by how quickly inflationary pressures followed his expansion of 1986–87). In 1990 the economy was subjected to a large deflationary monetary shock that lacked credibility (see below for more on this), and unemployment increased.

The question for the Beveridge curve is whether the fact that the 1989 to 1993 increase in unemployment is to the right of the 1979 to 1981 increase is evidence of more mismatch in the labor market in the 1990s than in the early 1980s. There can be no clear answer to this question, but my interpretation of it is that it is not. The Phillips curve discussion in the next section gives more support. Inflation was much higher in the early 1980s but in the early 1990s external pressures forced a contractionary aggregate policy that stopped the economy short of returning to its 1979 to 1980 position.

The loop traced from 1989 to 1997 is another textbook Beveridge curve. But once in the low unemployment equilibrium of 1997, no contraction took place, despite a small fall in the GDP growth rate. Unemployment continued to fall, and by 2000 and 2001 it reached its late 1970s position. Is this evidence of an inward shift or is it a return to the steady-state position of the late 1970s, after the long recession and recovery of the 1980s and 1990s? There is evidence to support both lines of reasoning. From 1994 onward growth was steady or falling, vacancies were steady, inflation was steady, and yet unemployment was falling. Viewed in this light, this is evidence that something happened in the labor market which improved the natural rate. One can look for institutional reform in the labor market, but these were also years of fundamental reforms to monetary policy, which did not allow inflationary pressures to build up. The claim can be made that the monetary policy regime can be important in labor markets beyond the short run, and that the dynamics of the natural rate observed in the 1990s can be attributed to the reform of monetary policy. This argument introduces an old fashioned, yet currently neglected "institution" in the dynamics of unemployment, monetary policy, but it introduces it as an influence on the NAIRU, not on the short-run deviation between the NAIRU and actual unemployment. To see the importance of this, let us turn to the Phillips curve.

9.4   The British Phillips Curve

Before the advent of supply shocks and the Lucas critique of the Phillips curve, the dynamics of unemployment in Britain were described in terms of the "stop–go" cycle. The Phillips curve played a key role in this description. Starting from recession, the economy was given the "go," to bring unemployment down. But after a brief fall, inflation picked up. The "brakes" were applied, to bring it under control. Both expansionary and contractionary policies were real—fiscal policy, the regulation of hire-purchase[5]—although interest rate policy was also used as an anti-cyclical tool.

In modern language the stop–go cycle describes the interplay between a "shock," real aggregate policy, and an "institution," the monetary policy regime. The monetary policy regime determines expectations, and expectations determine the point at which inflation picks up to check a further decline in unemployment. Inflation is a constraint on low unemployment, and because inflation differentials across the world cannot be large for long periods, countries with more inflationary bias in their monetary policy regime have to operate at a higher level of average unemployment than countries with lower inflationary bias. A close look at the British Phillips curve tells this story. It is shown in figure 9.8 for the years 1965 to 2001. The Phillips curve

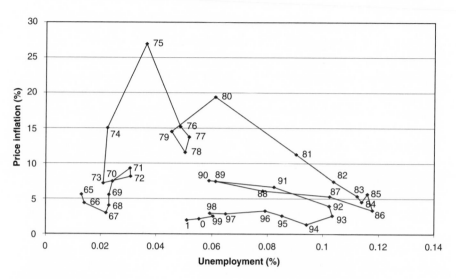

Figure 9.8
UK Phillips curve.

with corrected unemployment tells a similar story, except that the recovery of 1986 shown in figure 9.8 starts in 1983.

In 1973 to 1975 the supply shocks hit and moved the economy in a
northeastern direction, increasing both inflation and unemployment.
There have been three cycles in Britain since 1975 and each one traced
a path in inflation–unemployment space that was increasingly flatter
and closer to the horizontal unemployment axis than the previous one.
From 1975 to 1986 (or to 1983 with corrected unemployment) the path
traced by the economy is a textbook example of a short-run Phillips
curve, with a minor exception in 1979–80, when another oil shock
moved the economy northeastward. The predominant move from
1975 to 1986 is one of a fall in demand and a move down, along a fairly
steep curve. Inflation fell from 26 to nearly 3 percent, but unemployment rose from 3 to 12 percent. The period 1986 to 1993 traces another
textbook Phillips cycle, but now along a flatter curve. The trade-off
improves. Unemployment went down from 12 to 6 percent, but inflation increased only from 3.3 to 7.5 percent. Then, in 1993, unemployment falls again, and the fall continues to the end of the sample, along
an even flatter Phillips curve. Unemployment fell from 10.5 to 5 percent with hardly any move in inflation.

Thus, excluding the oils shocks, we can trace three "Phillips curves"
in Britain with increasing flatness: the less favorable curve of the 1975

to 1986 period, the flatter and more favorable trade-off of the 1986 to 1993 period, and the most favorable trade-off of the post-1993 period. A natural interpretation of this downward shift of the Phillips curve is in terms of inflation expectations. In the late 1970s inflation became so entrenched that a fall in demand—justified by "monetarism," which, despite popular belief, started in 1976 with the visit of the IMF and not with Thatcher—caused a lot of unemployment before inflation could be brought down. By 1986 the recession and the monetarist policy followed by the government finally brought inflation expectations down, but they did not eliminate their cause. When the government expanded the economy again in 1987, with an election imminent, unemployment fell along a flatter Phillips curve. But inflation increased to a level that was still inconsistent with government policy objectives. The objectives of monetary policy changed in the late 1980s to an exchange rate target, with sterling shadowing the deutchemark, first from outside and then from inside the European Exchange Rate Mechanism (ERM). An inflation rate of 7.5 percent was inconsistent with this target, necessitating disinflation and a new policy switch.

Late in 1992 Britain exited the ERM and the Bank of England introduced inflation targeting. Although independence was not granted to the Bank until 1997, when inflation expectations fell dramatically, the exit from the ERM and introduction of inflation targeting did not increase expectations except perhaps slightly at first, which may explain the move of inflation from 1.4 in 1994 to 3.3 in 1996. But inflation targeting soon brought inflation expectations down, and the granting of independence to the Bank in 1997, with low inflation as the only objective, made the short-run Phillips curve essentially flat.[6] The monetary policy regime became an "employment-friendly" institution. The growth of the second half of the 1990s did not hit the inflation constraint but allowed unemployment to fall to the levels of the high inflation era of the late 1970s.

Is it reasonable to attribute so much sluggishness to inflation expectations as is apparent in the 1970s and 1980s? If we think of inflation expectations in the way that economists used to think of them when they were estimating Phillips curves, as either adaptive or rational, the plausible answer is no: it is unlikely that inflation expectations take so long to adjust to events. But if we rethink the issue in terms of the credibility of monetary policy, the answer changes. In the 1970s and early 1980s the public could not believe that the inflation bias in British monetary and fiscal policy was taken out of the system. The Treasury refused to change the institutional rules of monetary policy and monetary policy was discretionary and completely under Treasury control. The Thatcher disinflation lacked credibility. It took a massive recession and a large increase in unemployment to bring inflation down, and it took four years to do it.

In 1987, when the expansion was obviously politically motivated and the operational ways of the Bank of England did not change, inflation fears built up, as unemployment fell. But the fear of a complete return to the high-inflation era of the late 1970s was averted, partly because by this time the government established better anti-inflation credentials and partly because of the switch to the exchange rate target. But the fears were enough to push prices up to unsustainable levels, albeit much below the inflation levels of a decade earlier. In 1990 another policy-induced recession aimed at the high inflation led to an increase in unemployment.

But in 1993 the change in the target was an important operational change, and in 1997 it virtually acquired the force of law, with the establishment of the independent Monetary Policy Committee. The economy could then be allowed to expand and bring unemployment down beyond the levels of the late 1980s, because inflation was removed as an obstacle to the expansion. From the Beveridge diagram in figure 9.7, it is apparent that the critical era began in 1997, when the economy returned to where it was in 1989. But whereas in 1989 inflation rose to 7.5 percent and the policy brakes had to be applied, in 1997 inflation was still on target, below 3 percent, and expansion could be allowed to continue.

9.5   Labor Market Institutions

Are there any other institutional changes that can explain the fall in the UK natural unemployment rate?

Panel regressions for the OECD show that the important labor-market institutions that influence unemployment are the unemployment insurance system and unionization.[7] Employment protection legislation is also sometimes found to be restricting employment growth, but the results are not robust, and usually (as suggested by theory) employment protection's influence on unemployment is ambiguous.[8] More recently product market regulation has been found to be at least as important as labor market regulation in its influence on unemployment,[9] whereas general taxation, in the form of the tax wedge between labor costs and take-home pay, has failed to show up significantly in unemployment regressions.[10]

Product market regulation includes entry costs for new enterprises, taxation of entrepreneurial activity, state control of industry, and regulation of domestic and international trade. Britain has always been one of the least regulated countries in Europe across the board. The OECD published a comprehensive ranking of 20 economies in 1997 in terms of their performance along a number of dimensions of product market regulation (see Nicoletti, Scarpetta, and Boylaud 2000). Britain came top, beating even the United States. Of the major European economies Germany was eighth, France was eighteenth, and Italy was twentieth. Unfortunately, there is no time-series information on product market regulation to draw on. But, with the exception of the privatization program of the 1980s, which reduced the British government's state control of industry, there is no obvious reason to believe that the relative ranking of Britain has changed in this respect. It is also unlikely that the privatization program led to a big reduction in unemployment, although it could have contributed to the decline of unions and the moderation of wage demands.

The tax wedge grew in Britain between 1974 and 1981 but declined virtually monotonically since then (figure 9.9). Although the timing is

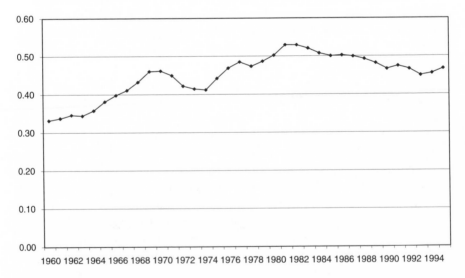

Figure 9.9
Tax wedge.

approximately right for the underlying changes in unemployment, it is unlikely to be a major contributor to the fall of unemployment in the 1990s. First, the fall in taxes from 1987 to 1990 was at about the same order of magnitude as the fall between 1982 and 1985, and in the 1982 to 1985 period unemployment experienced its biggest rise. Second, the fall in the 1990s was of a much smaller order of magnitude than in earlier periods. Finally, panel regressions of unemployment do not find a significant influence of the tax wedge on unemployment.

We turn now to a discussion of the two labor market institutions that usually are found to be significant in panel regressions, unemployment insurance and unionization. Two parameters are usually used to capture the influence of the unemployment insurance system, the ratio of compensation to the mean wage and the duration of entitlement. However, since the most frequently used measure of duration is the percentage of benefit that an unemployed worker retains after one year of claiming, this is equivalent to using two replacement ratio measures, one that applies to the typical unemployed person with less that 52 weeks unemployment and one applying to those with more than 52 weeks. The two series for Britain are shown in figure 9.10.

The replacement ratios shown in figure 9.10 do not tell a very convincing story. Replacement ratios are generally low by European

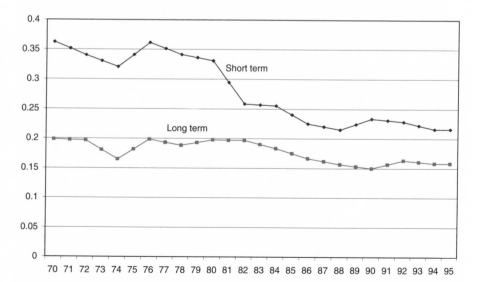

Figure 9.10
Replacement ratio for short-term and long-term unemployed.

standards. In the 1970s they fell and then rose again but no major changes took place. Beginning in 1980, the replacement ratio for the short-term unemployed declined fast, from its 1980 value of 33 percent to 26 percent in 1982 and to 21.5 percent in 1988. The ratio for the long-term unemployed also declined, but the decline started later and it was smaller, from nearly 20 percent in 1982 to 15 percent in 1990.

Since unemployment was rising fast in Britain up to 1984, the time of the biggest fall in the replacement ratio, unemployment insurance policy cannot explain the rise in unemployment. In 1983 the recovery started and unemployment benefits were falling. But, whereas unemployment fell fast, replacement ratios after the mid-1980s declined very little. It would require a large impact of replacement ratios on unemployment and a very large elasticity to explain the fall in unemployment, if UI is to be the driving force. Elasticities estimated in micro studies are usually small. The fall in the replacement ratio from the mid-1980s could have contributed to the decline in unemployment, but it could not have been the cause.

Unemployment insurance could, however, have played a role through other channels, as appear to have come into play in Britain in the second half of the 1980s. One is the buildup of long-term unemployment and another is trade unionism.

The buildup of long-term unemployment in the United Kingdom was blamed for the persistence of unemployment in the mid-1980s. Without generous and long-lasting unemployment benefits, the argument goes, long-term unemployment would not have built up and unemployment would not have persisted. The United States is again used as an example of a country with limited duration benefits that has no long-term unemployment. Empirical evidence is not very convincing, but those who looked at it became convinced that the duration of benefits is critical in the buildup of long-term unemployment.[11] The claim that long-term unemployment causes persistence is also probably justified, although this requires duration dependence in exit probabilities, which has not been established beyond doubt in micro studies. It might therefore be argued that the reforms to unemployment insurance at the end of the 1980s, including the fall in the level of benefits and the introduction of active policies targeted to the long-term unemployed, helped contain the rise in long-term unemployment in the recession of 1990 to 1993. Figure 9.4 shows that long-term unemployment was falling throughout the 1990s.

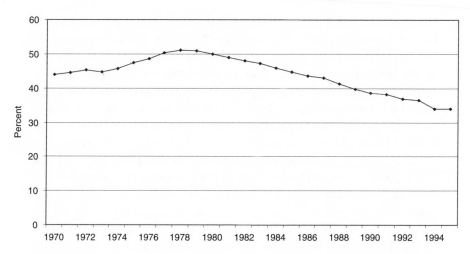

Figure 9.11
Union density.

The second institution that is found to be important in empirical studies is unionization. Unionization expanded in the 1970s and reached its peak in the late 1970s (figure 9.11). Beginning in 1979 union power declined, and in the 1990s unions became ineffective. Legislation that curtailed union power was passed in the early 1980s, with the most important measure probably being the 1986 legislation that prohibited the closed shop.[12] There has been a long debate whether the legislation was responsible for the decline of unions in Britain, since unions declined also in other large European countries that did not pass anti-union legislation. Checchi and Lucifora (2002), who looked at union density in a large number of countries, concluded that the decline of public sector employment in Britain and the Thatcher government's anti-union legislation contributed to the decline of unions. But in their summary evaluation the United Kingdom appears to be exactly at the median of the sample. The absence of state insurance provision (in the form of generous unemployment benefits, employment protection legislation, and wage indexation clauses) predicts that Britain should have about 6 percentage points more union coverage than the mean, but a large country fixed effect predicts that it should have 6 percentage points less than the mean. The reason for the large fixed effect is not explained.

Has the decline of trade unions been important in the fall in unemployment in the late 1990s? The empirical research of Nickell et al.

(1999) and others appears to make this the most important factor in the fall of unemployment. The decline of unions alone, however, is not enough to explain the job creation of the 1990s. What was different in the 1990s expansion was that inflation did not rise to provoke a reaction from government policy. The fact that unions were weak reinforced the low-inflation environment created by the reform of monetary policy. When unemployment was falling in the 1970s and early 1980s, unions put in large wage claims, which were either accommodated by policy or caused unemployment. In the 1990s they did not put in large claims. Whether they did not because they expected the Bank of England to keep inflation low, or whether they did not because they did not have the power to do it, is a moot point. Given empirical results by others, however, some of the employment gains in the 1990s must be due to the inability of unions to appropriate the gains from the expansion of labor demand for their employed members.

9.6   Identifying the Causes of Employment Growth

There have been three periods of cyclical GDP growth in Britain since the mid-1970s, roughly in 1976 to 1979, 1982 to 1989, and 1993 to 2001. In each unemployment fell, but in the first expansion the employment rate did not rise. In the other two it rose very rapidly. Another feature of each expansion is more interesting. In the first two expansions labor productivity grew above trend. In the last it grew below trend, with the exception of two years, 1994 and 1995. If instead of labor productivity we look at TFP, the difference is even more striking. TFP grew above trend in the first two expansions and below trend in each and every year since 1993. This information is useful for the following reason: If unemployment falls because of new job creation that is caused by an external shock to output, we should expect labor productivity to rise above trend. The external shock raises labor productivity, increases the demand for labor, and leads to more job creation. But, if employment is growing because of some institutional reform that increases the demand for labor, employment becomes the driving force of output growth, and so productivity should be rising below trend.

The behavior of labor productivity appears to suggest that the 1990s expansion was different from the previous ones, and driven by institutional reform. But there are more convincing ways of applying this taxonomy. Growth accounting exercises decompose the growth in output

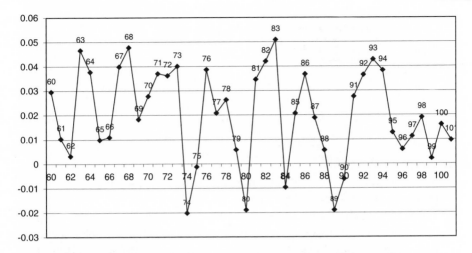

Figure 9.12
Growth accounting: Difference between the contribution of TFP and capital and the contribution of labor.

into one of three reasons, employment growth, capital growth, or TFP. If institutional reform is important in driving employment growth, the contribution of employment to output growth should be above historical levels. Figure 9.12 shows precisely this indicator. It is the difference between the contribution to output growth of the combined TFP growth and capital accumulation, on the one hand, and employment, on the other. The variable shown is cyclical, rising in periods of output expansion and falling in recession. But in the growth years of the 1980s the difference is large, indicating relatively more important productivity growth. With the exception of one year, 1984, the contribution of capital and TFP growth to output growth is more important in the 1980s expansion than in the expansion of the late 1990s.

This is confirmed by table 9.1, which shows the average contribution of each factor to output growth for selected periods since 1960. On average, employment growth contributed 9.6 percent to output growth. In the expansion of the 1960s the contribution of employment was smaller and it was negative in the contraction of the 1970s. But it increased to 17.1 percent in the expansion of the 1980s and to 19.6 percent in the expansion of the 1990s. Thus in the more recent cycles firms relied more on job creation than on investment and new technology as vehicles for output growth. They could do this because of institutional changes that reduced their expectations of wage growth: the decline of

Table 9.1
Growth accounting for the United Kingdom (% contribution)

Period	GDP growth	Employment	Capital	TFP
1960–2001	2.5	9.6	49.9	40.5
1960–1973	3.3	7.5	55.3	37.2
1974–1983	1.1	−34.2	79.7	54.5
1983–1992	2.5	17.1	39.1	43.8
1993–2001	3.0	19.6	33.1	47.2

union power and the anti-inflation credentials of the new monetary policy regime are again key to this.

But not much should be made of this difference because there are only two cyclical upswings, and they exhibit very similar behavior in the growth accounting sense. The most important influence on output is still productivity growth. The biggest contrast to emerge from the growth accounting exercises is between the period before the mid-1980s and the period after. This will prove useful in another context, to which we now turn.

9.7 Possible Objections

Our claim that the key to the British success story is the combination of monetary policy reform and the decline of trade union power needs to deal with two objections. First, it has to explain why unemployment in European countries that have had credible low-inflation institutions since the 1960s did not have the same unemployment history as Britain did. Germany is a case in point. Unemployment in Germany is now among the highest in Europe. Second, Britain had the inflation bias before 1974, but unemployment did not take off. Why?

The answer to the first question is to be found in other labor market institutions. Institutions such as high minimum wages, generous unemployment insurance, and stringent product market regulation can cause high unemployment whatever the monetary policy regime. British institutions, especially since the mid-1980s, have been closer to those of the United States than to those of Europe. Britain did not have minimum wages to speak of, always ranked low on product market regulation, and the level of its unemployment benefits has been below other European countries' levels. Yet Britain's unemployment history until the early 1990s was the history of Europe. The reason is the British economy's inability to come out of the 1970s supply shocks with low inflation at prevailing unemployment rates. Union demands in the 1970s and early 1980s were aggressive and created industrial strife, with which the government was unable to deal without causing a big rise in unemployment. It was also unable to deal with the price rises caused by the supply shocks with the prevailing monetary policy regime. Other European countries could deal with inflation more effectively, but their labor markets were not flexible enough to adapt quickly to the new conditions without causing high unemployment. So, although the unemployment history of Britain was similar to that of Europe, the causes for the rise in unemployment were different. By the early 1990s unions lost their power to push for big wage rises in the face of falling unemployment, and monetary policy was addressed specifically to inflation. The history of unemployment and inflation in Britain since then has had more features in common with the history of unemployment and inflation in the United States than with their history in continental Europe.

The answer to the second question, why was unemployment low in the 1960s, has to be found in the type of shocks that hit the British economy. The problems that surfaced in the 1970s and 1980s were present in 1960s Britain, but were overshadowed by a buoyant economy, protected from foreign competition, and growing fast to reconstruct after the war. The shocks that hit Britain in the 1960s and up to 1973 were positive productivity shocks. In table 9.1 the period up to 1963 is one of growth but of very small contribution from employment and a large contribution from TFP progress and investment. The employment rate in 1971 and 1972 was at the same level as it was in 1965 and 1966 (see figure 9.2). Between 1962 and 1973 the GDP growth rate exceeded 2 percent in each and every year, and the rate of growth of labor productivity was rising faster than trend from one year to the next. The economy was operating at full employment, but despite the buoyant conditions employment was not growing. When the negative supply shocks hit in the mid-1970s and the rate of growth of productivity declined, neither the full employment nor the previous rate of increase of real wages could be sustained at low inflation rates. Unions became more aggressive in their demands, and the Bank of England accommodated wage demands and public deficits. It was realized that the policy was unsustainable as early as 1976, but the strong disinflation and waning of union influence did not take place until after the election of a new government in 1979.

9.8 Conclusions

The recent history of British unemployment is a success story, essentially because the reforms of monetary policy that took place after 1993, combined with the decline of trade union power, removed the inflation constraint from a prolonged expansion in real aggregate demand. There is some evidence from growth-accounting calculations that the reforms also contributed independently to output growth, but it is doubtful whether the reforms alone were the significant driving force of employment growth. More likely they enabled a larger fall in unemployment in the face of rising aggregate demand than would have been possible under the regimes of the 1970s and 1980s.

The view that unemployment in Europe has been structural has been so entrenched in the minds of economists that monetary factors no longer receive a mention in papers on the rise and fall of unemployment. Yet there is a fundamental difference between monetary factors as reflected in temporary deviations between actual and expected prices and monetary factors as reflected in the institutional structure of monetary policy. In a world where inflation differentials between countries cannot deviate for very long, an institutional structure that has the reputation that it accommodates union wage demands and large budget deficits can act as a constraint on the expansion of economic activity. A change in the credibility of the regime, backed by legal reforms, can have a large long-term impact on the real labor market outcome.

This appears to be the factor behind the recent successes in the United Kingdom. With respect to labor-market institutions, Britain has always been at the less interventionist end of the European spectrum, resembling in many respects the United States. The reason its employment performance failed to mimic employment performance in the United States was the combination of strong trade unions and accommodating monetary policy. In the 1980s it required a large increase in unemployment to bring inflation down, because strong trade unions and the absence of institutional reforms to monetary policy led to large wage demands, in the face of built-in expectations that inflation would erode real earnings. The decline of union power and the reforms to the monetary policy regime that took place in the 1990s removed inflation expectations from the labor market and allowed unemployment to fall without causing big wage demands and inflation.

Notes

I am grateful to Vassileios Gkionakis of the CEP for excellent research assistance, and to Paloma Lopez Garcia and Giovanna Vallanti for help with the data. I have also benefited from the comments of the discussant at the conference, Pietro Garibaldi. The UK ESRC provided partial financial assistance through its grant to the CEP.

1. This goes back at least to Bruno and Sachs (1985). The work of Layard and Nickell (e.g., see Layard et al. 1991; Nickell 1997; Layard and Nickell 1999), Phelps (1994), Blanchard and Wolfers (2000), as well as mine (Pissarides 1986, 1999) also reaches similar conclusions.

2. See, for example, Blanchard and Summers (1986), Layard et al. (1991), and Pissarides (1992).

3. Evidence on job satisfaction can be found in the European Household Panel. See Pissarides et al. (2005) on this and other issues relating to the female labor market in Europe and Britain. The "women's" literature dismisses part-time jobs as secondary, but without evidence beyond some anecdotes (e.g., see Franks 1999, pp. 79–86).

4. For example, there has been a large rise in the number of full-time students holding part-time jobs, which needs more research.

5. Before the widespread use of credit cards, most durables were financed by hire-purchase, essentially a loan arranged by the seller of the durable and repaid in installments. Policy controlled the minimum downpayment, namely the cash amount that the buyer had to put up initially, and used this downpayment as a means of cyclical control of the economy.

6. See Johnson (2002) and references therein for the negative influence of inflation targeting on inflation expectations in Britain and elsewhere. Nelson and Nikolov (2002) show that if monetary policy after the 1973 shocks was run on the same principles as after 1992, the high inflation of the mid-1970s would have been avoided.

7. See, among others, Scarpetta (1996), Nickell (1997), Nickell et al. (1999), and Blanchard and Wolfers (2000).

8. Blanchard and Wolfers (2000) find it to be significant, but they are the exception rather than the rule. See OECD (1999), Bertola (1999), and Pissarides (2001) for more discussion.

9. See Nicoletti et al. (2000), Fonseca et al. (2000), Pissarides (2003), and Lopez-Garcia (2003) for some OECD results and Bertrand and Kramarz (2002) for a more detailed study of the French retail sector.

10. Another possible candidate for the fall in the natural rate after 1997 is active labor market policy in the form of the New Deal program for the unemployed, which was introduced by the new Labour Government in 1998. The program covered only young people aged 18 to 24, who had been unemployed for six months. Although its impact on the treatment group was large (Blundell et al. 2002 estimate that, on average, it increased the transition from unemployment to employment by about five percentage points, or 20 percent, in the first four months of treatment), the treatment group was too small and the program too recent to have had an impact on aggregate unemployment dynamics.

11. Layard et al. (1991) and Pissarides (1999).

12. See Booth (1995).

References

Bertola, G. 1999. Microeconomic perspectives on aggregate labor markets. In O. Ashenfelter and D. Card, eds., *Handbook of Labor Economics*, vol. 3C. Amsterdam: Elsevier/North-Holland.

Bertrand, M., and F. Kramarz. 2002. Does entry regulation hinder job creation? Evidence from the French retail industry. *IZA Discussion Paper* 415.

Blanchard, O. J., and J. Wolfers. 2000. The role of shocks and institutions in the rise of European unemployment: The aggregate evidence. *Economic Journal* 110: C1–C33.

Blanchard, O. J., and L. H. Summers. 1986. Hysteresis and the European unemployment problem. In S. Fischer, ed., *NBER Macroeconomics Annual*. Cambridge: MIT Press.

Blundell, R., M. Costa Dias, C. Meghir, and J. Van Reenen. 2002. Evaluating the employment impact of a mandatory job search assistance program. Institute for Fiscal Studies, *Working Paper* 01/20.

Booth, A. 1995. *The Economics of the Trade Union*. Cambridge: Cambridge University Press.

Bruno, M., and J. D. Sachs. 1985. *Economics of Worldwide Stagflation*. Cambridge: Harvard University Press.

Checchi, D., and C. Lucifora. 2002. Unions and labour market institutions in Europe. *Economic Policy* 17: 363–408.

Fonseca, R., P. Lopez-Garcia, and C. A. Pissarides. 2001. Entrepreneurship, start-up costs and employment. *European Economic Review* 45: 692–705.

Franks, S. 1999. *Having None of It*. London: Granta Books.

Jackman, R., C. A. Pissarides, and S. Savouri. 1990. Labour market policies and unemployment in the OECD. *Economic Policy* 11: 449–90.

Johnson, D. R. 2002. The effect of inflation targeting on the behavior of expected inflation: Evidence from an 11 country panel. *Journal of Monetary Economics* 49: 1521–38.

Layard, R., and S. Nickell. 1999. Labor market institutions and economic performance. In O. Ashenfelter and D. Card, eds., *Handbook of Labor Economics*, vol. 3C. Amsterdam: Elsevier/North-Holland.

Layard, R., S. Nickell, and R. Jackman. 1991. *Unemployment: Macroeconomic Performance of the Labour Market*. Oxford: Oxford University Press.

Lopez-Garcia, P. 2003. Labour market performance and start-up costs: OECD evidence. *CESifo Working Paper* 849.

Nelson, E., and K. Nikolov. 2002. Monetary policy and stagflation in the UK. Bank of England, *Working Paper* 155.

Nickell, S. 1997. Unemployment and labor market rigidities: Europe versus North America. *Journal of Economic Perspectives* 11 (3): 55–74.

Nickell, S. J., L. Nunziata, W. Ochel, and G. Quintini. 2001. The Beveridge curve, unemployment and wages in the OECD from the 1960s to the 1990s. Centre for Economic Performance, *Discussion Paper* 502.

Nicoletti, G., R. C. G. Haffner, S. Nickell, S. Scarpetta, and G. Zoega. 2001. European integration, liberalization, and labor-market performance. In G. Bertola, T. Boeri, and G. Nicoletti, eds., *Welfare and Employment in a United Europe*. Cambridge: MIT Press.

Nicoletti, G., S. Scarpetta, and O. Boylaud. 2000. Summary indicators of product market regulation with an extension to employment protection legislation. *OECD Economics Department Working Paper* 226.

OECD. 1993. Active labour market policies: Assessing macroeconomic and microeconomic effects. In *OECD Employment Outlook 1993*. Paris: OECD.

OECD. 1999. Employment protection and labour market performance. In *OECD Employment Outlook 1999*. Paris: OECD.

Phelps, E. S. 1994. *Structural Slumps*. Cambridge: Harvard University Press.

Pissarides, C. A. 1986. Unemployment and vacancies in Britain. *Economic Policy* 3: 499–559.

Pissarides, C. A. 1992. Loss of skill during unemployment and the persistence of employment shocks. *Quarterly Journal of Economics* 107: 1371–91.

Pissarides, C. A. 1999. Policy influences on unemployment: The European experience. *Scottish Journal of Political Economy* 46: 389–418.

Pissarides, C. A. 2001. Employment protection. *Labour Economics* 8: 131–59.

Pissarides, C. A. 2003. Company start-up costs and employment. In P. Aghion, R. Friedman, J. Stiglitz, and M. Woodford, eds., *Knowledge, Information, and Expectations in Modern Macroeconomics: In Honor of Edmund S. Phelps*. Princeton: Princeton University Press.

Pissarides, C. A., P. Garibaldi, C. Olivetti, B. Petrongolo, and E. Wasmer. 2005. Women in the labour force: How well is Europe doing? In T. Boeri, D. Del Boca, and C. A. Pissarides, eds., *European Women at Work*. A report for the de Benedetti Foundation. Oxford: Oxford University Press.

Scarpetta, S. 1996. Assessing the role of labour market policies and institutional settings on unemployment: A cross-country study. *OECD Economic Studies* 26.

Data Sources

The main sources are the UK Office of National Statistics (available on line at http:// www.statistics.gov.uk/) and the OECD. Statistics are generally comparable in the two sources. The institutional variables (tax wedge, replacement ratio for short and long-term unemployed, and union density) are not available at either site and were obtained from Nickell et al. (2001).

10

The Surprising French Employment Performance: What Lessons?

Jean Pisani-Ferry

10.1 Introduction

From the mid-1970s until the late 1990s France looked like the textbook case of a rigid European economy, where employment was essentially flat and ever-rising unemployment could only experience temporary breaks. International organizations routinely estimated the NAIRU to be perilously close from actual unemployment, and most outside observers confidently asserted that anything short of a radical labor market overhaul would fail to remedy this dismal situation.

Yet within five years France has been able to increase employment by 10 percent and to cut down unemployment by more than a fourth. In some respects the French economy of the early 2000s resembled more the slow productivity–high job creation US economy of the 1980s than the standard fast productivity–low job creation European economy of the same period.

France's recent performance is not unique. In the second half of the 1990s aggregate employment growth has significantly improved in the European Union, and some member states, such as Spain, have experienced record job creation. Yet France is very specific in some respects: its labor market institutions are frequently at odds with existing European models, and the policies it has adopted—especially but not only the working time reduction—have generally not been implemented elsewhere.

This chapter examines the French employment and unemployment record with particular emphasis on the recent performance. Section 10.2 provides an overview of what has happened and puts recent years in historical perspective. Section 10.3 is devoted to discussing what can account for the observed changes in employment and unemployment

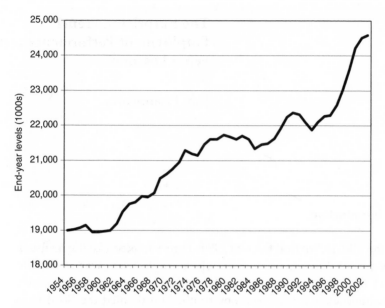

Figure 10.1
Total employment, 1954 to 2002. Source: INSEE.

trends. Section 10.4 focuses on current policy issues. Section 10.5 offers some conclusions.

10.2 Facts

Between 1900 and 1960 the French economy barely created a single job. According Marchand and Thélot (1997), total employment fluctuated around 19 million. Job destruction was taking place in agriculture while new jobs were created in industry and services, but the aggregate figure remained remarkably flat.

As the labor force started to expand again, the 1960s saw a noticeable increase in employment (figure 10.1). Two million jobs were created until 1974 in a high-growth, low-unemployment context. But from the mid-1970s to the late 1990s the picture changed dramatically: average annual employment growth did not exceed 0.2 percent and only one million new jobs were created between 1973 and 1996. Unemployment, which was virtually nonexistent in France as in most other European economies until the early 1970s, rose throughout that period, with only one significant interruption in the late 1980s (figure 10.2). From the 1970s on, each of the major macroeconomic shocks—the

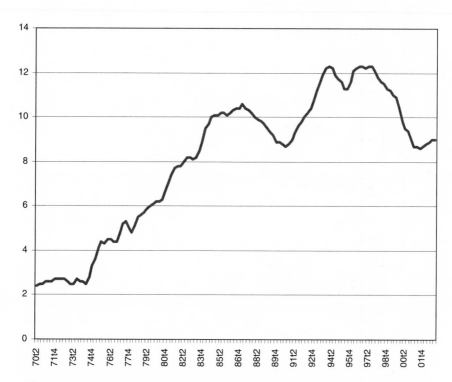

Figure 10.2
Unemployment rate, ILO definition, 1970 to 2002. Source: INSEE.

oil prices hikes, the rise in real interest rates, disinflation, German unification, and the ERM crisis—was associated with an increase in unemployment. In the mid-1990s, the perception that any temporary
increase in unemployment would tend to become persistent was widespread among economists and policy makers. France was a perfect example of the Blanchard-Wolfers (2000) view that unemployment could
be ascribed to the perverse interaction of shocks and institutions.

The employment expansion of the late 1990s to the early 2000s
was thus remarkable. Within five years, from end-1996 to end-2001, 2
million jobs were created and unemployment (ILO definition) was
reduced from 12.1 to 8.6 percent of the labor force before picking up as
a consequence of the economic slowdown that started in 2001. This
evolution came as a surprise to virtually all observers.[1]

The reduction in unemployment affected all categories, but it was especially pronounced for youth unemployment, as apparent in table
10.1 which provides unemployment rates by age and sex for January

Table 10.1
Unemployment rates by age and gender, 1997 to 2002

	Men				Women				All			
	15–24	25–49	>49	All	15–24	25–49	>49	All	15–24	25–49	>49	All
January 1997	25.1	9.8	7.9	10.7	34.8	13.2	8.5	14	29.4	11.3	8.2	12.2
May 2001	17.1	6.5	5.1	7.1	23.1	10.1	6.6	10.4	19.7	8.1	5.8	8.6
December 2002	19.7	7.5	5.9	8.2	24.3	9.4	6.6	10.1	21.7	8.4	6.2	9.1
1997–2001	–8.0	–3.3	–2.8	–3.6	–11.7	–3.1	–1.9	–3.6	–9.7	–3.2	–2.4	–3.6
2001–2002	2.6	1.0	0.8	1.1	1.2	–0.7	0.0	–0.3	2.0	0.3	0.4	0.5

Source: INSEE.
Note: Unemployment is by the ILO definition.

Table 10.2
Unemployment rates by education level, 1990 to 2002

	1990	1997	2002
Total	*9.2*	*12.3*	*8.9*
Primary	13.0	17.5	14.1
Short secondary	8.4	11.4	8.3
Long secondary education	6.5	11.4	8.2
Two years of university	3.7	8.2	5.6
University degree	3.5	7.3	5.7

Source: INSEE, annual employment survey.
Note: Data are for the month in which the survey is conducted (usually March, but January in 1990).

1997 (when unemployment reached a maximum), May 2001 (the recent minimum) and end of 2002.

The reduction in unemployment was also rather evenly distributed among employees of different education levels. In fact it was more pronounced in the low-skilled segment of the labor force, although its level remained extremely high for that category, especially for women (table 10.2). Unemployment decline was less significant in the skilled segment in comparison to 1990, a period in which this category of labor was close to full employment. Two reasons for those evolutions are (1) a significant change in the skill composition of the labor force, as more than two-thirds of the recent entrants have completed secondary education, and (2) a shift in the demand for low-skilled labor, which is discussed in detail below.

Unemployment data give a somewhat distorted picture as participation rates at the two ends of the age distribution are among the lowest in the OECD. A look at employment–population ratios leads to a more sober view: between 1996 and 2001 employment rates rose by about 3 percentage points for the three age groups, but nonemployment remained massive. While the low participation rate of younger persons may reflect the rise in educational enrollment and a preference for studying full time (possibly also statistical problems), the same cannot be said for senior workers, whose participation is low and declining.

COR (2002) indicates that only 45 percent of men and 42 percent of women are in employment at the time of retirement. The majority are enrolled in an early retirement scheme (32 percent of men and 21 percent of women), unemployed (but as they are generally not requested to look for a job, and have a very low probability to being hired anyway, this is practically equivalent to being on early retirement), or inactive. As a consequence, although the average retirement age was just below 60 years for the private sector employees of the 1932 to 1936 cohort that reached retirement age in the 1990s, the average age at which they effectively stopped being employed stood at 57.5 (COR 2002). This gap was virtually inexistent for the older cohorts and did not exceed one year for the 1912 to 1916 cohort. There is no indication that it has been reduced in recent years. In addition CERC (2001) points out that participation is only 60 percent for persons between 25 and 60 without a secondary education, while it is 75 percent on average for all education level. For this category participation has continued to decline in recent years.

Among employed persons a significant proportion of part-time employees indicate that they would wish to work full time. "Constrained part-time," as it is known in France, has receded in the context of a tighter labor market, but according to the annual employment survey it still affected a third (32.6 percent) of the part-time workers in 2002. It should also be mentioned that some 300,000 persons are on government-sponsored contracts in local communities, 60 percent of which part-time. The number of those contracts fluctuates contracyclically, which is a clear indication that they do not correspond to permanent needs but are rather used as an employment policy instrument.

How large is hidden unemployment? Table 10.3 suggests that taking into account part-time workers seeking a full-time job and senior workers on early retirement or not seeking a job would have increased by some 60 percent the number of people experiencing underemployment. A report by Pisani-Ferry (2000) used a different approach. It relied on a rough calculation of the number of jobs that would have to be created for the French economy to reach full employment in 2010

Table 10.3
Indicators of unemployment and underemployment, 2000

	Millions	Percentage of labor force
Unemployment, ILO definition	2.63	10.0
Part-time workers seeking full-time job	1.1	4.1
Senior workers not seeking a job	0.35	1.3
Senior workers on early retirement schemes	0.2	0.9

Source: INSEE, DARES.

(defined as 5 percent unemployment rate plus an increase in participation resulting in a 68.5 percent employment ratio, still below the 70 percent objective set at the EU Lisbon summit). The study reckoned that reaching that target would imply creating 420,000 jobs per year (+1.6 percent per year on average) instead of 300,000 in a constant participation rate scenario and 160,000 on the basis of the labor force projection previously in use, which envisaged a steady decline in the participation rates. In other words, it was assessed that nonparticipation contributed in a major way to underemployment.

10.3 Accounting for the Surprises

The unexpected labor market improvement of the late 1990s raises two main questions: First, how can the rise in labor demand be explained? Second, why did inflation remain subdued? These puzzles are the focus of this section.

10.3.1 A Shift in Labor Demand

France is known for having a large government sector. However, despite the *emplois jeunes* (a scheme introduced in 1997 with the aim of creating jobs for persons under 25 in the nonprofit and government sectors, which resulted in some 225,000 job creations), the net increase in employment in the nonbusiness sector only accounted for some 15 percent of total job creation in 1996 to 2001 (table 10.4). Most new jobs were created in the business sector.

The next usual suspect is economic growth. As was more generally the case in the euro zone, but to a more significant extent, French output growth accelerated markedly in the late 1990s. The contrast with

Table 10.4
Job creation in France, 1996 to 2001 (millions)

Total job creation 1996–2001	1.96
Non–farm business sector	1.80
Agriculture	−0.09
Non–business sector	0.28
• Government and nonprofit (excluding special schemes)	0.37
• Government and nonprofit (special schemes)	0.09
• Military call-up	−0.19

Source: DARES.

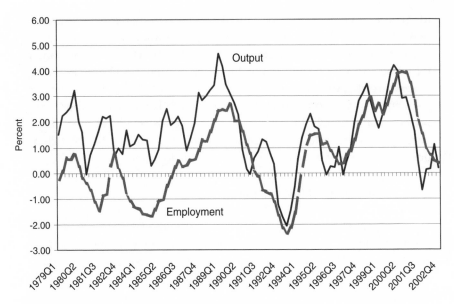

Figure 10.3
Year-on-year output and employment growth, business sector, 1979Q1 to 2002Q4.
Source: Direction de la prévision, INSEE.

the dismal growth performance of the early and mid-1990s was striking. But this performance cannot be deemed exceptional in comparison
to the late 1980s. As figure 10.3 indicates, the difference between the
two periods was that employment growth was significantly higher in
the 1990s while output growth was roughly comparable.

Suspect number 3 is part-time work. Until the early 1990s part-time
work was not widespread in France. At that time French governments
attempted to emulate the Dutch experience. In 1992 and 1993 the
hourly cost of a part-time worker at the level of the minimum wage
was reduced to 85 percent of the cost of a full-time worker through
targeted cuts in social security contributions. Part-time work then
expanded rapidly in services, from 12 percent in 1990 to 16.6 percent
in 1997 (Gonzalez-Demichel et al. 2002), but those jobs were frequently
taken up by persons wishing to work full-time, which gave rise to dis-
satisfaction. Incentives were progressively cut down and they were
eliminated altogether in 1998, as the socialist-led government of Lionel
Jospin chose to foster general working time reduction instead. From
1997 to 2002 the share of part-time work actually declined (to 16.2 per-

cent). While its development certainly has a role in explaining employment in the mid-1990s, it cannot be regarded as relevant for the late 1990s. There is thus evidence that the French economy experienced a significant labor demand shift in the late 1990s.

The most direct explanation for the increase in labor demand is that this is precisely what employment policy had attempted to achieve. Until the early 1990s employment policy had essentially been devoted to containing the rise in unemployment through early retirement and training schemes, and as recently as in 1990, 80 percent of public employment expenditures went to unemployment benefits and early retirement schemes. New priorities emerged in the 1990s, and while political changes introduced some instability in the definition of targets and instruments, there was a high degree of continuity in the broad direction of policy: most of the effort was devoted to fostering labor demand.

10.3.2 Social Security Contribution Cuts

A lasting component of this effort has been the introduction of targeted cuts in the employers' social security contributions. They were initiated by the right-wing Balladur government in 1993 after an influential report (Charpin 1993) had pointed out that although the cost of labor was not especially high in France, it was above average for unskilled workers. The exemption was initially modest, but it was amplified in 1995 and 1996 to reach 18 percent of gross wage at the level of the minimum wage, linearly decreasing to zero for 1.33 minimum wage. In the late 1990s the left-wing Jospin government introduced additional cuts, which were phased-in progressively as companies moved to the 35 hour week. The short-term aim was to use them as a carrot, but the government also regarded those cuts as a structural measure justified in its own right. Finally one of the first measures of the government appointed by president Jacques Chirac after the Right's return to office in 2002 was to amplify the cuts again while making them fully unconditional. This was partly done in order to offset the impact of the planned rise of the minimum wage as the complex multiminimum system resulting from asynchronous working time reduction is being eliminated,[2] but partly also because the government regards the reduction in nonwage costs as a key element of its employment policy. As a result cuts in employers' social security contributions at the level of the

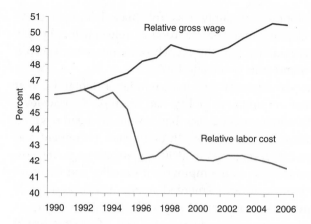

Figure 10.4
Minimum to average wage ratios, 1990 to 2006 (projected). Source: Direction de la prévision.

minimum wage should reach 26 percent of the gross wage in 2006, linearly decreasing to zero for 1.7 minimum wage.

The relative level of the unskilled workers' take-home pay has ended up being disconnected from the relative cost of unskilled labor (figure 10.4): although the former has risen from 46 percent in 1990 to 49 percent in 2002, the latter has decreased from 46 to 42 percent. This very substantial reduction in the tax wedge at the level of the minimum wage entails a significant cost for the budget, which amounted to 14.4 billion euros in 2002 (1 percent of GDP) and is expected to increase to 19.6 billion euros (1.2 percent of GDP) in 2005.

This policy was bound to affect significantly labor costs, since the French wage distribution is heavily skewed: 14 percent of private sector employees are on the minimum wage and 38 percent of them (including part-timers) earn less than 1.3 times the full-time minimum wage (INSEE 2002). This is the natural result from a long-standing policy of using increases in the minimum wage as an income policy instrument. For a large part of the employed population, changes in nonwage costs directly translate into labor cost reductions.

Most of the existing research on the effects of this policy has relied on ex ante simulations based on estimated labor demand parameters. Those evaluations that frequently rely on a three-factor production function, where unskilled labor is regarded as substitutable to a capital-skilled labor aggregate, estimate the effect of the cuts in place before the 1998 reform to be around 250,000 to 300,000 jobs, a 2 percent increase in private employment (see the surveys in Cahuc 2002, Campens et al. 2001, and Pisani-Ferry 2000).[3] The government services' own evaluations are consistent with this order of magnitude.

Crépon and Desplatz (2001) provide the first, and so far only, attempt at an ex post evaluation of the impact of the cuts on the basis of micro data. They base their research on a comparison between the employment behavior of the companies who benefited from the cuts and those who did not (or only benefited to a minor extent). Their point estimate, 460,000 jobs already in 1997 (but with a wide confidence interval), has been disputed because it was regarded as implausibly high (L'Horty 2001; Sterdyniak 2002; Crépon and Desplatz 2002).

Evidence from employment surveys suggests that the reduction in the cost of labor at the level of the minimum wage effectively halted the decline in the proportion of unskilled *jobs* after the social security contribution cuts were introduced in 1993 and 1994. However, in the stagnant context of the mid-1990s, unskilled *workers* were frequently crowded out by more educated workers who had been unable to find a job corresponding to their skills (Audric 2001). This phenomenon only began to recede after unemployment had declined for several years. Recent research suggests it is still present (Nauze-Fichet and Tomasini 2002).

Summing up, available evidence suggests that the cuts in social security contributions have contributed to increasing employment. The obvious downside has been that measured labor productivity has slowed down as more low-productivity workers were included in employment. While in the 1980s and early 1990s high productivity gains (especially in comparison to the United States, where economists were puzzled by the decline in labor productivity and the public alarmed by the spread of McJobs) resulted from the exclusion of those workers from employment, from the mid-1990s on the opposite evolution took place (unsurprisingly, the French began lamenting about McJobs, while economists started to be puzzled by low productivity gains). Labor input in France is still measured without correcting for changes in quality, but a back-of-the envelope calculation suggests this effect could be significant: assuming the share of unskilled labor in total employment was stabilized instead of declining by 0.4 to 0.5 percentage points per year, and that the productivity of an unskilled job is half that of an average job, the evolution that has been observed since the mid-1990s could account for a quarter of a percentage point decline in measured labor productivity growth.[4]

10.3.3 The 35 Hours Experiment

Although inspiration was different, the working time reduction implemented by the Jospin government also aimed at boosting labor demand. There were three main rationales for it.[5] The first was simply work sharing, for which support was strong (although economists had warned against the fallacy that the available amount of labor could be considered as given, their arguments carried little weight in the stagnant employment of context of the mid-1990s). A more sophisticated version of the argument started from the observation that the historical trend toward reducing working time had come to a halt in the 1980s. Provided the legislated reduction in working time only anticipated the natural trend, it could reduce unemployment and limit hysteresis in the medium run without affecting the long-run choice between income and leisure.

The second rationale was to use the 35-hour week as a banner for the overriding priority of job creation. A recurrent policy theme of the 1990s was that in France, as in several other European countries, priority had consistently been given to individual wage gains at the cost of stagnating employment. For the left, working time reduction could be an acceptable quid pro quo for wage moderation.[6] In a way the 35 hours were a metaphor for a wider employment-oriented social compromise.

The third rationale was a more indirect one. France's industrial relation system combines weak and fragmented unions (at least in the private sector) and a relatively rigid and, above all, complex system of labor laws, which in large part result from collective agreements negotiated at the industry or the national level that are given the force of law by government decision. Contrary to what is frequently assumed, those agreements have little bearing on wage formation, for which negotiation (if any) is extremely decentralized.[7] As a result negotiations are infrequent and rarely ambitious: before the working time reduction process was initiated, less that one-fourth of private sector employees were covered by a firm-level collective agreement (Barrat and Daniel 2002). Against this background the working time reduction was regarded as an occasion to encourage decentralized negotiations at the company level where discussions could be held simultaneously on work organization, wages, and employment. The aim was to foster "efficient" agreements involving productivity-enhancing reorganization or the adoption of more flexible arrangements, wage moderation, and job creation. The justification was that those efficient agreements were prevented from happening spontaneously for two reasons: first, because of ossified industrial relations and, second, because employment creation involves an externality in the form of a reduction of the unemployment insurance contributions burden.

In this spirit significant changes to labor regulation were made possible by law on the occasion of the move to the 35 h workweek: for example, working time could be defined in annual terms rather than weekly terms. An incentive element was also added through conditional cuts in social security contributions that were intended to internalize the job creation externality.

Working time reduction actually started in 1996 with the Robien law introduced under the right-wing government of Alain Juppé. At that time the approach was based on social contribution incentives and did not involve changes in the legal working time. After a new majority had come to power with the aim of moving to a 35 h workweek, it was phased in two steps: In 1998, additional incentives were introduced for companies moving to 35 h. In 2000, the legal working time was lowered from 39 h to 35 h per week, but additional overtime leeway was temporarily introduced and small business was given supplementary delays. After the presidential and general elections of 2002 the new government decided not to change the legal working time. Nevertheless, the overtime leeway was extended, and all social security contribution cuts were made unconditional. Both sticks and carrots were thus eliminated, and companies were left with no incentive to reduce working time.[8]

At mid-2002 about 60 percent of employees in the business sectors had moved to a new working time schedule (Ministry of Finance 2002). The breakdown was 80 percent in companies with 20 employees or more, and only 20 percent in companies with less than 20 employees. As a consequence average working time in the business sector was reduced by 4.5 percent between 1998 and 2002.

The actual experience was very far from mere work sharing. Total hours worked expanded significantly at the time the workweek was reduced (figure 10.5). But the impact of the 35 h on employment is still controversial. Most estimates of its effects, even careful ones (e.g., see Heyer and Timbeau 2000), are based on a similar methodology and suffer from the same shortcomings. They inject back-of-the envelope calculations of the ex ante effects of work sharing—based on estimates of the proportion of companies effectively implementing working time

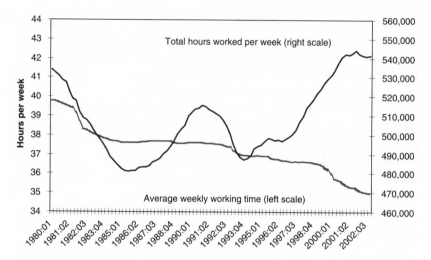

Figure 10.5
Work time and total hours worked, 1980 to 2002. Source: DARES, Mission analyse économique.

reduction and the efficiency gains brought by reorganization—into a macroeconometric model. The ex post effects thus differ to the extent that (1) working time reduction entails an increase in unit labor costs and (2) the decrease in unemployment gives rise to wage and price increases. Depending on assumptions and parameters, the expected employment gains range between 200,000 and 500,000. These are obviously short- and medium-term effects. In the long run, working time reduction cannot have positive effects on unemployment in such a setting, as the unemployment rate converges toward the NAIRU, unless there is significant hysteresis (Cette 2000).[9]

No comprehensive ex post evaluation of the impact of the 35h initiative has been published so far, but partial indications are available based on the comparative behavior of the companies that embarked early on working time reduction (Rouilleault 2001). They suggest that those companies have effectively achieved significant productivity gains and increased employment. When corrected for selection bias, corresponding estimates of the overall effect of the working time reduction are on the order of magnitude of 300,000 jobs (Jugnot 2002). But they are surrounded by significant uncertainty.

Table 10.5 decomposes the effects of working time reduction on unit labor costs as estimated by the Ministry of Finance. As the table shows, thanks to a combination of wage moderation, productivity gains, and

Table 10.5
Effects of working time reduction, 1998 to 2002

Impact of the working time reduction on average	
Working time $(1) = (2) - (3)$	−4.5%
• Labor productivity per head (2)	−2.1%
• Hourly labor productivity (3)	+2.4%
Monthly wage (4)	−1.1%
Unit labor costs before social security contribution cuts $(5) = (1) + (4)$	+1.0%
Impact of social security contribution cuts (6)	−1.3%
Impact on unit labor costs $(7) = (5) + (6)$	−0.3%

Source: Ministry of Finance.

social security contribution cuts, the 35h week has not given rise to an increase in unit labor costs. Assuming that it has had no effect on output (which is consistent with the result that unit labor costs have remained roughly constant), it suggests employment could have risen by 2.1 percent in 1998 to 2002 (the opposite of the decline in productivity per head), which also corresponds to 300,000 jobs.

This evaluation is fragile. First, it is not based on an explicit methodology for correcting selection bias. Second, the measured effects are short and medium term. Long-term effects should be less favorable, after the full effects of working time reduction on the cost of labor and labor market equilibrium conditions are taken into account. This especially applies to the minimum wage, which is going to increase by more than 10 percent in real terms as a consequence of the elimination of the multiminimum system. Finally, as for (unconditional) social security contributions cuts, the approach remains a partial equilibrium one. Nevertheless, it suggests that working time reduction has played a significant role in the recent employment record of the French economy.

10.3.4   How Welcome Is the Productivity Slowdown?

Social security contribution cuts and the working time reduction both contributed to reducing output per head, thereby temporarily increasing the "job content of growth." However, they do not suffice to explain the slowdown in labor productivity gains that was observed in France as in several other European countries.

Two other candidates are (1) labor market deregulation and (2) wage moderation. As a result of legislations introduced in the 1980s

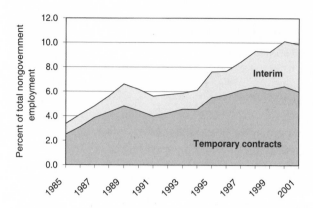

Figure 10.6
Employees on nonstandard work contracts, 1985 to 2001. Source: INSEE, Employment survey.

and despite some regulatory tightening in the 1990s, nonstandard work contracts (fixed-term contracts or *contrats à durée déterminée*—CDD—and interim) have experienced a significant development (figure 10.6). Although their share somewhat diminished when a tighter labor markets improved the bargaining position of employees, they represent some 10 percent of total employment—less than in other European countries such as Spain, because CDDs cannot be renewed, but still a noticeable development. Their impact on labor productivity is through two different channels. First, as severance costs and non-monetary costs of separation are typically lower than for standard contracts, CDDs reduce the present value of the cost of hiring an employee. Second, as discussed by Blanchard and Landier (2002), CDDs have the effect of encouraging high turnover for entry-level jobs, with potentially detrimental consequences on efficiency. The first of these effects is comparable to that of a reduction in the cost of un-skilled labor and should not affect total factor productivity (if properly measured), but the second one may lead to lowering TFP.

A more general reason for the productivity slowdown is labor deepening as a consequence of protracted wage moderation. Wage moderation has been consistently encouraged by governments since the 1980s, resulting in a correction of the initial "wage gap" and a medium-term drop in the share of labor in value added. This evolution may have resulted in a reversal of the capital deepening that had been observed throughout the 1980s and the early 1990s (Carnot and Quinet 2000).

Table 10.6
Decomposition of the labor productivity slowdown

Labor productivity per head, of which:	−0.5
Labor deepening	−1.2
Working time reduction	−0.4
TFP	+0.6
Cyclical factors	+0.4

Source: Cette, Mairesse, and Kocoglu (2002).
Note: 1995 to 2000 compared to 1990 to 1995, average annual growth rates.

Turning to the evidence, Cette, Mairesse, and Kocoglu (2002) provide a decomposition of the productivity slowdown, which is reported in table 10.6. As the table shows, labor deepening could have played an important part in the productivity slowdown, but these is no evidence of TFP slowdown. In fact TFP could have been accelerated (which would imply that the transition to a "job-rich growth" has not been detrimental to efficiency).

10.3.5 Why Did Wage Increases Remain Restrained?

The second major puzzle of the late 1990s to early 2000s is the persistence of wage moderation despite unprecedented employment gains. At the end of the previous phase of expansion, in 1990 wage accelerated markedly as unemployment was approaching 9 percent. But this did not happen until 2001, at least for monthly wages, and the acceleration observed in 2001 remained modest by historical standards (figure 10.7). Even hourly wage inflation, which was affected by the reduction in working time, remained below the level reached in 1990.

In 1999 and 2000 most available estimates put the NAIRU between 9 and 11 percent (OECD 2000; Pisani-Ferry 2000), which is consistent with the empirical evidence of the late 1980s. The risk of wage inflation is confirmed by quantity indicators: labor market tensions were visibly on the rise as a growing number of firms reported hiring difficulties, including for low-skill categories.

Figure 10.8 provides pseudo–Beveridge curve.[10] Several interesting observations can be made. First, from the mid-1970s to the late 1980s reported hiring difficulties remained at a low, roughly constant level while unemployment was almost continuously on the rise. When it receded in 1988 to 1990, there was an almost immediate increase in the

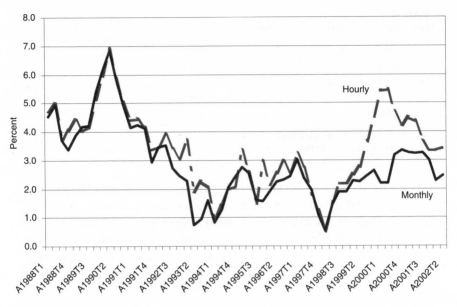

Figure 10.7
Monthly and hourly nominal wage growth, 1988Q2 to 2002Q2. Source: INSEE.

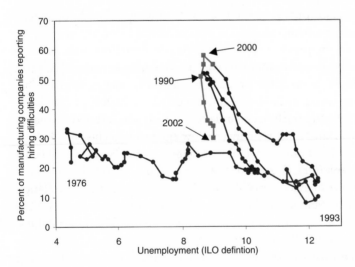

Figure 10.8
Beveridge curve, 1976 to 2002. Source: INSEE

proportion of firms reporting hiring difficulties, a clear indication that the Beveridge curve had shifted to the right. Together with wage increases, this was strong evidence that structural unemployment was effectively close to 9 percent. The same kind of behavior reappeared in the late 1990s as the proportion of firms reporting hiring difficulties reached 58 percent in 2000, an all-time record. However, wages did not rise as in 1990.

There are basically two potential explanations for this. The most favorable one is that the NAIRU had declined because social security contribution cuts had priced in low-productivity workers who were previously excluded from employment. According to Laroque and Salanié (2000), those cuts should have reduced classical unemployment by 2 percentage points (which is on the high side of estimates). Other active employment measures targeted at long-term or youth unemployment may have contributed to the improvement.[11] Finally increased competition within the European market and lower real interest rates should have played in the same direction.[12] With this optimistic interpretation, we can take comfort by the fact that hiring difficulties dropped rapidly in 2001 and 2002, which suggests that the further shift in the Beveridge curve was more apparent than real: reported hiring difficulties could have reflected problems in adjusting to a high flow of recruitments.

The less optimistic interpretation is that the absence of significant wage inflation should be attributed to a specific factor. As the legal working time reduction took effect on 1 January 2000 for larger companies, most of them had already undertaken or concluded negotiations on its implementation. A large proportion of the agreements (around 73 percent for those concluded before 2000 and 47 percent for those concluded in 2000) included a two to three year wage freeze or a wage moderation clause (Bloch-London, Pham, and Zilberman 2002). Wage inflation was thus paradoxically contained by the 35h week. When the wage moderation clauses expired, the economic context had already deteriorated.

Whatever the interpretation, the coexistence of a high unemployment rate and hiring difficulties cannot be taken as an indication that the labor market is working properly. In the early 2000s, realization that the French economy was moving fast from a demand-constrained to a supply-constrained environment prompted a reorientation of labor market policy priorities.

10.4   The Emergence of New Policy Issues

While the overriding priority of employment and unemployment policy in the 1990s was to encourage the demand for labor, new priorities began to emerge in the 2000s. As employment picked up and unemployment receded, the focus moved to new issues: inactivity traps, their impact on labor supply, and the possible remedies; the reform of the unemployment insurance system; and job security.

10.4.1   Inactivity Traps

France introduced in 1988 a universal minimum income, the *revenu minimum d'insertion* (RMI). It was initially supposed to conditional, but in the high-unemployment context of the 1990s, the number of beneficiaries rapidly exceeded all forecasts to reach one million at the end of the decade. By that time the incentive component of the RMI had been forgotten, and for all practical purposes it could be regarded as an unconditional income support.

The level of the RMI was initially set at roughly 50 percent of the net full-time monthly minimum wage for a single person, with additional income support depending on the structure of the family. This was considered a reasonable compromise between the two objectives of alleviating poverty and encouraging participation in the labor force. But as part-time work developed in the 1990s, a larger number of recipients were confronted with a choice between remaining on the minimum income and taking up a part-time minimum wage job. Because the RMI was designed as a differential income, meaning any labor income up to its level was effectively taxed at 100 percent, the gain for taking up such a job was nil. What had been conceived as compatible with encouraging participation had in effect become an inactivity trap.

The very strong labor supply reduction triggered by a parental income for nonworking mothers with children introduced in 1994 had warned that significant effects could be expected.[13] Significant research was thus devoted to reaching a precise diagnosis. It has revealed that the RMI was actually only part of the problem, as a number of other benefits such as housing allowances and allowances for single parents had the same characteristics. Laroque and Salanié (1999) have pointed out that four million persons were confronted with marginal tax rates on labor income above 90 percent. Taking into account the quality of the jobs that persons on the minimum income could be expected to find, Gurgand and Margolis (2001) have shown that the net expected long-term gain from taking up a job was inferior to 100 euros per month for one-fourth of the minimum income recipients and between 100 euros and 200 euros for another fourth. Recent research gives an even grimmer picture: many municipalities provide supplementary benefits to minimum income recipients, so obstacles on the way to employment can be significantly higher. A survey of ten local situations by Anne and L'Horty (2002) indicated that moving from the minimum income to a full-time job on the minimum wage actually frequently implied an income loss![14]

In 1998, a new policy direction was taken, and a series of measures were introduced to reduce the disincentive effects of effective marginal labor income taxation. The possibility of cumulating the minimum income in 1998, and a wage income for up to one year, was offered to minimum income recipients. In 1999, the housing tax was reformed in order to limit the disincentive effects of existing exemptions. In 2000, housing allowances were reformed in the same direction. Finally, a tax credit on labor income, the *prime pour l'emploi*, was introduced in 2001, together with a reform of the income tax exemption regime for low-income households. Of those measures the most symbolic and therefore the most controversial one was the *prime pour l'emploi*. Although a major union supported it, several others opposed vehemently to what they perceived as an intrusion of the state in the wage-bargaining process and as a threat to the minimum wage. The measure was also controversial within the socialist-led parliamentary majority. But it was nevertheless legislated and is now part of the landscape.

According to Hagneré and Trannoy (2002), those reforms have had a substantial effect on the incentive to take up a job.[15] First, they have eliminated many peaks in the effective marginal tax rate on labor income, making thereby disposable income a monotonic function of the primary income. Second, taking up a job, even part time, always increases disposable income in the first year: effective marginal tax rates on labor income are below 25 percent as recipients keep the minimum income for the entire year. For example, the annual gain from working full time is increased by 3,500 euros in comparison to the pre-reform situation. Third, in the long run moving to a part-time job still involves a very modest gain, but the annual gain from working full time is increased by 1,500 euros. Fourth, other things being equal, effective marginal tax rates are always higher for part-time jobs than for full-time jobs. The tax and benefit system thus provides incentives to work full time: part-time work can only pay as a labor market entry strategy.

Although the improvement is significant, there are two noticeable downsides. The first one is the high budgetary costs of the reforms: around 4.5 billion euros, close to a third of a percentage point of GDP (the cost was in fact higher before it was decided in 2002 not to implement the third planned increase in the *prime pour l'emploi*). This would be a high price to pay if only efficiency gains had to be expected. The labor supply effects of the reforms have not been studied extensively yet, but they are generally expected to be modest, as the *prime pour l'emploi* may have ambiguous effects on the participation of women (Cahuc 2001; Laroque and Salanié 2001). However, the reforms, especially the *prime pour l'emploi* which was introduced simultaneously with a cut in the marginal income tax rates, also had distributional objectives.

The second downside is that the design of the reforms signals a disputable aversion for part-time work. It is frequently claimed that public policy should not "subsidize" part-time work. However, as effective marginal tax rates on part-time labor income are significantly higher than on full-time income, this is far from being the case. Neutrality with respect to individual choices would imply having the same effective tax rate. The government has signaled an intention to go in this direction.

10.4.2 Unemployment Insurance

Another focus of recent discussions and reforms has been the functioning of the labor market. French policy in this field has been noticeably prone to instability. Before 1992, unemployment benefits were typically constant for fourteen months, then dropped to a level equivalent to that of the minimum income. The sudden drop was replaced in 1992 by a step-by-step decline: benefits were reduced by 17 percent every four months until they reached the minimum level. In 2001, employers and unions[16] agreed on a new system that has two main characteristics. First, it puts a new focus on the balance between rights and responsibilities. Each recipient must sign a contract which spells out its obligations. No new legally binding obligations are introduced, but the contract signals a willingness to enforce the existing obligation of active job search.[17] The contract also spells out the responsibility of the employment services. Second, the step-by-step decline in the level of the benefits is eliminated. Benefits are now constant without duration limits, provided the recipient fulfills its obligations.

The effects of the 1992 reform have been studied by Dormont, Fougère, and Prieto (2001). They find that the sudden benefit drop after fourteen months was associated with a peak in the rate of exit from unemployment, which was unsurprisingly eliminated by the reform. Their other finding is that the average exit rate has declined with the reform, especially for skilled persons. No research on the new reform has been published yet. Preliminary findings by Crépon point to a positive effect of signing the contract. However, anecdotal evidence suggests enforcement is frequently lacking, in part because of a scarcity of resources. The credibility of the system is thus uncertain. Furthermore, as deteriorating economic conditions have led to a deficit in the unemployment insurance system, its sustainability is also questionable.

10.4.3 Employment Protection

French governments have in recent years consistently refrained from reducing employment protection for employees on permanent contracts (if anything, legislation introduced in 2002 increased the delays for companies undertaking collective layoffs). Liberalization has basically taken place through the development of temporary contracts. As a consequence France ranks high as regards the strictness Employment Protection Legislation (EPL) as measured by the OECD.

In this respect governments essentially respond to popular demand. Public opposition to layoffs is widespread and vocal, especially in small towns, in manufacturing, and among senior workers. It has not been weakened by the introduction of temporary contracts as employees perceive permanent contracts as a guarantee against the risk of unemployment. It has not receded in the years of high-employment creation either.

The rationale for opposition to layoffs is that they generally imply remaining out of employment for a long period (50 percent of employees are still without a job after twenty months) and entail a durable income loss (Margolis 2001, 2002). Furthermore the probability of finding a new job is very low for workers above 50.

Discussions on alternative security concepts based on employability, training and placement have started but have not yet resulted in reform proposals.

10.5   Conclusions

In the last decade successive left-wing and right-wing French governments have introduced important changes in labor market policy. Despite significant differences a noticeable degree of continuity has prevailed in their approach. Common characteristics include:

• a refusal to consider radical reform in areas such as employment protection legislation, unemployment insurance, and minimum wage legislation;[18]

• a sympathy for active labor market policies;

• a strong focus on fostering labor demand, especially for unskilled workers;

• a heavy reliance on tax or social security incentives;

• a willingness to contemplate unconventional measures such as working time reduction.

The implicit diagnosis behind this approach was that the French labor markets suffered more from insufficient labour demand than from high firing costs, excessive unionization, or overgenerous welfare benefits. Judging from the job creation of the late 1990s and the early 2000s, this approach has produced better results than anticipated by policy makers (not to speak of the view of outside observers). While the level of employment remains modest in comparison to the achievements of some other European countries, this can be taken as an encouragement for unconventional active labor market policies.

There are, however, three important caveats.

First, direct evidence on the effect of French labor market policy remains scant. Some other European countries that have not made similar choices have also experienced favorable developments. Why labor productivity has slowed down simultaneously in several European countries remains a puzzle for research.

Second, the budgetary cost of this strategy is far from trivial. Table 10.7 gives some orders of magnitude. Although it does not include data after 2000 and does not take into account the cost of tax and benefits reforms, the size of the effort and the degree to which expenditures have been reoriented toward active policies is already noticeable. As developed in the text, expenditures on the financing of social security contribution cuts should increase from 0.8 percent of GDP in 2000 to 1.2 percent by the mid-2000s; the (gross) cost of the reforms in the tax-

Table 10.7
Public spending on employment programs, 1990 to 2000 (% of GDP)

	1990	1997	2000
Unemployment benefits	1.32	1.55	1.46
Subsidies to labor supply reductions	0.56	0.36	0.27
Support to nonbusiness sector employment	0.07	0.24	0.41
Support to business sector employment	0.22	1.13	1.23
with cuts in social security contributions	0.00	0.58	0.82
Training programs for unemployed persons	0.34	0.39	0.27
Functioning of the labor market	0.06	0.07	0.08
Total	2.57	3.74	3.73

Source: DARES.

benefits system through the *prime pour l'emploi* and related measures amounts to another 0.3 percentage points; finally, the cost of reforming the unemployment insurance system can be evaluated in the neighbourhood of 0.1 percent of GDP. The cost of supporting business sector employment through social security contribution cuts and tax incentives, which amounted to 1.2 percent of GDP in 2000 (table 10.7) should thus reach some 2 percent of GDP in 2005.

Third, new priorities must be addressed if unemployment is to be further reduced. The experience of 2000 and 2001 suggests some issues that should rank high in the priority list: the functioning of the labor market and the efficiency of the employment agency in contributing to the labor demand–labor supply matching process; the retraining system, which is notoriously inefficient; the participation of older workers, which remains exceptionally low; mobility; and alternative approaches to workers security that do not rely on employment protection legislation. Adopting the same kind of strategy to address or at least alleviate these problems would require significant additional resources against the background of a deteriorating budgetary situation. In a context of increasing strains linked to the ageing of the population and intra-European tax competition, it is doubtful that those resources will be readily available, even if cyclical conditions improve.

In other words, France has been able to achieve noticeable results in the reduction of mass unemployment while preserving essential tenets of its social and labor relation models, but at a significant budgetary cost. Whether this strategy is financially and politically sustainable is likely to be increasingly an issue in the years to come.

Notes

I thank the *Direction de la prévision* as well as Frédéric Lerais and the DARES for both data and discussions. I am grateful to Gilbert Cette, Juan Jimeno, and Bertrand Martinot for stimulating comments.

1. In 1997, a medium-term projection released by the Ministry of Finance (1997) envisaged 3 percent annual growth in 1998 to 2002 but, despite this optimistic assumption, reckoned that the unemployment rate would still stand at 11 percent at end-2002. In a report to the prime minister, Olivier Blanchard and Jean-Paul Fitoussi (1998) reached somewhat less pessimistic but qualitatively similar conclusions.

2. In order to ensure that minimum wage workers would not suffer a reduction in their monthly wage as a consequence of the work time reduction, a legal minimum guaranty was introduced at the level of $(39/35) \times$ the minimum wage at the time of the move from a 39- to a 35-hour workweek schedule. As companies were given latitude to choose at what date they would implement the work time reduction, the minimum wage at the time of the move was not identical for the different cohorts. Hence the coexistence of five, nonconverging guarantees, whose level all exceed $35 \times$ the minimum wage. They will be replaced by a single (but higher) minimum wage.

3. These are partial equilibrium simulations that do not take into account the impact of financing the contribution costs. It is often claimed that this policy is self-financing because it essentially activates passive labor market policies. However, the revenues accrue to the social security (which is managed by social partners) while the costs are supported by the state budget.

4. Recent research by Melka et al. (2003) finds that the growth rate in the quality of employed labor has declined by this amount between the first and the second half of the 1990s.

5. The rationale for a working time reduction is presented in Cette and Taddei (2000) and Taddei (1997).

6. This is why the process was launched by a conference on employment, wages and working time chaired by the prime minister, whose aim was to emulate the famous Dutch Wassenaar agreements. The conference, however, ended in a bitter dispute between the government and the employers federation, and no further negotiations took place at the central level.

7. Apart from public-sector pay, the only way centralized decisions affect wage formation is through setting the minimum wage, which increases annually according to a formula combining 100 percent ex post price indexation and 50 percent indexation on average hourly real wage gains, plus a discretionary increase decided by the government.

8. For those remaining on a 39h schedule, the only practical consequence is a 10 percent surcharge on hours worked beyond the 35th.

9. Working time reduction has also been studied in a long-run setting (d'Autume and Cahuc 1997; Cahuc 2001) where labor demand is determined by an explicit profit-maximization behavior and wages result from a bargaining process. Results depend on the choice of parameters. Long-run positive effects on employment are possible if significant productivity gains are realized on the occasion of the work time reduction and if it is supported by public subsidies, but negative effects can easily be found.

10. As French statistics do not record vacancies in a time-consistent manner, it is not possible to construct a standard Beveridge curve for the French labor market. However, a proxy can be built using surveys on hiring difficulties reported by manufacturing companies. There are two shortcomings in this approach. First, the data only cover a fraction of the labor market, which may be subject to specific shortages. Second, survey results can be influenced by the respondent's recent experience: after a period of protracted labor market slack, companies may tend to overestimate the difficulties they are facing in finding suitable candidates to fill vacant positions.

11. As for the United States (Katz and Krueger 1999), demographic changes may also account for a half a percentage point reduction (Pisani-Ferry 2000).

12. This is not to say that other factors, such as inactivity traps, have not had a negative role (more on this below).

13. Piketty (1998) has shown that the participation rate in the eligible population has dropped by 15 percentage points.

14. Anne and L'Horty compute a "reservation working time" that for single persons stands at 26h before taking into account local benefits but at 44h after they are taken into account.

15. Hagneré and Trannoy, however, do not take local benefits into account. They also assume full implementation of the *prime pour l'emploi*, which was supposed to be phased in three steps. However, the 2003 budget does not implement the third step as initially planned.

16. Not all unions agreed, but this was not necessary to make the agreement valid.

17. In the previous regime, benefits were conditional on active job-seeking behavior, but in practice, the conditionality was low.

18. The creation of a minimum wage for young workers was attempted in the early 1990s, but the government had to backtrack in face of strong student opposition.

References

Anne, D., and Y. L'Horty. 2002. Transferts sociaux locaux et retour à l'emploi. *Economie et statistique*, no. 357–358 (www.insee.fr).

Audric, S. 2001. La reprise de la croissance de l'emploi profite-t-elle aussi aux non-diplômés? INSEE, *Document de travail* G2001-02 (www.insee.fr).

Barrat, O., and C. Daniel. 2002. La négociation d'entreprise de 1995 à 2000. *Données sociales*, INSEE.

D'Autume, A., and P. Cahuc. 1997. Réduction de la durée du travail et emploi: Une synthèse. In P. Cahuc and P. Granier, eds., *La Réduction du temps de travail: Une solution pour l'emploi?* Paris: Economica.

Blanchard, O., and J.-P. Fitoussi. 1998. Croissance et chômage. Conseil d'analyse économique, report 4. Paris: La Documentation française.

Blanchard, O., and A. Landier. 2002. The perverse effect of partial labour market reform: Fixed-term contracts in France. *Economic Journal* 112: 214–44.

Blanchard, O., and J. Wolfers. 2000. The role of shocks and institutions in European un-employment: The aggregate evidence. *Economic Journal* 110: C1–C33.

Bloch-London, C., T.-H. Pham, and S. Zilberman. 2002. La mise en oeuvre des 35 heures. *Données sociales*, INSEE.

Bourguignon, F., and D. Bureau. 1999. L'architecture des prélèvements en France: État des lieux et voies de réforme. Rapport du Conseil d'analyse économique 17. Paris: La Documentation française (www.cae.gouv.fr).

Cahuc, P. 2001. L'expérience française de réduction du temps de travail: Moins d'emplois et plus d'inégalités. *Revue française d'économie* 15 (3).

Cahuc, P. 2002. Baisser les charges sociales: Jusqu'où et comment? Centre d'observation économique de la Chambre de commerce de Paris, *Document de travail*.

Campens, E., S. Doisy, S. Duchêne, and C. Gianella. 2001. Allégements de charges au voisinage du SMIC et chômage structurel: Une modélisation à partir d'un modèle de matching avec hétérogénéité des qualifications. Mimeo.

Carnot, N., and A. Quinet. 2000. L'enrichissement du contenu en emploi de la croissance: Une tentative de clarification. In J. Pisani-Ferry, ed., *Les Chemins du plein emploi*. Rapport du Conseil d'analyse économique 30. Paris: La Documentation française.

Conseil de l'Emploi, des Revenus et de la Cohésion sociale (CERC). 2001. *Accès à l'emploi et protection sociale*. Rapport 1. Paris: La Documentation française.

Conseil d'Orientation des Retraites (COR). 2002. *Retraites: Renouveler le contrat entre les générations*, Premier rapport 2001. Paris: La Documentation française.

Cette, G. 2000. Les 35 heures: Quels effets et quels risques? In J. Pisani-Ferry, ed., *Les Chemins du plein emploi*. Rapport du Conseil d'analyse économique 30. Paris: La Documentation française.

Cette, G., and D. Taddei. 1998. *La Réduction de la durée du travail: Les 35 Heures*. Paris: Le Livre de Poche.

Cette, G., J. Mairesse, and Y. Kocoglu. 2002. Diffusion of ICT and growth of the French economy over the long term, 1980–2000. *International Productivity Monitor*, no. 4.

Charpin, J.-M. 1993. *L'Économie française en perpective*. Rapport du Commissariat Général du Plan. Paris: La Découverte.

Crépon, B., and R. Desplatz. 2001. Une nouvelle évaluation des effets des allégements de charges sur les bas salaires. *Economie et statistique*, no. 348.

Crépon, B., and R. Desplatz. 2002. Reply to Sterdyniak (2002). *Revue de l'OFCE*, no. 82.

Dormont, B., D. Fougère, and A. Prieto. 2001. L'effet de l'allocation unique dégressive sur la reprise d'emploi. *Economie et statistique*, no. 343 (www.insee.fr).

Gonzalez-Demichel, C., E. Nauze-Fichet, and S. Seguin. 2002. Les performances du marché du travail au tournant du XXI° siècle. *Données sociales*, INSEE.

Gurgand, M., and D. Margolis. 2001. RMI et revenus du travail: Une évaluation des gains financiers à l'emploi. *Economie et statistique*, no. 308/309/310 (www.insee.fr).

Hagneré, C., and A. Trannoy. 2001. L'impact conjugué de trois ans de réforme sur les comportements d'activité. *Economie et statistique*, no. 346 (www.insee.fr).

Heyer, E., and X. Timbeau. 2000. 35 heures: Réduction réduite. *Revue de l'OFCE*, no. 74.

INSEE. 2002. *L'Économie française 2002–2003*. Paris: Le Livre de Poche.

Jugnot, S. 2002. Combien d'emploi créés par la réduction du temps de travail? *Données sociales*, INSEE.

Katz, L., and A. Krueger. 1999. The high-pressure US labor market of the 1990s. *Brookings Papers on Economic Activity* 1: 1–87.

Laroque, G., and B. Salanié. 2000. Une décomposition du non-emploi en France. *Economie et statistique*, no. 331 (www.insee.fr).

L'Horty, Y. 2001. Commentaire sur Crépon et Desplatz (2001). *Economie et statistique*, no. 348.

Marchand, O., and C. Thélot. 1997. *Le Travail en France, 1800–2000*. Paris: Nathan.

Margolis, D. 2000. Workers displacement in France. *Document de travail CREST-INSEE* 2000-01 (www.crest.fr).

Margolis, D. 2002. Licenciements collectifs et délais de reprise d'emploi. *Economie et Statisique*, no. 351 (www.insee.fr).

Melka, J., L. Nayman, S. Zignago, and N. Mulder. 2003. Skills, technology and growth: Is ICT the key to success. *CEPII Working Paper* 2003-04 (www.cepii.fr).

Ministry of Finance. 1997. Tendances de long terme de l'économie française. In DARES/ DP/INSEE, *Bilan économique et social de la France*. Paris: La Documentation française.

Ministry of Finance. 2002. *Rapport économique, social et financier*. Paris: Ministère de l'Economie, des Finances et de l'Industrie.

Nauze-Fichet, E., and M. Tomasini. 2002. Diplôme et insertion sur le marché du travail: Approches socioprofessionnelle et salariale du déclassement. *Economie et Statistique*, no. 354.

OECD. 2000. *Economic Survey of France*. Paris: OECD.

Piketty, T. 1998. L'impact des incitations financières au travail sur les comportements individuels: Une estimation sur le cas français. *Economie et prévision*, no. 132-133.

Pisani-Ferry, J. 2000. *Les Chemins du plein emploi*. Rapport du Conseil d'analyse économique 30. Paris: La Documentation française (www.cae.gouv.fr).

Rouilleault, H. 2001. *Réduction du temps de travail: Les Enseignements de l'observation*. Paris: Commissariat Général du Plan.

Sterdyniak, H. 2002. Fiche de lecture (on Crépon and Desplatz 2001). *Revue de l'OFCE*, no. 81.

Taddei, D. 1997. La réduction du temps de travail. Rapport du Conseil d'analyse économique 1. Paris: La Documentation française.

11 Unemployment in Germany: Reasons and Remedies

Norbert Berthold and Rainer Fehn

11.1 Introduction

In contrast to a number of other European countries and especially in contrast to the United States, Germany has made almost no progress in reforming labor market institutions and the welfare state in order to reduce stubbornly high unemployment rates. In fact persistently high unemployment rates are just one side of the coin of the overall economic performance that is far from satisfactory. The other side is the lackluster performance with respect to growth rates, where in the course of the 1990s Germany was outperformed not only by the United States but also by a number of other European countries. This has been the case even though, according to standard growth theory, eastern Germany should witness particularly high growth rates based on a catch-up process just as West Germany did in the 1950s and 1960s. The German economy now lacks the robustness and vitality of that era. It still relies mostly on its competitive edge in medium–high technology trade, but it is weak in areas of high technology, such as computers, communication technology, and biotechnology. It should therefore not be surprising that Germany, which used to be the economic powerhouse in the European Union, is increasingly called the "sick man of Europe" suggesting that something is rotten in its institutional setting.

The German concept of *Soziale Marktwirtschaft* used to be very successful with respect to both labor market performance and growth

---

Editor's note: Rainer Fehn died in the summer of 2003 (after having prepared a revised version of this manuscript). He had suffered from a severe disease for several years, but his death came unexpectedly for all his colleagues and friends. Aged 34, he left a wife and two small children. Rainer Fehn will remain in our memories as a bright and promising young scholar. We deeply regret the loss for his family.

rates, at least until the 1970s and maybe even until the 1980s, reconciling the interests of organized labor and capital. Some thirty years ago Germany's institutions, along with its low unemployment rates and social cohesion, were the envy of the world. Its unemployment rate was about one-fifth of that in the United States, which was then about the same as it is today. Today Germany has an unemployment rate about twice as high as that of the United States. Other European countries such as Britain, Switzerland, the Netherlands, or Denmark have been much more successful in keeping unemployment at acceptable levels.

Considering that well-designed institutions are a key factor for good economic performance in the long run, there are two main types of explanations for this discrepancy between the past and present economic performance of Germany relative to other OECD countries. First, German institutions' worsening over time relative to other countries, or even in absolute terms, might reflect the negative influence of special interest groups on political decision making. Second, the economic environment has changed, so a formerly appropriate German institutional setup fostering GDP growth and high employment might no longer be conducive to achieving these goals. There is widespread evidence that the economy of the twenty-first century, which has globalization and great technological advancement as its hallmarks, is characterized by greater variability and heterogeneity besides the more rapid change, so more institutional flexibility is called for (Heckman 2002). By and large German labor market institutions have not become much more rigid over the last thirty years. However, their lack of interaction with changes in the economic environment must be the prime reason for the rising unemployment. This is a fact explored in a number of recent papers.[1]

Arguing along similar lines, the chapter proceeds as follows: Section 11.2 highlights some stylized facts about German unemployment. Section 11.3 points out which major shocks have occurred and how they interact with German labor market institutions to produce rising unemployment. Section 11.4 provides some conclusions.

11.2   Some Stylized Facts on German Unemployment

Unemployment has ratcheted upward over the last three decades in Germany (figure 11.1). At the beginning of the 1970s Germany enjoyed a situation of full employment with negligible officially recorded un-

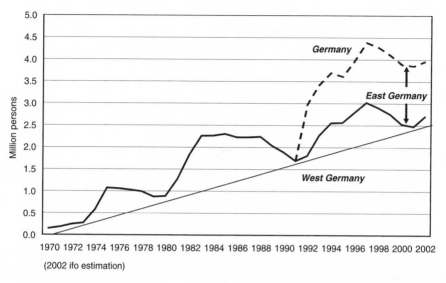

Figure 11.1
Unemployment in Germany. Source: Sinn (2002).

employment rates. This was in marked contrast to the United States, which then had a nonaccelerating inflation rate of unemployment (NAIRU) on the order of 5 percent. Afterward, as in other countries, unemployment jumped upward with each negative shock, such as the two oil price shocks and the changes in monetary policy toward a more restrictive, anti-inflationary course. Unlike a number of other countries, when economic conditions improved again, Germany has been almost completely unable to reduce its unemployment rate back to pre-shock levels. The total official number of unemployed in spring 2003 is around 4.7 million, so at least 6 million jobs are missing if additionally unemployment hidden in active labor market policy programs and early retirement schemes are considered. According to the latest OECD figures, the standardized unemployment rate in Germany in 2002 is 8.3 percent.

Structural unemployment in Germany has shown a strongly rising trend over the last thirty years as can be seen by the straight line in figure 11.1 that connects the troughs of unemployment during the boom periods. Thus unemployment has displayed a high asymmetric persistence, or hysteresis, in Germany. Furthermore it is striking to note that Germany's unemployment rate has continually increased over the 1990s and into the twenty-first century, whereas the United States, the

Table 11.1
Development of structural unemployment

	1980	1985	1990	1995	1999
France	5.8	6.5	9.3	10.3	9.5
Finland	4.3	3.9	5.6	10.6	9.0
Germany	3.3	4.4	5.3	6.7	6.9
Japan	1.9	2.7	2.2	2.9	4.0
Netherlands	4.7	7.5	7.5	6.1	4.7
Great Britain	4.4	8.1	8.6	6.9	7.0
United States	6.1	5.6	5.4	5.3	5.2

Source: Eichhorst, Profit, and Thode (2001).
Note: Structural Unemployment is measured by the concept of NAIRU (OECD 2000).

United Kingdom, and the Netherlands, for example, are much more successful over this time period in producing employment growth and in reducing their unemployment rates.

There is widespread consensus that the bulk of the rise in unemployment in Germany is due to structural causes (table 11.1), meaning that it is related to excessive real wage costs to firms, lack of wage differentiation, rising mismatch problems, and so forth, and that it cannot be successfully fought by simply expanding goods demand even if that were possible. Estimates for the NAIRU in Germany indicate that 80 to 90 percent of total unemployment is due to structural causes. Hence, to fight unemployment, emphasis must be put on the question of which institutions are to blame for this assessment and how these institutions should be reformed to obtain better results for the labor market. Institutions directly related to the labor market such as direct regulation and welfare state schemes should naturally be put under scrutiny (Siebert 1997), but they may not be the only relevant points of interest. There is sometimes the naïve belief that unemployment must be due to a defect in the labor market, as if the hole in a flat tire must always be at the bottom because that is where the tire is flat (Solow 2000). A. Marshall emphasized that the institutional structures on goods and capital markets also affect labor market performance (Heckman 2002).[2]

A look at the development of the Beveridge curve for Germany reveals that primarily there has been a massive movement downward; that is, the officially recorded unemployment rate has increased much more than the officially recorded vacancy rate (figure 11.2).[3] Such a downward movement along a given Beveridge curve can have two reasons. First, lack of goods demand can simultaneously depress

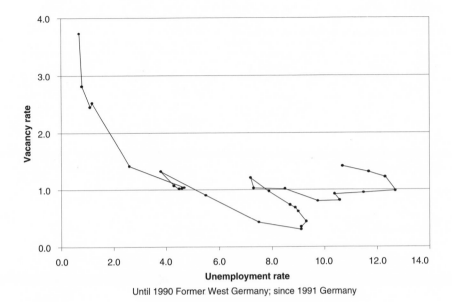

Figure 11.2
Beveridge curve for Germany from 1970 to 2000. Source: Bundesanstalt für Arbeit.

vacancies and increase unemployment. Given the brief discussion in the preceding paragraph, this is unlikely to be the major cause of this marked downward movement over the last thirty years. To be more precise, even if the original push toward higher aggregate unemployment came from the demand side, hysteresis mechanisms convert an originally cyclical rise into structural unemployment after a few years if the cyclical downturn cannot be reverted quickly enough. Second, a rise in real wage costs to firms exceeding trend productivity growth reduces vacancies and raises unemployment, which is then typically called classical unemployment. Given the rapid rise in wage costs in Germany relative to other countries and the marked tendency in Germany to substitute labor by capital (Berthold, Fehn, and Thode 2002), this is more likely to be the ultimate cause for the observed downward movement in the *uv*-plane.

In addition there has been an outward shift of the Beveridge curve; that is, the same vacancy rate corresponds to a considerably higher unemployment rate today than ten or twenty years ago. Such an outward shift of the Beveridge curve is usually caused by rising mismatch problems, where the characteristics of the unemployed fit less well with the

Table 11.2
Unemployment rates by German states, October 2002

	Unemploy-ment rate		Unemploy-ment rate
North		Sachsen	16.4
Bremen	12.3	Sachsen-Anhalt	18.5
Hamburg	8.9	Thüringen	14.6
Niedersachsen	8.8	*South*	
Nordrhein-Westfalen	9.1	Baden-Württemberg	5.5
Schleswig-Holstein	8.4	Bayern	5.8
East		Hessen	6.8
Berlin	16.9	Rheinland-Pfalz	6.9
Brandenburg	16.7	Saarland	8.7
Mecklenburg-Vorpommern	17.3	Germany	9.4

Source: *Bundesanstalt für Arbeit.*

available vacancies than in the past. All three standard types of mismatch unemployment seem to play a major role in Germany, namely mismatch with respect to region, sector, and qualification. Reunification led to a substantial regional mismatch problem in Germany as unemployment shot up in eastern Germany due to a number of reasons, some of the important ones are related to clear policy mistakes such as the conversion of the *Ostmark* into the DM at a highly overvalued rate, and a policy of rapid wage equalization between the east and the west of Germany. However, even before reunification Germany had a non-negligible rise in regional mismatch problems because unemployment had already started to increase more in the north than in the south (table 11.2).

Rising unemployment must also be attributed to increasing sectoral mismatch. Employment in the industrial sector has been shrinking more in Germany than in most other OECD countries without an equivalently strong rise in employment for the service sector (Eichhorst, Profit, and Thode 2001). There is a strong unsatisfied demand, in particular, for household-related services, while it is very difficult for unemployed industrial workers to find a new job in their original field of employment. Still it is much more attractive for people to work in the strongly unionized high-productivity industrial sector because a typical industrial worker can earn a much higher wage there than in the service sector. Of course, this assessment hinges on the realistic

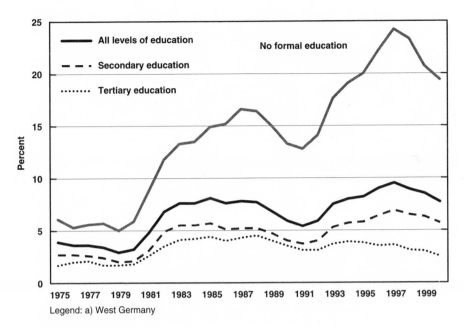

Figure 11.3
Unemployment rates by qualifications (West Germany). Source: Sinn (2002).

assumption that jobs in the service sector with a high-qualification profile, such as auditing or consulting, are not available for the industrial
workers concerned. Unemployed industrial workers are very reluctant
to work in the service sector, and especially young males still prefer to
enter into an apprenticeship in the industrial sector.

As in many other countries, unemployment in Germany is also
largely, and increasingly, concentrated among people with little or no
formal qualification for the labor market, pointing to rising qualifica-
tional mismatch (figure 11.3). The fact that this concentration has
increased over time reflects a shift of labor demand toward more
skilled labor, possibly due to globalization and/or labor-saving technical progress, since the relative supply of skilled labor has risen in
the course of the last few decades. In Germany the main divide still
appears to be made by the apprenticeship system, implying that the
probability of being unemployed or of ending up in long-term unemployment is much lower if someone has successfully finished formal
training. Roughly 50 percent of the long-term unemployed have no
such formal qualification via the apprenticeship system. However,
unemployment rates among the group with intermediate levels of

Table 11.3
Long-term unemployment (% total unemployment)

	1983	1990	2000	2002
Finland	19.2	9.2	29.0	24.4
France	42.2	38.0	42.6	33.8
Germany	41.6	46.8	51.5	47.9
Italy	57.0	69.8	61.3	59.2
Netherlands	47.8	49.3	na	26.7
Spain	52.4	54.0	47.6	40.2
United Kingdom	45.2	34.4	28.0	23.1
EU15	na	48.6	46.9	41.4
Japan	13.3	19.1	25.5	30.8
United States	13.3	5.5	6.0	8.5

Source: OECD.

qualifications have also increased quite a bit more than among those with university degrees.

Long-term unemployment, with individual unemployment spells exceeding one year, is an especially severe problem in Germany. The probability that someone who has lost his job will not find a new job over the next year has been hovering around 50 percent for a number of years now according to OECD numbers, which is exceptionally high by international comparison (table 11.3). Hence, the labor market is very much segmented in Germany between insiders, who have regular, well-protected and well-endowed jobs, and long-term unemployed outsiders, whose chances of ever getting back into the regular labor market are not only slim but also diminishing by each additional month spent in unemployment.

Long-term unemployment is not only draining the resources of the welfare state, but it also constitutes a huge economic waste. In contrast to frictional short-term unemployment, this cannot be justified by matching arguments, implying that this kind of unemployment would be necessary to allow for an optimal search for a new job. As a rule, the individuals affected are forced to stay idle against their will. Financing them via taxes and social security contributions actually reduces output due to the resulting distortions of work incentives. It is noteworthy in this respect that the total marginal rate of taxation of labor is extremely high in Germany compared internationally (figure 11.4). Last but not least, high rates of long-term unemployment are socially divisive and tend to undermine political stability.

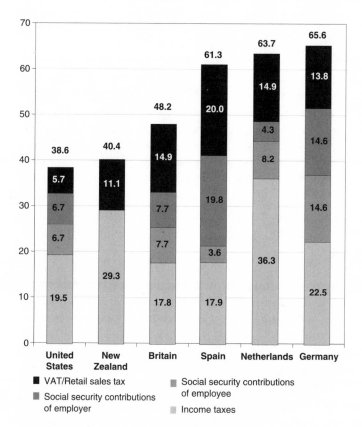

Figure 11.4
Total marginal taxation of labor. Source: Sinn (2002).

Germany has a very peculiar age profile among the unemployed (Heckman 2002). Unemployment among teenagers is low compared to most other OECD countries. Unemployment rates increase markedly among individuals in their twenties when the apprenticeship ends and when, as a rule, collectively negotiated wages have to be paid by firms. Firms therefore naturally restrict offers for continuing employment under regular terms to apprentices who have made sufficient progress in terms of their productivity to increase the net value of the firm later on even when they receive union wages. Also German unemployment or nonemployment rates are strikingly high at the other end of the age spectrum, among people aged 55 and above, which is a result of still generous rules of the welfare state concerning unemployment benefits and early pension rules for elderly people. The low participation

rate among elderly workers is unsustainable considering the combination of low fertility rates and increasing life expectancy.

These stylized facts contrast with the development of real wage costs
of firms and of wage differentiation. Real wage costs of firms rose
much more over the last three decades in Germany than in most
other OECD countries (Sinn 2002). This hardly reflects an equivalently
higher trend growth rate of labor productivity in Germany, considering that technological knowledge spreads quickly at least among
OECD countries and also that recent international comparisons of education tests such as PISA revealed that Germany is not in the top group
in preparing its young people well for working life. This development
must rather be attributed to higher wage cost pressure, be it due to
union wage demands or to rising costs for financing an overly generous welfare state.

Germany is furthermore among the few OECD countries where
wage differentiation according to qualification did not increase over
the 1990s but actually decreased (Eichhorst, Profit, and Thode 2001).
There has been no noticeable increase even in sectoral wage differentiation, probably due to pattern bargaining of the different sectors of
the economy, making wage bargaining more centralized than strictly
sectoral wage bargaining. Regional wage differentiation among the
western states of Germany is negligible in firms that pay union wages.
In terms of bargained wages there is still some wage differentiation
between the west and east regions. Unions are fighting hard to get rid
of even this little regional wage differentiation. Wages have therefore
been growing faster in the east even though employment in eastern
Germany is exhibiting a strong downward trend.[4]

11.3   The Interaction of German Labor Market Institutions with Shocks

11.3.1   Which Shocks?

Wages that are inappropriate for attaining full employment in all their
different facets—with excessive real wage cost pressure on firms, wage
rigidities of all kinds, lack of wage differentiation, excessive reservation
wages, and so forth—lead to rising structural unemployment. From
a policy point of view, however, it is crucial to find out which labor
market institutions primarily give rise to these inappropriate wages. A
large number of investigations, such as those done by the OECD, concerning the evolution of labor market institutions show that there has

been very little change in labor market institutions over the last decades in continental European countries and especially in Germany.
The United Kingdom with its substantial labor market reforms in the
Thatcher era is the exception rather than the rule. Hence there must
have been some major economic shocks in this time period that conflict, for example, with the German institutional setting on the labor
market, causing wages to be inappropriate and unemployment to rise.
There are at least five major candidates for such shocks.

First, there are the well-known oil price shocks of 1973 and 1979 that
constituted negative aggregate supply shocks for a country like Germany. Total factor productivity growth along with labor productivity
growth slowed down in the wake of these shocks, reducing the scope
for real wage increases without employment losses or even requiring
real wage cuts. Countries with labor market institutions that give rise
to real wage rigidities were bound to experience lasting increases in
unemployment rates as a result.

Second, in their monetary policy stance in the early 1980s the Fed in
the United States under Paul Volcker and the German *Bundesbank*, as
well as monetary authorities in a number of other OECD countries,
made the fight against inflation their top priority. As inflation only
decreased gradually over time, it was not possible to reverse the negative demand shock quickly enough to prevent hysteresis mechanisms
from setting in. Hence the scope for employment-neutral real wage
increases was further reduced. Subsequently there was a lasting rise in
real interest rates that would have made it necessary for unions to accept a falling labor share. Unemployment increased where labor market institutions were such that workers resisted this change in relative
factor rewards.

Third, substantial shifts in the structure of labor demand took place
over the 1980s and 1990s and increased the importance of flexible
wage structures. Labor demand has shifted not only from the industrial to the service sector, but firms have increased their skill requirements when hiring employees. Both movements are closely linked to
the ongoing process of globalization and to labor-saving technical
progress. Labor market institutions that tend to make wage structures
rigid and also to compress wage differentials have thus become more
costly in terms of employment. Through reunification Germany was
hit by a particularly severe shock concerning the regional structure of
labor demand. Due to disastrous economic policies during the socialist
era in the GDR, labor demand relative to working age population was
much lower in East Germany than in West Germany. Labor market

institutions such as centralized wage bargaining, which tend to compress regional wage differentials, have therefore become particularly problematic for Germany.

Fourth, the economic environment appears to have become more volatile during the 1980s and 1990s with an increasing likelihood of firm-specific shocks. This is also reflected in the rising instability of workers' earnings and the falling ability of firms to offer their employees lifetime employment (Gottschalk and Moffitt 1994). In particular, there has been a large increase in both the permanent and transitory components of earnings variation, leading to a rise in cross-sectional earnings inequality in the United States with its relatively unregulated labor market. In addition earnings losses of workers who have been involuntarily separated from their jobs have increased, indicating a reduced transferability of human capital across firms. Labor market institutions that conflict with this greater microeconomic turbulence give rise to increasing unemployment.[5]

Fifth, the 1990s was marked by the arrival of the so-called new economy based on the IT revolution, the Internet and the rising importance of such sectors as biotechnology, telecommunication, and knowledge-based industries in general. The new economy not only reinforced the trend toward greater economic turbulence, but it also further raised the importance of human capital in a broad sense, including cognitive and communication skills, proficiency in working with computers, as well as versatility in performing different tasks and in working in teams. Interestingly soft skills that are harder to prove via certificates gained in weight relative to hard skills, conflicting with labor market institutions that enforce wage equality across individuals belonging to identical categories based on certificates and tenure. In a nutshell, this was an era of creative destruction with greater risks but also potentially larger returns, destroying the old ways of producing and trading but also creating vast new opportunities for entrepreneurial success. At the same time the new economy raised the costs in terms of output and employment losses of large systems of social insurance and of clinging to the status quo.

11.3.2 Which Labor Market Institutions?[6]

German labor market institutions are heavily criticized these days for being outdated and far too rigid. In fact the Fraser Institute, in its ranking of both OECD countries and emerging countries on labor market flexibility, has put Germany last among all the 58 countries it considered (Gwartney and Lawson 2001). While it may be debatable whether this ranking of Germany is justified, the message is clear: rigid labor market institutions are stifling Germany's GDP and employment growth. In the following, two key labor market institutions are put under closer scrutiny, insurance benefits and other transfer payments to the unemployed and employment protection legislation.[7]

Insurance Benefits and Transfer Payments to the Unemployed
International comparative studies show that the generosity of insurance benefits and transfer payments to the unemployed is a key determinant for the extent and duration of unemployment in a given country.[8] The longer benefits are paid, the higher these benefits are and the less restrictive the rules are that govern what is expected of an unemployed person in order to receive these benefits, the higher the level of unemployment is and in particular long-term unemployment.

First of all, generous unemployment benefits simply lead to a reduction in the search intensity of the unemployed and subsequently to a drop in the probability of their being hired. In addition, the wedge of taxes and insurance contributions that increases gross wage costs for firms over the net wages that workers receive becomes larger with the higher costs of the welfare state. Incentives shift toward non-employment and irregular employment. This results in more aggressive wage-bargaining behavior on the part of trade unions, whose interest is in the net wage that their members receive and not in the corresponding employment losses. Trade unions and firms know that excessive wage increases and rash dismissals entail less serious consequences for workers who are made redundant. After all workers fall into a generous safety net that guarantees them a considerable part of the net income they last earned. With unemployment assistance, this is actually the case in Germany for an unlimited time (table 11.4). In such an institutional environment, unions and employer associations can roll over substantial parts of the consequences of their inappropriate wage-setting behavior to society at large and to future generations. The generosity of the German welfare state has thus induced behavior that is detrimental to employment and encourages so-called moral hazard.

Because of the aforementioned shocks a system that was relatively stable, but generous, has become damaging over the last thirty years. More workers were fired for a given size of any of these shocks as a

Table 11.4
German unemployment insurance and unemployment assistance

	Individuals covered	Qualifying conditions	Rate of benefit	Duration
Unemployment insurance	All employees (except civil servants)	12 Months of contributions during the last 3 years	With children 67%, without children 60% of average weekly net earnings over the last 52 weeks	6–32 Months, depending on periods of compulsory insurance coverage and age
Unemployment assistance	All employees (except civil servants)	Unemployment insurance benefits expired, means-tested	With children 57%, without children 53% of net earnings	Unlimited

Source: CESifo DICE.

Editor's note: These are key features of the German system of unemployment benefits as of 2003. Starting in 2005, unemployment assistance is merged with social assistance, the general basic welfare benefit. Starting in 2006, maximum duration of unemployment insurance benefits will be 18 months, depending on the period of compulsory coverage and age.

generous safety net for the unemployed increased real wage rigidities. The resulting rise in unemployment has lasted longer and part of the rise has even become permanent in this institutional environment due to the reduced job-finding rate of the unemployed.

So far in Germany there have been only minor changes in the generosity of the unemployment benefit system over time (Fehn 1997). There was a substantial extension of the maximum benefit duration for older workers that took place in the mid-1980s. Workers aged 57 and older are now allowed to draw unemployment benefits for up to 32 months. This measure along with the introduction of relatively lax rules for early retirement were supposed to smooth the process of structural change and to facilitate the substitution of older workers by younger ones. The predictable result has been a very low participation rate of workers aged between 55 and 65, which creates a heavy burden for the social security system and is unsustainable in view of the shrinking population.

There is no individual choice whatsoever concerning the size and structure of the insurance package, so individual preferences and any opportunities for self-insurance are completely neglected. This ineffi-

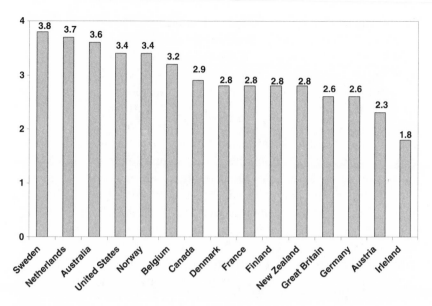

Figure 11.5
Strictness of eligibility criteria for unemployment insurance. Source: Eichhorst, Profit, and Thode (2001).

ciency is reinforced by a marginal tax rate of almost 100 percent in transition from receiving benefits to working on the regular labor market, so work incentives for those with low to medium qualifications are systematically destroyed. At the same time, recipients of insurance benefits and transfer payments have de facto no obligation to work.[9] Above all, the benefits are not only relatively high, but they are paid for an unlimited time, and the criteria for which type of jobs unemployed persons are expected to accept are still rather lax, with the result that the incentives to work are further weakened (figure 11.5).[10]

In reforming the system, a key issue should be the duration of benefits that are linked to previous net wages.[11] The maximum duration of receipt of unemployment insurance benefits could be substantially reduced, for instance, to one year for workers of all ages, so that entitlements to receive these benefits expire with the transition into long-term unemployment. In addition high replacement rates aggravate moral hazard problems. Here too the incentives should be set up in a way that unemployment and dismissals are avoided as far as possible without losing sight of the insurance aspect. A general waiting

period of, say, two months after a worker's dismissal before unemployment benefits can be received could help in this respect.

Furthermore the criteria for which kind of job offers unemployed
persons can reject without losing benefits could be made more restrictive. From the high regional concentration of unemployment in Germany (Decressin and Fatas 1994), it appears particularly important
that unemployed persons looking for a full time job become more mobile. They could thus be expected to move to different places after a
certain duration of unemployment, for example, after six months. The
maximum commuting time could be increased again to 180 minutes
of daily travel. German employment services are still relatively lax in
monitoring whether the unemployed are really searching intensively
for a new job. This is reflected in the low number of cases where
employment services interrupt the payment of benefits because individuals are not trying hard enough to obtain a new job (figure 11.6).
Since exit rates from unemployment are not higher in Germany than
elsewhere, it is unlikely that this low rate of penalization is due to the

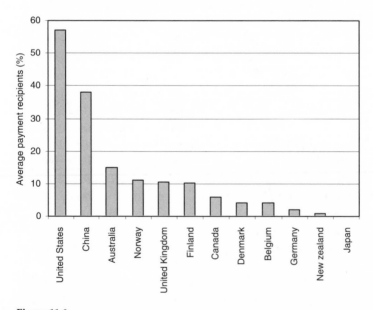

Figure 11.6
Suspension of unemployment insurance payments. Possible reasons are lack of search,
refusal to participate in active labor market policies, refusal of job offer, and noncompliance with administrative rules. Source: Eichhorst, Profit, and Thode (2001).

unemployed searching more intensively for a new job than their foreign counterparts.

There are further reasons why the peculiar system of unemployment assistance is deeply flawed from the perspective of reintegrating the unemployed into the regular labor market as quickly as possible. Unemployment benefits are financed from the federal government's budget, but recipients are led to believe that the benefits are based on insurance because they are linked to last net earnings and, depending on family status, are only 7 to 10 percentage points less than unemployment insurance benefits. Despite a means test it is therefore often the case that unemployment assistance substantially exceeds the social assistance administered by municipalities and represents the basic safety net. Furthermore the coexistence of these two types of benefits creates incentives to move individuals from one scheme to another as long as the funding of benefits and the responsibility for reintegrating the long-term unemployed in the regular labor market is shared by different institutions. One of the options that exist is to abolish unemployment assistance altogether. Anyone who has still not found a job when unemployment benefits expire after, say, one year, could be treated as a candidate for social hardship benefits rather than insurance benefits.

If unemployment assistance were abolished and the maximum duration of unemployment benefits were reduced at the same time, further questions arise as to what should happen to unemployed people who still have not found a new job after their unemployment benefit entitlements have expired. It should be clear that in a *Soziale Marktwirschaft*, needy people who are either unable to work or willing to work but not able to find a job would be entitled to social assistance. But this leads to moral hazard. Compared to people in regular employment, unemployed people have the "advantage" of having far more free time at their disposal. In particular, this creates the opportunity to earn money in the shadow economy. Far worse, depending on family size, benefit entitlements are already close to net wages earned by a single earner on average wages. This is especially the case in eastern Germany.[12]

One should therefore distinguish between two groups of people, those who are able to work and those who are not, often because they are handicapped or because they have to take care of household members such as small children or elderly people. The latter group of people could continue to receive the current level of social assistance. In contrast, the standard rate of social assistance for long-term unemployed who are, in principle, able to work should be substantially cut to reduce reservation wages and to increase the incentive to work on the regular labor market. Earned income tax credits defined along the lines of the system in the United States could then be put on top of the reduced social assistance level to strengthen work incentives and establish the incentive for unions to install a low-wage sector.[13] Reforms in the direction of workfare would reduce the problem that the current social assistance scheme effectively sets a lower limit for net wages which the long-term unemployed are prepared to accept for a regular job, also affecting collective wage agreements between unions and employer associations. This implicit wage threshold is a first-degree job killer in the regular labor market especially in eastern Germany, and with respect to families with several children and only one potential bread winner with less than average qualifications. This approach would be radically different from the current system where virtually all income earned in addition to social assistance triggers a one-for-one reduction in benefits.

However, even under a system with much stronger work incentives not all recipients of social assistance who are able and willing to work will be able to find jobs on the regular labor market. Paying them only a reduced rate of social assistance is therefore bound to be considered a violation of the German constitution, assuming that the current level of social assistance is indeed equivalent to the so-called sociocultural subsistence level at which recipients are just able to participate "adequately" in the life of society. As a consequence recipients of social assistance should be offered job-creation and/or qualification measures by local authorities. When participating in such activities on a full-time basis, they could earn the equivalent of the current level of social assistance. In contrast to existing job-creation schemes, entitlements to receive unemployment benefits should not be renewed through participation. The idea is to provide a strong incentive to accept a job in the regular labor market which, due to the earned income tax credit, would always lead to higher effective earnings per hour worked compared to the programs offered by the local authorities.

Such a rigorous policy of give and take in the system of benefit payments to the long-term unemployed could substantially reduce the opportunity to exploit the welfare state and to work in the shadow economy while receiving transfers, thus increasing once again the general acceptance of supporting the needy among the public at large.

Employment Protection Legislation

Another important and highly controversial labor market institution that differs greatly across OECD countries is employment protection legislation (EPL). In general, EPL is much more restrictive in continental Europe than in Anglo-Saxon countries (Nickell, chapter 1 of this volume). In particular, the United States with its "employment at will" principle is usually ranked very low concerning firing costs. Within continental Europe firing costs tend to be higher in the southern countries than in the northern ones. The latter usually protect workers against negative shocks via relatively generous unemployment insurance and welfare assistance (Buti et al. 1998). In the late 1960s and early 1970s firing costs increased substantially in some continental European countries like Germany and France and have stayed roughly on this higher level since then (Caballero and Hammour 1997).

It is not obvious how EPL affects overall labor market performance because there are opposing effects at work. Several arguments exist for why some EPL might be superior to a laissez-faire solution not only for reasons of equity but also on efficiency grounds (Bentolila and Bertola 1990). First, EPL in the form of severance pay forces firms to internalize some of the costs that they impose on workers who are dismissed and on society at large. Second, EPL smoothes employment over the business cycle because firms then are more reluctant to fire workers in recessions, since they can avoid firing costs by simply hoarding workers over the downturn. Third, EPL protects workers against arbitrary dismissals by firms, thus possibly creating a more trusting work relationship between firms and workers and making workers more willing to invest in firm-specific human capital.

It can be argued on these grounds that continental European firms are specialized in activities that require long-term work relationships, trust, and firm-specific human capital, whereas US firms specialize in activities that require no human capital, like hamburger flipping, or in activities that require a high level of nonspecific human capital like software development or auditing/consulting. A more volatile economic environment and faster structural change then constitute a great challenge for continental European countries. Along with the jobs the employees' firm-specific human capital and a rent-sharing component are destroyed, and the resistance of workers against dismissals can therefore be expected to be fiercer as their outside options are worse. By and large, the empirical literature confirms the interpretation that firm-specific human capital plays a greater role in continental Europe, with the associated problems under the current turbulent economic conditions (Wasmer 2002).

Regardless of the economic conditions there are also a couple of fundamental arguments against raising EPL too much. First, EPL increases total labor costs, thus reducing labor demand at given wage costs. As a result wage demands can become more aggressive because the potential of insiders to appropriate firms is raised (Caballero and Hammour 1997). Insiders will not be dismissed by firms as long as wages plus firing costs do not exceed their marginal productivity (Lindbeck and Snower 2002). The negative effect on labor market performance can be greater, the larger the long-run elasticity of substitution between capital and labor is. Recent empirical evidence pointing to a long-run elasticity of substitution that exceeds unity suggests that the negative effects in the long run of expanding EPL are very large (Berthold, Fehn, and Thode 2002).

Second, EPL makes firms more reluctant to hire workers at given wage costs. Flows in and out of unemployment are unambiguously reduced by EPL. While there is, in theory, no clear-cut effect on total unemployment from lower labor market flows, the reduced hiring rate due to EPL makes unemployment more persistent and raises long-term unemployment. Once dismissed, it is more difficult for workers in countries with high EPL to obtain a regular job compared to a laissez-faire country such as the United States. EPL therefore increases the segmentation of the labor market into insiders and outsiders.[14]

In addition to these general arguments against EPL, the transition to the new economy makes it likely that countries with relatively lax EPL fare better nowadays in terms of labor market performance. EPL is especially bad for employment when big structural breaks occur because firms are then very reluctant to hire new workers, and EPL cannot prevent dismissals in firms or sectors that will perish anyway. EPL is especially harmful to firms that are largely financed via debt rather than via equity because labor becomes a quasi-fixed production factor, whose utilization cannot be quickly adjusted to changing economic conditions. Thus quasi-equilibrium unemployment is raised if unions do not exercise sufficient wage restraint in return.[15]

Furthermore it can be shown that firms in high-EPL countries are induced to specialize in relatively secure goods at later stages in their product life cycles in order to avoid paying firing costs (Saint-Paul 2002a). The new and innovative goods with a high failure risk that are essential for the transition to the new economy are first developed and produced in low-EPL countries, such as the United States, and only later move to high-EPL countries, such as Germany. The negative effect of EPL on innovation and growth (Caballero and Hammour 1997) is reinforced by the fact that growth based on radical product innovations is less dependent on having experienced workers and managers. Rather, it depends on selecting the right group of innovative people and on being able to lay off people who have turned out to be incompetent without much hassle. The importance of selection relative to experience rises when approaching the frontier of economic development, thus making rigid EPL less efficient (Acemoglu, Aghion, and Zilibotti 2002).

Finally large-scale creation of new firms has been a hallmark of the new economy in the United States. However, newly founded firms often face financial restrictions, and having a high rate of new firms per period depends on a well-functioning venture capital market in order to circumvent these restrictions. Venture capitalists often help their portfolio firms to survive the particularly risky start-up period by counseling and advising them. However, empirical studies show that the growth of the venture capital market, which clearly helps a country to be a successful player in the new economy, depends greatly on labor market flexibility. So countries with a rigid labor market due to high EPL have less chance of benefiting from a positive new economy effect than countries with low EPL and a more flexible labor market.[16]

The countervailing effects of EPL on labor market performance and the direction and size of the net impact on unemployment, and to a lesser extent on employment growth, are in the end an empirical issue. There are now numerous cross-country studies on the effect of labor market institutions on unemployment,[17] often finding that the strictness of EPL is insignificant or that the relevant coefficient is relatively small. However, most of these studies suffer from important shortcomings. First, the time period that is investigated often only extends to the early 1990s so that most of the period when the transition to the new economy got under way is left out.[18] Second, they either include institutional variables concerning the labor market only or supplement them merely with goods market variables; as a rule, capital market variables are completely left out. If these shortcomings are avoided, EPL turns out to have a significant negative effect on labor market performance across OECD countries, raising the standardized unemployment rate and lowering employment growth. The impact of EPL on the unemployment rate is also more pronounced than the effect on employment growth (Belke and Fehn 2001).

In sum, reducing the strictness of EPL can help fight unemployment and raise employment in the age of the new economy by facilitating the hiring decisions of firms. From the perspective of achieving higher employment growth, it is best to completely substitute current EPL by a legal financial solution that is unambiguous. Firms that need to lay off workers due to firm-specific reasons, and not due to, say, the misconduct of workers, will then be legally obliged to make severance payments to these workers based on the annual salaries and tenure of the individual workers. Such simplification of EPL has the advantage of creating certainty with respect to the legal consequences of layoffs. Furthermore, it can substantially reduce the role of labor courts, which are notorious in Germany for not considering the consequences of their jurisdiction for the economy at large as well as for employment creation (Heckman 2002).

11.4 Conclusions

Only a broad set of fundamental institutional reforms, affecting not only the labor market but also the welfare state and the goods and capital markets, will enable Germany to overcome its persistent unemployment problem and successfully meet the challenges posed by the new global economy. The same is true for Germany's tax and social security systems, which should spur rather than stifle entrepreneurial incentives.[19] Institutional reforms are the only way for Germany to leave its current position as one of the most sclerotic European countries in its record of economic and employment growth. However, complacency and political inertia are widespread in Germany, so institutional reforms are a risky undertaking that will hurt a large part of the electorate in the short run. There is to be expected strong resistance to applying the appropriate supply-side policies to the labor market, and also to the goods and capital markets. The walls of the fortress protecting insider prerogatives in all markets of Germany are so high as to crumble in times of a deep crisis, which in itself would be desirable. Yet the current economic decline is so severe that the traditional policy approach of muddling through is no longer feasible. The time is now for Schumpeterian politicians to issue in a broad coalition of reform supporters. The government must resist the temptation to give in to lobbying efforts of special interest groups and create confidence in the public that in the near future bold structural reforms will pay off for almost everyone by reanimating the dynamic of the economy.

This is an era of creative destruction. Greater risks can bring greater returns in countries that are prepared for both consequences. Economic opportunities arise in institutional environments that do not aim to preserve obsolete economic activities but foster entrepreneurship and the creation of new modes of production by motivating firms to invest in skills or in new technology. Unfortunately, the institutional setting in Germany is geared too much toward preserving the status quo and fostering stability, long-term relationships, and an egalitarian income distribution. Thus Germany has been kept from making full use of the opportunities created by the new global economic environment. In a nutshell, too much "social insurance" and too little reward for entrepreneurial risk taking has stifled Germany's economic creativity and growth (Heckman 2002).

Notes

1. See Blanchard and Wolfers (1999), Ljungqvist and Sargent (2002), and Chen, Snower, and Zoega (2002).

2. The longer working paper version of this chapter (Berthold and Fehn 2003) contains a discussion on how German labor market performance has been negatively affected also by insider-oriented goods and capital markets.

3. There was, of course, a structural break in 1990 due to reunification, which complicates a comparison of the pre-1990 data with the post-1990 data.

4. Setting the number of individuals employed subject to the German social insurance system at 100 in January 1994 (to exclude a first period of transition in eastern Germany), employment stays largely constant until the end of 2002 in West Germany, while it continuously falls to 83 percent (-1.8 percent p.a.) in eastern Germany (Sinn 2002).

5. See Bertola and Ichino (1995), Ljungqvist and Sargent (2002), and Wasmer (2002).

6. The dismal outlook for the German labor market seems to have triggered a willingness on the part of policy makers to overhaul labor market institutions, so substantial changes may soon occur. This chapter reflects the situation at the beginning of 2003.

7. An extended version of this chapter (Berthold and Fehn 2003) also argues in favor of decentralizing the wage-bargaining system.

8. See, for example, Hunt (1995), Nickell (1997), and Bertola, Blau, and Kahn (2001).

9. De jure, this is not the case for recipients of unemployment assistance or social assistance. Municipalities can legally require these people to do community work or to participate in qualification programs. In the case of (repeated) noncompliance, authorities can reduce payments or even stop them altogether. However, up until now municipalities appear to be very reluctant to use this instrument for monitoring the actual willingness to work of recipients of transfer payments.

10. Reforms that are currently under way are designed to impose stricter work availability criteria.

11. Editor's note: See the notes to table 10.4 indicating that starting in 2005 and in 2006, some reforms of this kind are being undertaken with respect to unemployment insurance benefits and unemployment assistance.

12. In the west (in parentheses: east) social assistance plus housing benefits are about 36.5 (41.6) percent of the net wage derived from *average* gross wages of employees in manufacturing, trade, banking, and insurance in the case of a single adult. In the case of a married couple with three children, they climb to no less than 71.9 (81.6) percent of average net wages (Sinn 2002).

13. For a detailed description of a proposal along those lines, see Sinn et al. (2002).

14. See Lindbeck and Snower (2002) and Saint-Paul (2002b).

15. See Bertola and Ichino (1995) and Fehn (2002).

16. See Jeng and Wells (2000) and Fehn (2002).

17. See, for example, Nickell (1997) and Blanchard and Wolfers (1999).

18. Chen, Snower, and Zoega (2002) find that the empirical effect of firing costs depends on the time period under investigation because firing costs do have especially adverse employment effects in periods of economic instability with many negative shocks and low growth rates.

19. See, for example, Boeri, Nicoletti, and Scarpetta (2000) and Fehn (2002).

References

Acemoglu, D., P. Aghion, and F. Zilibotti. 2002. Distance to frontier, selection, and economic growth. *NBER Working Paper* 9066.

Belke, A., and R. Fehn. 2001. Institutions and structural unemployment: Do capital-market imperfections matter? *IFO Studies* 47 (4): 405–51.

Bentolila, S., and G. Bertola. 1990. Firing costs and labour demand: How bad is eurosclerosis? *Review of Economic Studies* 57: 381–402.

Berthold, N., and R. Fehn. 2003. Unemployment in Germany: Reasons and remedies. *CESifo Working Paper* 821.

Berthold, N., R. Fehn, and E. Thode. 2002. Falling labor share and rising unemployment: Long-run consequences of institutional shocks? *German Economic Review* 3 (4): 431–59.

Bertola, G., and A. Ichino. 1995. Wage inequality and unemployment: United States versus Europe. *NBER Macroeconomics Annual*. Cambridge: MIT Press.

Bertola, G., F. Blau, and L. Kahn. 2001. Comparative analysis of labor market outcomes. European University Institute, Florence, mimeo.

Blanchard, O., and J. Wolfers. 1999. The role of shocks and institutions in the rise of European unemployment: The aggregate evidence. *NBER Working Paper* 7282.

Boeri, T., G. Nicoletti, and S. Scarpetta. 2000. Regulation and labour market performance. *CEPR Discussion Paper* 2420.

Buti, M., et al. 1998. European unemployment: Contending theories and institutional complexities. European University Institute, Florence, *Policy Papers* 98/1.

Caballero, R., and M. Hammour. 1997. Jobless growth: Appropriability, factor substitution, and unemployment. *NBER Working Paper* 6221.

Chen, Y., D. Snower, and G. Zoega. 2002. Labour market institutions and macroeconomic shocks. *CEPR Working Paper* 3480.

Decressin, J., and A. Fatás. 1994. Regional labour market dynamics in Europe. *CEPR Discussion Paper* 1085.

Eichhorst, W., S. Profit, and E. Thode. 2001. *Benchmarking Deutschland: Arbeitsmarkt und Beschäftigung.* Bericht der Arbeitsgruppe Benchmarking und der Bertelsmann Stiftung an das Bündnis für Arbeit, Ausbildung und Wettbewerbsfähigkeit. Berlin: Springer.

Fehn, R. 1997. *Der strukturell bedingte Anstieg der Arbeitslosigkeit in Europa: Ursachen und Lösungsansätze.* Baden-Baden: Nomos.

Fehn, R. 2002. *Schöpferische Zerstörung und struktureller Wandel: Wie beeinflussen Kapitalbildung und Kapitalmarktunvollkommenheiten die Beschäftigungsentwicklung.* Baden-Baden: Nomos.

Gottschalk, P., and R. Moffitt. 1994. The growth of earnings instability in the U.S. labor market. *Brookings Papers on Economic Activity* 2: 217–54.

Gwartney, J., and R. Lawson. 2001. *Economic Freedom of the World: 2001 Annual Report.* Vancouver: Fraser Institute.

Heckman, J. 2002. Flexibility and job creation: Lessons for Germany. *NBER Working Paper* 9194.

Hunt, J. 1995. The effect of unemployment compensation on unemployment duration in Germany. *Journal of Labor Economics* 13 (1): 88–120.

Jeng, L. A., and P. C. Wells. 2000. The determinants of venture capital funding: Evidence across countries. *Journal of Corporate Finance* 6 (3): 241–89.

Lindbeck, A., and D. Snower. 2002. The insider-outsider theory: A survey. *IZA Discussion Paper* 534.

Ljungqvist, L., and T. Sargent. 2002. The European employment experience. *CEPR Discussion Paper* 3543.

Nickell, S. 1997. Unemployment and labour market rigidities: Europe versus North America. *Journal of Economic Perspectives* 11 (3): 55–74.

Saint-Paul, G. 2002a. Employment protection, international specialization, and innovation. *European Economic Review* 46 (2): 375–95.

Saint-Paul, G. 2002b. The policital economy of employment protection. *Journal of Political Economy* 110 (3): 672–704.

Siebert, H. 1997. Labor market rigidities—At the root of unemployment in Europe. *Journal of Economic Perspectives* 11 (3): 37–54.

Sinn, H.-W. 2002. Die rote Laterne—Die Gründe für Deutschlands Wachstumsschwäche und die notwendigen Reformen. *IFO Schnelldienst* 55, no. 23/2002 (special issue).

Sinn, H.-W., et al. 2002. Aktivierende Sozialhilfe: Ein Weg zu mehr Beschäftigung und Wachstum. *IFO Schnelldienst* 55, no. 9/2002 (special issue).

Solow, R. 2000. Unemployment in the United States and in Europe: A contrast and the reasons. *CESifo Working Paper* 231.

Wasmer, E. 2002. Interpreting Europe and US labor market differences: The specificity of human capital investments. *IZA Discussion Paper* 549.

12

The Structure and History of Italian Unemployment

Giuseppe Bertola and Pietro Garibaldi

12.1 Introduction

In this chapter we review the Italian unemployment experience, analyzing in particular the time-series behavior of unemployment rates along the path that brought Italy into Europe's economic and monetary union, and their disaggregated structure across geographical and demographic dimensions. While we will refrain from cross-country comparisons, we note at the outset that Italy's institutional characteristics and labor market performance fit very well the empirical perspective of many recent cross-country panel studies. This holds true with regard to aspects we focus on, such as the relationship between labor market institutions, public employment, and unemployment dynamics, as well aspects we neglect for lack of space and data, such as the employment and productivity effects of product market regulation, other industrial organization features, and financial arrangements.[1]

Moreover the "shocks and institutions" approach of Blanchard and Wolfers (2000) and others to cross-country evidence is relevant to analysis of developments within Italy, a very heterogeneous country. As discussed in more detail below, the range of unemployment rates across Italian regions is very wide, indeed just about as wide as that observed across regions over all the European Union and across all OECD countries. And unemployment rates across Italian regions fanned out over time, with unemployment rising fast in some regions and fluctuating along a stable level in other regions. Such dynamics are similar to those observed across countries in standard panel studies that rationalize the evidence in terms of increasingly different impact of unchanged institutional heterogeneity interacting with similar macroeconomic shocks. Such shocks–institution interactions appear as important within Italy as across the OECD: institutional constraints had increasingly adverse effects in some regions, and remained consistent with near–full employment in others.

The theoretical perspective of standard cross-country panel regressions is also useful when interpreting the role of shocks and institutions in shaping the time-series history of Italian unemployment and employment rates. When considering an individual country, however, it is possible to draw on a larger information base regarding the dynamic development of labor market institutions and disaggregated unemployment outcomes. To the extent that reforms and outcomes interact through endogenous channels, it would be difficult and potentially misleading to estimate time-series relationships between slowly evolving institutions and labor market outcomes influenced by forward-looking behavior by workers and firms. However, guidance from existing panel studies makes it possible to assess the extent to which standard explanatory mechanisms are applicable to Italy, both over time and across disaggregated dimensions.

The chapter proceeds as follows: Section 12.2 presents the main facts on the evolution of Italian unemployment, with a focus on both regional and age dimensions. Section 12.3 presents the institutional framework, aiming at presenting a complete if abbreviated picture of collective bargaining arrangements, employment protection legislation, and active and passive labor market policies. Section 12.4 aims at interpreting the historical evolution as the natural outcome of the combination of adverse macroeconomic interacting with the complex institutional framework described in section 12.3. Section 12.5 reviews recent developments, and concludes.

12.2 Facts

This section reviews a set of stylized facts on Italian unemployment over the last thirty years, focusing on the large and persistent regional and age unemployment differentials. First, we look at the historical evolution of the aggregate unemployment rate. Next, we define the main structural characteristics of unemployment, and analyze them in cross section and over time. Throughout this section we just report key unemployment statistics and stylized facts, postponing most assessment and interpretation.

12.2.1   The Evolution of the Aggregate Unemployment Rate

As currently defined, the Italian unemployment rate stood at 9.1 percent of the labor force in December 2001, much lower than the 12 percent reached in the late 1990s. Official statistics for longer time periods were occasionally redefined, but the two self-consistent series[2] indicate that the current unemployment rate is rather high from a long-run viewpoint. Unemployment rates were as low as 3 percent in 1963 on the basis of a willingness-to-work measure close to the current definition (or 4 percent on the basis of a broader definition giving more weight to administrative indicators, such as registration at employment offices). The series increase, especially fast after 1974, up to 10 to 12 percent in the late 1980s. After a small fall to the 9 to 11 percent range, the two definitions of unemployment surged quickly to 12 to 16 percent in 1998.

The evolution of the unemployment rate is displayed in figure 12.1 on the basis of current definition data, available since 1977 and until 2001. The two episodes of increasing unemployment both lay within

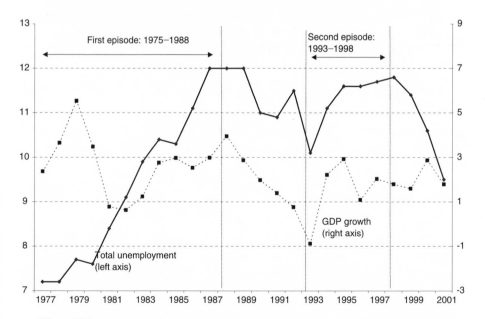

Figure 12.1
Total unemployment rate and GDP growth in Italy from 1977 to 2001. Source: Istat and Bank of Italy.

this 25-year period, and are marked by vertical lines in the figure. In section 12.4 we will examine how these large and persistent increases in unemployment can be attributed to an interaction of national and international shocks coupled with country specific institutions. In section 12.5 we will review recent reforms and discuss their possible relationship to the other notable feature of figure 12.1, namely the recent and quite remarkable unemployment decline by 2.5 percentage points between 1998 to 2001.

12.2.2 The Current Structure of Unemployment

Beneath the broad time-series picture of figure 12.1, Italy features a complex structure of disaggregated unemployment rates. Focusing on disaggregated dimensions of the unemployment problem offers important insights into the interaction of market and institutional features in shaping the structure and dynamics of Italian unemployment. The latter is characterized by three key dimensions of heterogeneity: a *regional differential*, an *age differential* and a *gender differential*. As shown in table 12.1, the unemployment rate in the north is as low as 4 percent. But the unemployment rate in the south is as high as 18 percent of the labor force. Indeed, more than 60 percent of the two million unemployed workers estimated by the labor force surveys live in the

Table 12.1
Structure of unemployment in Italy, 2002

	Percentage of labor force	Thousands	Shares[a]
All	8.70	2,096	1.00
Male	6.70	1,107	0.53
Female	11.70	988	0.47
Regional			
North	4.00	467	0.22
Centre	6.60	311	0.14
South	18.20	1,384	0.64
Youth[b]	26.10	852	0.41
Male	23.00	426	0.20
Female	30.30	426	0.20

Source: Istat.
a. Total number of unemployed.
b. First time unemployed.

southern regions. In the regions in the center–north portion of Italy, the unemployment rate is lower than the national average, but still much larger than that of northern regions. To the extent that high national unemployment is a reflection of pockets of concentrated unemployment, aggregate statistics should always be read from a regional perspective.

Table 12.1 also offers evidence of large age differentials: 40 percent of the unemployed are young labor market entrants (never employed). Finally table 12.1 shows that the Italian unemployment rate has an important gender dimension. While the female unemployment rate is close to 12 percent of the labor force, the male unemployment rate is "just" 6.7 percent. However, more than 53 percent of the unemployment workers are male, because the female participation rate is low: only 34 percent of the working age female population participated in Italy as a whole on average in the 1991 to 2001 decade, and only 27 percent in the south (source: Istat). Obviously the three dimensions outlined in table 12.1 are interrelated, and the youth unemployment rate in the south reaches a remarkably high 50 percent of the labor force.

The structure of unemployment in Italy is only very mildly related to skill differentials as measured by formal education. Table 12.2 reports 2001 unemployment rates by region, age, and five educational attainment levels. Very low skilled workers are more likely to be unemployed, but higher education does not reduce the unemployment rates of young workers by much. In fact it may even slightly increase them, as is the case in the north–east and north–west regions. And in the south, the youth unemployment rate is larger for individuals with university degrees than in the aggregate of the age class (respectively 28 and 26.8 percent). Only among older workers the more educated individuals are mildly less likely to be unemployed. In summary, to be protected from unemployment in Italy, it is much more important to be old than to be well educated. Overall, after controlling for age, education differentials do not appear to be structurally related to the Italian unemployment problem.[3]

12.2.3 Regional and Age Differentials over Time: 1977 to 2001

The strong increase in Italian unemployment is mainly a regional phenomenon. Indeed, male unemployment in the north hardly increases over time, as illustrated by the simple regressions of unemployment

Table 12.2
Unemployment rates by age, regions, and educational attainment

Age group	Highest degree	Northwest–northeast		Center	South
25–34					
	University degree and PhD	5.6	7.9	14.1	28
	High school diploma	3.8	3.6	9.8	27.3
	Professional diploma	4.1	3.2	8.3	26.6
	Secondary degree	5.9	4	10.5	24.7
	Primary degree	11	5.8	14.5	35.6
	Total	5	4.3	10.6	26.8
35–64					
	University degree and PhD	1.1	1.3	2	2.3
	High school diploma	1.8	2	3	6.3
	Professional diploma	2.5	2.4	3.6	9.9
	Secondary degree	3.6	2.7	4.7	12.3
	Primary degree	3.9	2.9	5.8	16.3
	Total	2.7	2.4	3.9	10
Total					
	University degree and PhD	2.7	3.7	5.6	9.7
	High school diploma	2.6	2.7	5.6	14.4
	Professional diploma	3.1	2.7	5.2	15.1
	Secondary degree	4.4	3.1	6.6	16.6
	Primary degree	4.4	3.1	6.4	18.6
	Total	3.5	3	6	15.3

Source: ISTAT; computed from Labor Force Survey (2001).

rates on a time trend reported in table 12.3. Conversely, as we move to southern macro regions, the male unemployment rate not only is larger in magnitude but also significantly trended. The trend coefficient on male unemployment in the south is as large as 0.47, and the level of unemployment ranges from 6.4 percent in 1977 up to 17.4 in 1999. Quantitatively the north–south male unemployment differential rose from 3.3 percentage points in 1977 to almost 14 points in 1998, and is still 12 percentage points in 2001. To summarize, the increase in male unemployment rates is not an Italian phenomenon but mainly a southern Italy phenomenon. Interestingly table 12.3 shows that Italian female unemployment is not significantly trended. Over the twenty-five years of our analysis, the north–south unemployment differentials rose from 10 percentage points in the late 1970s, up to a remarkable 22 percent in the late 1990s. But since the female labor force participation in

Table 12.3
Unemployment rates by macro region, gender, age, 1977 to 2001 range and trends

	Average	Maximum	Minimum	Time trend	t-Statistic
Italy					
Male	7.26	9.1	4.6	0.17	8.22
Female	15.76	18.8	12.6	0.05	1.14
North	0	0.3			
Male	3.82	5.1	2.7	−0.08	−0.38
Female	10.1	14	5.9	−0.12	−2.59
Center					
Male	6.06	7.2	4.8	0.05	4.41
Female	14.3	17.4	10.3	−0.05	−1.34
South					
Male	12.6	17.5	6.4	0.47	13.13
Female	26.82	33.2	18.1	0.49	5.59
15–24					
Male	26.62	29.9	20.4	0.29	4.7
Female	36.71	42.2	28.2	0.2	1.97
25–39					
Male	6.24	9.5	2.4	0.31	16
Female	14.15	17.9	8.7	0.33	6.24
40–59					
Male	2.48	4.2	1	0.13	13.25
Female	5.84	7.4	4.2	0.11	9.54

Sources: Istat, Bank of Italy, and authors' calculations.

the south is rather small, that upward trend does not translate into a clear trend in the aggregate female unemployment statistics.

As to the age dimension in table 12.3 the unemployment rate appears to be significantly upward trended for both the youth and the prime-age groups.[4] Indeed, in a regression of youth unemployment on a constant and a time trend, the coefficient of the latter is approximately 0.3 for both male youth unemployment (age 15–24) and male prime-age unemployment (25–39). This suggests that the unemployment differential between youth and prime-age workers has not increased over time. This seems to be the case for both male and female workers: the youth/prime-age male unemployment differential increased from 20 to 26 percent up to the late 1980s, but it then returned to a value of 20 percent in the late 1990s. For female workers there seems to be actually a slight decrease in the age differential.

It is rather puzzling to see most of the historical increase in unemployment concentrated in the 25 to 39 age bracket used to define "prime-age workers" in table 12.3, since Bertola, Blau, and Kahn (2002) and other cross-country studies establish that structural unemployment tends to be concentrated in secondary portions of the labor force. To investigate this further, we use the national source data collected for Italy by Bertola, Blau, and Kahn (2002), which provide a finer age decomposition. These data are not strictly comparable to those discussed above but distinguish individuals aged 25 to 29 from individuals aged 30 to 39. These two age groups turn out to have very different unemployment dynamics. Figure 12.2 plots the shares of unemployment over time for five age groups. Three features of this graph are important. First, there is a substantial reallocation of the unemployment pool toward the age group 25 to 29, whose share among the unemployed rises from 12 to 25 percent. Second, there is a decline in the shares of unemployment accounted for the very young workers. Third, prime-age individuals (30–39) do experience an increase in the share of unemployment, but such increase is just from 6 to 12 percent of the total. Overall, 65 percent of the absolute increase in unemployment is accounted for by the increase in unemployment of individuals aged 20 to 29. Thus young workers (but not as young as in other countries) have been mostly hit by the increase in unemployment that took place over the last twenty-five years. Consistent with the theoretical perspective of Bertola, Blau, and Kahn (2002), the contribution to aggregate unemployment of very young (14–19) and mature (40–65+) individuals declined quite sharply over the 1980s and 1990s. If not working, these individuals are likely to be in education or retirement rather than unemployed, and the share of mature unemployed individuals was further restrained by Italy's stringent employment protection legislation (discussed below) that has largely prevented job loss until recently. The share of unemployed workers over 40 years of age, however, has increased from 10 to 15 percent over the 1990 to 1997 period, and this may reflect recent institutional developments in the direction of labor market flexibility.

12.2.4   Labor Market Flows

Flow data are scarce in Italy. However, Bertola and Ichino's (1995) analysis of entry and exit rates in manufacturing firms with over 100 employees indicate that the Italian labor market was far from turbulent

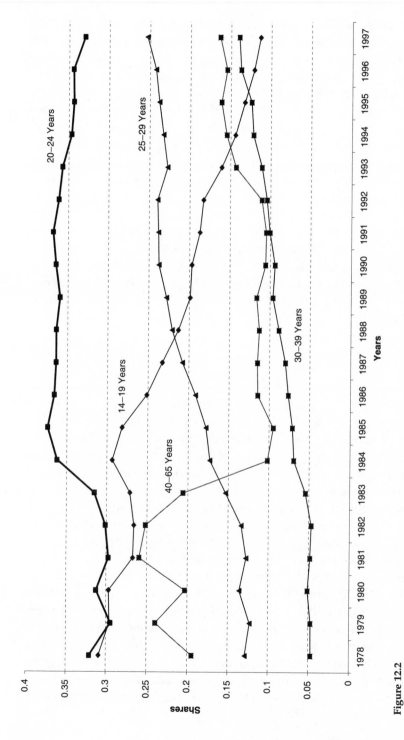

Figure 12.2
Shares of unemployment by age groups. Source: Database compiled by Bertola, Blau, and Kahn (2002) from national source data reported in *OECD Labor Force Statistics*, various issues.

in the 1970s, when monthly exit and entry rates hovered around 0.8 percent. Not surprisingly (in light of stringent employment protection legislation) few workers were dismissed, and few were hired, to imply that the brunt of unemployment fell on young labor market entrants. The 1975 and 1977 recessions both featured parallel drops of entry and exit rates: the (very limited) employment losses of large firms resulted from hiring freezes and minimal quits, with extensive labor hoarding. Data from the 1980s and, especially, from the 1990s offer an increasingly different picture. Entry and exit rates now diverge from each other during recessions, so that employment losses are due to higher (involuntary) exit rates rather than to hiring freezes, consistent with institutional evidence of increasing flexibility starting from the mid-1980s. The recession of 1993 and 1994 stands out for an unprecedented amount of job destruction: monthly exit rates reach a maximum of about 12 per thousand at the end of 1992 and, while decreasing at the end of the recession, remain extraordinarily high in historical perspective. All this confirms that the Italian labor market became more flexible in the 1990s, a fact that we will bring to bear on recent experience in section 12.5 below.

12.2.5 Shadow Economy

The definition of unemployment is unavoidably less than clear-cut (see Jones and Riddell 1999). In Italy, as we discuss below, several types of temporary layoff, nonmarket employment, and "activation" programs make up a gray area of individuals who are not really employed but (as is the case for ALMP participants in other countries) are not counted as unemployed.

Further official employment statistics (though not, at least in principle, the survey-based ones) may be imprecise due to undeclared or "black" employment pools. The shadow economy is important in Italy, and as in other European countries, its size trends up in time: different estimates suggest that shadow activity increased by some 10 to 15 percent of GDP in the 1970s to some 30 to 40 percent in the 1990s. This upward trend parallels that of Italy's aggregate unemployment rates. Not surprisingly, and quite interestingly from the institutional perspective we lay out below, the incidence of the shadow economy varies importantly within Italy, again quite like unemployment. Regions with low productivity and high unemployment display significantly larger shares of unregistered activities and employment than the country averages. Boeri and Garibaldi (2002) offer a detailed account and analysis of this phenomenon. They show that shadow employment varies between 10 percent in Piedmont (north–west) and more than 30 percent in Sicily (south), that the proportion of irregular employment may be as high as 30 to 35 percent in the south (but only around 20 percent in the center, and less than 10 in the north–west and the north–east), and that this can only very partially be explained by the regional heterogeneity of production structures.

12.3   Institutions

We begin by interpreting high and persistent unemployment in light of labor market regulation, which we review in the first subsection for the case of Italy. Of course, we recognize at the outset that regulation is not meant to increase unemployment. Rather, unemployment is an important side effect of rules meant to improve the welfare of workers, and a not unintentional side effect of higher wages from the perspective of unions, whose role in Italy is reviewed in the second subsection.

12.3.1   The Character and History of Italian Labor Market Regulation

Bertola and Ichino (1995) offer an extensive review of Italian labor market institutions and reforms up to the early 1990s. Briefly, the 1970 Charter of Workers' Rights (*Statuto dei Lavoratori*) introduced very stringent regulation of employment relationships, including hiring and firing procedures, the compensation structure, rules for workers mobility and promotions within firms, and safety of working environment. "Rigidity" of the Italian labor market was furthered by subsequent legislation, including a 1974 reform of labor litigation that made it easy for workers to sue employers for noncompliance with the Charter. The character and evolution of Italian employment protection legislation is reviewed in detail by Bertola and Ichino (1995). In essence, dismissal is possible (for employers subject to the Charter, and workers on regular employment contracts) only if appropriately motivated. Article 18 of the Charter prescribes that following an unjust dismissal: employers are obliged to compensate the dismissed workers in kind, restoring their employment status and paying back wages for all the period of litigation plus other monetary penalties.

Wage contracts were also strongly centralized around 1970, when previous provisions for regionally differentiated wages were abolished, and industry-specific negotiated wage structures were extended to all workers and all employers. Further, the wage indexation system introduced in 1975 (*Scala mobile*) stipulated the same cost-of-living allowance for all workers, regardless of pay. Hence low-wage workers were more than fully compensated for inflation, and wages were strongly compressed, especially at the low end of the distribution. The wage differential between the median and the 10th percentile of the earnings distribution declined from almost 100 percent in the late 1970s to only 40 percent in the early 1980s (the indexation system was reformed in 1983).[5] In the absence of centralization and wage-compressing indexation, wage differentials would, of course, have differed across regional and demographic dimensions. To the extent that they were not allowed to do so, it is unsurprising to see wide divergence in various groups' regional and demographic unemployment rates.

Since wage rigidity and strong dismissal restrictions were problematic for the employers' profitability, employers were allowed to dismiss redundant employees by a variety of schemes introduced in the 1970s and the early 1980s, such as CIG and CIGS.[6] The role of these (at least nominally) temporary layoff schemes is broadly similar to that of other countries' Unemployment Insurance systems, which relieve downward pressure on wages at the same time as they offer income support to job losers. The Italian income support system is peculiar in various respects, however. First, workers need to be previously employed by relatively large firms in order to be entitled to these nonemployment subsidies; second, those drawing such benefits would not be counted among the unemployed, since the prospect of reinstatement is supposed to eliminate their incentives to search for new jobs. In the 1970s and 1980s these systems involved a substantial pool of quasi-unemployed individuals: use of the CIG and CIGS temporary-layoff programs peaked at some 160 million hours in 1984, equivalent to some 80,000 full-time equivalent subsidized unemployed.

The institutional framework of "passive" subsidies mentioned above is still in place, but since the early 1980s several flexibility-oriented features have been introduced. On the wage front the indexation system was progressively reformed and eventually abolished in 1992. Employment protection remained quite stringent, and in 1990 was extended to small firms. However, it was somewhat weakened by labor courts' less restrictive interpretation of justifiable dismissals and, especially, by the collective redundancy procedures introduced in 1991 along with restrictions on entitlement to "temporary" income support schemes, both the pre-existing CIG and a new "special" unemployment subsidy. A 1993 law partially backtracked on that reform, however, to imply that the evolution toward greater flexibility was generally perceived to be hesitant, with adverse effects on employers' incentive to hire (see Bertola and Ichino 1995 for a detailed analysis). To the extent that labor market regulation is at least partly endogenous to labor market conditions, such hesitancy is not surprising in light of the surge in unemployment experienced by Italy in the early 1990s and quite apparent in figure 12.1 above.

The unsustainable character of the 1970 to 1980s regime of subsidized "temporary" layoffs, however, also led to introduction of more "active" policy instruments, meant to foster employment of workers made redundant by declining sectors and of young long-term unemployed market entrants. Space does not make it possible to review the character of these instruments (see box 2 of the working paper version): briefly, Italy's "active" labor market policies appear extremely underdeveloped from a cross-country comparative perspective.

Regulation of hiring, however, also became less stringent, especially over the 1990s. While employment protection remained largely unreformed for regular employment relationships, a variety of nonstandard contracts were exploited more widely. In particular, possibilities of temporary employment were extended by several legislative provisions that we cannot review here in detail (see box 3 of the working paper version) but will mention when discussing the implications of this institutional evolution for Italy's recent experience in section 12.5.

12.3.2   The Role of Unions

In the postwar period three union confederations played a major role in the Italian labor market, and until recently acted together in wage negotiations as well as in exerting pressure on legislative processes. Within each of the three confederations different political orientations coexist, but CGIL was formerly Communist, CISL was formerly Christian Democrat, and UIL was "lay." In addition a number of smaller unions became increasingly important (COBAS). As shown in figure 12.3, union membership rose sharply in the late 1960s to early 1970s season of industrial unrest, peaked around 1980, and has been declining since (even more sharply than would appear from these statistics,

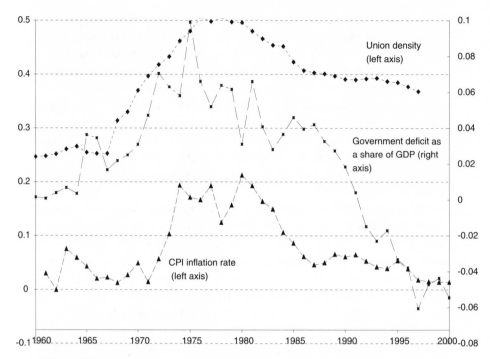

Figure 12.3
Union density, government deficit, and CPI inflation in 1977 to 2001. Source: Primary
government deficit/surplus: OECD; inflation (consumer prices): Bank of Italy; union density (percentage of union members among dependent employees): Checchi and Lucifora
(2002).

since up to 50 percent of the main union confederations' members are
now retired).

Union wage pushes (supported by mandatory extension of centrally
bargained contracts, and by automatic indexation and wage compression) certainly played an important role in fostering unemployment
growth in the 1970s and early 1980s. Since the early 1990s, however,
unions have played a very different role. Strike activity was very intense in the 1970s (when up to 100 percent of dependent workers were
involved in at least one strike per year). It subsided sharply in the
1980s, however, and especially in the 1990s (when 20 percent or fewer
workers were on strike at least once per year) when the central bargaining framework was reformed so as to privilege inflation stabilization (a prerequisite for EMU membership) and peaceful industrial
relations. Briefly (see box 4 of the working paper version for more de-

tail), wages were set on the basis of "programmed" inflation rates, and employment-oriented fiscal instruments (as well as employers' commitments to investment and employment) were bargained together with wage platforms. As a result the 1990s were a decade of wage moderation in Italy.

12.4 History and Shocks

It is easy to interpret Italy's aggregate and disaggregate unemployment experience in terms of the interaction of institutional features with such shocks as the oil price hikes and productivity slowdown of the 1970s to 1980s, and the fiscal and monetary restrictions in the 1990s run-up to EMU. It is, of course, no coincidence that the two episodes of sharp and sustained unemployment increase were observed in 1975 to 1988 and 1993 to 1998. However, it is important to note that the character of shocks and of their interaction with institutions was quite different in the two episodes.

12.4.1 Two Episodes of Increasing Unemployment

When Italy was hit by the oil shock and productivity slowdown in 1973, unemployment rose only modestly because wages were high and rigid and employers were largely prevented from dismissing redundant employees. As mentioned above, both hiring and firing remained quite subdued initially. Young labor market entrants began to find it difficult to obtain employment, and the remarkable growth of unemployment over the following fifteen years was largely concentrated on those among the young who did not exit the labor force to pursue education. It is not surprising, in light of strong regional wage equalization, that the largest increase in unemployment should be observed in the less productive south, with a particularly pronounced divergence increase in 1985 to 1989. The latter mechanism is a simple and striking force or widespread regional dimension of Italian unemployment, as reported in tables 12.1 and 12.2.

1975 to 1988: Fiscal Crowding out and the Cost of Disinflation

To understand the character of the first episode, which we dated 1975 to 1988, two key macroeconomic developments seem particularly important, namely the dynamics of government spending and the disinflation process. Figure 12.2 reports the dynamics of public primary deficits, which grow sharply in the 1980s and decline equally sharply toward a surplus position in the 1990s. Public employment (as a share of dependent employees) also grew from about 10 percent in the early 1960s to about 16 percent in the late 1980s, but then was stabilized and declined slightly. The theoretical framework and cross-country panel evidence of Algan, Cahuc, and Zylberberg (2002) are readily applicable to the interaction of these variables with Italy's labor market institutions and performance. In general, public employment can reduce unemployment at given wages, and both the growth of public employment and the aggregate demand stimulus of government deficits arguably contributed to limiting unemployment growth in the 1970s and 1980s. Wage rigidity, in the face of supply shocks, would potentially have resulted in much sharper unemployment increases in Italy. But public employment generally increases unemployment when it increases equilibrium wages (destroying private jobs and drawing additional workers in the labor force). This phenomenon helps explain the high unemployment rates among well-educated individuals in the south. Public jobs pay the same wage everywhere, and life is cheaper in the south where private jobs are scarce. Hence unemployment should be (and was) concentrated in that region, where it took the form of wait-unemployment for highly educated individuals.

Following the supply shocks of the 1970s, which resulted in a simultaneous increase in inflation and unemployment from the mid-1970s up to the early 1980s, throughout the 1980s Italy experienced a remarkable disinflation process, which brought CPI inflation down from 21 percent in 1980 to less than 5 percent in 1988 (figure 12.3). Monetary policy became more independent in 1981, when the Bank of Italy ceased automatic financing of budget deficits (the *divorzio*). In addition the indexation system was reformed in 1983, and Italy was also forced to slowly open its capital market, as required by participation in the European monetary system (EMS), which was introduced in 1978. These various developments obviously helped the disinflation process, but the tightening in monetary policy over the 1980s was accompanied by a significant sacrifice ratio, despite the very loose fiscal policy implemented in that period. Between 1980 and 1988, while the inflation rate fell by 17 percentage points, the unemployment rate rose from 7.6 to 12 percent, with a sacrifice ratio of 0.25: each percentage point fall in inflation was accompanied by an increase in unemployment of around a fourth of a percentage point.

1992 to 1998: Fiscal Retrenchment and the Road to EMU

Serious budgetary problems, however, lead public employment to flatten out. Privatization also arguably has employment consequences (in 1988, government-owned firms accounted for 84 percent of employees in the energy and extraction sector and for 64 percent of employees in transportation and communications: the partial or complete privatization of state firms in those sectors certainly put pressure on those jobs). Thus, far from buffering the short-run consequences of wage rigidity in the face of supply shocks, government spending and unemployment have in recent years exacerbated employment losses. Despite wage moderation and limited flexibility-oriented reforms, the recession of the early 1990s resulted in a sharp increase in unemployment. Overall, there is a significant negative correlation over time between the size of the primary budget deficit and the overall unemployment rate (figure 12.4). In the mid-1970s the primary budget deficit was as large as 8 percent, and unemployment was still 8 percent. When unemployment reached its peak in 1998, Italy experienced a 6 percent primary surplus: a remarkable fiscal adjustment effort that, accompanied by some creative accounting, opened the gate to EMU membership.

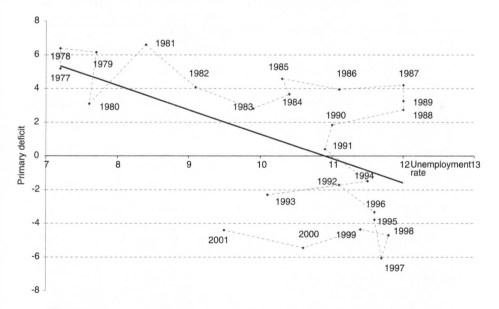

Figure 12.4
Primary budget deficit and total unemployment in 1977 to 2001. Source: OECD and Bank of Italy.

While the time correlation between the budget deficit and unemployment is overall clear and significant, the time evolution highlighted in figure 12.4 also illustrates the different nature of the two increasing unemployment episodes. The points corresponding to the first episode are all positioned above the regression line, suggesting that the increase in unemployment was accompanied by loose fiscal policy. Conversely, the points corresponding to the second episode are all below the regression line, since the increase in unemployment took place at a time of substantial fiscal retrenchment. The second episode also features important regional developments. The divergent pattern of unemployment rates between northern and southern Italy is particularly striking in the aftermath of the aggregate shocks that hit Italy in the early 1990s. In the more dynamic and competitive regions, effects of the fiscal retrenchment required by the Maastricht Treaty were offset by the 1992 devaluation and by Italy's subsequent excursion out of the European monetary system. In the south, conversely, the unemployment rate rose from 16 to over 23 percent in the first half of the 1990s, and employment and GDP both fell by over 10 percent as wages and productivity remained roughly unchanged.

To summarize, the divergent dynamics of unemployment in the 1970s and 1980s were largely explained by different reactions (in light of wage rigidity) to similar aggregate shocks, partly buffered by government policies. In the early 1990s, conversely, shocks were different in the north and in the south, and the still very limited (especially along regional lines) flexibility-oriented reforms of labor market institutions did little to prevent unemployment from diverging again.

12.4.2   Regional Productivity Differentials

As discussed in more detail by Bertola (2000), relative wage and productivity indicators for the manufacturing sectors of southern and northern Italy display a convergent productivity pattern until around 1970, when national contracts began to impose stringent lower bounds on each sector's wages throughout Italy. After some divergence relative productivity remained lower in the south and flat from 1975 to the present. In the manufacturing sector, take-home pay was only about 10 percent lower in the south than in the other regions, and not sufficient to induce migration in light of cost-of-living differentials and of fairly small job-finding rates in the north. Productivity differentials are twice as large, at about 20 percent: only a smaller fiscal wedge, largely reflecting social security contribution exemptions, makes it possible for employers' unit labor costs to be roughly equalized throughout Italy (as must be the case, of course, if firms are free to choose where to produce). While employed southerners earn almost as large a wage as their compatriots do, few are indeed employed because their productivity remains lower. But few migrate (e.g., see Brunello, Lupi, and Ordine 2001) because centralized wage bargaining does not allow them to put pressure on wages in the north where their standard of living would not be higher. Migration outflows from the south have been sharply higher in recent years, and this may be evidence of a permanently higher responsiveness to wage and unemployment rate differentials, as may be caused by reduced government expenditure overall and especially in the south.

12.4.3   Taxation and the Upward Trend of the Shadow Economy

Over the last twenty years Italy experienced a remarkable increase in income tax, consumption tax, and payroll tax revenue as a share of GDP. In terms of labor market impact, the most important development may have been that of payroll taxation, whose total revenue increased from 11 percent of GDP in the early 1970s up to more than 15 percent in the late 1990s (source: OECD). In the last few years a substantial decline is observed, and it could have contributed to the recent developments discussed in the concluding section below.

The role of labor taxes in determining unemployment is theoretically unclear and empirically controversial (see Pissarides 1998; Daveri and Tabellini 2000). Microeconometric studies of Italian data suggest that labor participation is very inelastic (Aaberge et al. 1999), and most of the burden of payroll taxation should be shifted to labor. But labor taxes have unambiguous effects on two important labor market aspects: participation and the shadow economy. In theory, higher payroll taxation can affect participation importantly even when it leaves unemployment unchanged (Garibaldi and Wasmer 2001), and the fall in the Italian employment rate is empirically correlated with the rise in payroll taxes. The heavy and increasing tax, social security, and administrative burdens imposed on activities that are officially registered tends not only to decrease overall employment but naturally to increase the share of shadow employment, both in theory and in the Italian experience (see Boeri and Garibaldi 2002).

12.5   Recent Developments and Policy Tensions

In this chapter we argued that interpreting Italy's unemployment experience in light of standard theoretical approaches is not difficult, and quite insightful. Our necessarily brief review of time-series and cross-sectional aspects finds that both can be explained readily by the interaction of institutions and shocks. Of course, inference cannot be univocal when analyzing an individual country's history, since very little can be kept fixed when both evolving institutions and more or less dramatic macroeconomic developments are allowed to play a role. Hence it should be, in principle, possible to interpret the same data in terms of other theoretical frameworks. Viewing Italy as a particular set of observations within a coherent data set of industrialized countries, however, offers statistical support to our perspective, and can discipline our effort to offer a more detailed assessments of disaggregated and time-series relationships between macroeconomic dynamics and labor market institutions.

In the second half of the 1990s, employment rates increased rather sharply. The south benefited marginally more than the north from the cyclical upswing, and labor productivity growth declined. In 2002, Italian GDP is growing very slowly, perhaps at a 0.6 percent rate for the year. Yet employment is growing at some 1.2 percent annual rate, and the unemployment rate at 9 percent is the lowest in ten years. As repeatedly mentioned, the Italian labor market problems are mainly to be found in the south, and even across regions recent positive experiences mirrors previous negative developments: in the south, employment is growing at 2 percent per year, much faster than the national average. And even the previous trend away from regular employment is not confirmed in recent experience, as the share of term contracts is stable at 10.4 percent of dependent employment and many of the newly created jobs are standard, protected ones. For Italy, growth used to be jobless. Now, if anything, growth-less hiring is observed, and slow productivity growth may replace nonemployment as a cause of policy concern. Why should such this be the case now and, indeed, since the mid-1990s? There are at least three possible (and interrelated) reasons for this apparent regime change.

First of all, the Italian labor market has become *more flexible* since the mid-1990s: a "package" law in 1997, the 2000 law relaxing regulation of part-time employment, and the 2001 deregulation of term contracts all made it possible to create "atypical" jobs. Moreover the quasi-dependent (but formally self-employed) *Collaborazione coordinata e continuativa* employment relationships have grown substantially throughout the 1990s. All these flexible employment relationships played a very important role in the 1997 to 2000 boom years, when GDP was growing at over 2 percent per year. Flexibility, however, cannot explain the resilience of employment creation in the 2001 and 2002 slowdown: if anything, a more flexible labor market should destroy more jobs during a downturn. Second, and also very important, *wage moderation* has prevailed in Italy since the early 1990s. The pre-set planned inflation rate was ex post lower than actual inflation throughout Italy's disinflation, so real wages did not keep up with productivity (and employment grew, along the labor demand curve). The slowdown that followed the late 1990s boom was accompanied by continued (if less pronounced) wage moderation.

However, a third important mechanism is at work, and explains an important feature of recent experience: the strong growth of regular, open-ended, protected employment relationships, especially in the south, and probably at the expense of continued growth in temporary employment. This phenomenon is probably a reflection of *hiring subsidies*, in the form of tax credits, that were introduced in the second half of the 1990s. Workers over 25 years of age, not employed on a regular contract in the previous two years, would entitle the employer hiring them to a tax credit amounting to 413 euros per month (620 euros in the south). The scheme was temporary, for a three-year period originally scheduled to end in December 2003 (the current government repealed this tax credit, and may or may not reinstate it). Since the fiscal burden was substantially reduced by the scheme, it may be the case that part of observed employment growth is just due to legalization of previously "black" employment relationships. Evidence is lacking, however, and employers have largely ignored an even more generous fiscal treatment (provided by a parallel "amnesty" program) of employment relationships resulting from ones that were previously existing but undeclared.

In summary, recent institutional changes are sensibly linked to recent labor market developments. In the last six years Italy has been able to generate many jobs, despite still rather restrictive fiscal policy (in figure 12.4, where unemployment moves horizontally) and despite a sharp cyclical slowdown. This is welcome, since Italy's employment rate (even after its strong recent increases) stands at only 55.8 percent of working-age population, far below the EU target of 70 percent by 2010. Of course, productivity growth (sustaining wage growth) is needed to make high employment appealing, and this has been lacking in recent years. It remains to be hoped that appropriate reforms (not only in the labor market but also in product and financial markets) will be able to deliver positive developments in coming years. The lessons of the past forty years are quite relevant to current policy debates, but European economic and monetary integration poses new challenges to Italy's labor market. In Italy, which is a fraction of an integrated eurozone, the reform tension can be largely summarized in terms of a need to restructure labor market interactions to address the microeconomic efficiency and arising distribution issues rather than the macroeconomic stability issues that were preeminent in previous years. Before EMU the unemployment problem was addressed by macro policies, largely based on wage indexation and bargaining coordination schemes. These are clearly less relevant in the new millennium when Italy needs to foster microeconomic flexibility in order to compete with other economic and social systems. The relevant reform process has just begun, and the lessons of historical experience will remain relevant for many years to come.

Notes

For comments we thank Paloma Lopez-Garcia. We are also grateful to Saverio Scaramuzzo for competent research assistance.

1. For example, product-market regulation and firm dynamics datasets such as that analyzed by Scarpetta et al. (2002) feature Italy as a country with particularly small firm size.

2. Reconstructed and kindly made available by Paola Casavola for the 1954 to 1998 period; see Bertola (2000).

3. More generally, education does not appear to have important labor market implications in Italy: perhaps as a reflection of higher education institutional quality, the return to higher education is estimated by the OECD to be lowest in Italy among all countries considered in the *Education at a Glance* studies. The microeconometric analysis of Boero et al. (2002) finds that university performance has little or no impact on employment and earnings in Italy.

4. The age groupings in table 11.2 are unfortunately not the same as those in table 11.3, which is based on a different source.

5. See Manacorda (2004) for a fuller account of the indexation system's institutional structure and for evidence that it did affect wage inequality. In particular, the 1983 reform was associated with the end of a previous phase of increasing wage compression, which was reversed in the following year as the cost-of-living adjustment was no longer the same across all wage levels.

6. CIG (*Cassa Integrazione Guadagni*) and CIGS (*Cassa Integrazione Guadagni Straordinaria*) provide income support to redundant employees of large firms, up to a ceiling, for a limited period of time. More detail is available in the working paper version of this chapter.

References

Algan, Y., P. Cahuc, and A. Zylberberg. 2002. Public employment and labour market performance. *Economic Policy* 34: 9–65.

Aaberge, R., U. Colombino, and S. Strom. 1998. Labour supply in Italy: An empirical analysis of joint household decisions with taxes and quantity constraints. *Journal of Applied Econometrics* 14: 403–22.

Bertola, G. 2000. Labor markets in the European Union. *ifo Studien* 1: 99–122.

Bertola, G., F. D. Blau, and L. M. Kahn. 2002. Labor market institutions and demographic employment patterns. *CEPR DP3448, NBER Working Paper 9043.*

Bertola, G., and A. Ichino. 1995. Crossing the river: A comparative perspective on Italian employment dynamics. *Economic Policy* 21: 359–420.

Blanchard, O. J., and J. Wolfers. 2000. The role of shocks and institutions in the rise of European unemployment: The aggregate evidence. *Economic Journal* 110: C1–C33.

Boeri, T., and P. Garibaldi. 2002. Shadow activity and unemployment in a depressed labor market. *CEPR Discussion Paper* 3433.

Boero, G., A. McKnight, R. Naylor, and J. Smith. 2002. Graduates and graduate labour markets in the UK and Italy. *Lavoro e Relazioni Industriali* 2: 87–124.

Brunello, G., C. Lupi, and P. Ordine. 2001. Widening differences in Italian regional unemployment. *Labour Economics* 8 (1): 103–29.

Checchi, D., and C. Lucifora. 2002. Unions and labor market institutions in Europe. *Economic Policy* 35: 361–408.

Daveri, F., and G. Tabellini. 2000. Unemployment, growth and taxation in industrial countries. *Economic Policy* 30: 49–104.

Garibaldi, P., and E. Wasmer. 2001. Labor market flows and equilibrium search unemployment. *IZA Discussion Paper* 406.

Jones, S., and W. J. Riddell. 1999. The measurement of unemployment: An empirical approach. *Econometrica* 67 (1): 147–61.

Manacorda, M. 2004. Can the Scala Mobile explain the fall and rise of earnings inequality in Italy? A semiparametric analysis, 1977–1993. *Journal of Labor Economics* 22: 585–614.

Pissarides, C. A. 1998. The impact of employment tax cut on unemployment and wages: The role of unemployment benefits and tax structure. *European Economic Review* 42 (1): 155–83.

Scarpetta, S., P. Hemmings, T. Tressel, and J. Woo. 2002. The role of policy and institutions for productivity and firm dynamics: Evidence from micro and industry data. *OECD Economics Department Working Paper* 329.

13

Spanish Unemployment:
The End of the Wild Ride?

Samuel Bentolila and Juan F.
Jimeno

E31 J65 E32
J52 E24 E32

13.1 Introduction

Over the last quarter century Spain has stood out for having the highest unemployment rate in the OECD. In the 1960s, by contrast, Spain shared with the rest of Europe unemployment rates of 2 to 3 percent. As figure 13.1 shows, since the second half of the 1970s Spain has experienced a wild ride compared with the largest four European Union economies—France, Germany, Italy, and the United Kingdom (the EU4). Only since the mid-1990s has the unemployment rate decreased significantly. In this chapter we describe this extraordinary evolution and offer an explanation of the unemployment experience based on existing economic research.

In the last few years the joint analysis of shocks and labor market institutions has become popular for explaining European unemployment. It is therefore natural to ask whether we can account for the differential behavior of unemployment in Spain by unusually bad shocks with average institutions, by average shocks with exceptionally unemployment-prone institutions, or by unusually bad shocks and institutions. To do so, we use Blanchard and Wolfers's (2000) model of equilibrium unemployment in the OECD, which allows us to exploit comparable measures of shocks and institutions.

After describing the evolution of the unemployment rate (section 13.2), we show that Spain experienced similar shocks as other OECD countries, except for stronger labor demand shifts (section 13.3). Thus our explanation relies mostly on Spain having a set of exceptionally unemployment-prone labor institutions, in particular, employment protection, unemployment benefits, and collective bargaining (section 13.4). We also argue that a peculiar type of interaction between shocks and institutions was at work, namely that labor institutions

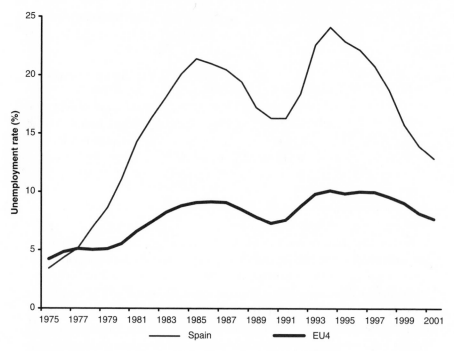

Figure 13.1
Unemployment rate in Spain and the EU4.

were established in the transition from dictatorship to democracy and in the midst of the sharp recession of the 1970s. This environment induced attempts to compensate for the lack of social protection, leading to excessively protective labor institutions. We end by discussing how our story can account for the recent drop in unemployment and argue that it is to some extent structural—due to labor market reforms—although further reforms will be needed (section 13.5).

13.2   Unemployment Evolutions

Before we describe the evolution of the aggregate unemployment rate in Spain since 1975, and then a few breakdowns, we should point out that official Spanish unemployment figures have been questioned in the past. A common suspicion is that they are overstated, given the presumed large underground economy. We discuss this issue in the appendix. Here let us note that several methodological revisions have led to increases in measured employment, but since the estimated labor force has gone up too, the unemployment rate has hardly changed.

The OECD standardized unemployment rate is on average 3 percentage points below the official figure for 1976 to 2001, but it is still very high.

The latest revision of the Spanish labor force survey (LFS), however, *has* significantly altered the measured unemployment rate. Due to an EU directive redefining job search intensity, since 2002 the jobless who reply that their only job search method in the preceding month was to visit the public employment office and that this visit was not for job-seeking purposes are considered nonparticipants. Surprisingly this has shaved 2.4 points off the official unemployment rate. Our analysis stops in 2001, to avoid the survey changes of 2002.

13.2.1 Aggregate Unemployment Rate

At the end of 1975 the Spanish unemployment rate stood at 3.4 percent. As figure 13.1 shows, it then rose for ten years, peaking at 21.4 percent, fell back to a through of 16.3 percent in 1990 and 1991, and shot up again to 24.1 percent in 1994. Since 1995 it has fallen, to 12.9 percent in 2001.

The trend is clearly up and the volatility is remarkable. Table 13.1 presents the ratio of the standard deviations of Hodrick-Prescott (HP) de-trended unemployment, employment, and GDP for Spain vis-à-vis the EU4 countries. For unemployment, they range from 1.4 to 2.8. This *excess volatility* does not stem from output volatility alone, which is also higher but not as much as for unemployment. A related fact is that Spanish Okun's law shows a very high effect of the change in output on the change in unemployment.[1] One reading of these facts is that labor institutions amplify shocks more in Spain than elsewhere. This is surprising because labor market rigidity—which is high in Spain—should induce lower, not higher, volatility in (un)employment with respect to output. We return to this issue in section 13.5.

Table 13.1 also highlights that the unemployment rate grossly underestimates the degree of labor underutilization in Spain. The employment rate fell all the way to 47 percent in 1985 and its current value of 62 percent is among the lowest in the European Union.[2]

13.2.2 Key Breakdowns

Unemployment has a very different impact across population groups in Spain. The difference between the male and female rates, for prime-age workers, is now around 7 percentage points. The rate for male

Table 13.1
Labor market variables in Spain and the EU4 (1976–2001)

		1976–1985	1986–1990	1991–1994	1995–2001
Unemployment rate	*Spain*	12.6	18.9	20.4	18.1
	EU4	6.6	8.4	9.1	9.2
GDP growth[a]	*Spain*	1.6	4.5	1.2	3.5
	EU4	2.4	3.2	1.1	2.2
Employment growth[a]	*Spain*	−1.5	3.3	−1.5	3.9
	EU4	0.2	1.1	−1.0	1.0
Employment rate[b]	*Spain*	53.8	50.3	50.6	54.8
	EU4	62.8	61.9	61.0	62.0
Relative volatility in Spain vis-à-vis:[c]		*France*	*Germany*[d]	*Italy*	*United Kingdom*
Unemployment rate		2.8	1.9	2.7	1.4
Employment		3.2	0.8	2.5	1.5
GDP		1.5	1.1	1.6	1.0

Sources: OECD Economic Outlook (via dX for Windows), Encuesta de Población Activa (EPA), Instituto Nacional de Estadística (INE) (www.ine.es), and Boletín Estadístico of the Banco de España (www.bde.es).
Note: Data are averages for the periods shown. EU4 denotes the unweighted averages of the variables for France, Germany, Italy, and the United Kingdom. All variables are percentages, except for relative volatility, which is a ratio.
a. For Germany in 1991 to 1994 we use only the growth rate over 1992–1994, to avoid the distortions induced by the 1991 reunification.
b. For Germany, starting in 1990, we construct a counterfactual level by imputing the growth rates of the average employment rate of the other three countries, to avoid the level change induced by the 1991 reunification.
c. Ratio of standard deviations of the Hodrick-Prescott annual detrended series (with $\lambda = 100$) for Spain and each of the other four countries.
d. For the comparison with Germany, the period is 1976–1990 due to reunification.

workers aged 16 to 24 years old is about 10 percentage points higher, and for females about 20 percentage points higher, than for prime-age males; see table 13.2. Unemployment of males with a college degree is 6 percentage points lower than of those without a college degree, while for females the difference is 14 percentage points. Across regions, unemployment rates range from around 6 percent in the Ballearic Islands to about 22 percent in Extremadura and Andalusia.[3]

Unemployment differentials are related to changes in the relative demand and supply of each population group. The usual suspects for demand are—as elsewhere—skill-biased technological progress and international trade, though macroeconomic shocks probably also played a role. Some Spanish specificities can, however, be found for la-

Table 13.2
Unemployment differentials and demographic variables in Spain and the EU4 (%)

	Spain			EU4		
	1975	1985	2001	1975	1985	2001
A. Unemployment differentials						
Youth (16–24) versus males (25–54)						
Males	6.4	23.9	9.8	6.0	13.2	9.3
Females	4.4	35.6	20.7	6.4	18.3	11.7
Females (16–24) versus males (25–54)	−1.6	0.6	7.4	0.4	2.8	2.2
Tertiary versus nontertiary education						
Males			6.1			3.6
Females			13.6			5.1
B. Demographic variables						
Youth population[a]	85.3	88.5	67.6	77.3	81.1	55.4
University graduates[b]						
Males	25	29	53	26	26	47
Females	14	29	62	19	25	58
Participation rates[c]						
Males	96.5	94.2	91.6	95.3	94.3	91.6
Females	27.9	35.0	61.2	49.1	60.0	72.2

Sources: Unemployment differentials: Spain: EPA, INE; EU4: OECD Employment Outlook. Youth population: United Nations and Eurostat. University graduates: UNESCO. Participation: Labour Force Statistics, OECD.
Note: EU4 denotes the unweighted average of the variables for France, Germany, Italy, and the United Kingdom.
a. Youth population (16–24 years old) over the male population aged 25 to 54 years old.
b. Gross enrolment rates at tertiary level of education for population aged 18 to 22 years old.
c. Population aged 25 to 54 years old.

bor supply. Table 13.2 gives a few facts. In particular, the baby boom took place in Spain later than in the EU4, whereas recently the share of youth has decreased; the educational buildup also took place later, and female labor participation increased, closing the gap with male rates by 40 percent.

13.3 Explanations: Shocks

We now describe macroeconomic events from 1976 to 2001. Our theme is that besides worldwide shocks Spain had a few of its own. For the sake of clarity, we break down the period into three cycles, corresponding to the periods shown in table 13.1.

13.3.1 The Long Recession (1976–1985)

The turbulence of the second half of the 1970s coincided in Spain with the transition from the Franco dictatorship (1939–1975) to democracy (Portugal shares this trait).[4] The dictator's economic legacy was a balanced budget and very low gross public debt (13 percent of GDP) but also relatively low income (80 percent of the EU15 average, at PPP), an underdeveloped welfare state (with public spending at 24 percent of GDP), an obsolete industrial structure (with 22 percent of employment still in agriculture), and a relatively closed economy (with exports plus imports at 19 percent of GDP). The labor market was heavily regulated: unions, strikes, and lockouts were forbidden, and the government determined labor conditions. In 1976 Spain embarked on a path of democratization and decentralization, welfare state expansion, and rising economic openness. New labor institutions were established in the Workers' Statute (1980).

Due to political instability there was little policy response to the two oil price shocks until the early 1980s. And there was a large wage push as unions competed to get established, which was stopped in 1977, when the first of a series of social pacts was introduced. The first half of the 1980s saw a strong wave of industrial restructuring.

Monetary policy was lax until 1977 and then restrictive: the real long-term interest rate went from −9 percent in 1978 to 3.2 percent in 1981.[5] On the other hand, public spending rose to 40 percent of GDP and the budget deficit to 6 percent, bringing gross public debt to 50 percent of GDP by 1986.

13.3.2 The EU (1986–1994) and EMU (1995–2001) Cycles

The 1986 to 1990 boom was marked by two events. There was another specific shock (shared with Portugal): entry into the European Community (EC) in 1986, which entailed, inter alia, lower barriers to trade. Spain also joined the European monetary system in 1989 and the European single market in 1993. And there was a huge increase in temporary jobs. In the 1991 to 1994 recession Spain followed the European cycle. An aggravating factor was the overvalued exchange rate of the peseta, which triggered several realignments in 1992 and 1993.

The 1995 to 2001 expansion was influenced by the arrival of a Center-Right party to power in 1996. Its 1997 labor market reform and its determination, shared by the central bank, to meet the Maastricht

Treaty conditions for economic and monetary union (EMU) fostered wage and price moderation. In the run-up to EMU, real interest rates fell sharply.

13.3.3 A Benchmark Model

We now use the observable shocks model of Blanchard and Wolfers (2000) (BW hereafter) to quantify the contribution of shocks to the increase in equilibrium unemployment. The dependent variable consists of five-year averages of unemployment rates in twenty OECD countries, u_{it}, over the period 1960 to 1999. The explanatory variables are country-specific shocks interacted with institutions:

$$u_{it} = c_i + \left(\sum_k a_k Y_{kit} \right) \left(1 + \sum_j b_j X_{ij} \right) + e_{it}, \tag{1}$$

where the indexes are i for country, t for five-year periods, k for shocks, and j for institutions. c_i are country effects and e_{it} is random noise. The shocks Y_{kit} are TFP growth, the long-term real interest rate, and labor demand shifts (the labor share purged of the impact of factor prices). Labor institutions, X_{ij}, are described in section 13.4.

Since most institutions were established around 1980, the model makes less sense for Spain before that time. To retain transition to democracy, we examine changes between 1970 to 1974 and 1995 to 1999. Figure 13.2 presents the observed and fitted values and table 13.3 shows the data. The last two columns show changes in shocks for Spain and the average of the other 19 countries in the sample. Changes in TFP growth and real interest rates in Spain were in line with those elsewhere, while labor demand shifts were about twice larger. The model accounts for only 11 of the 17 percentage-point increase observed, attributing 6 percentage points to changes in TFP growth, 4 percentage points to labor demand shifts, and 1 percentage point to interest rates.

These results are not robust, however. Monetary policy was loose up to 1977 and restrictive afterward, and there was a large drop in TFP growth in the second half of the 1970s. For the change between 1975 to 1979 and 1995 to 1999, the fit is much better: the model predicts a 14.6 percentage-point increase vis-à-vis the 14.2 percentage points observed, attributing a 7.6 percentage-point unemployment increase to real interest rates, 4.3 percentage points to labor demand shifts, and 2.7

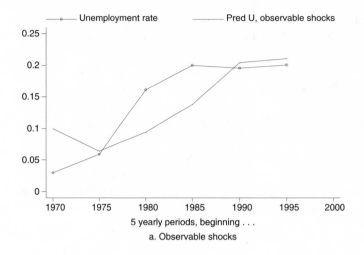

a. Observable shocks

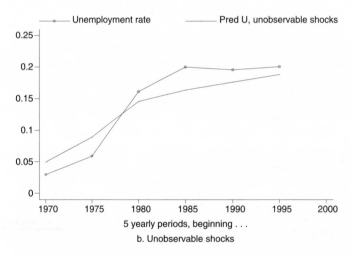

b. Unobservable shocks

Figure 13.2
Unemployment rate and fit of Blanchard-Wolfers models: (a) Observable shocks; (b) unobservable schocks.

Table 13.3
Accounting for Spanish unemployment à la Blanchard-Wolfers, 1995 to 1999 versus 1970 to 1974 (%)

	Change in unemployment[a]	Change in shocks	
		Spain	OECD[b]
Actual change	17.1		
Observable shocks model	11.1		
Total factor productivity growth		6.0	−2.1	−2.3
Real interest rate		0.9	0.9	0.8
Labor demand		4.1	−10.3	−4.6
Unobservable shocks model	13.9		
Shocks (at average institutions)	6.7		
Institutions (interacted)[c]	7.2		
Unemployment benefits		3.3	
Employment protection		2.3	
Unions and bargaining		0.5	
Taxes and labor policies		1.1	

Source: Own estimation using the model in Blanchard and Wolfers (2000) (econ-wp.mit .edu/RePEc/2000/blanchar/harry_data) and updated unemployment rates for 1995 to 1999. There are changes unemployment definitions in 1995 to 1999 in Belgium, Denmark, Germany, Greece, and Spain.
a. Change in the average unemployment rate from 1970–1974 to 1995–1999. Unemployment based on national definitions.
b. Countries: Australia, Austria, Belgium, Canada, Denmark, Finland, France, Germany, Ireland, Italy, Japan, the Netherlands, New Zealand, Norway, Portugal, Sweden, Switzerland, the United Kingdom, and the United States.
c. Unemployment benefits includes both replacement rates and benefit length. Unions and bargaining includes union coverage, union density and bargaining co-ordination. Taxes and labor policies includes the wage tax wedge and active labor market policy.

percentage points to TFP growth. These decompositions include as effects of shocks both their direct impact and their interaction with institutions. In the next section we separate the two.

13.4 Explanations: Institutions

We return to BW for a first look at labor institutions, namely the unemployment benefit replacement rate and length, union contract coverage and union density, the union and employer coordination of bargaining, employment protection, the wage tax wedge, and active labor market policies. The measures are 1983 to 1994 country averages from Nickell (1997), entered as deviations from the overall average.

Table 13.4
Comparison of labor market institutions in Spain, the OECD, and Portugal

		OECD[a]				
Variable	Spain	Mean	Mini-mum	Maxi-mum	Portugal	Units
Replacement rate	75	56.5	11	90	63	% of previous wage
Benefit length	3.5	2.4	0.5	4	0.7	Years[b] (1)
Employment protection	19	10	1	20	18	Ordinal
Union coverage	3	2.7	1	3	3	Index[c] (2)
Union density	14.5	43.6	11.8	81.8	39.1	% of employees
Coordination	3	4	2	6	4	Index[d]
Tax wedge	52.2	47.4	29.8	69.8	35.6	% tax rate[e]
Active labor policy	7.5	12.3	2.6	59.3	9.3	% spending[f]

Source: Blanchard and Wolfers (2000). The variables are simple averages of the values for 1983 to 1988 and 1989 to 1994 given in Nickell (1997).
a. See the list of countries in note 2 to table 13.3.
b. 4 means indefinite.
c. 1 = under 25%, 2 = 25–70%, 3 = over 70%.
d. Sum of union and employer coordination, each ranked as low (1), medium (2), or high (3).
e. Sum of payroll, income, and consumption tax rates.
f. Active labor market spending per unemployed person as a percentage of GDP per member of the labor force.

Table 13.4 presents the values of institutions for Spain and the average of the other countries. It reveals that (1) the unemployment benefit replacement rate and length, and employment protection, are all high, (2) union coverage is high and coordination low, though union density is also low, (3) the wage tax is slightly above the average, and (4) active labor market policy is symbolic. Thus, apart from low union density, the overall impression is one of unemployment-prone labor institutions.

To isolate their role, we use BW's model with common, unobservable shocks captured by time dummies, d_t, interacted with time-invariant measures of institutions:

$$u_{it} = c_i + d_t \left(1 + \sum_j b_j X_{ij}\right) + e_{it}. \tag{2}$$

Figure 13.2 shows the observed and fitted values. Note in table 13.3 that the model underpredicts the increase between 1970 to 1974 and 1995 to 1999 by 3 percentage points. The model implies that had Spain had labor institutions like the average country in the sample, its unemployment rate would have risen by 6.7 percentage points, from the effect of shocks, rather than the 13.9 percentage points predicted. Unemployment benefits and employment protection jointly account for more than three-quarters of the institutions-induced increase. Thus, the story that Spain had a set of strongly unemployment generating institutions, which amplified macroeconomic shocks, can account for the evolution of unemployment.

Although we give only a first approximation (institutions are constant, shocks are not properly identified, etc.), potentially suffering from data mining (measures of institutions that do well survive) and reverse causality, we think this is a very useful benchmark. But measures of institutions are likely to contain sizable measurement error, and so we now describe the key institutions in Spain.

13.4.1 Employment Protection

Contrary to other institutions, employment protection existed under Franco and the new legislation (1980) did not depart much from the Francoist one.[6] For workers on indefinite or *permanent* contracts, individual dismissal carries severance pay of 20 days of wages per year of service (p.y.o.s., hereafter) with a ceiling of one year, unless it is based on disciplinary grounds. However, most dismissals are actually disciplinary, for two reasons. First, the firm does not need to give advance notice of disciplinary dismissals. Second, economic reasons for dismissal were not recognized until 1994, and in this case, if the worker appeals, the firm has to prove its reasons in court. Most dismissals are appealed because the cost of appealing is low. The severance pay is raised this way to 45 days of wages p.y.o.s. (with a ceiling of 3.5 years[7]), and the worker can get paid interim wages up to the date of the ruling if the dismissal is ruled unfair, which happens in about 72 percent of cases going to court. As a result about 85 percent of dismissals are settled out of court.

Collective dismissals, entailing severance pay of twenty days of wages p.y.o.s., involve 18 percent of fired workers. They require administrative authorization, which is given only upon agreement between the parties, and this often leads to higher severance pay.

These are very high figures, but several reforms have altered the picture. In late 1984, provisions limiting the use of fixed-term contracts to temporary activities were suppressed. New fixed-term contract types were created, with low (12 days p.y.o.s.) or no severance pay, renewable for up to three years. The temporary jobs' share in hiring shot up, from 12 to 96 percent, and the share in the stock of employees from 11 to around 33 percent. The 1994 reform, which reintroduced the principle that fixed-term contracts should be used only for temporary activities, had no effect on that share.

The 1997 reform reduced severance pay for unfair dismissals of new hires from 45 to 33 days of wages p.y.o.s. with a ceiling of two years, via a new permanent contract with reduced social security contributions.[8] Workers aged 30 to 45 with less than one year of unemployment were ineligible for the contract, so as not to subsidize all workers (forbidden by law). After the reform the share of temporary contracts in hires fell from 96 to 91 percent and from 34 to 31 percent of the stock of employees.

Lack of direct data on firing costs has hampered the analysis of their impact on employment. But the introduction of fixed-term contracts spurred many studies providing related evidence. The main effects found are as follows:[9] (1) Fixed-term contracts have raised employment volatility. (2) They sharply raised labor flows; for instance, the ratio of annual hires to the labor force grew from an average of 12 percent in 1977 to 1983 to 76 percent in 2001. (3) They have probably helped reduce long-term unemployment (over one year), which has fallen from 61 to 40 percent. (4) They lowered labor costs, since temporary employees get 7 to 15 percent lower wages than comparable permanent employees, and thus contributed to wage inequality. (5) They raised wage pressure until the early 1990s, by providing a buffer for permanent workers, but appear to have reduced unemployment hysteresis since then (through lower long-term unemployment). (6) Since fixed-term contracts are seldom upgraded to permanent, they have probably lowered human capital investment and led to more frequent accidents at work. (7) They have reduced youth unemployment vis-à-vis adult unemployment.[10]

13.4.2 Unemployment Benefits

Unemployment benefits exist in Spain since 1961, but their modern form was established in 1976 and consolidated in 1984.[11] The unemployment insurance (UI) replacement ratio was, up to 1992, equal to

80 percent for months 1 to 6 of unemployment, 70 percent for months 7 to 12, and 60 percent thereafter. Benefit duration was equal to one-half of previous job tenure (from six months), with a maximum of two years. In 1992 the replacement ratio was cut to 70 percent in months 1 to 6 and to 60 percent thereafter, and benefit duration to one-third of tenure (from one year). In 1993 benefits became taxable.

Unemployment assistance (UA) pays 75 percent of the minimum wage to workers with dependants whose average family income is below that threshold, for up to two years.[12] Since 1989 more generous conditions apply to workers aged 45 or older, and benefits are paid until retirement to workers aged at least 52. In 1993 UA also became taxable. There is a special UA for agricultural workers in the regions of Andalusia and Extremadura. They get 75 percent of the minimum wage for 90 to 300 days within the year if they have been employed for at least 40 days (20 days if already in the system in 1983). Since May 2002 no new workers were allowed to join the system, but this change was undone due to a successful general strike.

The 1992 reform was a turning point, reinforced by the short employment durations caused by temporary employment. In particular, benefit coverage, which had risen from 23 percent in 1984 to 50 percent in 1992, fell again to around 37 percent in 2001.

As for the effects of benefits, the macroeconomic literature for Spain has found that replacement ratios raise wages and, through this channel, equilibrium unemployment.[13] Work on microeconomic data shows that unemployment benefits reduce the exit rate from unemployment but not that they lead to better matches, at least in terms of tenure, once a job is found.[14]

13.4.3 Collective Bargaining

Under Franco labor conditions were bargained in so-called vertical unions that included both workers and employers, with the government having the final say. In 1975 standard collective bargaining was established, with legal regulations set in 1980 and 1985. But departure from initial conditions has been slow in many respects.[15]

Workers have a constitutional right to be covered by a collective bargain, independently of union affiliation. Indeed, unions obtain their representation from firm-level elections, rather than affiliation. If they obtain 10 percent of the representatives at the national level or 15 percent at the regional level, they have the right to negotiate in *any* industry-level bargain. Absolute majority of representatives is required for agreement validity. Conditions set in above firm-level agreements are automatically extended by law to all firms and workers in the relevant industry or geographical area, and firm-level agreements cannot overrule broader ones.

Thus there is little incentive for workers to unionize and union density is largely irrelevant. Large organizations are at a premium: there are two major unions and one employers' association. Above firm-level agreements cover around 80 percent of employees and firm-level agreements only 11 percent (2000). Bargaining takes place mostly at the industry level, and there is geographical fragmentation. There has been no real reform of collective bargaining regulation.

The legal minimum wage has gone from representing 45 percent of the average wage in the early 1970s to 30 percent now. Minimum wages set in collective bargains are, however, binding for low-skill workers.[16]

Empirically, in aggregate equations, the unemployment rate, benefit replacement ratios, and taxes are all significant determinants of wages, as well as often the change in unemployment, the long-term unemployment share, and mismatch measures. The estimated coefficient of the effect of unemployment on wages is typically low, around -0.2, and Spain is normally ranked among the high real wage rigidity countries.[17]

Union activity is badly measured. Estimates of insider worker hysteresis from Spanish firm-level data are in between those for countries where bargaining is highly centralized or decentralized. Unions have managed to reduce wage inequality, across both skills and regions, through national pacts in 1977 to 1986 and through bargaining afterward. The evidence indicates that industry coverage of collective bargaining raises wages in medium and large firms and reduces returns to skill, while firm-level bargaining partly offsets wage compression, presumably by allowing employers to bring wages closer to productivity. Overall, wage inequality seems to be high above the median (comparable to the United States) and low below the median (comparable to continental Europe). Last, both the national minimum wage and minimum bargained wages appear to have induced higher youth unemployment.[18]

13.4.4   Other Issues

Two final issues worth mentioning are geographical mobility and family ties. Interregional migration rates, around 0.5 percent of the population, are about half in Spain as in other European countries. This is partly endogenous to high national unemployment but also related to unemployment benefits and housing prices.[19] Indeed, the regions with the lowest income per capita and the highest unemployment rates, Andalusia and Extremadura, receive net immigration from the rest of Spain, which is probably related to their special unemployment benefits for agricultural workers. The lack of mobility is also related to the uniformity of wages across regions, so that relative regional wages do not seem to respond much to regional unemployment rates.[20] By creating mismatch, low migration is likely to have raised equilibrium unemployment.

A related fact is that the welfare impact of becoming unemployed is mitigated by extended family networks. In Spain family networks provide income support to unemployed heads of households to a larger extent than in northern Europe. Young workers represent a larger share of the unemployed than in most of Europe, and they also suffer higher job instability. They have responded by postponing parental home leaving. As a result they may have higher reservation wages and lower geographical mobility, again leading to higher unemployment.[21]

These factors make wage adjustments harder and employment adjustments more likely, thus contributing to higher equilibrium unemployment. But they are shared with countries with lower unemployment rates, like Italy, and we are lacking an assessment of their contribution to the differential Spanish experience.

13.5 Interpretation and Policy Implications

Taking stock at this point of our discussion, our explanation for the rise in unemployment in Spain from 1975 to 1995, say, runs as follows: Spain chose a set of labor market institutions conducive to high unemployment, in particular, unemployment benefits and employment protection. These institutions amplified the effects of aggregate shocks, which seem to have been similar in the rest of the OECD, except for more severe labor demand shifts (and stronger disinflation from the mid-1970s) in Spain.

Let us add two caveats. First, two other country-specific shocks were present: the transition from dictatorship to democracy and joining the EC. While the second was beneficial in integrating the economy to goods, labor, and capital flows, the first seems to us more important.

Second, we believe that firing costs and unemployment benefits get too much blame for the rise in unemployment, while collective bargaining gets too little. As is well known, the relationship between firing costs and aggregate unemployment is theoretically ambiguous and empirical results are not conclusive.[22] Moreover, the incidence of firing costs was reduced by deregulating fixed-term contracts. Unemployment insurance benefits are relatively high at the beginning of the spell, but unemployment assistance is much less generous and coverage rates are low. On the other hand, unions have an undisputed grip on collective bargaining, whose regulation remains unchanged since the early 1980s.

Why did Spain choose those institutions? An important reason is that it had a low level of social protection expenditure when the oil shocks hit. To compensate, firing was kept expensive, and the unemployed were provided with generous income support. This may also explain why it was possible to reform the institutions in the 1990s. By 1991 the gap in expenditures on social protection with respect to the EU12 had fallen to 4 percent of GDP. Simultaneously, the unemployed plus the temporary workers overtook permanent employees as a fraction of the labor force,[23] making it politically viable to reduce protection on other margins.

For this story to be plausible, however, we need to discuss why Portugal, with apparently similar starting conditions and institutions, has much lower unemployment.

13.5.1 Spain versus Portugal

As Layard (1990) once stated, any convincing story for Spanish unemployment must account for the difference with Portugal. The initial conditions were similar (e.g., in industrial structures), both underwent a transition to democracy and joined the EC simultaneously, and it is widely thought that both shocks and institutions have been similar. However, their respective average unemployment rates were 13.6 and 6.6 percent in 1976 to 2001 (OECD standardized rates). What is missing? We now argue that, in fact, shocks and institutions have *not* been the same in the two countries.

First of all, BW measures of shocks were, on average, more favorable for Portugal over 1975 to 1994 (later data being unavailable): the change in TFP growth was equal to 0.6 percent in Portugal as opposed to −2.3 percent in Spain, and labor demand shifts to 23.8 percent as opposed to −9.7 percent in Spain. On the other hand, real interest rates rose more in Portugal, 4.3 versus 3 percent.

More important, standard measures of institutions, presented in table 13.4, do not look so similar, except for high employment protection and minimal active labor market policies. In Portugal labor taxes are lower, and unemployment benefit replacement rates and length were much lower than in Spain.[24]

Table 13.4 presents union coverage as being the same and coordination as being higher in Portugal. Union density is higher in Portugal, but this is a bad measure of union power. There are only two coordinated unions in Spain, while in Portugal there are many uncoordinated unions. The outcomes are telling: Spanish unions achieve wages far above the national minimum wage, while Portuguese unions cannot for many categories. Wage dispersion is also higher in Portugal.[25]

Why is union power lower in Portugal than in Spain? Political developments could have been important. For a few months after the Carnation Revolution the Communist party run the government. But in November of 1975 a military countercoup led to normalization of political institutions and weakened labor unions.[26] Spain had no revolution: Franco died in bed, and then a party of reformists from the old regime ruled for seven years, maintaining social peace by improving social protection.

Thus the idea that Spanish labor institutions are less conducive to low unemployment than Portuguese institutions, collective bargaining in particular, helps explain the unemployment differential. Does it also help us understand why unemployment has fallen so much in Spain in the 1990s? We now take up this question.

13.5.2   Has the NAIRU Fallen?

How structural is the recent fall in unemployment? A fraction is clearly cyclical: average GDP growth was 1.2 percent in 1991 to 1994 and 3.5 percent in 1995 to 2001. But while in the latter period the unemployment rate fell from 24.1 to 12.9 percent, inflation went from 3.9 to 3.8 percent. This suggests a significant reduction in structural unemployment. Let us now list the factors leading to the unemployment reduction and then present estimates of the change in structural unemployment.

One cause of the fall in unemployment was wage moderation, in particular, since 1993: a simple wage equation for 1981 to 2002 delivers residuals of around 2 percent between 1986 and 1992, close to zero between 1993 and 2000, and around −1.5 percent in 2001 and 2002.[27]

Table 13.5
Inflation-unemployment trade-off

Dependent variable: Annual change in inflation[a]		
Cyclical unemployment rate[b]	−0.040	−0.022
	(0.032)	(0.033)
Cyclical unemployment rate × Dummy 1997–2001	−0.009	−0.022
	(0.103)	(0.102)
Δ Unemployment rate		−0.124
		(0.058)
Δ Unemployment rate × Dummy 1997–2001		0.120
		(0.100)
Growth rate of price of imports (lagged)	0.019	0.027
	(0.008)	(0.008)

Sources: Wage increases: Boletín de Estadísticas Laborales, Spanish Ministry of Labor and Social Affairs. Unemployment: INE. Price of imports: SERIES Database, Spanish Ministry of the Economy.
a. Quarterly data on the GDP deflator. Sample period: 1978:1 to 2002:2. Standard errors in parentheses.
b. Cyclical unemployment is measured as the deviation of the unemployment rate from a third-order polynomial.

Further evidence of a structural change in wage and price setting comes from analyzing the trade-off between unemployment and inflation. In Spain inflation is not very responsive to cyclical unemployment, but it is to the change in unemployment.[28] Estimating the trade-off (see table 13.5), we find evidence that after 1997 the response of changes in inflation to cyclical unemployment has increased, while the response to changes in unemployment has fallen (though neither effect is statistically significant).

What factors could account for a change in wage setting? Figure 13.3 presents time-varying measures of six labor institutions in Spain and the EU4 countries: unemployment benefit replacement rates and duration, employment protection, union density, coordination of wage bargaining, and the wage tax wedge.[29] It reveals convergence of Spain toward the EU4 in the second part of the sample.

But there were other events. First, the employment losses of 1991 to 1994, leading to unemployment at 24 percent, affected union behavior in wage setting. Second, since 1994 wage moderation has been exchanged by unions for the nonapplication (1994) or nonapproval (2001) of labor reforms. Third, the nominal convergence Maastricht Treaty criteria imposed some discipline on price and wage setting. Fi-

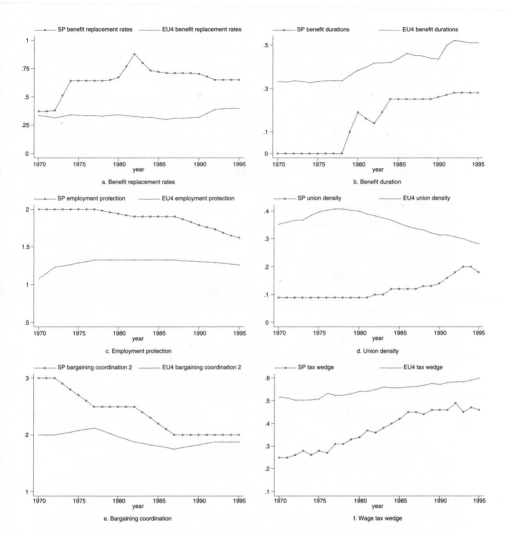

Figure 13.3
Labor market institutions in Spain and the EU4: (a) Benefit replacement rates; (b) benefit duration; (c) employment protection; (d) union density; (e) bargaining coordination; (f) wage tax wedge.

nally, some mild product market reforms could have lowered price markups. Since these are all one-time events, it is hard to assess their contributions to wage moderation. In any event, it is risky to award all the merit to labor reforms.

Macroeconomic policy also helped unemployment to fall. Mostly due to EMU, the real interest rate went from 7.4 percent in 1995 to 1.8 percent in 2001, while it had averaged 5.1 percent in 1985 to 1994. There were also reductions in income tax rates in 1999 and in social security contributions for permanent contracts in 1997.

Let us now try to disentangle cyclical from structural changes. We look at two indicators of structural unemployment: the third-order polynomial series used for computing cyclical unemployment in table 13.5 and the equilibrium unemployment rate, or NAIRU, implied by the aggregate price and wage equations in Estrada et al. (2000). The two measures indicate a reduction of structural unemployment in 1995 to 2001 of about 7 percentage points—to around 14.5 percent in 2001—while actual unemployment fell by about 11 percent. As to the sources of the 7.4 percentage-point estimated NAIRU fall, the wage and price equations attribute 3.6 percentage points to the fall in the wage taxes, 2.9 percentage points to the fall in unemployment benefits, and 0.9 percentage point to the fall in price–cost markups.

13.5.3   Looking Ahead

We conclude with a discussion of forces challenging the achievements in the 1990s and the institutional changes needed to cope with them.

EMU Challenges

Since its entry into EMU, Spain has maintained annual GDP growth and inflation rates of about 1 and 2 percentage points, respectively, above eurozone averages. An argument can be made that both are equilibrium phenomena coming from the fall in equilibrium unemployment (excess growth) and the adjustment of relative prices (excess inflation) associated with growth (the Balassa-Samuelson effect). As for the fall in equilibrium unemployment, we have argued that it may be overestimated, given the concurrence of several one-time events. Regarding the Balassa-Samuelson effect, we may note that labor productivity in the business sector grew at an annual rate of 0.7 percent from 1999 to 2001, the same rate as in the eurozone.

Another warning comes from the current account balance, which has gone from 0.4 percent of GDP in 1997 to around −3 percent since 2000. Spain can surely afford to run deficits for a while, especially if the real interest rate remains below the GDP growth rate. But eventually the restoration of external equilibrium will require a substantial real depreciation that, given the common currency, can only be achieved through lower inflation than in the eurozone. Further reductions in equilibrium unemployment and higher productivity growth rates will therefore be very much needed.[30]

Going for Low Unemployment

Current labor institutions will probably allow Spain to sustain unemployment rates 1 or 2 points above those of the largest continental European economies. We very much doubt, however, that with a NAIRU of 14.5 percent (12 percent with the new official definition) Spain can join the club of low unemployment economies.

Starting with employment protection, preliminary evidence indicates that the 1997 reform raised employment rates for young workers, though we cannot disentangle the effects of lower severance pay from those of lower social security taxes.[31] We believe that further reform, aimed at reducing the role of labor courts, would be beneficial. If this was not politically viable, including workers aged 30 to 45 years old in the lower unfair dismissal pay regime would be a minimal step to take.

Regarding unemployment benefits, the worst feature is its lax administration: enforcement of criteria for benefit receipt, in particular, work availability, is practically nonexistent. Increasing strictness could prove effective, and we believe there would be a large constituency for this measure. This should be combined with more intense active labor market policies, mostly in job search assistance,[32] and specially for workers over 45 years old.

Last, but not least, the real policy challenge is to re-regulate collective bargaining. Real wage flexibility and wage dispersion are both relatively low. We wondered in section 13.2 how could it be that in a country with stringent employment protection, employment and unemployment has been more volatile than in the EU4. This could be attributed to acute industrial restructuring in the early 1980s and to high turnover caused by temporary contracts after 1984. But a third factor is the lack of wage flexibility, which has probably caused excess firing of permanent employees as well.[33]

Wage bargaining is in the hands of a small number of agents who mostly represent the interests of large firms and their permanent workers, in detriment of small firms and fixed-term employees. Despite their limited representativeness, unions have prevented any change in the regulations. We believe that a reform that fosters decentralization would help reduce unemployment. Rules like the automatic extension of both the right to negotiate and of labor conditions negotiated in industry agreements to all firms belonging to an industry or area, or the inability of firm-level agreements to affect broader agreements, should be lifted.[34]

In sum, the Spanish unemployment experience shows that choosing certain labor market institutions can lead to very high unemployment rates but also that it can be reversed if those institutions are reformed. We hope that this lesson will be applied in future so that Spain will go back to a low unemployment equilibrium.

Appendix: Measuring Unemployment in Spain

The official unemployment rate is computed from the labor force survey (LFS), which is of comparable quality to the surveys in other European countries. The LFS is a long-established survey, and its sample is large (60,000 households). Since 1987 its design is adequate, its questions are similar to those in other surveys, and it follows the ILO guidelines in defining unemployment.

The official figures have, however, been questioned several times. The main criticism is that the LFS does not capture the underground economy. While the underground economy is probably large in Spain, the relevant issue refers to the incentives that individuals may have to hide their employment status. Comparisons with other sources suggest that *irregular* unemployment did not account for more than 2 to 3 percentage points of the official unemployment rate around 1985. The reason is that the majority of irregular jobs were held by people who had another fully registered job, were retired, or were disabled (see Blanchard et al. 1995).

Technical problems were present in the 1980s and early 1990s because the 1981 census on which the LFS sampling was conducted became obsolete. Neither attrition nor the treatment of nonresponses was corrected, and the population aged 25 to 45 years old was underrepresented. According to some estimates this resulted in an underestimation of employment and the labor force by about one million people,

Table 13A.1
Unemployment rates: Alternative definitions (%)

Period	Old definition	New definition
2001:1	13.3	10.9
2001:2	12.8	10.4
2001:3	12.6	10.3
2001:4	12.7	10.5
2002:1	—	11.5

but it had little effect on the unemployment rate (Toharia 2000). In 1995 and 1996 the 1991 census was adopted, which led to an overestimated employment growth then. Further improvements took place in 2000.

In 2002:1 an EU directive changing the job search requirements to be classified as unemployed was implemented in the LFS. Up to then, being registered in the public employment office was enough. Since then, absent other methods, going to the employment office needs to have happened over the preceding four weeks, and the purpose must be job searching. The initial effect (see table 13.A1) was to reduce the unemployment rate by about 2.4 percentage points. But the rise in unemployment rate by 1 percentage point in 2002:1 and the narrowing gap between the two series suggest that the impact of the change is being undone. This is not certain, however, because new population data and a new weighting scheme were also introduced in 2002:1.

Notes

We thank Manuel Arellano, Olivier Blanchard, Tor Eriksen, and Bertil Holmlund for comments. We are grateful to Olivier Blanchard, Ángel Estrada, Ignacio Hernando, J. David López-Salido, Steve Nickell, Luca Nunziata, and Justin Wolfers for making their data available to us, and to Emma García for excellent research assistance.

1. See Blanchard and Jimeno (1999).

2. The *OECD Employment Outlook* gives a figure of 59 percent for Spain and 64 percent for the EU4 in 2001.

3. The standard deviation across regions in 1985 to 2000, 5.3, is higher than in France (2.0), the United Kingdom (2.7), or Germany (3.3), though lower than in Italy (6.0).

4. See Bentolila and Blanchard (1990) for a description of this period.

5. Measured as the long-term interest rate minus the once-lagged GDP deflator growth rate.

6. See Bover et al. (2000) for details.

7. With Franco it was equal to 60 days of wages p.y.o.s.

8. See Kugler et al. (2002).

9. See Dolado et al. (2002) for a survey.

10. See Jimeno and Rodriguez-Palenzuela (2002) for related evidence on firing costs.

11. See Bover (2002) for a description.

12. The benefit duration figure in table 12.4 accumulates UI and UA.

13. See the references in note 17.

14. See Bover et al. (2002a) and García-Pérez (1997), respectively.

15. See Blanchard et al. (1995) for a description.

16. See Dolado et al. (1997).

17. Layard et al. (1991) report an estimate of −0.17, and Estrada et al. (2000) −0.2 for the private sector. However, De Lamo and Dolado (1991) obtained −1.17. Most real wage equations are static, but the dynamic ones show a higher response in the long than in the short run. Layard et al. (1991) rank Spain fifth out of 19 OECD countries in the degree of real wage rigidity.

18. See Bentolila and Dolado (1994) for insider effects, Bover et al. (2002b) for wage inequality, Dolado et al. (1996) for the national minimum wage, and Dolado and Felgueroso (1997) for minimum bargained wages.

19. See Bover and Velilla (2004), Bentolila and Dolado (1991), and Antolin and Bover (1997).

20. See Jimeno and Bentolila (1998).

21. See Bentolila and Ichino (2003) for networks and Becker et al. (2002) for youth emancipation.

22. See OECD (1999) for a survey.

23. See Dolado et al. (2002).

24. Blanchard and Jimeno (1995) singled out benefits as the key institutional difference. But reforms increasing coverage in Portugal (1989) and reducing it in Spain (1992) have shortened the gap.

25. See Bover et al. (2000b) and Cantó et al. (2002).

26. We owe this point to Pedro Portugal.

27. The equation is: $\Delta(w - p)_t = -0.07 - 0.24u_t + 0.05(w - (p + \hat{y} - l))_{t-1}$ (standard errors: 0.04, 0.10, and 0.02, respectively), where $\Delta(w - p)_t$ is the real wage growth rate in collective bargaining, u the unemployment rate, and $w - (p + \hat{y} - l)$ the log of the ratio of the wage to productivity predicted from a regression on a time trend and its square (see Blanchard and Katz 1997).

28. Dolado and Jimeno (1997) argue in favor of hysteresis in the dynamics of Spanish unemployment.

29. From S. Nickell and L. Nunziata, Labor Market Institutions Database (cep.lse.ac.uk/pubs).

30. See Blanchard and Jimeno (1999).

31. See Kugler et al. (2002).

32. See Nickell et al. (2002).

33. See Bertola and Rogerson (1997).

34. See Bentolila and Jimeno (2002).

References

Antolin, P., and O. Bover. 1997. Regional migration in Spain: The effect of personal characteristics and of unemployment, wage and house price differentials using pooled cross-sections. *Oxford Bulletin of Economics and Statistics* 59: 215–35.

Becker, S., S. Bentolila, A. Fernandes, and A. Ichino. 2002. Job insecurity and children's emancipation: The Italian puzzle. CEMFI, Madrid, mimeo (www.cemfi.es/~sbc).

Bentolila, S., and O. Blanchard. 1990. Spanish unemployment. *Economic Policy* 10: 233–81.

Bentolila, S., and J. J. Dolado. 1994. Labour flexibility and wages: Lessons from Spain. *Economic Policy* 18: 53–99.

Bentolila, S., and J. J. Dolado. 1991. Mismatch and internal migration in Spain, 1962–1986. In F. Padoa-Schioppa, ed., *Mismatch and Labour Mobility*. Cambridge: Cambridge University Press.

Bentolila, S., and A. Ichino. 2003. Unemployment and consumption: Why are job losses less painful than expected near the Mediterranean? CEMFI, Madrid, mimeo (www.cemfi.es/~sbc).

Bentolila, S., and J. F. Jimeno. 2002. La reforma de la negociación colectiva en España. In J. Aurioles and E. Manzanera, eds., *Cuestiones Clave de la Economía Española. Perspectivas Actuales, 2001*. Seville: Centro de Estudios Andaluces (centrA) y Ediciones Pirámide.

Bertola, G., and R. Rogerson. 1997. Institutions and labor reallocation. *European Economic Review* 41: 1147–71.

Blanchard, O., et al. 1995. *Spanish Unemployment: Is There a Solution?* London: Centre for Economic Policy Research.

Blanchard, O., and L. Katz. 1996. What we know and do not know about the natural rate of unemployment. *Journal of Economic Perspectives* 11: 51–72.

Blanchard, O., and J. F. Jimeno. 1995. Structural unemployment: Spain and Portugal. *American Economic Review (Papers and Proceedings)* 85: 212–18.

Blanchard, O., and J. F. Jimeno. 1999. Reducing Spanish unemployment under the EMU. *FEDEA Working Paper* 1999-02.

Blanchard, O., and J. Wolfers. 2000. The role of shocks and institutions in the rise of European unemployment: The aggregate evidence. *Economic Journal* 110: C1–C33.

Bover, O., M. Arellano, and S. Bentolila. 2002a. Unemployment duration, benefit duration, and the business cycle. *Economic Journal* 112: 223–65.

Bover, O., S. Bentolila, and M. Arellano. 2002b. The distribution of earnings in Spain during the 1980s: The effects of skill, unemployment, and union power. In D. Cohen, T. Piketty, and G. Saint-Paul, eds., *The New Economics of Rising Inequalities*. Oxford: CEPR and Oxford University Press.

Bover, O., P. García-Perea, and P. Portugal. 2000. Labor Market Outliers: Lessons from Portugal and Spain. *Economic Policy* 31: 379–428.

Bover, O., and P. Velilla. 2004. Migrations in Spain: Historical background and current trends. In K. Zimmerman, ed., *European Migration: What Do We Know?* Oxford: CEPR and Oxford University Press.

Cantó, O., A. R. Cardoso, and J. F. Jimeno. 2002. Earnings inequality in Portugal and Spain: Contrasts and similarities. In D. Cohen, T. Piketty, and G. Saint-Paul, eds., *The New Economics of Rising Inequalities*. Oxford: CEPR and Oxford University Press.

De Lamo, A., and J. J. Dolado. 1993. Un modelo del mercado de trabajo y la restricción de oferta en la economía Española. *Investigaciones Económicas* 17: 87–118.

Dolado, J. J., and F. Felgueroso. 1997. Los efectos del salario mínimo: Evidencia empírica para el caso Español. *Moneda y Crédito* 204: 213–61.

Dolado, J. J., F. Felgueroso, and J. F. Jimeno. 1997. The effect of minimum bargained wages on earnings: Evidence from Spain. *European Economic Review* 41: 713–21.

Dolado, J. J., C. García Serrano, and J. F. Jimeno. 2002. Drawing lessons from the boom of temporary jobs in Spain. *Economic Journal* 112: F270–95.

Dolado, J. J., and J. F. Jimeno. 1997. The causes of Spanish unemployment: A structural VAR approach. *European Economic Review* 41: 1281–1307.

Dolado, J. J., F. Kramarz, A. Manning, S. Machin, and C. Teulings. 1996. The economic impact of minimum wages in Europe. *Economic Policy* 23: 317–72.

Estrada, A., I. Hernando, and J. D. López-Salido. 2000. Measuring the NAIRU in the Spanish economy. Banco de España, Servicio de Estudios, *Working Paper* 0009.

García Pérez, J. I. 1997. Las tasas de salida del empleo y el desempleo en España (1978–1993). *Investigaciones Económicas* 19: 29–53.

Kugler, A., J. Jimeno, and V. Hernanz. 2002. Employment consequences of restrictive permanent contracts: Evidence from Spanish labor market reforms. Universitat Pompeu Fabra, *Working Paper* 651.

Jimeno, J. F., and S. Bentolila. 1998. Regional unemployment persistence (Spain, 1976–1994). *Labour Economics* 5: 25–51.

Jimeno, J. F., and D. Rodriguez-Palenzuela. 2002. Youth unemployment in the OECD: Demographic shifts, labour market institutions, and macroeconomic shocks. *FEDEA Working Paper* 2002-15.

Layard, R. 1990. Comment to "Spanish Unemployment" by S. Bentolila and O. Blanchard (1990). *Economic Policy* 10: 271–73.

Layard, R., S. Nickell, and R. Jackman. 1991. *Unemployment: Macroeconomic Performance and the Labor Market*. Oxford: Oxford University Press.

Nickell, S. 1997. Unemployment and labor market rigidities: Europe versus North America. *Journal of Economic Perspectives* 11 (3): 55–74.

Nickell, S., L. Nunziata, and W. Ochel. 2002. Unemployment in the OECD since the 1960s: What do we know? Bank of England, London, mimeo.

OECD. 1999. Employment protection and labour market performance. In *OECD Employment Outlook*. Paris: OECD.

Toharia, L. 2000. El Paro en España: ¿Puede Ser tan Alto? *Revista Gallega de Empleo* (February): 75–104.

Index

N/A